Fodor's 90

Scotland

Fodor's Travel Publications, Inc.
New York & London

ISBN 0–679–01823–9

Fodor's Scotland

Area Editor: Gilbert Summers
Editorial Contributors: Robert Brown, Leslie Gardiner
Editor: Richard Moore
Maps: C. W. Bacon, Brian Stimpson, Swanston Graphics
Drawings: Lorraine Calaora
Photographs: Scottish Tourist Board
Cover Photograph: Brandenburg/West Light

Cover Design: Vignelli Associates

SPECIAL SALES

Fodor's Travel Publications are available at special discounts for bulk
purchases (100 copies or more) for sales promotions or premiums. Special
editions, including personalized covers, excerpts of existing guides, and
corporate imprints, can be created in large quantities for special needs. For
more information, write to Special Marketing, Fodor's Travel Publications, 201
East 50th Street, New York, NY 10022. Enquiries from the United Kingdom
should be sent to Fodor's Travel Publications, 30–32 Bedford Square,
London WC1B 3SG.

CONTENTS

SUPPLEMENTS

FOREWORD

Scotland is a natural destination for the traveler of taste, the visitor with a well-developed sense of wonder. Not that it is entirely easy to come to realistic grips with Scotland—the country is so heavily disguised by a swirling reputation for high romance. It is a reputation of fairly recent date, the result of a massive operation mounted by the powerful public-relations firm of Scott and Hanover—Sir Walter Scott and Queen Victoria. Scott began it by devising, virtually single-handed, a new and instantly successful appreciation of the violent and complex history of his native land. Victoria added her own infallible touch to the process by creating Balmorality and the tartanitis virus which, from her day down to the present, has infected untold millions.

We hope that we have managed in this Guide to hold a balance between fact and fantasy, while paying due respect to the fascination of the country's legends and lore—though, where Scotland is concerned, the border between reality and embroidery is sometimes hard to define.

A pair of simple, but very revealing, statistics are that Scotland is three-fifths the size of England (30,405 square miles against 50,333 square miles) but that it has a population of only just over five million—most of which is in the southern half of the country. Not only is Scotland justly known as one of the most beautiful countries on earth but, as these figures show, it also has great tracts which are virtually unpopulated. Indeed, it is still possible to discover places where, in all likelihood, yours will be the first human foot to tread. To find a country of such magnificent scenery and to be able to enjoy it in peace is increasingly rare these days.

The Scots are a friendly, welcoming people who have, by and large, managed to preserve a courtesy and warmth that may sometimes be lacking south of the border. Their understanding of the needs of tourism has noticeably sharpened over the last few years and standards of hotel accommodations and restaurant food have improved greatly. The Book-a-Bed-Ahead scheme to which we refer in *Facts at Your Fingertips* is just one of the enterprising ideas that are in full swing. It is a particularly valuable scheme, too, as it gives visitors a chance not only of staying in hotels but of trying the delights of bed-and-breakfast, of seeing how the Scots live and sampling their home fare.

While Scotland suffers the same drastic cutbacks in public transport that afflict the rest of Great Britain, it is still a country that can be explored to great advantage by bus and train—and, of course, by boat, since the coastal waters and the islands are linked by a spider's web of ferry routes. To explore this way needs a lot of planning, but if you are the kind of traveler to whom a railway timetable is more evocative than a book of poetry, then you are in for a wonderful time.

We would like to thank the many staff members of the Scottish Tourist Board who gave us invaluable help while we were compiling this book. We know that our readers will be greeted by the same enthusiasm that welcomed us when they visit one of the Board's offices.

We would also like to thank Gilbert Summers, who has put his knowledge and understanding of Scotland at our disposal for the preparation of this edition, and Leslie Gardiner, for his sterling work in the past.

We would also like to thank Peter McArthur and Co. of Hamilton for their considerable help in the matter of tartans.

While every care has been taken to insure the accuracy of the information contained in this guide, the publishers cannot accept responsibility for any errors that may appear.

All prices that we quote are based on those available to us at the time of writing. In a world of rapid change, however, the possibility of inaccurate or out-of-date information can never be totally eliminated. We trust, therefore, that you will take prices quoted as indicators only, and will double-check to be sure of the latest figures.

Similarly, be sure to check all opening times of museums and galleries. We have found that such times are liable to change without notice, and you could easily make a trip only to find a locked door.

When a hotel closes or a restaurant produces a disappointing meal, let us know, and we will investigate the establishment and the complaint. We are always ready to revise our entries for the following year's edition should the facts warrant it.

Send your letters to the editors of Fodor's Travel Publications, 201 E. 50th Street, New York, NY 10022.

FACTS AT YOUR FINGERTIPS

SOURCES OF INFORMATION. The principal source of information in North America on all aspects of travel, including tours and tour operators, to Scotland is the British Tourist Authority. Much of the information they are able to supply is free; all of it is to the point and well laid out. The B.T.A.'s addresses are:

In the U.S.: 40 West 57th St., New York, NY 10019 (212–581–4700); 875 North Michigan Ave., Chicago, IL 60611 (312–787–0490); World Trade Center, Ste. 450, 350 S. Figueroa St., Los Angeles, CA 90071 (213–628–3525); 2305 Cedar Springs Rd., Suite 210, Dallas, TX 75201–1814 (214–720–4040).

In Canada: 94 Cumberland St., Toronto, Ontario M5R 3N3 (416–925–6326).

In the U.K.: Thames Tower, Blacks Rd., London W6 (01–846 9000). The Scottish Tourist Board has an office at 19 Cockspur St., London SW1Y 5BL (01–930 8661). Its head office at 23 Ravelston Terrace, Edinburgh EH4 3EU (031–332 2433) handles telephone enquiries only. Edinburgh's downtown Travel Centre, 14 South St. Andrew St., EH2 2AZ (same telephone number), gives out free brochures and detailed travel and transport information. You can buy travel literature, change money, rent a car, and book touring vacations.

Scotland's network of tourist information centers, "TICs," are run by more than 30 area tourist boards. See the *Practical Information* sections of our regional chapters. Most are open Monday–Friday, 9–5, with shorter hours on Saturday and Sunday and longer hours in midsummer. Some are open April to September only.

Scotland's main information point is the Edinburgh Travel Centre. There is also a large Information Centre at Southwaite (Cumbria) for the benefit of motorists approaching Scotland on the M6 motorway.

There are about 160 tourist information centers sited strategically throughout the country. They bear the distinctive "i" sign and provide information about their own districts as well as operating accommodations services for their localities and, in most cases, a "Book-A-Bed-Ahead" scheme for other districts. These centers are supported by a number of miscellaneous information offices run by organizations such as the Forestry Commission, the National Trust for Scotland and others; and by "tourist points"— kiosks or notice boards at viewpoints, picnic sites and the like.

TRAVEL AGENTS AND TOURS. The range of tours to Europe is so immense, and the savings many represent over independent travel so significant, that it is well worth investigating those on offer. A reliable and efficient travel agent is a considerable advantage in this respect. Even those who prefer to travel independently may well find that at the very least a good agent is able to advise on the tangle that currently constitutes the air fares scene. But for those on a limited budget or who wish to combine a trip to Scotland with one to England, or perhaps elsewhere in Europe, or who are interested in the many special interest vacations on offer, there is little doubt that a good agent can save you time and money.

If you are uncertain about which agent to go to, the British Tourist Authority or Scottish Tourist Board will be able to point you in the right direction. Similarly, the American Society of Travel Agents, 1101 King St., Alexandria, VA 22314, and the Association of British Travel Agents, 55 Newman St., London W1, can help.

Below we list some of the best ways of finding out about tours in Scotland, and give a few examples.

Tours from the U.S. The Scottish Tourist Board's own overseas marketing activities have included the setting up in the U.S. of SCOTS—Specialist Counselors on Travel to Scotland. This organization is open to all travel agents in the U.S. who then receive special training. This takes the form of an education course and series of tests which have themselves been put together by STB in conjunction with the Education Department of Edinburgh University! If this sounds a little serious, then at least it means that customers using a SCOTS travel agent can be assured that they will be dealing with professionals with a good knowledge of Scotland. Scottish travel queries are handled by the British Tourist Authority (addresses above). They will also supply names of SCOTS travel agents, published quarterly in the Scottish Tourist Board's U.S. magazine *Scottish Quest*. However, remember that the BTA are far from exclusively Scottish and are in the business of promoting other parts of the United Kingdom.

Amongst the huge choice of other tour operators is Abercrombie and Kent International who have made a big impact in recent years with their "Royal Scotsman" luxury train travel around Scotland. (Prices start from £1080 per person, 3 days, in a luxury twin cabin). They also offer such delights as "The Highlands and Lochs of Scotland," 13 days chauffeur or self-drive (for the independent traveler) from $2510 per person. Full details from Abercrombie and Kent International Inc., 1420 Kensington Road, Oak Brook, IL 60521–2106, or 312–954–2944. Among other possibilities: *Globus Gateway/Cosmos'* Bonnie Scotland, seven days in England and Scotland, with overnight stops in Edinburgh, Inverness, and Fort William, for about $499–$549. They also offer "The Highlander," 15 days—though it includes some travel in England—taking in Edinburgh, Royal Deeside, Inverness, Skye and Glasgow. $1028–$1078.

For those with a keen interest in golf the British Tourist Authority in New York supplies free information about the game in Scotland. British Airways and Aer Lingus, in co-operation with tour operators, offer golf packages. Many golf tours, including weeks or weekends at the famous resort hotels of Gleneagles and Turnberry, may be booked once you are in Scotland.

Golf *and* fishing fans generally might wish to check the advertisements in specialty magazines—especially the classified ads—for listings of tour operators and individual guides living in Scotland but whose services can be contracted prior to your departure.

U.S.-based tour operators whose Great Britain packages take in Scotland include:

American Express, 822 Lexington Ave., New York, NY 10021.
Barclay Travel Ltd., 767 Third Ave., New York, NY 10017.
C.I.E. Tours International, 122 East 42nd St., New York, NY 10168.
Globus Gateway/Cosmos, 95–25 Queens Blvd., Rego Park, NY 11374.

Maupintour, 1515 St. Andrews Dr., Lawrence, KS 66046.

Villas International, 71 W. 23rd St., New York, NY 10010.

Please note that all quoted rates vary with international currency fluctuations.

U.K.-based tour operators offering special-interest tours include:

Accomotel (Scotland), 2d Churchill Way, Bishopbriggs, Glasgow G64 2RH. Golf holidays, fishing, automobile tours, summer cottages.

Cadies, 1 Upper Bow, The Royal Mile, Edinburgh EH1 2JN. Personally conducted walking tours of historic Edinburgh.

Fairway Tours, 8D Roseberry Place, Gullane, East Lothian EH31 2AN. Golf, shooting, fishing and sightseeing. Estate-car transport.

Ghillie Personal Travel, 64 Silverknowes Road East, Edinburgh EH4 5NY. Complete à la carte service by automobile or coach.

Grampian Tours, 27 St. John Street, Perth PH1 5SH. Bus and special interest tours, sporting, skiing, farming, heritage of Scotland.

Henry James Steven Tourism, 27 Drummond Place, Edinburgh EH3 6PN. Prompt and reliable specialists in Scottish sojourns from campus hostels to castles, and in upmarket tours from private steam trains to Hebridean cruises. Special arts tours are planned for 1990 to celebrate Glasgow's nomination as European City of Culture. Linked in U.S. with *Villa Leisure,* P.O. Box 1016, Fairfield, CT 06430.

Ian Dickson Travel, 50 Dundas Street, Edinburgh EH3 6JN. Industrial, study, sporting and special interests. Friendly and efficient travel agencies in several Lothian towns.

Paton's Travel Services, 5 Crown Street, Aberdeen AB1 2HA. Custom-made itineraries, fishing and shooting in Grampian Region.

Thomas Cook, 9–11 Castle Street, Edinburgh EH2 3BD and 79A Princes Street, Edinburgh EH2 2ER. Complete travel service for overseas visitors. Seven-day Highland bus tour from Edinburgh every Wednesday in summer.

Tours and Travel Promotions, 25 Brunstane Drive, Edinburgh EH15. Luxury vacations in Scottish castles and country houses, Edinburgh Festival arrangements, cultural and genealogical tours.

Treasures of Scotland Tours, 3 Silk Street, Paisley PA1 1HG. Medium-priced packages covering castles, historic monuments, art galleries and museums, concerts and theaters. Also custom-made tours and vacations.

HANDICAPPED TRAVEL. A growing number of travel agencies and societies for the disabled specialize in holidays for the handicapped. Generally their tours parallel those for the non-handicapped traveler, but at a more leisurely pace, with everything checked out in advance to eliminate all inconvenience, whether the traveler happens to be deaf, blind or in a wheelchair. For a complete list of tour operators who arrange such travel, write to the Society for the Advancement of Travel for the Handicapped, 26 Court St., Brooklyn, New York, NY 11242. An excellent source of information in this field is the book *Access to the World: A Travel Guide for the Handicapped,* by Louise Weiss, published by Henry Holt & Co.; order through your local bookstore. This book covers travel by air, ship, train, bus, car and recreational vehicle; hotels and motels; travel agents and tour operators; destinations; access guides; health and medical problems; and travel organizations.

Another major source of help is the Travel Information Service, Moss Rehabilitation Hospital, 12th St. and Tabor Rd., Philadelphia, PA 19141. Also helpful is the Information Center for Individuals with Disabilities, 2743 Wormwood St., Boston, MA 02210.

In the U.K., the Royal Association for Disability and Rehabilitation (RADAR), 25 Mortimer St., London W1N 8AB (tel. 01–637 5400), in addition to publishing its excellent handbook, *Holidays for Disabled People,* also acts as an information service. Within Scotland the best source of information is the Disability Foundation, Princes House, 5 Shandwick Place, Edinburgh (tel. 031–229 7324). They produce an annually updated information list giving details of hotels, places of interest, transport facilities and the like that are suitable for the disabled. They also have a considerable number of contact addresses. Among their publications they produce an invaluable *Access to Public Conveniences* guide. The S.T.B. also produces the publication *Holidays with Care* and uses, wherever helpful, the disabled logo in its other publications.

CLIMATE. The Scottish climate has been much maligned; sometimes with justification. You can be unlucky: you may spend a summer week in Scotland and experience nothing but low cloud and drizzling rain. But, at the same time, you can be lucky: you may enjoy month-long spells of calm Mediterranean-like weather even in early spring and late fall.

Generally speaking, Scotland is three or four degrees cooler than southern England. The east is drier, and colder, than the west; Edinburgh's rainfall, for example, is comparable to Rome's, while rainfall in Glasgow is more like that in Vancouver—yet the cities are only 44 miles apart and both are at sea level.

All visitors comment on the long summer evenings, which grow longer still as you travel north. Dawn in Orkney and Shetland in June is at around 1 A.M., no more than an hour or so after sunset. The other side of this coin, though, are the very short winter days.

Scotland has few thunderstorms and little fog, except for local sea mists near coasts. But there are often variable winds which reach gale force even in summer. But they do at least blow away the hordes of gnats and midges (the curse of the western Highlands). On the subject of which, if you plan to visit the western Highlands, bring or buy a repellent.

The following are average temperatures for central Scotland in degrees Centigrade:

	Jan.	Feb.	Mar.	Apr.	May	Jun.	Jul.	Aug.	Sep.	Oct.	Nov.	Dec.
Daily temp.	3	3	4.5	7	11	14.5	17	15.5	13	9.5	5	4
Humidity	85	82	79	75	73	73	73	75	80	85	86	86
Days with rain	11	13	14	13	14	15	16	15	12	14	13	13
Sea temp.	4.5	5	5	7	8	10	12	13.5	12.5	10.5	8	6

SPECIAL EVENTS. The Scottish Tourist Board, P.O. Box 15, Edinburgh EH1 1UY, will send you on request a free booklet of *Events in Scotland* for the forthcoming year (it is usually available in November). Here we note the principal activities for each month without specifying precise dates since most of them change every year. In addition there are always one-time-only events—special celebrations and commemorations.

January. Kirkwall, Orkney: Ba' Games (mass street football); New Year's Day.

Glasgow, Ayr, Dumfries, Edinburgh, and many other towns and villages: Burns Night dinners and entertainments on the 25th.

Lerwick, Shetland: Up Helly Aa, ancient Viking festival; end of month.

February. Perth: Aberdeen-Angus Show, important cattle sales; early in month.

March. Tobermory, Mull: Drama Festival; end of month.

Edinburgh: Edinburgh Folk Festival, an international event in city halls and clubs; end of month.

April. Edinburgh: Royal Scottish Academy; annual exhibition starts mid-month.

Hamilton: Hamilton Races (Flat).

St. Andrews: Kate Kennedy procession, historic university pageant.

May. Fort William: Scottish Six-day Motor-cycle Trials; first week.

Glasgow: Mayfest; first three weeks.

Strichen: Buchan Heritage Festival.

June. Hawick: Common Riding, historic patroling of boundaries, general vacation in locality, first of several similar events in Borders towns; second week.

Lanark: Lanimer Day, historic festival; second week.

Selkirk: Common Riding; second week.

Dumfries: Guid Nychtburris, traditional festival; mid-month.

Kirkwall, Orkney: St. Magnus Festival, arts and music; mid-month.

Isle of Skye: Skye Week; third week.

Edinburgh: Royal Highland Show, principal agriculture, commerce and outdoor displays. At Ingliston showground, seven miles from city; third week.

Peebles: Beltane Festival, traditional observance of midsummer, of pagan origin; around 21st.

Galashiels: Braw Lads' Gathering, part of the Borders' program of Common Ridings; end of month.

July. Jedburgh: Jethart Callants Festival, traditional processions and entertainments; first week.

Glasgow: Folk Festival; second week.

Langholm: Common Riding; end of month.

Kelso: Gala Week. Also Border Union Show, large exhibition and horse racing; end of month.

August. Lauder: Common Riding; first week.

Various centers in rotation: National Sheepdog Trials, big social occasion for farmers and shepherds; first week.

Muir of Ord: Black Isle Agricultural Show; first Sat.

St. Andrews: Lammas Fair (medieval market); first week.

Glasgow: World Pipe Band championships; mid-month.

Edinburgh: International Film Festival; last two weeks of month. International Jazz Festival; third week. Military Tattoo, colorful international regimental ceremonial; mid-month to early Sept. International Festival of Music, Drama and the Arts, famous annual *kulturfest;* mid-month to early Sept. Festival Fringe, a festival-within-the-festival for off-beat and avant-garde entertainments in and around the city; mid-month to early Sept.

September. Fort William: Mountain race, Ben Nevis; first Sat.
Leuchars (Fife): Military and Civil Air Show; mid-month.
Glasgow: Marathon; second or third weekend.
October. Oban: Highland Cattle Autumn Show; mid-month.
Perth: Aberdeen-Angus Fall bull sales and cattle show; third week.
November. Edinburgh: Winter Antiques Fair; third week.
Aberdeen: Christmas Shopping Festival; from third week.
St. Andrews: International St. Andrews Day Dinner; 30th.
December. Comrie (Tayside): Flambeaux procession (traditional torchlight parade); 31st.

Highland Games. The principal Games and Gatherings (see our chapter on Sports in Scotland) are held in the following months, usually on a Saturday: **June,** Aberdeen, Grantown-on-Spey; **July,** Dufftown, Dundee, Elgin, Forres, Kenmore, Inveraray, Inverness, Lochaber (Fort William), Lochearnhead, Dingwall; **August,** Mallaig, Aberfeldy, Glasgow, Perth, Crieff, Oban, Dunoon, Birnam, Strathpeffer, Aboyne, Rothesay (Bute), Portree (Skye); **September,** Braemar, Pitlochry.

WHAT TO TAKE. Lightweight clothing is usually adequate in summer, but add a jacket, sweater or cardigan for evenings. A waterproof coat or parka (anorak) is essential. In Scotland casual clothes are *de rigueur* and you will find very few hotels or restaurants which insist on jackets and ties for men in the evenings. If you expect to attend some gala occasion (a premiere at the Edinburgh Festival for example) men should have a tuxedo, women an evening dress. Many visitors to Scotland appear to think it necessary to adopt a Scottish costume. It is not. Scots themselves do not wear tartan ties or Balmoral "bunnets" and only an enthusiastic minority prefer the kilt for everyday wear.

Drip-dry and crease-resistant fabrics are a good bet. If you are touring, it is almost impossible to get any laundering or cleaning done, except in the most prestigious hotels.

The golden rule is to travel light; generally, try not to take more than you can carry yourself. Not only are porters more or less wholly extinct in Europe these days (and where you can find them they're very expensive anyway), the less luggage you take the easier checking in and out of hotels becomes, similarly airports (the number one nightmare of all modern travel) become much easier to get through and, if you only take one piece of luggage, the less risk there is of it being lost en route, and, in theory anyway, the less time you need to wait for it to appear when you get off the plane. It's an excellent idea also to make sure that your luggage is sturdy; there's no worse way to start or finish your vacation than by discovering that your clothes are generously distributing themselves along a station platform or, even worse, have already scattered themselves around the hold of a 747. It can also be a good idea to pack the bulk of your things in one large bag and put everything you need for overnight, or for two or three nights, in a smaller one, to obviate packing and repacking at brief stops.

TRAVELER'S CHECKS. These are probably the safest and best way to carry money abroad. The best known are issued by American Express, Bank of America, Barclay's and Cook's, but there are a number of other brands as well. Most charge a small commission for issuing them. It's as well to keep a written record of the check numbers in a place other than that where you keep them, or give the numbers to a companion or friend. In the event the checks are lost or stolen this will greatly facilitate obtaining replacement checks.

Credit Cards. These are readily accepted at most Scottish hotels, restaurants, garages and multiple stores. Their use is less widespread in small shops and country districts. Access, Visa and to some extent American Express are generally recognized; you may have difficulty with others. Some credit cards allow you to cash personal checks or draw cash.

A point that should be watched with those useful pieces of plastic is the problem of the rate at which your purchase may be converted into your home currency. We have ourselves had two purchases made on the same day in the same place charged ultimately at two totally different rates of exchange. If you want to be certain of the rate at which you will pay, insist on the establishment entering the current rate onto your credit card charge at the time you sign it—this will prevent the management from holding your charge until a more favorable rate (to them) comes along, something which could cost you more dollars than you counted on. (On the other hand, should the dollar or pound be revalued upward before your charge is entered, you could gain a little.)

We would advise you, also, to check your monthly statement very carefully indeed against the counterfoils you got at the time of your purchase. It has become increasingly common for shops, hotels or restaurants to change the amounts on the original you signed, if they find they have made an error in the original bill. Sometimes, also, unscrupulous employees make this kind of change to their own advantage. The onus is on you to report the change to the credit card firm and insist on sorting the problem out.

TRAVEL DOCUMENTS. Passports for Americans. Major post offices throughout the country are now authorized to process passport applications; check with your local post office for the nearest one. You may also apply in person at U.S. Passport Agency offices in various cities; addresses and phone numbers are available under governmental listings in the white or blue pages of local telephone directories. Applications are also accepted at most County Courthouses. Renewals can be handled by mail (form DSP-82) provided that your previous passport is not more than 12 years old. In addition to the completed application form (Form DSP-11), new applicants will need:

1) Proof of citizenship, such as a birth certificate;

2) two identical photographs, two inches square, in either black and white or color, on non-glossy paper and taken within the past six months;

3) $35 for the passport itself plus a $7 processing fee if you are applying in person (no processing fee when applying by mail) for those 18 years and older, or if you are under 18, $20 for the passport plus a $7 processing fee if you are applying in person (again, no extra fee when applying by mail). Adult passports are valid for 10 years, others for five years;

4) proof of identity that includes a photo and a signature, such as a driver's license, previous passport or any governmental ID card. When you receive your passport, write down its number, date and place of issue separately. The loss of a valid passport should be reported immediately to the

local police and to the Passport Office, Department of State, 1425 K St. NW, Washington DC 20524; if your passport is lost or stolen while you're abroad, report it to the local authorities and apply for a replacement at the nearest U.S. Embassy or consular office.

Passports for Canadians. Canadian citizens may obtain application forms for passports at any post office; these are to be sent to the Bureau of Passports, External Affairs, Ottawa, Ont. K1A OG3, with a remittance of $25, two photographs, a guarantor, and evidence of Canadian citizenship. You may apply in person to the regional passport offices in Edmonton, Halifax, Montreal, Toronto, Vancouver or Winnipeg. Canadian passports are valid for five years and are non-renewable.

Visas. Americans, Canadians, citizens of EEC countries and most Commonwealth countries do not require visas to enter Scotland or any other part of the U.K. Similarly, if entering Scotland from elsewhere in the U.K., there are no immigration or customs formalities.

VACATION TRAVEL INSURANCE. The different varieties of travel insurance cover everything from health and accident costs, to lost baggage and trip cancelation. Sometimes they can all be obtained with one blanket policy; other times they overlap with existing coverage you might have for health and/or home; still other times it is best to buy policies that are tailored to very specific needs. Insurance is available from many sources, however, and many travelers unwittingly end up with redundant coverage. Before purchasing separate travel insurance of any kind, be sure to check your regular policies carefully.

Generally, it is best to take care of your insurance needs before embarking on your trip. You'll pay more for less coverage—and have less chance to read the fine print—if you wait until the last minute and make your purchases from, say, an airport vending machine or insurance company counter. If you have a regular insurance agent, he or she is the person to consult first.

Flight insurance, which is often included in the price of the ticket when the fare is paid via American Express, Visa or certain other major credit cards, is also often included in package policies providing accident coverage as well. These policies are available from most tour operators and insurance companies. While it is a good idea to have health and accident insurance when traveling, be careful not to spend money to duplicate coverage you may already have . . . or to neglect some eventuality which could end up costing a small fortune.

For example, basic U.S. Blue Cross-Blue Shield policies do cover health costs incurred while traveling. They will not, however, cover the cost of emergency transportation, which can often add up to several thousand dollars. Emergency transportation *is* covered, in part at least, by many major medical policies such as those underwritten by Prudential and Metropolitan Life. Again, we can't urge you too strongly that in order to be sure you are getting the coverage you need, check any policy carefully before buying. Another important example: Most insurance issued specifically for travel does not cover pre-existing conditions, such as a heart condition.

Recently, several organizations have appeared which offer coverage designed to supplement existing health insurance and to help defray costs not covered by many standard policies, such as emergency transportation. Some of the more prominent are:

Carefree Travel Insurance, c/o ARM Coverage Inc., 120 Mineola Blvd., Box 310, Mineola, NY 11501, underwritten by the Hartford Accident and Indemnity Co., offers a comprehensive benefits package that includes trip cancellation and interruption, medical, and accidental death/dismemberment coverage, as well as medical, legal, and economic assistance. Trip cancellation and interruption insurance can be purchased separately. Call (516–294–0220 or 800–654–2424) for additional information.

International SOS Assistance Inc. has fees from $25 a person for seven days, to $195 for a year (800–523–8930).

IAMAT (International Association for Medical Assistance to Travelers), 417 Center St., Lewiston, NY 14092 in the U.S.; or 188 Nicklin Rd., Guelph, Ontario N1H 7L5 in Canada.

Another frequent inconvenience to travelers is the loss of baggage. It is possible, though often a complicated affair, to insure your luggage against loss through theft or negligence. Insurance companies are reluctant to sell such coverage alone, however, since it is often a losing proposition for them. Instead, it is most often included as part of a package that would also cover accidents or health. Remuneration is often determined by weight, regardless of the value of the specific contents of the luggage. Should you lose your luggage or some other personal possession, be sure to report it to the local police immediately. Without documentation of such a report, your insurance company might be very stingy. Ask about purchasing "excess valuation," offered by some airlines; basically, this coverage increases the airline's liability. Also, before buying baggage insurance, check your homeowners policy. Some such policies offer "off-premises theft" coverage, including the loss of luggage while traveling.

The last major area of travelers' insurance is trip cancellation coverage. This is especially important to travelers on APEX or charter flights. Should you get sick abroad, or for some other reason be unable to continue your trip, you may be stuck having to buy a new one-way fare home, plus paying for space on the charter you're not using. You can guard against this with "trip cancellation insurance," usually available from travel agents. Most of these policies will also cover last minute cancellations.

TIME. Scotland operates on Greenwich Mean Time (G.M.T.), which is five hours ahead of (later on the clock than) Eastern Standard Time. From March to October, in common with the rest of the U.K., Scotland switches to British Summer Time, which is six hours ahead of Eastern Standard Time.

GETTING TO SCOTLAND FROM NORTH AMERICA. By air. Air services to Scotland from North America are extensive and regular. International flights go to Prestwick Airport, Glasgow, about 30 miles from the city center. (Don't confuse it with Glasgow airport, eight miles from the city, which is used for domestic and European flights.) Among airlines currently flying to Scotland are Northwest and Air Canada (from Canada only). Alternatively, you can fly to London and make connection to Glasgow, Edinburgh or other Scottish cities. Budget travelers should investigate Virgin Atlantic flights to London.

Air fares are in a constant state of flux, and our best advice is to consult a travel agent and let him or her make your reservations for you. Agents are familiar with the latest changes in fare structures as well as with the rules governing various discount plans. Among those rules: booking (usually) 21 days in advance, minimum stay requirements, maximum stay, the amount that (sometimes) must be paid in advance for land arrangements. Lowest prices overall will, of course, be during the off-season period between November and March (with the exception of Christmas and New Year holidays).

Generally speaking, on regularly scheduled flights, you have the option, in descending order of cost, of First Class, Club or Business Class, Economy or APEX. Budget travelers with fixed schedules will want to meet the requirements for APEX. Some charters are also still available; here again, an agent will be able to recommend which ones are reliable. Sometimes it is also worth investigating package tours even if you do not wish to use the tours' other services (hotels, meals, etc.); because a packager can block book seats, the price of a package can be less than the cost when air fare is booked separately.

If you have the flexibility, you *can* sometimes benefit from last-minute sales tour operators have in order to fill a plane; if in the U.S., check the travel pages in Sunday newspapers for such advertisements, but do try to find out whether the tour operator is reputable and whether you are tied to a precise round trip or whether you will have to wait until the operator has a spare seat in order to return.

By boat. Sad to say, there are no passenger services between North America and Scotland. The only regular sailings over the Atlantic are on the *QE2,* and even these are summer only and go to England (Southampton) rather than Scotland. At between $1,350 to $8,500 for a cabin, plus the added expense of subsequently making your way to Scotland, it is a pricey way to travel.

The persistent can be rewarded with passage on the rare freighter offering relatively comfortable one-class accommodations for a maximum of 12 people. What they lack in the way of entertainment and refinement these ships make up for by way of informality, relaxation and cost (though flying is almost always cheaper).

GETTING TO SCOTLAND FROM ENGLAND AND WALES. By air.
There is a "bus-service" of flights from London to Scotland. British Airways and British Midland operate from London Heathrow to Edinburgh and Glasgow. Between them they operate some 17 flights to Edinburgh and 18 to Glasgow each weekday. Business Air, Air Ecosse, Dan Air and Air U.K. also connect Scotland with English airports including London Gatwick. Inside Scotland, British Airways, Air U.K., Air Ecosse and Loganair operate a network of routes covering Glasgow, Edinburgh, Aberdeen and the Highlands and Islands. Stand-by tickets are offered on most flights.

By train. There are two main rail routes from the south to Scotland. Firstly there is the west coast main line which runs from London Euston to Glasgow Central via Rugby, Crewe, Preston and Carlisle. These frequent and reliable services cover the 401 miles to central Scotland in just over five hours. The standard service is of one train per hour, and some have portions for Edinburgh which are detached at Carstairs. For daytime travel to the Scottish Highlands the *Highland Chieftain* is a very useful train, taking you direct to Stirling and Aviemore and terminating at Inverness. The train also carries an excellent restaurant car to cater for the inner needs. Sleeper services run overnight from London Euston to Glasgow Central, Perth, Stirling, Aviemore, Inverness and Fort William. All of the trains are formed of the new sleeping carriages which are airconditioned and sound-proofed. Family compartments are available. These services allow you to leave London in the late evening and arrive refreshed at your destination early the following morning. They obviously offer a restful way of getting into the heart of the Scottish Highlands. Special overnight *Inter-City Nightriders* connect London with Dumfries, Glasgow, Edinburgh and Aberdeen. Fares are less than half normal fares (e.g. £22 London-Aberdeen). All seats are first-class and must be reserved in advance at a station or Travel Center. The *InterCity Saver* (see below) may be used on *Nightrider* but you *must* reserve the seat.

Secondly, there is the east coast main line from London King's Cross to Edinburgh via Newcastle and Durham, crossing into Scotland at Berwick on Tweed. This line (full electricification due in 1991) is the quickest way of reaching the Scottish capital. Between 8.00 in the morning and 6.00 in the evening there are 15 trains to Edinburgh of which three run through to Aberdeen. Limited-stop expresses like the *Flying Scotsman* take a little under five hours for the 393-mile London-Edinburgh journey. Connecting services from Edinburgh to most other parts of Scotland are much better than from Glasgow. For travel to Glasgow Queen Street there is a half hourly service with the fast trains taking only 45 minutes. Travelers bound for the Western Highlands and Islands—Mallaig, Oban and Fort William—will find it easier to travel via Edinburgh to Glasgow Queen Street as this cuts out the need to cross between stations in Glasgow. The nightly east coast *Nightrider* service calls at the same cities, and offers the same level of comfort as the west coast train. Reservation on both the traditional sleeper trains and Nightrider is essential.

Trains from elsewhere in England are good: there are regular services from Birmingham, Manchester, Liverpool, Bristol, Southampton, and Penzance to Glasgow and Edinburgh. For travelers entering Britain via Harwich (ships from Holland, Germany and Denmark) there is the *European,* which runs through to Glasgow via North London and Birmingham. For faster connections catch the new train the *Rhinelander* and change at Peterborough for the East Coast Main Line to Edinburgh.

Train fares vary according to the type of ticket purchased as well as class. The fare system is complex. Always go to the Information Office/Travel Center first and ask about the cheapest way to travel and if there are any special offers. Ask about *InterCity Savers,* and about the *Family Railcard* if children are with you. For visitors from outside Western Europe, the *BritRail Pass* is unbeatable value. This gives unlimited travel over the entire system. For young people aged 16 to 23 there is the *Young Person's Railcard* which is slightly cheaper. Both passes must be bought before you arrive in Britain. They are available for first-class or standard travel and obtainable from principal travel agents *outside* the United Kingdom. They cover periods of 8, 14 and 22 days, or one month. Tickets for children aged 5 through 15 cost half the price of the adult ticket. For those who arrive without a BritRail pass, British Rail offer numerous travel bargains.

There is the *Freedom of Scotland* ticket, standard only, for periods of 7 or 14 days (£44 or £72). It may be bought at railroad stations and travel agents in Scotland. The *Highlands and Islands Travelpass,* available from mainline London and Scottish rail stations or Travel Centers or by post from Hi-Line, Dingwall, Ross-Shire IV15 9SL, offers unlimited travel on most trains, buses and ferries in the Highlands, plus the trip from and to Glasgow, Edinburgh, or Aberdeen. Valid 7 or 14 days, it costs £54 or £75 high season (June–Sept.) and £33 or £50 low season.

For full information on these passes (costs are subject to change) in North America apply to BritRail Travel International, 630 Third Avenue, New York, NY 10017; Suite 603, 800 South Hope St., Los Angeles, CA 90017; Suite 210, Cedar Maple Plaza, 2035 Cedar Springs, Dallas, TX 75201; 409 Granville St., Vancouver, B.C. V6C 1T2; 94 Cumberland St., Toronto, Ontario M5R 1A3.

By bus. Buses (or coaches, as the long-distance and touring buses are usually called) provide the cheapest method of transport between England and Scotland. About 20 coach companies operate services between English cities, especially London, and Scottish towns and cities, especially Glasgow and Edinburgh. The best-known operators are Scottish Omnibuses, Eastern Scottish, National Express, Western SMT, Stagecoach, Cotter's and Parks of Hamilton. Journey time between London and Glasgow or Edinburgh is 8 to 8½ hours and the coaches run day and night. Most are quite comfortable, some offer catering facilities and videos on board. Fares on the long-distance coaches are approximately one-third of the rail fares for comparable trips.

The main London terminal is Victoria Coach Station but some Scottish companies use Gloucester Road Coach Station in west London, near the Penta Hotel. Many people travel to Scotland by coach; in summer a reservation three or four days ahead is advisable. Scottish Bus Group timetables are obtainable from the Group's offices at 114/116 George Street, Edinburgh EH2 4LX, or in London from Scottish Citylink Coaches, 298 Regent Street, London WIR 6LE, or from the Coach Travel Center, 13 Regent Street, London SW1Y 4LR (tel. 01–730 0202). Travel centers and travel agents also have details, and some travel agents sell tickets.

CUSTOMS. Entering Scotland from any other part of the U.K., you will face no customs formalities. But anyone coming from Northern Ireland may face a security check. Otherwise, there are two levels of duty free allowance for people entering the U.K.; one, for goods bought outside the EEC or for goods bought in a duty free shop within the EEC; two, for goods bought in an EEC country but not in a duty free shop.

In the first category you may import duty free: 200 cigarettes or 100 cigarillos or 50 cigars or 250 grammes of tobacco (*Note* if you live outside Europe, these allowances are doubled); plus one liter of alcoholic drinks over 22% vol. (38.8% proof) or two liters of alcoholic drinks not over 22% vol. or fortified or sparkling or still table wine; plus two liters of still table wine; plus 50 grammes of perfume; plus nine fluid ounces of toilet water; plus other goods to the value of £28.

In the second category you may import duty free: 300 cigarettes or 150 cigarillos or 75 cigars or 400 grammes of tobacco; plus 1½ liters of alcoholic drinks over 22% vol. (38.8% proof) or three liters of alcoholic drinks not over 22% vol. or fortified, still table or sparkling wine; plus five liters of still table wine; plus 75 grammes of perfume; plus 13 fluid ounces of toilet water; plus other goods to the value of £207 (*Note* though it is not classified as an alcoholic drink by EEC countries for Customs' purposes and is thus considered part of the "other goods" allowance, you may not import more than 50 liters of beer).

In addition, no animals or pets of any kind may be brought into the U.K. The penalties for doing so are severe and are strictly enforced; there are *no* exceptions. Similarly, fresh meats, plants and vegetables, controlled drugs and firearms and ammunition may not be brought into the U.K. There are no restrictions on the import or export of British and foreign currencies.

Anyone planning to stay in the U.K. for more than six months should contact H.M. Customs and Excise, Dorset House, Stamford Street, London SE1 9PS (tel. 01–928 0533) for further information.

DUTY FREE is not what it once was. You may not be paying tax on your bottle of whisky or perfume, but you are certainly contributing to somebody's profits. Duty free shops are big business these days and mark ups are often around 100 to 200%. So don't be seduced by the idea that because it's duty free it's a bargain. Very often prices are not much different from your local discount store and in the case of perfume or jewelry they can be even higher.

As a general rule of thumb, duty free stores on the ground offer better value than buying in the air. Also, if you buy duty free goods on a plane, remember that the range is likely to be limited and that if you are paying in a currency different from that of the airline, their rate of exchange often bears only a passing resemblance to the official one.

MONEY. Britain's currency is the pound sterling, which is divided into 100 pence (100p). Notes are issued to the values of £50, £20, £10, and £5 (also £1 in Scotland). Coins are issued to the values of £1, 50p, 20p, 10p, 5p, 2p, and 1p. Scottish coins are the same as English but Scottish notes are issued by three banks: the Bank of Scotland, the Royal Bank of Scotland and the Clydesdale Bank. They have the same face values as English notes, and English notes are interchangeable with them in Scotland. Scottish £1 notes are no longer legal tender outside Scotland. English banks and post offices will exchange them for you at present, but fewer and fewer shops are accepting them.

Except on public holidays, banks open Mon.–Fri. 9.30–3.30, some days to 4.45. Some close for an hour at lunchtime. No Saturday or Sunday openings. The larger travel agents, the more expensive hotels, the biggest multiple stores and the independent *bureaux de change* in the cities will change money for you and cash checks. But it is best to compare the rates they offer and the commissions they charge: they do vary. Banks offer the best deal. The major airports operate 24-hour banking services seven days a week.

As we write, the exchange rate for the pound sterling is around $1.60, but it fluctuates from day to day so it is as well to study the trends in order to get the best value for your dollar.

HOTELS. Scotland was the first part of the U.K. to run a national "Classification and Grading Scheme" to take some of the guesswork out of accommodation booking. Make sure when you are considering a hotel, guest house or bed & breakfast that you pay close attention to classification and its grading. The classification part is easy. A number of crowns from zero to five tells you the range of the establishment's facilities. Zero crowns (confusingly described as "Listed") is basic, five crowns luxury. The grading part is actually more important. It objectively assesses the quality of the place. Very roughly, the ordinary is "Approved," the good "Commended," and the very good "Highly Commended." Thus a two crown "Highly Commended" is probably better value all round than a four crown "Approved." The awards are part of the accommodation listing in the *Where to Stay* Guides (see below) and are also in local accommodation leaflets, available from tourist information centers. Not all establishments participate, but the scheme is becoming popular. In many small towns and villages there are excellent value inns and hotels offering reasonable comfort (central heating, rooms with bath or shower and telephone and television) at competitive prices. But rural Scotland is also bed-and-breakfast land, and, as Scottish breakfasts are usually nothing if not hearty, these are pretty good value. Indeed, for anyone planning to tour Scotland they can be hard to beat, especially as most offer genuinely warm hospitality as well as home cooking and comforts. The Scottish Tourist Board's *Scotland—Hotels and Guest Houses (£5.60 by post) and Where to Stay Bed and Breakfast* (price £3.60) together give details of more than 4,000 bed and breakfasts.

Hotels in the larger cities are generally also good. Glasgow and Edinburgh boast a number of very superior hotels as well as an extensive range of good hotels in all other prices categories. Both have active and helpful accommodations offices should you arrive without reservations (see *Practical Information* sections for both cities for details).

Bookings are generally easy to make as, in recent years, even in the height of the season—July and August—only some 80% of all available accommodations have been booked. So if you are touring around you are not likely to be stranded unless you arrive in Edinburgh at Festival time or some place where a big Highland Gathering or golf tournament is in progress. Your choice of accommodation will then be extremely limited. Try if possible to make reservations in advance either through a travel agent at home or in England, or from one of the many STB booklets listing accommodations when you arrive in Scotland and have decided what your itinerary will be. Telephone bookings should be confirmed by letter and country hotels expect you to turn up by about 6 P.M. You can also make reservations through local Information Centres (which we list in the *Practical Information* sections of our regional chapters) making use of their "Book-a-Bed-Ahead" facilities. Grand Metropolitan Hotels Ltd. (Inter-Continental and Forum Hotels; 800–327–0200) and Trusthouse Forte Hotels Inc. (800–225–5843) can reserve accommodations for you in Scotland and for your onward trip in Britain and Europe in one of their hotels.

We have graded hotels and guest-houses solely according to the cost of one night's accommodations for *two* people sharing a room: Deluxe (L), Expensive (E), Moderate (M) and Inexpensive (I). As well as a note of their classification and grading, the STB's *Scotland: Where to Stay* books referred to above give up-to-date tariffs for most establishments. Note that the following figures are based on high-season rates. Before June and after September you would expect to pay less. A two- or three-night stay is also more economical (see next paragraph); and the nightly rate normally includes a substantial breakfast. Double occupancy is usually significantly cheaper per head than single.

Category	Edinburgh, Glasgow, Aberdeen	Elsewhere
(L)	£85+	£65+
(E)	£65–£85	£45–£65
(M)	£30–£65	£25–£45
(I)	under £30	under £25

Budget Tip. The vacation scene in Scotland is changing. The Briton's traditional two-week summer vacation is giving way to shorter, more frequent breaks. Many hotels now offer three-day, midweek and off-season tourist packages at favorable inclusive rates. British Rail, the bus companies and ferry boat operators are into this business too. This is an aspect of Scottish tourism worth investigating. All British travel agents can help you seek out the bargains.

Self-catering. The STB publishes *Self-Catering Accommodation in Scotland,* £5.50 by post, a list of 2,000 places for do-it-yourself accommodations—furnished rooms, shepherds' and gamekeepers' cottages, chalets, caravans on fixed sites and so on. Many country cottages have been brought into tourist-renting schemes and some farmers and estate-owners have converted or custom built their own high class and low class lodges and log cabins for vacation use. As you tour Scotland you will see groups of log cabins in picturesque situations: forest or lochside refuges rented for self-catering, usually centered on a large house which is shop, laundry and social center for the vacationists.

At most travel agents and at all Tourist Information Centres in Scotland you can pick up the STB's brochure *Scotland 1990* for free. It includes 70 pages of advertisements by all kinds of establishments in the tourism business from luxury hotels to self-catering operators, plus a variety of holiday ideas and wide-ranging Scottish information.

If you like the idea of a "Highland home of your own," at least for a week or so, try to get advice from a local tourist office or from the STB if you cannot preview the property you have chosen. Some places are distinctly primitive and remote; while some, on the other hand, are particularly suitable for the elderly or disabled. Rates vary enormously, from £50 a week low season to £280 high season. From certain operators (see pages 2–3) you can rent a mansion or shooting lodge for up to £800 per week. The *National Trust for Scotland* has a few historic apartments and houses, in town and country, available for short- or long-term renting at from £75 to £230 per week. The address is 5 Charlotte Square, Edinburgh EH2 4DU.

University Accommodations. Universities and colleges in Edinburgh, Glasgow, Aberdeen, Stirling, and Dundee have accommodations to rent in their students' halls of residence during vacations, usually end-June to end-September but in some cases all year round. The normal arrangement is about five single (occasionally double) rooms centered on a kitchen, bathroom and lavatory. Some halls of residence provide a full meal service, others bed and breakfast, others cooking facilities and room. Daily rates may be as low as £16.25 inclusive. Details are in our hotels sections, under *Hostels.*

Youth Hostels. Youth Hostel membership cards are accepted at all British hostels and intending members may join at any hostel or, in Scotland, by contacting the Scottish Youth Hostels Association, 7 Glebe Crescent, Stirling FK8 2JA (tel. 0786–51181) or five other district offices. Hostel stays are usually unlimited for bona fide visitors. Hostel wardens may allocate "small duties" or chores. This helps costs: from £3.65–£4.25 at a grade 1 city hostel to £2.25–£2.65 grade 3. Note that hostels close for a period during the day, e.g. grade 1 hostels are closed from 11–2 in the summer. There are 80 youth hostels in Scotland.

For information and membership applications in North America, write to American Youth Hostels Inc., Box 37613, Washington, DC 20013; or Canadian Hostelling Association, 3rd Floor, Tower A, 333 River Rd., Ottawa, Ont. K1L 8H9.

Camping. The London-based Camping and Caravan Club has a major site on the A1 at Barns Ness (tel. 0368–63536), about 25 miles north of Berwick-on-Tweed. It also has sites on or near this highway, strategically placed for first arrivals in Scotland, at Gosford Park (tel. 087 57–487) and Yellowcraigs (tel. 062 085–217). The STB map *Camping in Scotland,* free from information centers, shows all the camping sites and caravan parks, together with their addresses and telephone numbers. Campers and caravanners are well catered for by the local authorities all over Scotland, especially in the Loch Lomond and Clyde coast areas: local telephone directories give addresses and numbers of sites. Outside the official sites, few landowners will object if you ask permission to park a caravan or pitch a tent; except that is, in the deer-stalking country of the Highlands and on the grouse moors, where even the sight of an automobile parked a few yards off the main road reduces ghillies and gamekeepers to apoplexy.

You may hire lightweight tents from Graham Tiso, 115–123 Rose Street, Edinburgh EH2 3DT (tel. 031–225 9486) and tents and camp beds from Banks of Perth, 29 St. John Street, Perth PH1 5SH (tel. 0738–24928). Among firms which rent out campers (motorized caravans) and trailers (trailer caravans) are Braids Caravan Park, Gretna near Carlisle CA6 5DQ (tel. 0461–37409); Dumfries Caravan Centre, Annan Road, Dumfries DG1 3JZ (tel. 0387–52917); and Sharp's Motorhomes, "Shangri-La," Culloden Road, Balloch near Inverness IV1 2HQ (tel. 0463–790543). Rental charges vary according to region, but you may expect to pay around £60 a week for a trailer, £190 for a camper.

The STB's booklet *Camping and Caravan Parks,* price £2.40 or £2.90 if sent through the mail, lists about 400 approved parks with full details of fees and facilities. Two people with automobile and tent or automobile and caravan will pay between £3 and £5 for overnight accommodation at an approved park.

RESTAURANTS. Our *Food and Drink* chapter deals with this subject and some specific examples are given in the *Practical Information* sections of our Regional chapters. Here we will just say that Scottish restaurants are noted for helpful attention and modest prices but not, in most places, for an exotic or imaginative cuisine. In all districts you will find restaurants which have risen, or are beginning to rise, above the old dull stereotyped level—but they are still in the minority.

City Scots usually take their midday meals in a pub, wine bar or bistro or in a department store restaurant which may be non-alcoholic and non-smoking. When traveling, the Scot generally eats inexpensively and quickly at a country pub or village tea-room. Places like Glasgow, Edinburgh and Aberdeen, of course, offer restaurants of cosmopolitan character and various price-levels. The more notable ones tend to open only in the evening. Most smaller towns and many villages have at least one restaurant where—certainly if a local is in charge—the service is a reminder of a Highland tradition which ensured that no stranger could travel through the country without receiving a welcome.

In a country so involved in the tourism industry, "all day" meal places are becoming quite widespread. The normal lunch period, however, is 12.30–2.30. As well as dinner, a few places serve "high tea"—one hot dish and masses of cakes, bread and butter and jam, served with tea only around 5.30–6.30.

You will come across restaurants which offer "A Taste of Scotland"—traditional dishes with peculiar names, often cooked and served in traditional pots and pans. The Taste of Scotland scheme, initiated by the STB, has helped—almost by accident—to preserve some of the Scots language, especially the names for a variety of traditional dishes.

The restaurants listed at the end of each of our Regional chapters—and they are only a selection, not necessarily the best or worst in the Region—are categorized (L), (E), (M) and (I) according to the prices they charge for a full meal for *two* persons, including a bottle of wine, VAT and service charges.

(L) £60+; (E) £40–£60; (M) £20–£40; (I) under £20

At an unpretentious main street department store or roadside café you will pay about £3 per head for lunch, at a selfservice snack bar or restaurant rather less. Motorway cafés have a poor reputation in Britain but those along the Scottish motorways are new and for the present generally tidy and good value for money.

You will pay up to £1.20 for a pint of beer, a glass of wine in a pub or restaurant or a 'nip' of spirits. Coffee for two adds about £1 to your bill. Water is supplied free on request: iced water is almost unheard-of. Cocktails and post-prandial liqueurs (rarely available in modest establishments) from £2 upwards.

DRINKING. The Scot's staple drink is tea, but coffee (of variable quality) is always available. In another sense the staple drink is whisky (note spelling—only the Irish variety is called "whiskey"); but it is worth remembering that some towns of the central belt built their prosperity on brewing and that Scots ale and lager is sold all over Britain. Connoisseurs drink 'real' ale. Scots lagers in Scotland are considered inferior to German, bottled or on draft. Most pubs sell wine by the glass. We deal more fully with whisky in our Grampian Region chapter.

Once more tightly controlled than anywhere else in Britain, drinking in Scotland is quite promiscuous. Long after English pubs have closed for the afternoon the tills are ringing merrily in Scotland. Subject to a local licensing authority's approval, rarely withheld, the publican may sell liquor from 11 A.M. to 11 P.M.

The nearest things to liquor stores in Scotland are the "off-licences." They too, like the wine merchants, may sell bottles all day long.

TIPPING. The Scots themselves are not over-generous tippers and most have no great expectations of tips. The barber, the waiter, the guide and bus-driver, even the taxi driver, may accept a tip if it is offered, but they do not expect it. There are now, of course, a good many non-Scots in the hotels and restaurant business to which the general Scottish attitude does not apply.

After a meal ask, or see from your bill, whether a charge has been made for service as well as for VAT (Value Added Tax). If it has not, a tip of not less than 10% is appropriate.

MUSEUMS, HOUSES AND GARDENS. In the *Practical Information* sections at the end of each regional chapter you will find details of museums, galleries, houses, castles and gardens in each area. Check opening times if possible: they do occasionally vary.

Most bookshops, stationers and tourist information centers sell the booklet *Scotland: More than 1001 Things to See*. It contains useful descriptions of museums, monuments and great houses. Price £3.20 or £3.70 by post from the *Scottish Tourist Board*.

Many historic Scottish castles and houses—not to mention islands, stretches of coastline, gardens, cottages and waterfalls—are in the care of the National Trust for Scotland. An annual membership fee of £15 (£24.50 for a family), with reductions for the young or the elderly, entitles you to visit most properties free. Application forms from the NTS at 5, Charlotte Square, Edinburgh EH2 4DU, or you may enroll at any NTS property. But entrance charges to houses and museums in Scotland are so small, and often non-existent, that the membership is of value only to the most dedicated stately-homes buffs.

A most agreeable organization called Scotland's Gardens Scheme operates from 31 Castle Terrace, Edinburgh EH1 2EL. Through its activities several hundred gardens, from the most elaborate and formal to the most quaint and wild, are periodically open to the public. A nominal admission charge covers owners' expenses and leaves a little over for charity. Teas are usually provided and tours of the house or some village-fête-like entertainment offered. The booklet *Scotland's Gardens* is available from the above address, price £1 or £1.30 including postage in the U.K., with details of openings for the current year. Opening times are also published week by week in the following Scottish newspapers: *Glasgow Herald, Scotsman, Edinburgh Evening News, Dundee Courier* and *Aberdeen Press & Journal*. They normally appear on Fridays, since most gardens open on Saturdays or Sundays. Where gardens are open in the locality you happen to be in, you will see yellow posters in shop windows, advertising the fact.

LANGUAGE. "Much," said Doctor Johnson (who else?), "much may be made of a Scotchman *if he be caught young.*" This quote sums up—even today—the attitude of some English people to the Scots language. They simply assume that their English is superior. As they speak the language of Parliament and much of the media, their arrogance is understandable. The Scots have for long been made to feel uncomfortable with their mother tongue and have only themselves to blame, being actively encouraged—at school, for example—to ape the dialect of the Thames Valley ("Standard English") in order to "get on" in life. The Scots language (i.e. Lowland Scots, not Gaelic) was a northern form of Middle English and in its day was the language of court and literature. It borrows from Scandinavian, Dutch, French and Gaelic. After a series of historical body blows—such as the decamping of the Scottish Court to England after 1603, and the printing of the King James Bible in English, but not Scots—it declined as a literary or official language. It survives, in various forms, virtually as an underground language spoken at home, in shops, the playground, the farm or quayside amongst ordinary folk, especially in its heartlands, in Northeast Scotland. (There they describe Scots who use the brayed diphthongs of the English Thames Valley as speaking with a "bool in the mou"—marble in the mouth!) Plenty of Scots speak English with only an accent and virtually all will "modulate" either unconsciously or out of politeness into understandable English when conversing with a non-dialect speaker. As for Gaelic, that belongs to a different Celtic culture and, though threatened, hangs on in spite of Highland depopulation.

SHOPPING. Shops are usually open 9–5 or 9–5.30; in country districts from 8.30; in popular tourist destinations you will find many shops open in the evenings as well as Sundays. Some shops, away from city-centers, close for one afternoon weekly. Every Scottish town has a "local" holiday on Monday two or three times a year and a "trades holiday" (which affects some shops) for two weeks in midsummer: the dates vary from place to place. On January 1 and 2 the Scots recuperate from Hogmanay (New Year) and these are blank days in the calendar for virtually everyone.

The best buys in Britain in general are antiques, craft items, woollen goods, china, men's shoes, books, confectionery and toys. In Scotland, many visitors go for tweeds, designer knitwear, Shetland and Fair Isle woollens, tartan rugs and materials, Edinburgh crystal, Caithness glass, Celtic silver and pebble jewelry. The Scottish Highlands bristle with old "bothies" (farm buildings) which have been turned into small craft workshops where visitors are welcome—but not pressured—to buy attractive hand-made items of bone, silver, wood, pottery, leather and glass. Handmade chocolates, often with whisky or Drambuie fillings, and the traditional "petticoat tail" shortbread in tin boxes are popular; so too, at a more mundane level, are boiled sweets in jars from particular localities—Berwick cockles, Jethart snails, Edinburgh rock and suchlike crunchy items. Dundee cake, a rich fruit mixture with almonds on top, and Dundee marmalades and heather honeys are among the other eatables which visitors take home from Scotland.

On most purchases VAT (Value Added Tax) at 15% is charged. Under retail export schemes, this charge may be refunded. Unfortunately, not all Scottish shops operate the scheme, but those which specialize in souvenir and peculiarly Scottish goods—kiltmakers, bagpipe makers and so on—will be familiar with the routine. If you have difficulty, and if the saving on the concession is worth your while, contact the VAT Office, H.M. Customs & Excise, 44 York Place, Edinburgh EH1 3JG (tel. 031–556 2433).

Clothing Sizes. Although you may see several charts with comparative U.S.–British sizings, in our experience these are not truly standardized. Best take along a tape measure, or rely on the shop assistant's assessment (in the first place) of your sizing. Always try on a garment before purchasing: an apparently correct sizing may prove to have arm-holes too wide or too narrow, sleeves too long or too short.

MAIL. British postage rates are: Inland (including islands and all Ireland), 15p slow rate and 20p fast (for letters and postcards up to 60g.). To E.E.C. countries in Europe 19p and to other European countries 23p for letters and postcards up to 20g.; Air Mail stickers are not required. To the U.S. and Canada: 32p for Air Mail letters up to 10g., 15p per 10g. thereafter; 27p for postcards; 27p for aerogram, on flimsy paper, obtainable at post offices.

Telegrams. You can send a telegram overseas from post offices or by telephone. If the latter, dial 100. Have plenty of small change to put in the slot if you do this from a public call box. There are no inland telegrams but you may send a telemessage (dial 100) which is delivered next day.

TELEPHONES. Red public call boxes are being replaced by tinted glass boxes with yellow 'T' sign. All coin boxes take 10p coins. The new boxes (with push-button numbers) take most other coins too, and will store them, giving you a refund of unused coins when you have finished the call. Some call boxes only accept a phone card, which you can buy from newsagents. They cost from £1, and save you having to worry about having the right change. Call boxes usually have a directory, dialing instructions, and a list of code numbers at hand. In some isolated places without call boxes you will see a blue sign on a shopfront: "You may telephone from here." Minimum cost for any call is 10p; if you speak for several minutes or to a number outside the area you will need several 10p coins.

Calls made before 8 A.M. and after 6 P.M. and at weekends and public holidays are significantly cheaper than others. Similarly, calls made to places within a 35-mile radius are significantly cheaper than those made over longer distances. IDD (International Direct Dialling) also varies in cost according to distance and time of day. You may dial direct from Scotland to about 50 U.S. and 40 Canadian cities, the rate being 63p–75p per minute. Country codes and international prefixes are listed in telephone directories.

For general enquiries dial 191; for directory enquiries dial 192; for international enquiries dial 100.

The telephone numbers that we quote in this Guide must all be prefixed with the code for the city, town or village mentioned in the address if you are calling from outside that locality. You do not need to use the code if you are calling from the same locality. The Roxburghe hotel in Edinburgh, for example, has the number 225 3921, and that is what you dial if you are calling from anywhere in Edinburgh. If you call from outside the city, you should dial 031–225 3921, 031 being the code for Edinburgh.

You are warned not to make long-distance phone calls from your hotel room without checking very carefully what the cost will be. Hotels frequently add *several hundred percent* to such calls. This is an international practice, not one confined to Britain. It is worthwhile utilizing your telephone credit card for these calls to avoid the massive hotel surcharge and certain U.S. cards are valid in Europe for this purpose.

PHOTOGRAPHY. American and Continental color films are obtainable in Britain. Processing, significantly cheaper than in the U.S., is generally available at city druggists on a next-day basis.

Don't leave already exposed film in your pockets or in any hand luggage while passing through airport X-ray machines. The process can sometimes fog the film and you may find a whole trip's photographs ruined. It is worth investing in a product called Filmashield, a lead-laminated pouch. It stores flat when not in use and holds quite a lot of film or, indeed, your camera with half-used film in it. It is available in many countries.

SPORT. For further information on sports in Scotland, see the sports chapter on page 74. Deer-stalking and shooting can be arranged on the spot by most Highland hotels or in advance by some of the tour operators and handling agents mentioned earlier in this section. We have included a summary of the golf scene in the regional *Practical Information* sections. Further details, including lists of golf-vacation operators and hotels, are available in *Scotland: Home of Golf,* price £2.25 by post. The publishers, Pastime Publications, 15 Dublin Street Lane South, Edinburgh EH1 3PX, also offer *Scotland for Fishing* (£2.25 by post). No special license is needed for fishing Scottish waters. All you need is a local permit from the neighborhood fishing tackle shop, post office or hotel—though for popular (and expensive) salmon beats you should enquire well in advance. We have further information in our *Practical Information* sections for each region.

The various winter sports developments in Scotland are described in the STB's free booklet *Ski Holiday Scotland:* best pick up the latest edition when you arrive; this is a rapidly changing scene. Wherever you come to a sizeable and reasonably accessible loch you will find water sports—sailing, canoeing, water-skiing and the like—going on under the control of some local hotel group. Details are in the STB's free booklet *Adventure and Special Interest Holidays*—which also offers other activity-oriented themes, such as archery, birdwatching, working holidays, winemaking, orienteering—or you can even learn Gaelic at a summer school.

All the booklets mentioned above are normally available in Scottish bookshops, newsstands and hotel kiosks, from information centers or by mail from the Scottish Tourist Board, P.O. Box 8, Wishaw ML2 7BN. Note: prices quoted include postage for U.K. and Republic of Ireland only.

TRAVELING IN SCOTLAND BY CAR. If you bring your own car you must also bring the vehicle's registration documents and a nationality plaque or sticker. Driving your own or hired car you must have a current driving license or International Driving Permit. Then you may drive in Britain for 12 months, after which you will have to pass a test and obtain a British driving license.

Membership of a recognized automobile club in your own country gives you access to certain facilities in the major automobile clubs of Britain. The Royal Automobile Club (RAC) has blue signs, vans and offices at 47 Pall Mall, London SW1Y 1HS and in several English cities; and at 200 Finnieston Street, Glasgow G3 8NZ; 17 Rutland Square, Edinburgh EH1 2BQ; and the Port Office, Stranraer in Scotland. The Automobile Association (AA) has yellow signs and vans, offices at Fanum House, Basingstoke, Hampshire RG21 2BR and in several English cities; and at 20 Melville Street, Edinburgh EH3 7PD; 269 Argyle Street, Glasgow G2 8DW; and the Port Office, Stranraer in Scotland. Both organizations offer literature, roadside help and get-you-home services. Foreign visitors and non-members will find the RAC helpful; the AA is strictly member-oriented.

There is also in Scotland a Royal Scottish Automobile Club (11 Blythswood Square, Glasgow G2 4AG), a social and motor-sporting organization.

Car Rental. Our *Practical Information* sections give details of places where you may rent an automobile. Many visitors to Scotland arrive in vehicles they have rented in England and the major car-rental firms allow you to pick up a vehicle in the south and leave it in a Scottish city, or vice versa.

To rent a medium-sized automobile in Scotland costs up to £25–£35 per day in high season—including insurance but not gas. Some firms insist on payment in advance; some will not rent to those under 21 or over 70.

Rules of the Road. Drive on the left, overtake on the right. Maximum permitted speeds are 70 m.p.h. on motorways, 60 on ordinary roads, 40 or 30 in built-up areas in and around towns. Traffic signs are similar to those in use all over Europe. In the centers of many towns parking is allowed only in metered spaces where you pay 40p–50p an hour by day, nothing at night. Where a single continuous line is painted parallel to the sidewalk, parking is restricted to the hours shown on adjacent time-plates. A double yellow line or zigzag markings indicate that parking is prohibited at all times. Most towns have off-street parking lots. Visitors to Scotland find city parking relatively easy, and motorways and other roads agreeably uncongested. It is compulsory for drivers and front-seat passengers to wear seat-belts.

Gasoline. Comes in two qualities, two-star and four-star. Prices vary from area to area but are currently around £1.75 per imperial gallon, the equivalent of 1.2 American gallons or 4.5 liters. Cheapest in central Scotland; most expensive in the western Highlands and islands. Environmentally-considerate unleaded gas is also becoming available.

Maps. From the Scottish Tourist Board, P.O. Box 8, Wishaw ML2 7BN, and its offices and information centers at home and abroad you may obtain a good *Touring Map of Scotland,* price £3.10 by post in U.K.; or the *Enjoy Scotland Pack* of useful material, including the map, price £6.90. This map is scaled 5 miles to the inch. Among more detailed maps (1 mile to the inch) are the Ordnance Survey's Scottish series, tourist maps of holiday areas and town plans, and Bartholomew's National maps, available at most booksellers.

TRAVELING IN SCOTLAND BY BUS. There is a very extensive bus network throughout the country. City bus services are comprehensive; not so in country districts. All the networks underwent privatization in 1986, with some initial difficulties, but these are mostly over.

Express services link main cities and towns; for example, Glasgow to Edinburgh, Inverness, Aberdeen, Perth, Skye, Ayr, Dumfries and Carlisle, and of course similar services from Edinburgh. From Inverness there are routes to Aberdeen, Wick, Thurso and Fort William. These express services are very fast, and the fares are quite reasonable.

Full details of all these services can be had from most bus stations or the Travel Center, Buchanan Street Bus Station, Glasgow G2 3NP (tel. 041–332 7133); Eastern Scottish, St. Andrew Square Bus Station, Edinburgh EH1 3DU (tel. 031–556 8464); and Scottish Travel Center, 14 South St. Andrew Street, Edinburgh EH2 2AZ (tel. 031–557 5522).

For town, suburban or short-distance journeys you normally buy your ticket on the bus, from paybox or driver. Sometimes the exact fare is demanded. For longer journeys, e.g. Glasgow–Inverness, it is usual to reserve and pay at the bus station booking office.

City tours, bus tours and excursions are run mainly by private companies. Among the latter are Silver Fox Coaches of Edinburgh; Cotters Tours Ltd. (Glasgow); Parks of Hamilton; Doigs Tours (Greenock) Ltd.; McIntyre's Coach Tours (Aberdeen). Details of these services and others on similar lines are available from travel agents.

There is no general runabout ticket for bus travel in Scotland. But each company issues its own in conjunction with the local tourist authority. These are based on cities or towns or resorts. Costs vary but range from around £2.50 for a day ticket to around £15 for a family ticket for a week, with unlimited travel within a fixed zone. Details from bus stations and local tourist offices.

TRAVELING IN SCOTLAND BY TRAIN. Scotland has a good rail network extending all the way to Thurso and Wick, the most northerly stations in the British Isles. Lowland services are generally reliable and fast. They radiate mostly from Glasgow and Edinburgh, between which there is a half-hourly shuttle taking some 45 minutes. Glasgow has two main stations, Central (for all services from England and southwest Scotland) and Queen Street (for services to Edinburgh, Aberdeen and the north). The city also has an extensive electrified suburban system and an Underground (subway) which serves the city center. Edinburgh has one main station, Waverley.

Although many routes in Scotland run through extremely attractive countryside, several are outstanding. The best are from Glasgow (Queen Street) to Oban via Loch Lomond; to Fort William and Mallaig via Rannoch (ferry connection to Skye); from Edinburgh to Inverness via the Forth Bridge and Perth; from Inverness to Kyle of Lochalsh and to Wick; and from Inverness to Aberdeen.

Some lines in Scotland—all suburban services and lines north and west of Inverness—are one class only, i.e. standard. Elsewhere both first and standard predominate. Long distance services carry buffet and refreshment cars. There are also sleeper services between Inverness and Glasgow and Edinburgh.

A luxury private train, the *Royal Scotsman,* does scenic tours, partly under steam. Gourmet banquets en route. Book with *Abercrombie & Kent,* Sloane Square House, Holbein Place, London, SW1W 8NS (tel. 01–730 9600) or in the U.S. at 1420 Kensington Rd., Oak Brook, IL 60521 (tel. 800–323–7308 or 312–954–2944), from $1,590 (three days) to $3,990 (six days). *British Rail* offer occasional pullman rail cruises, partly steamhauled, window seat guaranteed, overnights in sleeper or hotel, in the *Highlander* and *West Highlander;* from London (St. Pancras), P.M. Fri. to A.M. Mon., £215–£245 according to season. Details from London (Euston)

Travel Center. Book through *InterCity Scottish Land Cruises,* 104 Birmingham Road, Lichfield, Staffs. WS14 9BW (tel. 0543–254076).

The *Freedom of Scotland Rover* ticket, standard only, costs £44 (seven days) or £72 (14 days). Unlimited travel north of Berwick-upon-Tweed and Carlisle. Available from most Scottish stations and certain English ones, or from any British Rail travel agent, by personal or postal application. Don't forget that there are very few trains in the Highlands on Sundays.

Preserved Steam Railways. Among surviving steam railways, where historic locomotives periodically operate, usually at weekends from May to Sept. are: *Caledonian Railway,* Brechin, Angus; *Bo'ness & Kinneil Railway,* Bo'ness, West Lothian; *Strathspey Railway,* Aviemore, Invernessshire (every day in summer except Fri.). ScotRail, ironically, hire steam locos from preservation bodies to run frequent very popular summerseason excursions on their own Fort William to Mallaig rail link (in addition to their normal services). Full details from principal Scottish railroad stations.

TRAVELING IN SCOTLAND BY AIR. Although a small country, Scotland nonetheless has a significant internal air network. British Airways, the principal carrier, has fly/drive packages to Orkney and Shetland of four to 14 days from all main U.K. airports. British Airways' *Highland Rover* airpass, price £170 from BA travel shops and most travel agents, allows eight flights between mainland and/or island airports over 8–21 days. Loganair is another important carrier within Scotland.

TRAVELING IN SCOTLAND BY FERRY. With so many islands, plus the great Firth of Clyde waterway, ferry services in Scotland are of paramount importance. Most of these are now vehicle ferries, although a number of the smaller ones are passenger only. All vehicle ferries carry foot passengers.

The main operator is Caledonian MacBrayne Ltd., The Ferry Terminal, Gourock PA19 1QP (tel. 0475–33755). They are a state-owned company, known generally as Calmac. Their services extend from the Firth of Clyde, where they operate an extremely extensive network, right up to the northwest of Scotland and all of the Hebrides. Calmac offer a Car Rover runabout ticket which is ideal for touring holidays in the Islands as well as an island hopping scheme called Island Hopscotch. Western Ferries, 16 Woodside Crescent, Glasgow G3 7UT (tel. 041–332 9766) operate Dunoon–Gourock on the Clyde, and Iskay (Port Askaig) to Jura.

The Orkney Islands are linked to the mainland by car ferry from Scrabster (near Thurso) to Stromness (on the main island of Orkney, called Mainland). This is operated by P & O Ferries, Jamieson's Quay, P.O. Box 5, Aberdeen AB9 8DL (tel. 0224–572615). The ferry runs daily with an extra service from June to September. The Shetlands are linked to the mainland by car ferry from Aberdeen to Lerwick; three sailings weekly in each direction. The main ferry on this route, the *St. Clair,* has cabin accommodations. This service is operated by P & O, too.

There is also a series of inter-island ferries between the Shetlands and the Orkneys. Details of these are given in the comprehensive guide, *Getting Around the Highlands and Islands;* see below for details.

For a taste of Scottish sea air, take a daytrip on the Firth of Clyde in a charter yacht. Among several options (details in STB's *Adventure and Special Interests* free booklet) are the skippered voyages in the sailing ketch *Norsala* (write to Modern Charters Ltd., Shore Rd., Clynder G84 0QD).

TRAVELPASS. One of the most useful runabout tickets in the British Isles is the Travelpass, issued by the Highlands and Islands Development Board. This covers travel by train, bus and ferry within the entire region and also includes ferries to Orkney and of course all the ferries to the Outer Hebrides. In area it covers all Scotland north and west of a line joining (roughly) the Firth of Clyde and the Moray Firth. Services of Scottish Citylink and the Scottish Bus Group come into the scheme. You can use the pass to travel by train (standard) or bus from Glasgow, Edinburgh, or Aberdeen into the Highland region and back again.

Issued for 7 or 13 days consecutive travel, it costs £35 or £57; in high season (June–Sept.) £50 or £75. Apply in person to British Rail at Glasgow, Edinburgh, Aberdeen, Paisley, Stirling or Inverness stations; at main bus stations in Glasgow or Edinburgh; or to Caledonian MacBrayne, The Ferry Terminal, Gourock PA19 1QP. Postal or telephone applications to Hi-Line, Dingwall, Ross-shire IV15 9SL (tel. 0349–63434).

All holders of the Travelpass receive a free copy of the comprehensive guide-timetable *Getting Around the Highlands and Islands* which covers the entire transport system within the region by plane, train, bus and ferry. The guide can also be purchased (£3 including postage) from Travelguide, Information Services, H.I.D.B., Golspie, Highland and Islands. It is also on sale at many bookshops and tourist information centers in Scotland.

CUSTOMS ON RETURNING HOME. If you propose to take on your holiday any *foreign-made* articles, such as cameras, binoculars, expensive timepieces and the like, it is wise to put with your travel documents the receipt from the retailer or some other evidence that the item was bought in your home country. If you bought the article on a previous holiday abroad and have already paid duty on it, carry with you the receipt for this. Otherwise, on returning home, you may be charged duty (for British residents, Value Added Tax as well). In other words, unless you can prove prior possession, foreign-made articles are dutiable *each time* they enter the U.S. The details below are correct as we go to press. It would be wise to check in case of change.

U.S. Residents. You may bring in $400 worth of foreign merchandise as gifts or for personal use without having to pay duty, provided you have been out of the country more than 48 hours and provided you have not claimed a similar exemption within the previous 30 days. Every member of a family is entitled to the same exemption, regardless of age, and the exemptions can be pooled.

The $400 figure is based on the fair retail value of the goods in the country where acquired. Included for travelers over the age of 21 are one liter of alcohol, 100 cigars (non-Cuban) and 200 cigarettes. Any amount in excess of those limits will be taxed at the port of entry, and may additionally be taxed in the traveler's home state. Only one bottle of perfume trademarked in the U.S. may be brought in. Write to the U.S. Customs Service (Box 7407, Washington, DC 20044) for information regarding importa-

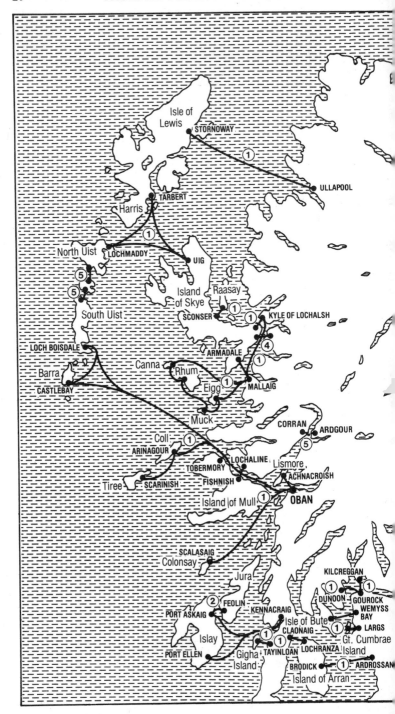

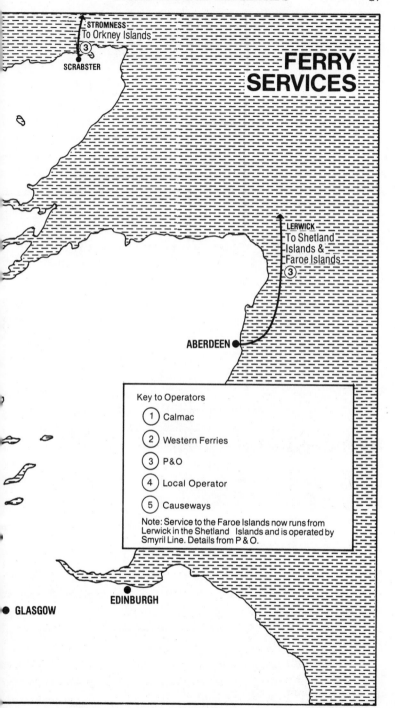

STROMNESS
To Orkney Islands
(3)
SCRABSTER

FERRY
SERVICES

LERWICK
To Shetland
Islands &
Faroe Islands
(3)

ABERDEEN

Key to Operators

(1) Calmac

(2) Western Ferries

(3) P&O

(4) Local Operator

(5) Causeways

Note: Service to the Faroe Islands now runs from
Lerwick in the Shetland Islands and is operated by
Smyril Line. Details from P & O.

EDINBURGH

GLASGOW

tion of automobiles and/or motorcycles. You may not bring home meats, fruits, plants, soil or other agricultural items.

Gifts valued at under $50 may be mailed to friends or relatives at home, but not more than one per day (of receipt) to any one addressee. These gifts must not include perfumes costing more than $5, tobacco or liquor.

Canadian Residents. In addition to personal effects, the following articles may be brought in duty free: a maximum of 50 cigars, 200 cigarettes, 2 pounds of tobacco and 40 ounces of liquor, provided these are declared in writing to customs on arrival and accompany the traveler in hand or checked-through baggage. These are included in the basic exemption of $300 a year. Personal gifts should be mailed as "Unsolicited Gift—Value Under $40." Canadian customs regulations are strictly enforced; you are recommended to check what your allowances are and to make sure you have kept receipts for whatever you have bought abroad. For details ask for the Canada Customs brochure, *I Declare*.

THE
SCOTTISH
SCENE

PRESENTING THE SCOTS

A Race Apart

In some old collection of phonographs, you may well turn up *Roamin' in the Gloamin'* or *I Love a Lassie* or one of the other comic songs of Harry Lauder, a star of the music halls of the 1920s. With his garish kilt, short crooked walking stick, rich rolling "r's" and "pawky" (cheerfully impudent) humor, chiefly based on the alleged meanness of the Scots, he impressed the Scottish character on the world. But it was, needless to say, a false impression and one the Scots have been trying to stamp out ever since.

So, how then do you characterize the Scots? Temperamentally, they are a mass of contradictions. They have been likened, not to a Scotch egg, but to a soft-boiled egg: a dour hard shell, a mushy middle. The Scot laughs and weeps with almost Latin facility, but to strangers he is reserved, non-committal, in no hurry to make an impression. Historically, fortitude and resilience are his hallmarks; and there are streaks of both resignation and pitiless ferocity in his make up, warring with sentimentality and love of family. Very Scottish was the instant reaction of an old lady of Edinburgh 200 years ago, when news arrived of the defeat in Mysore in India and of the Scottish soldiers being fettered in irons, two by two: "God help the puir chiel that's chained tae oor Davie."

The Scots are in general suspicious of the go-getter. Whizz kid is a term of contempt. But they are by no means plodders, though it is true to say that they are determined and thorough, respecting success only when it has been a few hundred years in the making. Praise of some bright ambitious youngster is quenched with the sneer: "Him? Ah kent (knew) his faither."

Yet this is the nation which built commerce throughout the British Empire and opened wild territories and was responsible for much of mankind's scientific and technological advancement, a nation boastful about things it is not too good at, shame-facedly modest about genuine achievements. From a hand-out about the Edinburgh school of medicine:

"If one excepts a few discoveries such as that of 'fixed air' by Black, of the diverse functions of the nerve-roots by Bell, of the anaesthetic properties of chloroform by Simpson, of the invention of certain powerful drugs by Christison and of the importance of antiseptic procedures by Lister, the influence of Edinburgh medicine has been of a steady constructive rather than a revolutionary type."

A further paradox is that, while Scotland always does badly compared with the rest of Europe when the crime, poverty, poor health and drunkenness statistics appear, Scotland is a land where old values are cherished, where honesty and plain dealing are the rule, where more children are brought up according to old-fashioned moral precepts than elsewhere. In country districts one still sees the effects of religious teachings and frugal habits: "porridge and the Shorter Catechism."

Among things which strike most newcomers to Scotland are: the generosity of the Scots; the narrowness of their minds; their obsession with respectability; their satisfaction with themselves and their desire to stay as they are; and above all their passionate love of Scotland.

The qualities which unite the English and Scots are more important than those which divide them. And when we travel through Scotland we may never meet a native who fits the descriptions we have outlined here: so diverse is mankind, even in a small, tightly-knit land. Glaswegians will tell us the Edinburghers are hardly Scots at all; Edinburghers will point out that if every Irishman in Glasgow walked out with a Jew under his arm there would be no one left; we shall observe that Highlanders look on Lowlanders as Sassenachs, no better than the English . . . Maybe it is best to come to Scotland without any preconceived ideas at all, but to take the Scots as you find them.

Education, Law and the Church

Obstinate refusal to go along with English ideas has led the nation to be accused of a head-in-the-sand attitude to progress. But the Scots have their own ideas of progress and they jealously guard the few institutions which remain unique to them.

Educationally, Scotland has a proud record. It is her boast that she had four universities—St. Andrews, Aberdeen, Glasgow and Edinburgh—when England had only two: Oxford and Cambridge. The "lad o' pairts" (parts, i.e. talents), the poor child of a feckless father and a fiercely self-sacrificing mother, sternly tutored by the village "dominie" (schoolmaster) and turned loose at the age of 13 with so firm a base of learning that he rose to the very top of his profession . . . this type of lad is a phenomenon of Scottish social history. The sacrifices that boys made as a matter of course to further their education are an old Scottish tradition. "Meal Monday," the mid-semester holiday at a Scottish university, is a survival of the long weekend that once enabled students to return to their distant homes—on foot—and replenish the sack of "meal" (oatmeal) which was their only subsistence.

As to university education, a reformer has written that nothing shows so clearly the Scots' passion for learning than the willingness of students to crowd into medieval lecture-rooms to listen to inaudible, inarticulate—but erudite—professors.

It is a British cliché that an English education teaches you to think and a Scottish education stuffs your head with information. The average Scot does appear to be better informed than his English neighbor and to discuss facts rather than ideas. Scots pride themselves on their international outlook and on being better linguists than the English. The Scots get on well with foreigners and they offer strangers a kindly welcome and a civility which is not often found in the modern world.

As the Scots have their own traditions in education, so is their legal system distinct from that of England's. In England the police both investigate crime and prosecute suspects. In Scotland there is a public prosecutor directly responsible to the Lord Advocate (equivalent to England's Attorney General), himself accountable to Parliament.

For the most part, however, you will notice few practical differences except in terminology. The barrister in England becomes an advocate in Scotland. Law-office name-plates designate their occupants "S.S.C." (Solicitor to the Supreme Court) or "W.S." (Writer to the Signet); cases for prosecution go before the "procurator fiscal" and are tried by the "sheriff" or "sheriff-substitute." The terms are different in England; and procedures are slightly different too, for Scotland is one of the few countries which still bases its legal system on the old Roman law.

Crimes with picturesque names from ancient times remain on the statute-book without precise equivalents in England: "hamesucken," for example, means assaulting a person in his home. In criminal cases Scotland adds to "Guilty" or "Not Guilty" a third verdict: "Not Proven." This, say the cynics, signifies "Don't do it again."

The Presbyterian Church of Scotland—the "Kirk"—is entirely independent of the Church of England. Up to the 20th century it was a power in the land and did much to shape Scottish character. There are still those who can remember when the minister visited houses like an inquisitor and put members of the families through their catechism, punishing or reprimanding those who were not word-perfect. On Sunday mornings the elders patrolled the streets, ordering people into church and rebuking those who sat in their gardens or stared idly out of the windows.

Religion in Scotland, as elsewhere, has lost much of its grip. But the Kirk remains influential in rural districts, where Kirk officials are pillars of local society. Ministers and their wives are seen in all their somber glory in Edinburgh in the springtime, when the General Assembly of the Kirk takes place and, for a week or more, Scottish newspapers devote several column inches daily to their deliberations.

The Episcopalian Church of Scotland has bishops, as its name implies (unlike the Kirk, where the ministers are all equal) and a more colorful ritual. It approximates to a Church of England north of the Border. Episcopalianism is considered genteel and has been described rather sourly by the Scottish novelist Lewis Grassic Gibbon as "more a matter of social status than theological conviction . . . a grateful bourgeois acknowledgment of anglicisation."

Of the various nonconformist offshoots of the established Kirk, the Free Kirk of Scotland is the largest. It remains faithful to the monolithic unity of its forefathers, promoting the grim discipline that John Knox promoted long ago. The Free Kirk is strong in parts of the Outer Hebrides—Lewis, Harris and North Uist. Here, no buses run on Sundays, all the shops are shut and there is a general atmosphere of a people cowering under the wrath of God.

Among the fishing communities, especially of the northeast from Buckie round to Peterhead, particularly including Gardenstown, evangelical movements such as the Close Brethren and Jehovah's Witnesses have made impressive inroads.

Outside religion, Scotland on the whole is mercifully free of that class-consciousness and social elitism which so often amuses or disgusts foreign residents in England. But her turbulent history has left Scotland a legacy of sectarian bigotry, comparable to that of Northern Ireland, which England grew out of centuries ago. Scotland's large minority population of Roman Catholics is still to some extent under-privileged. Catholics tend to stick together, Protestants to mix only with Protestants. Even the two most famous soccer teams in Scotland—Rangers and Celtic—are notorious for their sectarian bias.

Scots and Scotch

A word, finally, is needed on the vexed subject of nomenclature. A "scotchman" is a nautical device for "scotching" or clamping a running rope. It is not a native of Scotland. Though you may find some rather more conservative people refer to themselves as "Scotchmen" and consider themselves "Scotch", most prefer "Scot" or "Scotsman", and call themselves "Scottish" or "Scots."

There are exceptions to this rule. Certain internationally known Scottish products are "Scotch." There is Scotch whisky, Scotch wool, Scotch tweed, Scotch mist (persistent drizzling rain). A Scotch snap is a short accented note followed by a longer—a characteristic phrase in Scottish music, though certainly not unique to it. A modern addition to the list is Scotch tape. A snack food of a hard-boiled egg wrapped in sausage is a Scotch egg.

You may include the Scots in the broader term British. But they dislike the word Brits. And nothing infuriates them more than being called English. Nonetheless there are a lot of Anglo-Scots; that is, people of Scottish birth who live in England or the off-spring of marriages between Scottish and English people. But they are not to be confused with Sassenachs, a word applied jokily or disdainfully to all the English and which is the Gaelic word for Saxon. But at the same time, English people who live in Scotland remain English to their dying day, and their children after them. Similarly, the description of North Britain for Scotland, which crept in during Victorian times, has now crept out again. It survives only in the names of a few North British hotels. Scots feel that it denies their national identity and there are some who, on receiving a letter with "N.B." or "North Britain" in the address, will cross it out and return the envelope to the sender.

SCOTTISH HISTORY

The Rulers of the North

The preoccupation with genealogy that most Scots share has led some Scottish historians to trace links between the earliest Scots and the ancient civilizations of the Mediterranean. Thus "Gael" has been linked with Gaythelos, a mythical Greek warrior, and connections have been sought between "Scot" and Scota, daughter of an Egyptian pharaoh. Sadly, however, these antecedents have no very strong basis in fact. But on the other hand it is known, from monuments and artefacts dating from the Neolithic period (about 6,000 years ago), that numbers of short, dark immigrants from the Mediterranean did establish themselves in Scotland.

But they were, as might be imagined, very much in a minority among the other early settlers in Scotland. A very much larger body of peoples came from what is now Germany, while at the same time there were interminglings with ancient Britons from the south, with Irish from the west and with Norsemen from Scandinavia. In fact, Scotland was overrun by turbulent hordes from all quarters. Some liked it there and stayed on.

The Romans in Scotland

A more precise history begins with the arrival of the Romans in Scotland in A.D. 80, pushing north from Hadrian's Wall with the idea of consolidating absolutely the Empire's northwestern frontier. And at Mons Graupius in A.D. 84 the Roman general Agricola destroyed the Scottish tribes in what, in point of numbers involved, was the largest battle ever fought on British soil. The defeated leader of the tribes is credited with a quote which has rung down the ages: "They make a desert and call it peace."

Agricola built a number of forts in his newly-conquered territories, while his successor, the Emperor Antoninus Pius, piled up further barriers of stone and turf (the Antonine Wall) across the narrowest point of Scotland, from Bo'ness on the Firth of Forth to Old Kilpatrick on the Firth of Clyde. But as an outpost of Empire it proved difficult to hold and after 40 years the Romans abandoned it, retreating to the security of the more massive Hadrian's Wall. The best-preserved parts of the Antonine Wall are at Bearsden, on the outskirts of Glasgow and Rough Castle, west of Falkirk. These sites are in the care of Historic Scotland, the government agency with responsibility for a variety of castles, ancient sites and monuments. North of the wall, Tayside was a Roman center of activity, though much of the remains are grassed-over and sometimes not easy to spot. The best known Roman camps are at Inchtuthil and Ardoch, the latter perhaps the most impressive.

The Four Tribes

The curtain had hardly risen on Scottish history when it fell again. The Dark Ages—darker than most—saw disparate bands of violent peoples fighting, combining, splitting up and coming together again until, about A.D. 600, four recognizable tribal divisions emerged. They were the Picts, of unknown origin, in the north; the Scots, of Irish origin, in the west; the Britons, kinfolk of the Welsh, in the southwest; and the Angles, first of many Sassenach invaders, in the southeast. The Angles spoke low German and Saxon English, the Scots and Britons Gaelic dialects, and the Picts an aboriginal patois all their own. Very gradually, external pressures from England, a larger and more sophisticated country, from the seaborne invasions of the Norsemen, and, as much as anything else, from the growth of Christianity, molded these groups into something like a nation. (The painfully slow spread of Christianity, during this darkest of Dark Ages, received important impulses with the building by Ninian of his chapel at Whithorn (Dumfries and Galloway) around A.D. 400, Mungo preaching on the banks of the Clyde in A.D. 550 and the establishment in A.D. 563 by Columba, disciple of St. Patrick himself, of a community of monks and missionaries on the island of Iona.)

Enter Macbeth

The Declaration of Arbroath, which the Scots sent to the Pope in 1320, boasted the continuous reign in Scotland of 113 kings and queens of "royal stock, the line unbroken by a single foreigner." The bulk of them, however, (about 100) were shadowy figures, and monarchs of limited authority only. One such, for example, was Kenneth II, who, so it is said, adopted the thistle as the national emblem of Scotland after a Danish invader trod on one and let out a yell, thereby giving the alarm which saved the Scots at the battle of Luncarty near Perth. Unfortunately, there is no clear evidence that the battle took place, while the thistle did not appear as Scotland's emblem until many years later.

Kenneth MacAlpin, a chieftain of the Scots and Picts, is sometimes called the first king of Scotland (843). But strict genealogies begin only with Malcolm II (1005–1034), who recovered the southeastern territories from the English, received the southwest by inheritance and handed a more or less united land to his successor Duncan. The warring lines of the Atholls and Morays tore Scotland apart again, however, shortly afterwards. It was during this period, for example, that Duncan of Atholl was slain by Macbeth of Moray—an incident which, centuries later, was to provide Shakespeare with the idea for his play. Malcolm III, called "Canmore" (Great Head), ultimately secured victory for the house of Atholl in 1057, though his successors had to deal with Moray rebellions for another 200 years.

However, even then ambitious earls, claiming absolute sovereignty over certain districts, and Norwegian monarchs, who retained possession of their Scottish colonies, frequently ensured that these Scottish kings of the 11th and 12th centuries were rulers in name only. (The Hebridean islands did not become Scottish until 1263, Orkney and Shetland not until 1472; and constitutionalists say that Norway is entitled to buy these islands back whenever she cares to.)

In their troubles, the Scottish monarchs turned increasingly to England for help. Royal marriages with English princesses and pacts with the Norman rulers of England brought Scotland some domestic stability, but at the cost of making her a client state of England.

The "Sair Sanct"

"Sair Sanct" means "sore saint" or "sore saintly"—an expression applied ruefully to King David I, who almost bankrupted the kingdom by the building of great abbeys. Both before and after he became king he busied himself erecting tourist attractions of the future, notably the four graceful sisters of Tweedside: the abbeys of Jedburgh (1118), Kelso (1128), Melrose (1136) and Dryburgh (1150).

This "most courtly king," as an English chronicler called him, was brought up in the care of William the Conqueror and was eager to give his rough countrymen some Norman polish. For a start, he offered tax concessions to lairds who "agreed to dwell in a more civil manner, and be attired with more refinement, and be more particular about their food." He persuaded Norman friends of his youth to live in Scotland and set the natives an example. Some of the best-known Scottish family names— Seton, Fraser, Lamont, Lindsay and others—have stemmed from the "Norman invasion" which David encouraged.

David, in periodic bouts of warfare, nonetheless managed to keep Scotland reasonably unified: he was a man of his time, cunning and cruel as well as courtly. But after his death, the feuding and fighting between the rival factions increased. At the wedding of King Alexander III and Jolande de Dreux in Jedburgh Abbey a ghostly figure appeared, prophesying the sorrows of Scotland. To many, it must have seemed like a statement of the obvious.

Freedom Fighters

By the latter part of the 13th century, Scotland came more closely under the control of England, specifically in the person of the ambitious and successful Edward I, the "Hammer of the Scots." The death of Alexander

III in 1286 (he and his horse fell over a cliff at Kinghorn one dark night—some say they were pushed) gave Edward a wonderful opportunity to bind Scotland's fortunes to his own. He promptly betrothed his son to Alexander's granddaughter and successor, a small child called Margaret, envisaging a union of the crowns in due course. This plan, however, failed when the little girl died on the way home from the Norwegian court where she had been brought up.

But Edward was presented with another opportunity of bringing his northern neighbor under control when he was appointed to arbitrate among the new claimants to the Scottish throne, no fewer than 13 of them. Ignoring the native Pictish rules of lineage, he appointed John Balliol as king, having been assured of Balliol's support. Scotland's puppet-king (who did not survive long!) thereby gained the title ever after of "Toom Tabard"—empty coat.

But Scotland's affairs went no more smoothly than they had done before. The patriot William Wallace, a private citizen, organized a rabble into an army and gained surprising victories over the English forces in central Scotland. The stirring battle-hymn of Robert Burns, *Scots wha hae wi' Wallace bled,* an unofficial national anthem to this day, expresses the pride and passionate love of country which Scotland found under Wallace.

In 1305, William Wallace was hunted down and executed for breaking an oath of allegiance he had never sworn. The subsequent turmoil threw up another freedom fighter in the person of Robert Bruce. (He was sometimes known as Robert *the* Bruce, or simply as The Bruce.)

How Bruce learned patience and perseverance from a spider while he was in hiding in a cave on Rathlin Island (Northern Ireland) is a story every Scottish child is told. Whatever the truth of it, he certainly survived many defeats and disgraces before writing some of the most glorious pages of Scottish history. Luckily for him, the "Hammer of the Scots" had been succeeded by an ineffectual son, Edward II, in 1307.

In 1314, a date ever-memorable to true Scots, Bruce snatched Edinburgh Castle from Edward II and then vanquished the English army as it marched to the relief of its beleaguered comrades in Stirling Castle. The fight immortalized the field of Bannockburn, a place which is ready to sink today under the weight of its commemorative statuary; and a name which is still hurled defiantly at the "auld enemy"—England—whenever the two nations meet in sporting encounters.

"It Cam' wi' a Lass"

Robert the Bruce lived to see Scotland's nationhood confirmed by the Treaty of Northampton (1328) but, like his old antagonist Edward I, he produced a weak and vacillating son, David II. And during his long reign Scotland almost fell again under English domination.

The crown then passed through Bruce's daughter Marjory to her son, another Robert. Marjory had married Walter the Steward—the Stewardship of Scotland being one of the ancient high offices of state—and thus the name Steward, or Stewart, became the name of Scotland's royal dynasty. Later on, through French influence, the spelling was altered to Stuart.

The Stuarts ushered in an eventful and mainly unhappy era. Nearly every one of them—11 kings, three queens and two "pretenders" (claimants to the throne)—met bloody or miserable ends, fighting the English, unruly barons and obstinate churchmen.

James I, for years a prisoner in England, was brutally murdered at Perth; James II was killed when one of his cannon exploded at Roxburgh Castle; James III died by an assassin's hand after losing the battle of Sauchieburn; James IV fell at the battle of Flodden (Northumbria), along with the flower of Scottish chivalry; James V, vanquished at Solway Moss on the Border, died of a broken heart in Falkland Palace. Hearing, as he expired, that his Queen had given birth to a daughter in Linlithgow Palace he muttered: "It cam' wi' a lass and it'll gang (go) wi' a lass"—"it" being the House of Stuart; the two lasses being Marjory Bruce who began the dynasty and the newborn princess with whom, James supposed, it would come to an end.

The Monstrous Regiment of Women

Things did not turn out like that. The baby Mary, succeeding to the throne within a few days of her birth, revived Stuart hopes and Scottish fortunes. To protect her in her extreme youth an arrangement called the "auld alliance" was made use of: a mutual assistance pact between France and Scotland, two nations with little in common but their hatred and fear of England and love of good wine. Adhered to by the Scots with sentimental fervor and by the French with cynical opportunism, the "auld alliance" crops up at various turning-points of history down to our own times.

So Mary went to France for safety. At 16 she married the sickly Dauphin (crown prince). Her French mother ruled Scotland on behalf of the French king until Mary, now a bewitching widow of 18, returned to take over her realm. She and her mother were two of the ladies the Protestant agitator John Knox had in mind when he thundered against the "monstrous regiment (regime) of women."

Mary was universally acknowledged Queen of Scots. Thanks to a complex Anglo-Scottish family tree, she also had a better title to the throne of England than her cousin Elizabeth, the incumbent. But she was a Roman Catholic. In Scotland the Reformation was in full swing, in England it had already been accomplished. Both nations declared for a Protestant royal family. Mary faced the irreconcilable tasks of placating Queen Elizabeth, whom she had hopes of succeeding, and of restoring Catholicism to Britain. After five years her patience gave out and in 1565 she made a foolish marriage to Lord Darnley, another cousin, and allegedly another Catholic.

Disaster followed. Her Italian secretary David Rizzio was stabbed to death in her presence; Darnley her husband was booby-trapped and blown up in his lodging at Kirk o' Field near Edinburgh. (Tradition has it that Mary went off and played a round of golf at Seton (Lothian) when she heard the news—which showed a sense of priorities that some Scots would approve of.) Piling folly on folly she next married the uncouth Earl of Bothwell who was supposed to have arranged Darnley's murder and was reputed to be a practitioner of the Black Arts.

Abandoned by him and driven from Scotland, she became Elizabeth's prisoner. For the next 20 years she was moved from castle to castle in England, a captive of state whose life depended entirely on political whims. In 1587 Queen Elizabeth finally signed the death warrant and the Queen of Scots, lovely still though racked with rheumatism from damp apartments, was beheaded for treason. She had spent nearly half her life in prison.

Almost as much romantic ink has been spilled over Mary Queen of Scots as over that other fascinating leader of lost causes, her great-great-great-grandson Bonnie Prince Charlie. She was a sharp and wilful schemer, even when handicapped in prison, she was a Catholic and half a foreigner, her private life did not bear looking into . . . despite all that she is Scotland's heroine and she can still bring out the latent chivalry of a nation notorious for its sturdy chauvinism, stern Protestantism and respect for moral values.

A Counterblaste

Mary's son, another James, was crowned in Stirling while only a year old. John Knox preached the sermon. James' minority was a troubled time, but soon the young king proved himself an adept ruler, manipulative and full of guile. When he was only 17 he declared his desire to be a "universal king" who stood above factional interests. He balanced the politics of the old noble families with the use of his own special agents while, at the same time, managing to keep the Reformed Church of Scotland in check. Yet he also had a marked aversion for arms and bloodshed, having seen enough of it as a very small child. He developed a preference for the arts and science and was a minor poet of some distinction.

When Elizabeth of England died childless in 1603 the prize which had eluded his mother fell into his lap. He became James I of England. He was already James VI of Scotland and in the table of succession he is styled "James VI and I."

As King of England, Scotland and Ireland, James's power and prestige were greatly increased. His method of "ruling by the pen" seemed to work. Unusually for a Stuart he never fought a battle, never allowed the Kirk (the Scottish Presbyterian Church) to dictate to him—and died peacefully in his bed.

The End of an "Auld Sang"

Arrogance, obstinacy, extravagance, ingratitude and a firm belief in the divine right of kings were implanted in all the later Stuarts. Both England and Scotland suffered from their clumsy handling of economic problems and in addition they brought to England the bitterness of religious conflict with which Scotland was all too familiar.

In Scotland these were the years of the Solemn League and Covenant (1643) which called for a Presbyterian nation and a Presbyterian monarch; and of the Killing Times (1666 onwards) when the pendulum swung against Presbyterianism and the Covenanters, goaded into rebellion, were pursued and hacked to death wherever they could be found. Readers of Sir Walter Scott will remember "Old Mortality," the aged wanderer who went from place to place tidying up the Covenanters' neglected graves.

When in 1688 England forced the Catholic James II and VII to abdicate, no one north of the Border raised a hand to save the last Stuart king. The Protestants were now firmly on top. It was decreed that no Roman Catholic should henceforth sit on the English or Scottish throne—and none has ever done so. Joint sovereigns were brought over from Holland to share the vacant crown; one of them, Mary, was a Stuart and their successor, Anne, who came to the throne in 1702, was the last of the Stuart monarchs.

During Anne's reign, men and nations had time to let the dust settle and to contemplate their fortunes and their relationships. In a more mercantile age, Scotland wished to emulate her richer southern neighbor in expanding her commerce and trade, but England was unwilling to consider joint trading ventures. Towns and Parliament thus risked their finances in a national scheme to found a colony near Panama. This was known as the Darien Scheme and proved totally disastrous for the Scottish economy. An expedition left Scotland in 1698, but by 1700, the colony of "New Caledonia" had been abandoned through disease, mutiny and a Spanish blockade. England ordered her own colonies nearby to give no help.

Bankrupt and ailing, Scotland eventually accepted a Treaty of Union with England (by 110 votes to 67) in 1707. She kept her own Kirk and legal system and was promised a share in the benefits of England's colonial exploitations.

Charlie Was Their Darling

Historical novelists have mined glittering seams from the triumphs and troubles of the Stuarts, but the richest nuggets have been found in the adventures of two who never quite made it to the throne: the Jacobite pretenders of the early-18th century. ("Jacobite" signifies a follower of Jacobus, the Latin for James.)

Many people both in Scotland and England regarded the Hanoverian successors of Queen Anne (George I, the first of the Hanoverians, came to the throne in 1714) as usurpers. James, offspring of James II and VII, based his claim to the throne on his status as the senior surviving Stuart. His assets were the sympathy of Catholics everywhere; a general discontent in Scotland at the first effects of the Union; and, as always, France's eagerness to stir up trouble.

The Old Pretender, however, was not a very inspiring personality and his campaign of the Fifteen (1715) petered out after a few half-hearted skirmishes.

The Forty-five (1745) was a different matter. The Young Pretender, otherwise Prince Charles Edward or Bonnie Prince Charlie or the Young Chevalier—Jacobites gave him various affectionate names—enthusiastically embraced his father's cause.

He owed his chance to the French, who were again at war with Britain and seeking a diversion. Bonnie Prince Charlie landed on Eriskay in the Outer Hebrides, crossed to the mainland and set up his standard at Glenfinnan in August 1745. His youth (he was only 24), his courageous energy, his charm and vivacity (he was a mixture of Scot, Italian and Pole) attracted the Highland chiefs and their clans to his banner in satisfactory numbers: they were mostly Catholics and not averse to the idea of a little Lowland foray.

Marching south the small army took Edinburgh by surprise, installed the Prince at Holyroodhouse and proclaimed his father King James III and VIII. Government forces rallied, but the Jacobites brushed them aside. The rebel army marched rapidly towards London, gathering supporters as it went. Why it turned back at Derby, 140 miles from the capital, and whether it was wise to do so, are questions which right-wing romantics still debate.

Hanoverian troops under the Duke of Cumberland, who was also 24 years old, started in pursuit. The Jacobites retreated steadily north, growing increasingly demoralized. Large numbers deserted, pleading pressure of work at home: the spring sowing season was coming on. The government troops caught up with the rebels on Culloden Moor near Inverness.

As a tactician the Prince was no match for cold ruthless professionals like the Duke of Cumberland and Major James Wolfe (afterwards Wolfe of Quebec). In 40 minutes at Culloden 9,000 Hanoverians routed 5,000 Jacobites and left 1,000 dead on the moor.

The Prince escaped. For the next five months he was a fugitive in the western Highlands and islands, during which time a young lady from South Uist protected him—and so the Flora MacDonald legend was born. Eventually a French ship took him away from Borrodale, from the spot where he had landed the previous year.

Driven from Paris under the terms of an Anglo-French peace treaty, the Young Pretender set up house in Rome. Faithful Scottish followers bore stoically with his petulance and drunken rages until his death in 1788. Back in Scotland, Jacobite sympathizers suffered harsh reprisals and the myth of the "King over the water" was born, lairds symbolically passing their glasses over the water jug whenever they were required to drink the King's health. (Some still do.) Wits in Georgian England recited the Jacobite toast:

"God bless the King—I mean the Faith's Defender.
God bless (no harm in blessing) the Pretender.
But which the former is, and which the latter—
God bless us all! That's quite another matter."

Learning to Live Together

Rebellions apart, it took time for the Scots and English to settle into harness. Old scars were slow to heal, old antipathies persisted. In the Border counties pleas for "one nation" are stifled to this day by memories of centuries of viciousness and vendetta on both sides.

The Scots resented their neighbors' patronizing condescension, the assumption that a Scot was an inferior kind of Englishman. The English mocked the apparent poverty of Scotland and the readiness with which those super-patriotic porridge-eaters migrated to the south. When a London alderman complained to Doctor Johnson that "poor old England is lost" the sage answered that the tragedy was "the Scots have found it."

Scottish Genius

After the Union of 1707 Scotland's history was carried forward not by kings and queens but by pioneers in the arts and sciences. There had already been a few who had shown the world what Scotland could do. John Napier of Edinburgh (1550–1617) had invented logarithms and if that ingenious method of multiplying large numbers by simple addition was one day to be taken over by the computer and digital calculator it is worth remembering that the same mathematician also devised a set of rods ("Napier's bones") that anticipated modern calculating machines.

Among the Scots who helped organize the finances of Europe and laid the foundations of the national reputation for shrewdness in insurance and investment was William Patterson (1658–1719). He proposed, and afterwards directed, the Bank of England.

We shall deal with some outstanding writers and poets in a separate chapter, *Literature and the Arts.*

Since medieval times, Scotland, with her strong trading links with Europe, had been international in outlook. However, the Highlands, cut off by geography, language and culture, had been considered by Southerners (and by Lowland Scots) a backward and barbaric place. The Union, coming at the beginning of an industrial and scientific age, increased opportunity for the enterprising Scots. In the city of Edinburgh, for example, a flowering of intellectuals brought a new golden age—a period known as the Scottish Enlightenment (1730–90). Ironically, around the same time, the Highlands witnessed the destruction of their culture and way of life in the wake of the last Jacobite uprising in 1745.

From the beginning of the industrial revolution Scots were marching into the Hall of Fame in numbers out of all proportion to the population. David Hume (1711–1776) and Adam Smith (1723–1790) propounded theories of philosophy and economics that launched those sciences on their modern paths. James Hutton (1726–1797) wrote the seminal treatise for present-day geology, *Theory of the Earth.* John Hunter (1728–1793) pioneered modern surgery. Robert Adam of Kirkcaldy (1728–1792) was responsible for the neo-classical "Adam style" which gave much of England and Scotland their dignified Georgian architecture and urban planning.

James Watt of Greenock (1736–1819) devised the principles of steam propulsion while walking on Glasgow Green—not, as legend has it, by watching his mother's kettle boil. Watt is entitled to be called the Father of Industry, for without steampower the industrial revolution could not have proceeded. Among Scottish contemporaries who enabled mankind to profit from his inventions were David Dale (1739–1806), cotton-mill builder and philanthropist; Henry Bell (1767–1830), "hero of 1,000 blunders and one success," who designed and operated commercially the first steamship in Europe; Thomas Telford (1757–1834), "Colossus of Roads," who built the first highways, bridges and canals in various parts of the world; John Loudon Macadam (1756–1836), who gave his name to the ideal road-surfacing material; Robert Stevenson (1772–1850), lighthouse engineer and inventor of the lantern reflector. . . .

The list grows tedious. Suffice it to say that a few everyday items the 19th century owed to innovative Scots were the vacuum flask, the raincoat or macintosh, the first reaping and threshing machines, the coal-gas lamp, shale oil, pneumatic rubber tyres, the steam hammer, the bicycle and the telephone!

New Times in the Glens

Up to 1801 the population of Scotland had remained fairly stable at around 1½ millions. In the next 100 years it rose to more than 4½ millions. Industry moved to the towns and small elegant cities like Glasgow became the smoky workshops of the world. Most people were employed in the heavy industries of coal-mining, engineering, iron smelting and shipbuilding; or in the domestic industries of brewing, milling, paper-making, tanning and wagon-building, to which the Scots and their climate were well suited. Country craftsmen, weavers and woodworkers migrated to the urban fringes of central Scotland's towns. Emigration from the Highlands, both overseas and to the cities, had started in the aftermath of the last Jacobite rebellion.

The demand for labor brought Irish workers into the west of Scotland. Highland families too were tempted to move to Glasgow to look for a better life which, on the whole, they did not find. Pressure from their landlords forced many Highland folk out of their ancestral crofts (farm cottages). The discovery that mutton and wool yielded better profits and needed fewer workers than beef and dairy produce precipitated the infamous Clearances when large numbers of western Highlanders and islanders were evicted to make room for sheep pastures. The 1800s were years of mass emigrations overseas. A number of other economic factors prompted these movements, including a fall in the price of kelp (one of the few Highland "industries"), a failure of west coast fishings and, after the Napoleonic wars, a dramatic fall in the value of the small black Highland beef cattle, another important Highland export.

Emigration was a blessing for some young people. Scotland's superior education system was producing "lads o' pairts" (i.e. lads of talents) so fast that one small country could not accommodate their skills and thousands went off to seek careers abroad.

Scots in the New World

Thomas Edison, Samuel Morse, Edgar Allan Poe, Washington Irving, Robert E. Lee, Presidents Jefferson, Monroe, Jackson, Grant and Polk, Patrick Henry and James McNeil Whistler all claimed Scottish ancestry. Allan Pinkerton of the detective agency was born in Glasgow, John Paul Jones, founder of the U.S. Navy, came from the Solway shore. Samuel Wilson, whose parents sailed to America from Greenock on the Clyde, has been officially recognized as the original Uncle Sam.

The Scots John Macdonald and Alexander Mackenzie were Canada's first and second Prime Ministers. That country's Fraser and Mackenzie rivers are named for Scottish pioneers, as is her leading university, McGill.

Some pioneers carried royal blood to the New World, if the genealogists are to be believed. Jimmy Carter, through his alleged descent from King Henry III, must be linked with the Stuarts; the Irish Kennedys' Scottish cousins went back to Robert the Bruce, as did Thomas Jefferson, James Monroe and James Buchanan; while Ulysses S. Grant claimed descent from an earlier king, David I, and Theodore Roosevelt boasted three clan chieftains—a Stuart, a Drummond and a Douglas—in his ancestry.

Perhaps the most famous American Scot was Andrew Carnegie, steel baron and multimillionaire, who started work as a bobbin boy in a Pittsburgh mill. When Andrew was 13, in 1848, his father, a weaver, had taken the whole family from Dunfermline to Pittsburgh to make a fresh start.

Sir John Moore the general who was killed at Corunna (1809) and immortalized in the poem by Charles Wolfe was a Scot; so was Sir Ralph Abercrombie who achieved the first successes against Napoleon's "invincibles." Robert Douglas and Patrick Gordon built the armies of the King of Sweden and the Czar of Russia and another Scottish soldier of fortune, Samuel Greig, created the Russian Navy.

A patriotic historian, Agnes Mure Mackenzie, has claimed that in 40 years after 1797 the island of Skye (population 3,500) gave the British Army "21 generals, 48 colonels, 600 majors, captains and subalterns; and to the Civil Service in the same period one governor-general, four colonial governors, a Chief Baron of England and a high court judge." There is a hint here of another maxim that Scots live by: look after your friends and relations and help them up the ladder.

To complete the military tale, Britain's senior commanders of World War I, Earl Haig and Sir Ian Hamilton, were both Scots. Scottish-born sailors and airmen of World War II included Admiral Viscount Cunningham and Air Marshals Lords Tedder and Dowding. The inventors of the Lee-Enfield and Ross rifles (and, they say, the Bowie knife) were dyed-in-the-wool Scots. America's General MacArthur descended from a west-Highland family.

Tartanitis

As the 18th century drew to a close, the taste for the neo-classical, with its order and harmony, gave way to the Romantics, with their emphasis on the emotions. Instead of formal gardens, taste in landscapes began to incline towards the wild and grand. A cult of the 'Picturesque" developed. Travelers began to tell of the wildness of Scottish scenery. (As early as 1794, for instance, a Callander minister wrote that "The Trossachs are often visited by persons of taste . . . desirous of seeing nature in her rudest and most unpolished state.") Writers such as Wordsworth, Coleridge and—especially—Sir Walter Scott further popularized Scottish scenes.

The romance also focussed upon tartan, particularly after the visit to Scotland in 1822 of King George IV. This was organized by Sir Walter Scott, by then a famous writer and authority on Scottish matters. He helped push tartan as a romantic symbol of the now-subjugated Highlands.

Tartan became madly fashionable and the manufacturers invented patterns as a matter of course. The final seal of approval was given by Queen Victoria with the purchase of the Balmoral estate in Royal Deeside in 1852. This castle was rebuilt in Scots baronial style with tartan greatly in evidence. A nostalgic and romantic view of Scotland as a land of tartan-clad warriors rapidly developed. This rash of "tartanitis" was the most obvious aspect of a cult sometimes referred to as "Balmorality." Queen Victoria and her playboy son, afterwards Edward VII, made summer travel in Scotland fashionable and set examples in deer-stalking, salmon-fishing, grouse-shooting and pony-trekking which their subjects eagerly copied.

The Twentieth Century

Scotland's recent history is, generally speaking, the history of the United Kingdom of which she remains of course an integral part. In science and technology Scots continued to shine. Without going into a very long list of names, we might just look at the field of telecommunications. Along with the name of Alexander Graham Bell (first practical telephone) stand the names of Lord Kelvin (first Atlantic cable), John Logie Baird (first practical television), Sir Robert Watson Watt (radar) and James Clerk-

Maxwell (electro-magnetic theories which put Einstein and Marconi, as they said, "on the right track").

Scots have shown a peculiar aptitude for politics. Keir Hardie of Bellshill near Glasgow founded the Labour party and is regarded as Britain's first socialist. The first working man to become a member of the British Cabinet (John Burns) and the first British Marxist (John Maclean) were Scots. Since the beginning of this century six British Prime Ministers have been Scots: A.J. Balfour, Henry Campbell-Bannerman, Bonar Law, Ramsay Macdonald, Harold Macmillan and Lord Home.

Politically the nation has held her own with England. In 1745 the office of Scottish Secretary was abolished "in the interests of national unity" and until 1885 Scotland was merely North Britain. Not until 1928 was a Scottish Office established in Scotland with departments to administer the country from Edinburgh. About the same time the Scottish Secretary became a senior minister in the Westminster government and his prestige, cares and duties have increased ever since.

Industrially Scotland has known good times and bad. Venerable industries have declined. The great Clydebank shipyards which turned out the *Queen Mary* and *Queen Elizabeth* are now in public ownership or converted to other uses. Scotland once produced 43 different makes of automobile; the Depression of 1931 swept them all away and today she has none. Rightly or wrongly, Scots tend to blame England for their industrial troubles; and the Scottish labor unions are among the most left-wing and militant in the British Isles.

Numerous industrial and commercial operations with good Scottish names are controlled by English giants. The "dawn raiders" from the south have had more success with takeovers than their freebooting ancestors who operated when Robert the Bruce was a boy. It involves some swallowing of national pride, but it has given Scotland a high technology and a better communications system than almost any country in Europe.

The Oil Bonanza

In 1970 British Petroleum struck oil under the sea in an area known as The Forties, about 100 miles east of Aberdeen. Thus began the most significant industrial development in Scotland of the century.

Britain's new-found oil and natural gas reserves lie in a straggling line about 100 miles off the Scottish coast, approximately from the Firth of Tay to Shetland; most therefore comes within what might loosely be called Scotland's territorial waters. Visions of a race of tartan sheikhs have evaporated, but the British economy has received a boost and there is a separate spin-off for Scotland in the well-paid jobs available in rig, platform and module construction and repair, in specialist shipbuilding, transportation and pipe-laying, in technical services and in the processing of the crude product at Grangemouth. A variety of government agencies have also been active in bringing to Scotland new electronics industries, located in the so-called "Silicon Glen," mainly the central belt.

Scotland's traditional commodities have proved successful in the consumer society. Whisky distillers have created a world-wide demand. Textiles, especially the Border woollens and Shetland knitwear and Harris tweeds (now largely under multinational control) attract buyers from overseas. Scottish enterprise, self-confidence and inventiveness are still evident, though home-based companies complain of a lack of investment capital.

Shotgun Marriage

How is the Union, that shotgun marriage of 1707, getting along? Whenever polls are taken, most of the English are satisfied with the way things are, a majority of Scots would prefer some kind of Home Rule; a smaller number want complete independence and a separate seat at the United Nations.

The Scottish National Party was born out of the Great Depression of the 1930s and achieved its greatest strength to date in the late 1960s and early 1970s. At one period it had a dozen members of Parliament at Westminster out of a grand total of 635. After a period of eclipse in the early 1980s and an unspectacular performance in the 1987 general election, as the 1980s drew to a close, the Nationalists began to show signs of a revival. This took place in a Scottish political scene which was itself at its most volatile (and unpredictable) for some decades. In a UK context, the "center ground" parties had failed to achieve a breakthrough, while the Labour party still seemed unable to topple the governing Conservatives, who were left with no strong opposition. In 1987 Scotland voted into Parliament a large majority of Labour Members of Parliament, outnumbering Scottish Conservative members by about 5 to 1.

However, with Labour heavily defeated in England and the Conservatives firmly in control in Westminster, there was nothing to stop legislation being passed which was against the wishes of the majority of Scottish people. Inevitably, the Scots started thinking in a Nationalist context, uncertain about full independence, but adamant that some form of Home Rule was necessary. Also, with the failure of the center parties, an element of "protest voting" then attached itself to the Nationalists.

Perhaps another factor in reviving the Nationalists' fortunes has been the obvious wealth of London and the Southeast of England, as expressed in house prices. An increasing number of people from the south of England have sold up and "opted out," buying property in Scotland. Selling in the south and buying in Scotland, where property prices are much cheaper, has enabled incomers—not always sympathetic to Scottish culture—to acquire much "upmarket" property and land. This in turn has caused resentment in the native Scottish population.

The intransigence of the Conservative party in refusing to consider even a hint of devolving power to Scotland has resulted in a polarization or simplification of choices: either the Union remains unshakeable (the Conservative stance) or it is in some way renegotiated (the majority view in Scotland). With some opinion polls in Scotland showing the Scottish Nationalist Party running the Labour Party very close, the 1990s should prove a watershed in Scottish politics and Scotland's relationship with England.

Finally, after failing to ignite the Scots with their slogan of the 1970s—"It's Scotland's Oil"—the Scottish Nationalist revival owes much to a change of tack. With Scots becoming increasingly disenchanted with Westminster rule, the Nationalists campaign under a "Scotland in Europe" banner. They wish Scotland to take her place amongst the European nations, such as Norway, another small country with similar population size and natural resources. This also—by design or otherwise—harks back to Scotland in medieval times, when there was much trade and cultural exchange between the Lowlands of Scotland and continental Europe. More importantly, it also neatly avoids the charge of "isolationism" which has for long been leveled at the party both by faint-hearted Scots and the anxious English.

A MINI-HISTORY OF SCOTLAND

Reigning Monarch	*Dates*	*Events*
	A.D. 80	Romans arrive in Scotland
	392	Ninian founds the first Christian church on Isle of Whithorn
	c.400	End of Roman occupation
	c.500	First "Scots" arrive from Ireland
	563	St. Columba on Iona
	685	Pictish army defeats invading Angles at Nectansmere
Houses of Alpin, Atholl and Moray		
Kenneth MacAlpin, 843–58, first "king" of Scots and Picts		
Numerous short-lived "kings," drawn from descendants of MacAlpin. His great-great-grandson was:		
Kenneth II, 971–95	990	Supposed battle of Luncarty, Scots against Danes, adoption of thistle as national emblem
Constantine III, 995–97		
Kenneth III, 997–1005		
Malcolm II, 1005–34	1018	Battle of Carham. Lothian annexed to Scotland
Duncan I, 1034–40		
Macbeth, 1040–57		
Lulach, 1057–58	1057	England abandoned northern Northumbria to the Scots. The kingdom of Alba ("Alba" is still the Gaelic word for Scotland) took shape. King Malcolm III, by the time he murdered Lulach, had already begun to mold the old Scottish, Pictish and Anglian kingdoms into one, and to bring the tribes under one head and one law
Malcolm III, 1057–93, called Canmore (Great Head)	1093	Death of saintly Margaret, wife of Malcolm Canmore and founder of modern Edinburgh

Reigning Monarch	*Dates*	*Events*
Donald, 1093–4, displaced by Duncan	1093–1200	Kingdom torn by internal strife and threatened by Norse invasions
Duncan II, 1094–5		
Donald (restored) 1095–7		
Edgar, 1097–1107		
Alexander I, 1107–1124		
David I, 1124–53, the Sair Sanct	1118–50	Building of abbeys at Holyrood, Melrose, Kelso, Dryburgh and Jedburgh
Malcolm IV, 1153–65, called The Maiden		
William, 1165–1214, called The Lion	1174	Scotland becomes a vassal state of England
Alexander II, 1214–49		
Alexander III, 1249–86	1263	Battle of Largs. Scotland acquires the Hebrides from Norway
Margaret, 1286–92, called Maid of Norway		
John Balliol, 1292–1306	1297	Patriots under William Wallace defeat the English at Stirling Bridge
	1305	Wallace captured and executed
	1314	Battle of Bannockburn
Robert I, 1306–29, called The Bruce	1328	Treaty of Northampton, by which Scotland confirms her independence
David II, 1329–71	1368	Edinburgh Castle rebuilt

House of Stuart

Robert II, 1371–90	14th–15th centuries	The MacDonalds, Lords of the Isles, and the "Black" Douglases wage war on the crown
Robert III, 1390–1406	1388	Battle of Otterburn. "Black" Douglas repels the English
	1396	Battle of the Clans at Perth
James I, 1406–37	1411	St. Andrews University founded
James II, 1437–60	1451	Glasgow University founded
	1472	Scotland acquires Orkney and Shetland
James III, 1460–88	1482	Scots lords hang the King's favorites from Lauder bridge
	1488	Battle of Sauchieburn. King slain
James IV, 1488–1513	1494	Aberdeen University founded
	1513	Battle of Flodden. King slain
James V, 1513–42	1542	Battle of Solway Moss
Mary, 1542–67, called Queen of Scots	1544	Edinburgh burned by invading English

Reigning Monarch	*Dates*	*Events*
	1560	Reformation of the Church. Roman Catholicism abolished
James VI, 1567–1625	1582	Edinburgh University founded
	1587	Mary Queen of Scots beheaded
	1603	Union of Crowns. James VI of Scotland becomes James I of England
Charles I, 1625–49	1643	Solemn League and Covenant, making Presbyterianism compulsory in Scotland
(Interregnum, 1649–60)	1650	Cromwell's victory over Scottish royalists at Dunbar. Cromwell rules England and Scotland as Lord Protector
	1658	First stage-coach from Edinburgh to London
Charles II, 1660–85	1660–88	Episcopacy re-established. The Killing Times. Presbyterian Covenanters brutally persecuted
James II and VII, 1685–88		
William III (1689–1702) and Mary II (1689–1694), a joint monarchy	1689	Battle of Killiecrankie
	1692	Massacre of Glencoe
Anne, 1702–14	1707	Union of Parliaments, by which Scotland and England become one nation

House of Hanover

George I, 1714–27	1715	Jacobite rebellion. The Earl of Mar defeated at Sheriffmuir
	1736	Birth of James Watt
George II, 1727–60	1745	Last Jacobite rebellion
	1746	The Young Pretender defeated at Culloden. Wearing of the kilt forbidden
	1759	Birth of Robert Burns
George III, 1760–1820	1771	Birth of Sir Walter Scott
	1782	Wearing of the kilt permitted
	1788	Death of Bonnie Prince Charlie
George IV, 1820–30	c. 1820	Beginning of Highland Clearances
William IV, 1830–37		
Victoria, 1837–1901	1842	Edinburgh-Glasgow railroad opened

Reigning Monarch	*Dates*	*Events*
	1846	Edinburgh-London railroad opened
	1854	Construction of Balmoral Castle, the Queen's Highland home
House of Saxe-Coburg-Gotha		
Edward VII, 1901–10		
House of Windsor		
George V, 1910–36	1914–18	World War I
	1928	Scottish Office established as Government department in Edinburgh
Edward VIII, 1936, abdicated		
George VI, 1936–52	1938	St. Andrew's House opened in Edinburgh as center of Scottish administration
	1939–45	World War II
Elizabeth II, 1952	1959	Finnart Oil Terminal, Chapelcross Nuclear Power Station, and Dounreay Fast Breeder Reactor opened
	1964	Forth Road Bridge opened
	1967	First Scottish Nationalist candidate (Mrs. Winifred Ewing) elected to Parliament
	1970	Exploitation of North Sea oil begins off Scottish coast
	1973	Britain becomes a member of European Economic Community ("Common Market")
	1974	Seven Scottish Nationalist MPs elected to Parliament
	1975	Local government burghs and counties reorganized as Regions
	1979	"Devolution" debate. National referendum on a separate parliament for Scotland shows 33% in favor, 31% against; 36% do not bother to vote. Serious decline in Scottish Nationalist fortunes

Reigning Monarch	*Dates*	*Events*
	1981	Europe's largest oil terminal opened at Sullom Voe (Shetland)
	1986	Commonwealth Games, Edinburgh, boycotted by 32 nations
	1987	Only 3 Scottish Nationalist MPs elected
	1988	Unexpected by-election victory signals Nationalist revival
	1989	Campaign for a Scottish Assembly gains support

LITERATURE AND THE ARTS

Originality and Vigor

The English-reading world meets Scottish literature at an early age. Every child knows *Treasure Island* by Robert Louis Stevenson, scribbled on a sick-bed at Braemar. And every child makes the acquaintance of *Peter Pan,* the creation of Sir J.M. Barrie, while few are not familiar with *Robinson Crusoe:* the real-life hero, not the author, was a Scot named Alexander Selkirk from Largo.

In a literary tradition remarkable for its richness and diversity, two giants stand out: Robert Burns the poet and Sir Walter Scott the poet and novelist.

Not many outside Scotland appreciate the depth of affection that Scotland has for Robert Burns (1759–1796). To his fellow-countrymen he is more than a great lyric bard; he is the champion of the under-dog, the lover of noble causes, the hater of pomposity and cant, the prophet of social justice. "A man's a man for a' that" expresses a universal truth far beyond Scotland's shores. His love-songs warm the coldest Presbyterian hearts. His own mixed-up love life and untimely end evoke a curious sympathy in the "unco' guid," as Burns called the ultra-respectable pillars of society of his time. The man in the street still quotes Burns—which is more than can be said, south of the Border, of Shakespeare. Burns societies and federations abound all over the globe. Burns Night, 25th January, is an anniversary of some importance in Scotland.

Walter Scott (1771–1832) was an Edinburgh lawyer with aristocratic pretensions, an assiduous collector of old ballads and tales, an expert on rhyming couplets and later a novelist universally acclaimed. His long narrative poems included *The Lay of the Last Minstrel, Marmion, The Lady of the Lake* and *The Lord of the Isles.* The most widely-read of a long string of historical novels were *Waverley, Ivanhoe, The Talisman, Redgauntlet, The Heart of Midlothian* and *Old Mortality.* Told seriously and thoroughly documented, his works lifted fiction high above the Gothick romances of his contemporaries. Not many readers these days get through Scott without skipping pages, but when he was alive his popularity was tremendous and he has been described as Scottish tourism's best-ever propagandist.

Scotland's First Poet

Thomas of Ercildoune (c.1225–c.1300) was the sort of semi-mythical character whom Scott delighted in. Ercildoune is modern Earlston and Thomas was that "True Thomas" or "Thomas the Rhymer" who spent seven years in Elfland with the Fairy Queen. Whatever the truth of that, a few of Thomas's ballads and rhyming prophecies have survived and he is to be considered Scotland's earliest poet.

Over the next 200 years, the only outstanding names are those of the court poets William Dunbar (c.1465–c.1513), whose *Lament for the Makaris* (*makar* meaning poet) is well-known; and Sir David Lindsay (c.1490–c.1555), whose sprawling verse-drama *Ane Satire of the Thrie Estates* is a valuable critique of administrative systems under the Stuarts.

During that same period anonymous ballads of poignant simplicity became a vital element in Scottish literature. Most verse anthologies contain samples of them, and schoolchildren learn them by heart: *Otterburn, The Twa Sisters, Lord Randal, Tam Lin, Sir Patrick Spens* and scores besides.

Scottish literature dealt with everyday themes before that of most of Europe; the country's writers were expressing the life and character of ordinary people when most of Europe thought it proper to write and read only about lords and ladies. Allan Ramsay (1684–1758) wrote ballads and songs of rustic life; Robert Fergusson (1750–1774) gave liberal sentiments lusty voice and inspired Burns; Tobias Smollett (1721–1771) depicted the young Scot seeking his fortune abroad in novels such as *Roderick Random, Humphrey Clinker* and *Peregrine Pickle;* and James Boswell (1740–1795), companion and biographer of Dr. Samuel Johnson, established himself as one of the greatest diarists of all time.

The Golden Age

Then came the golden age of Scottish literature, represented by Burns and Scott and James Hogg (1770–1835). Hogg's poetry did not enjoy great popularity after his death, but during his life-time his writings and table-talk were thought much of. Recently, Scotland has rediscovered the "Ettrick Shepherd" as he was called—he was a friend and neighbor of Sir Walter Scott—and his tortured apology for a life oppressed with fears of Hell, *Confessions of a Justified Sinner,* is more appreciated today than when it was written.

In the era of Burns, Scott, Hogg and many lesser lights, Edinburgh became a hotbed of poetic talents and a metropolis of the printing, publishing and bookselling trades. Several long-running magazines were started, some of international repute. The brothers William (1800–1883) and Robert (1802–1871) Chambers of Peebles set up their first small shop in Edinburgh, taking it in turns to sleep under the counter at night to save the expense of a nightwatchman. They were to publish *Chambers' Journal* and eventually an issue of reference books, including *Chambers' Encyclopaedia* and *Chambers' Dictionary.* William Blackwood (1776–1834) launched *Blackwood's Magazine,* a conservative institution in Britain and the Empire for nearly 170 years. Francis Jeffrey (1773–1850), at the opposite extreme of the political spectrum, founded the influential *Edinburgh Review.*

From a tiny room in the Old Town of Edinburgh in 1771 the *Encyclopaedia Britannica* was issued. The first work of its kind, the model for encyclopedias the world over, it was written almost single-handed by the journalist James Tytler (c.1742–1806) on a washer-woman's upturned tub.

"Kailyard"

In the shadow which Burns and Scott had cast before them, a generation of regional writers appeared, facetiously christened the "Kailyard" (cabbage-patch) school for their parochialism and use of impenetrable local dialects. Head and shoulders above the rest stands John Galt (1779–1839), author of delightful tales about country life in Ayrshire in *Annals of the Parish, The Provost* and other works. As an antidote to kailyard sentimentality, perhaps the greatest of Scotland's 20th-century novelists, Lewis Grassic Gibbon (1901–35), scandalized his neighborhood with his book *A Scots Quair.* Set in Kincardineshire and Aberdeen, it is still highly praised and influential today.

Kailyard is not an adjective to be applied to William McGonagall (1830–1902) of Dundee, though more derisory terms have been heaped on him. McGonagall, the clown of Scottish literature, applied poor rhymes, worse meter and over-florid metaphor to grand subjects with a bathos that amounted almost to genius. He is a cult figure in some circles as the only truly memorable bad poet.

Monoliths of Scholarship

The survey of Scottish literature must cover a few of the works of immense scholarship which became standard text-books of the sciences and philosophy. Before the 1800s there had been David Hume's *Concerning Human Understanding* (1748) and Adam Smith's *The Wealth of Nations* (1776).

Thomas Carlyle (1795–1881), born at Ecclefechan, dominated literary scholarship in the 19th century. His rugged, powerful style in *Sartor Resartus* and the monumental *French Revolution* led Walt Whitman to say of him that "no man else will bequeath to the future more significant hints of our stormy era, its fierce paradoxes, its din." Carlyle's wife Jane (1801–1866), a native of Haddington, was almost as notable in her day. Her letters and critical essays reveal her to be one of the most accomplished women of the century.

The Scottish genius for laborious and painstaking research is exemplified in Hugh Miller (1802–1856), a stonemason from Cromarty and a self-taught journalist and geologist. *Old Red Sandstone* and *Testimony of the Rocks,* like the works of Hume, Adam Smith and Carlyle, are more than treatises on themes of narrow specialism: they are masterpieces of literature.

Long John Silver and Sherlock Holmes

Son and grandson of two famous Scottish engineers, Robert Louis Stevenson (1850–1894) wrote his memorable *Treasure Island* and *Kidnapped* as serials for boys' magazines while contemplating more serious works. With *Travels with a Donkey* and *An Inland Voyage* the owner of the second best-known set of initials in literature (R.L.S.) produced two short classics of travel writing. He was a genuine poet and his short stories of life in the Pacific islands where he lived for some years and died young are the finest any Scottish writer has written. And in his parable of the schizoid personality, *Dr. Jekyll and Mr. Hyde,* he demonstrated a psychological perception that would have interested his contemporary Sigmund Freud.

The same preoccupation with the darker forces existing within man is found in a number of Stevenson's short stories with a supernatural, or related, theme. Indeed, in their apparent predilection for morbidity and melancholy there is often more than a hint of that other master of fictional horror, Edgar Allan Poe, who of course had claims of his own to Scottish ancestry.

R.L.S. is not as popular in Scotland as he might be (he spoke slightingly of Sir Walter Scott), but his work shows an acute sense of Scottish life and history and he is one of the most stylish writers the English language has known.

Something of Stevenson's mastery of the craft appears also in Sir Arthur Conan Doyle (1859–1930), another Scot with a creative imagination and first class control over suspense and drama. His incomparable Sherlock Holmes stories ensure Doyle's immortality, but he wrote many other tales and a few novels on quite different subjects.

Modern Literature

The first half of the 20th century produced no British playwright more successful than Sir J.M. Barrie (1860–1937). Born very poor, his many successes ensured that he died extremely rich. As with Conan Doyle and Sherlock Holmes, his name will always be linked to one great work: *Peter Pan,* the perennial juvenile. His other great money-spinners—*Dear Brutus, What Every Woman Knows, Quality Street, The Admirable Crichton* and others—are considered lightweight for the modern theater. Though dismissed sometimes as cloyingly whimsical, they are marvelously constructed and infused with sure touches of humor which completely conquered the London theaters of Barrie's day.

James Bridie (1888–1957), a playwright who has achieved less success than he deserved, is best remembered for *Tobias and the Angel.* There are signs of a resurgence of interest in Bridie; he has become a favorite of the Pitlochry Theater in the Hills. Another author half-forgotten but recently revived—thanks to television—is Neil Munro (1864–1930). He wrote the romantic tale *John Splendid* but was most at home in the humorous *Para Handy Tales,* the adventures of the men who manned the puffers (small coasting vessels) of the Clyde.

Among 20th-century poets Edwin Muir (1887–1959) is better remembered as an essayist, critic and first translator of Kafka than for his rather turgid poetry. Poetry—perhaps one should say verse—is very much alive in Scotland today and, though wide in its choice of subject matter, tends to be underestimated by English critics uncomfortable with and unable to understand Scots poets' natural wish to express themselves in Scots. But Hugh MacDiarmid (1892–1979) will probably go down in history as the best Scots poet since Burns. Certainly no living poet is in the same class.

20th-century prose writers of stature are Compton Mackenzie (1883–1972)—in his time the Grand Old Man of Scottish letters—and Eric Linklater (1899–1974), author of *Private Angelo, Don Juan in America* and other novels. The work of both displays refined wit harnessed by incisive intelligence. A more passionate involvement with his Scottish heritage is found in the work of James Leslie Mitchell (1901–35), who also wrote under the pseudonym Lewis Grassic Gibbon. In the last seven years of his short life Mitchell produced the novels *Sunset Song, Cloud Howe* and *Grey Granite* which comprise *A Scots Quair,* the most ambitious work of Scottish literature.

Radio and television have reawakened interest in A.J. Cronin (1896–1981), best remembered for the novels *Hatter's Castle* and *The Stars Look Down,* and the adventures of the country medicos Finlay and Cameron. Based in Orkney and deeply versed in Orcadian mythology and folklore is the short-story writer George Mackay Brown (b. 1921).

Art and Architecture

Scotland has never been supreme in the visual arts, but she has produced four good painters and two great architects. Allan Ramsay (1713–1784), not to be confused with his father the poet, painted many portraits while active in London literary life. Sir Henry Raeburn (1756–1823) did many more—600-odd, it is said—and was knighted by King George IV. Alexander Nasmyth (1758–1840) is regarded as the father of the Scottish landscape school, although his best-known picture is a portrait of Robert Burns.

As Sir Walter Scott preserved the old life of Scotland on paper, so Sir David Wilkie (1785–1841) recorded it on canvas. *Pitlessie Fair, The Penny Wedding* and *John Knox Preaching* are examples of the homely scenes and historical reconstructions he specialized in. His work is comparable in sentiment and subject matter to the many pictures of Highland life, which did so much to promote the 19th-century popular image of Scotland, produced by his English near-contemporary Sir Edwin Landseer.

In architecture Robert Adam (1728–1792) of Kirkcaldy continued the impressive work of his father William and was assisted by his brother John. He originated the stately and rather fanciful Gothick and, later, the palatial neo-classical styles of most of Scotland's elegant 18th-century buildings, streets and squares. The best examples of the Adam style in Scotland are Edinburgh's Charlotte Square and Mellerstain House. But his success was equally great in England, especially London.

Charles Rennie Mackintosh (1868–1928), like Robert Adam before him, designed not only buildings but the furniture and fittings to go in them as well. Mackintosh was not well known at his death, least of all in Scotland, but he is now acclaimed as a phenomenon of innovative design, painting and architecture; and his deceptively stark furniture, which used to be broken up for firewood, commands extraordinary prices.

Music

Though the bagpipe is by no means the exclusive property of Scotland—in fact, it is one of the most ancient instruments in the world and species of bagpipe existed throughout the Ancient World—its elegiac wail is popularly identified with Scotland as part of the nation's tartan image. However, Scotland has a great body of folk music, with many tunes originally played on fiddle, with or without cello. This wealth includes bothy ballads (farming songs) and work songs from mill or quayside.

Everyone knows a few old Scottish songs—*Annie Laurie, Auld Lang Syne, The Braes of Yarrow, Auld Robin Gray, The Bonnie Earl o' Moray* and the rest—but musicians distinguish between deliberately-composed sentimental songs and the airs and ballads which sprang from a genuine folk tradition. Somewhere between the two categories lie the haunting melodies to which the songs of Allan Ramsay and Robert Burns were set. Great composers like Haydn, J.C. Bach and Beethoven did not disdain to use them in concertos and variations.

The Scots love music and the list of foreign virtuosi who visited Edinburgh and Glasgow in the 18th and 19th centuries is a long one. But native classical compositions, with one or two exceptions—Hamish MacCunn's (1868–1916) overture *Land of the Mountain and the Flood,* for example—have made little impact abroad. Nor are many Scots-born performers internationally known. Apart from Frederick Lamond (1868–1948) the pianist, Mary Garden (1877–1967) the operatic diva and Joseph Hislop (1884–1977) the tenor, it is hard to name one.

Of recent composers the following names appear regularly on the programs of Scottish concerts: Francis George Scott (1880–1958), noted for song settings of poems by Burns and MacDiarmid; Ian Whyte (1901–1960), composer of opera and ballet scores and some chamber music; Robin Orr (b. 1909) and Thea Musgrave (b. 1928), composers of operas on Scottish historical themes; and Cedric Thorpe Davie (b. 1913), best known for his music for films and plays.

An important modern composer, Lancashire-born but firmly attached to Scotland is Sir Peter Maxwell Davis (b. 1934). Until recently he was resident in Orkney, and his most acclaimed operas, such as *The Lighthouse,* are set in the cold northern climes.

Seeing and Hearing

The National Gallery of Scotland, the National Gallery of Modern Art, the National Portrait Gallery and the National Museums of Scotland are all located in Edinburgh. There are also superb picture galleries in Glasgow, including—at last!—a home for the famous Burrell Collection which, under the terms of its bequest, had to be housed in a pollution-free atmosphere. Aberdeen, Dundee and Perth also have excellent picture galleries.

The National Library of Scotland is in Edinburgh and the famous Mitchell Library in Glasgow. Thanks to benefactions by Andrew Carnegie, the 19th-century American steel tycoon, many small Scottish towns have remarkably large and well-stocked public libraries.

There are major touring theater companies in Glasgow, Edinburgh and Aberdeen and repertory theaters in Glasgow, Edinburgh, St. Andrews,

Dundee and Perth; and a summer season at the Pitlochry theatre. The MacRobert Arts Centre at Stirling University offers variegated and avant-garde fare in concerts, operas, drama, films and art exhibitions.

Scottish Opera and Scottish Theatre Ballet, though late-comers to the British musical scene, have over the past few years established their reputations and gained admirers at home and abroad. Both companies are partly financed by commercial and banking concerns. Some of the most famous 19th-century operas have Scotland for their setting (*Lucia di Lammermoor* and *The Fair Maid of Perth* are only two), but Scotland herself has no custom-built opera house and opera and ballet performances with full chorus and orchestra are seen only in the large theaters of Glasgow and Edinburgh.

The Scottish National and Scottish Symphony orchestras give regular concerts in the principal cities and towns. The Scottish Arts Council promotes and supports local artistic activities throughout Scotland and also provides about 12 annual touring exhibitions of painting, sculpture and crafts. The Council's program sums up the situation in Scottish arts and crafts when it says that "those who come in search of the past will be agreeably surprised by the vitality of the present."

CLANS AND TARTANS

Gaeldom's Savage Splendor

The word "clan" means children. That definition is the key to the social organization of the Scottish Highlands—not the Lowlands—in history and legend.

The clan system is archaic. It goes back to an era when savage tribes gave up their restless wanderings and chose places to settle down in. A clan chief was revered by his followers as the lineal descendant of him "who first raised smoke and boiled water in that place"—the first land-holder, the sacred embodiment of the race. But all the clansfolk, rich and poor, bore that patriarch's name and regarded themselves equally as his children.

This explains the extreme loyalty and docility of the clans towards their chiefs down the generations. It also explains the pride and arrogance which early travelers in the Highlands found so ludicrous in gangs of cattle-thieves who looked to them like the dregs of humanity.

There are about 90 clans, some old and some fairly new, and between them they cover every square inch of the Highlands and islands, excluding Orkney and Shetland. Their territorial boundaries were not always clearly defined: some clans mingled freely with others, some progressively enlarged their holdings and others lost the ground they claimed. Territorial boundaries have no significance at all today and the only survivors with any claim to the land are one or two great chiefs who still live on their ancestral acres. But the descendant of a clansman, wherever in the world he may be, regards the glen or island of his forebears as his native heath.

Lords of the Isles

Clan origins may be rooted in Norse and Celtic legends but their actual histories go back not much farther than the 13th and 14th centuries, when their names and deeds were first recorded. The Clan MacDonald is considered to be the oldest. The first MacDonald was, as his name implies, "son of Donald" and Donald was the grandson of a Norse adventurer named Somerled who flourished around 1100.

Donald's descendants took over much of the western Highlands and for centuries boasted the title of Lords of the Isles. Offshoots formed separate clans: MacDonalds of Sleat, MacDonells of Glengarry, MacDougalls and others. Many clans were interrelated. Some preserve venerable alliances, some are hereditary enemies. Not long ago a Mr. Campbell refused to have his son taught by a teacher named MacDonald. The hostility dated from the Glencoe massacre of 1692, when the clan chiefs got mixed up in national politics.

Causes of widespread strife were the Jacobite rebellions of 1715 and 1745. Some clans were pro-Jacobite because of their Catholicism and because, as the clansmen regarded the chief as their father, so the chiefs regarded the royal Stuart as *their* father. It was the natural order of the system. To this day you may hear arguments between those whose ancestors were "out" in the Forty-five and those whose ancestors stayed at home.

Names and Titles

If you bear a name which appears in the official table of the clans you are probably a member of that clan, though your family came from Glasgow in the Lowlands, or even from England or Ireland. Emigration and soldiering dispersed the clans into some far places.

Certain proud Highland names, by the way, described characteristics not at all flattering. Campbell was "crooked mouth," Cameron meant "bent nose" and Kennedy "ugly head."

Highlanders emphasize the exclusive nature of their culture by giving the word "the" a special dignity. "Do you speak Gaelic?" is wrong; "Do you have the Gaelic?" is correct. Similarly, "Do you wear a kilt?" is wrong; "Do you wear the kilt?" is correct.

"The" is part of the majestic style of the chief and he is so described in the telephone book although, through the vicissitudes of time, he may be a secondhand automobile salesman in the United States or a bank clerk in England. (By the old custom, chiefs descend in both male and female lines.) So the chief of the Mackintosh clan is "The Mackintosh." What is more, since he lives on an estate of the same name, he is "The Mackintosh of Mackintosh." In olden times he would have been styled "The Mackintosh of that Ilk." One or two reactionary chiefs still cling to "of that Ilk."

At clan gatherings and banquets a few high-and-mighty chiefs glory in sonorous Gaelic designations. MacGregor of MacGregor's followers call him "An t-Ailpeanach," "The Alpin," which recalls the Dark-Age chieftain who fathered the first kings of Scotland. The Duke of Argyll rejoices in the name of "MacCailein-Mhor," "Great Son of the Whelp," a name long associated with the Clan Campbell of which he is the head.

Shirt and Boots

If your Scottish family name is not in the list of clans it may be among the "septs." Septs were either collateral branches of the clan or groups of survivors from clans wiped out in battle or shipwreck who had attached themselves to the clan. The latter were known as "broken men."

The septs embrace a variety of names not obviously Scottish, which is a stroke of luck for the people who make and sell clan insignia. If your name is Brown you have a choice of the Lamont or MacMillan tartans. The Clarks claim kinship with the Camerons, the Cooks with the Stuarts. Lewises may wear the MacLeod colors, Millers the MacFarlane, Thomsons the Campbell and Wrights the Macintyre. Some Highland dress outfitters stock the Smith tartan.

The best authorities say we must not wear the tartan unless we belong to the clan. "To do so invites scorn and derision," says the book of rules. Not surprisingly, this is not a view shared by the manufacturers and retailers of all the paraphernalia of clannery. But in any case to insist on the prohibition in Scotland today is to be excessively punctilious. Tartan is not copyright.

If some pedantic person asks what right you have to the old Highland dress, remind them that the old Highland dress was shirt and boots—and not always boots. Kilt and sporran, badges, bonnets, brooches, buttons, belts and buckles are relatively modern mysteries. The clan societies themselves—the protocol departments of the clans—dispute the authenticity of the regalia.

Invention of the Tartan

The traditional dress of the Highlander included a "plaid," a large rectangle of material belted and hanging skirt-like below the waist and gathered in adaptable folds above. Various Highland costume authorities agree that the kilt as it is known today was invented by an Englishman. He was an ironmaster, called Thomas Rawlinson, working in Lochaber in the early 18th century. Noticing that his Highland workers were encumbered by the weight of material above the waist, he made the simple modification of cutting off the top part, thereby inventing the "little" kilt or philabeg. He often wore it himself.

Documentary evidence of the clan system in the 18th century around the time of Culloden suggests that clans did not identify themselves by tartan design, but by cap badge. (Hence the importance of the "white cockade," originally a wild white rose plucked by the Young Pretender, in the Jacobite campaigns.) There may have been regional variation in tartan designs, depending on which plants and other dye-stuffs were available locally, but it is part of the modern tartan mythology to promote "clan tartans." Nevertheless, the study of old tartans is an interesting project on any Scottish visit. They can be found in places such as as the Museum of Scottish Tartans in Comrie and the West Highland Museum in Fort William. The portraits of Raeburn also reveal much about 18th-century tartans. They all present an interesting contrast with the modern aniline dye tartan designs manufactured to meet the demands of the industry today.

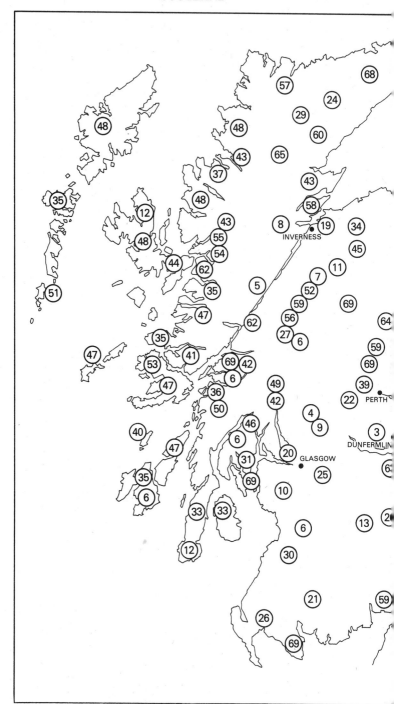

THE PRINCIPAL HIGHLAND CLANS AND LOWLAND FAMILIES OF SCOTLAND

1	Armstrong	37	MacDonell
2	Barclay	38	MacDuff
3	Bruce	39	MacFarlane
4	Buchanan	40	MacFee
5	Cameron	41	MacGillivray
6	Campbell	42	MacGregor
7	Chattan	43	MacKenzie
8	Chisholm	44	MacKinnon
9	Colquhoun	45	MacKintosh
10	Cunningham	46	MacLachlan
11	Davidson	47	MacLean
12	Donald	48	MacLeod
13	Douglas	49	MacNab
14	Duncan	50	MacNaughton
15	Elliot	51	MacNeil
16	Erskine	52	MacPherson
17	Farquharson	53	MacQuarrie
18	Forbes	54	MacRae
19	Fraser	55	Matheson
20	Galbraith	56	Menzies
21	Gordon	57	Morgan or Mackay
22	Graham		
23	Grant	58	Munro
24	Gunn	59	Murray
25	Hamilton	60	Murray or Sutherland
26	Hay		
27	Henderson	61	Ogilvie
28	Innes	62	Ranald
29	Keith	63	Ramsay
30	Kennedy	64	Robertson
31	Lamont	65	Ross
32	Lindsay	66	Scott
33	MacAlister	67	Shaw
34	MacBean	68	Sinclair
35	MacDonald	69	Stewart
36	MacDougall		

After the debacle of the Forty-five the clans were forbidden to wear the tartan. The order was rescinded after 36 years, but it had by then begun the process of degeneration among the clans: chief into landlord, warrior into peasant. It might be said that a process of degeneration had also occurred to Highland dress. During the time of the Proscription, the banning of Tartan was really an attempt to stamp out all things Highland—including kilts and weaponry. During this time, a kilted tradition had been kept alive by the British army. Scottish regiments were allowed Highland uniform. This seemed to have given ample scope for the basic dress to be gradually decorated in all sorts of ways—hugely ornate sporrans, for instance! All of this took the idea of Highland dress further and further away from the original simple, practical garment worn in rough country.

Tartanitis and Balmorality

During Queen Victoria's reign the Highland dress blossomed out magnificently. Accessories which would have struck old Highlanders with amazement were incorporated in the outfit. Arbiters of fashion ruled that those without clan connections might wear a kilt of "hodden gray" or heather mixture. Clanless subjects of the Queen claimed the right to the Royal Stuart tartan. The all-purpose Jacobite and Caledonia tartans were invented. The Prince Consort designed a Balmoral tartan, red, black and gray, for servants and retainers at the Queen's Highland home. On the Royal Deeside route there was even a tartan train—a locomotive with Royal Stuart paintwork.

Historians, or perhaps tartan manufacturers, discovered hunting, dress and mourning tartans to add to the everyday ones. Many books were written by self-styled experts, and much contradictory advice given.

The 40-odd "original" clans are those with the commonest Highland names. A few of them are: Cameron, Campbell, Forbes, Fraser, Gordon, Graham, Murray, MacCallum, MacDonald, MacFarlane, MacGregor, Mackintosh, MacLean, MacLeod, MacMillan, MacNeil, MacPherson, MacRae, Ross, Stewart or Stuart, Sutherland and others. These clans, down the ages, have built up quite a wardrobe of different tartans. If you want to wear the Stuart you have a choice of no fewer than 22 patterns!

The "new" clans, riding in on the mid-Victorian wave of tartanitis, were sometimes quite old clans which had never bothered much about tartans; or Lowland families—Kennedy, Hamilton, Hay, Scott, Johnstone, Elliot and others—getting into the act; or, as the late Duke of Montrose, an authority on Highland dress, put it, "so-called clans which came into existence how or when Heaven alone can say." They increased the number from around 40 to around 100.

From Queen Victoria's heyday to the present the number of clans has remained static; but in both civil and military life the tartans have continued to proliferate. Sir Walter Scott wore "shepherd's check"—a black and white pattern; it is now the Shepherd tartan. Not content with their 22 Stuart tartans, the royal family had special tartans woven for the Prince of Wales, later Edward VII, and Princess Beatrice (Queen Victoria's youngest child); and more recently for Princess Elizabeth (the present Queen), Princess Margaret Rose (the present Princess Margaret) and Princess Mary (the late Princess Royal). They are not exclusive designs; any kiltmaker will supply them.

Certain patriotic business houses have acquired "company" tartans. The Turnberry tartan sells well among golfers. There are Clergy and Green Clergy tartans for churchmen. During World War II, a regimental tartan was bestowed on the Royal Canadian Air Force and at the nuclear submarine base in the Holy Loch the American sailors have had woven for themselves a Polaris tartan. When the astronaut Neil Armstrong visited Langholm, the town of his forebears, there was already an Armstrong tartan available, but the local woollen mill produced a Moon tartan for him as well. Even the Scottish Tourist Board has its own specially-designed and officially-registered tartan. Purists resist such deviations. But nevertheless some modern "designer" tartans incorporate beautiful color harmonies, while some Victorian inventions now appear grim, garish and aesthetically chaotic.

Dressed to Kill

In Scotland's cities there are many outfitting shops which specialize in the Highland costume. They offer a choice of about 300 approved tartans. The kilt, of course, is only the beginning. A sporran (leather purse), knitted hose (stockings) and leather brogues (shoes) go with it; plus black or tweed jacket, tweed tie and plain shirt.

Evening dress is rather more elaborate. "Dressed to kill"—the original purpose of the free-and-easy Highland garb—has taken on new meaning. Your kilt of dress tartan is backed up with a light plaid, diamond-patterned stockings with scarlet garters and rosettes, a blue bonnet and a velvet doublet. The bonnet is adorned with clan badge, cock feather, crest and motto enclosed in a belt-and-buckle surround. The doublet has lace jabot and cuffs and its diamond-shaped buttons are set with the clan crest and perhaps semi-precious Cairngorm or Scotch topaz stones.

The dress sporran is hung with tassels and ornaments and may be faced with the head of a fox, badger, otter or some other creature appropriate to the clan; all mounted in silver. Shoe buckles, waist-belt, sword-belt and shoulder-brooch complete the essential part of the dress.

Pistol and powder-horn are obsolete now and the sword is worn only on very formal occasions; but you must have the *sgian dubh* (skeean doo) or black knife thrust down your stocking. The ensemble is best worn with an air of manly dignity.

While this peacock finery is strictly for the men, a Highland lady's evening wear is striking enough. She has a white blouse with Celtic or heraldic embroidery and a skirt of tartan silk. The silk *arisaid,* feminine version of the plaid, hangs down her back and is pinned with a brooch of antique design.

Glittering ostentation is the very essence of Highland dress. The authorities insist: "Attempts by self-conscious Lowlanders to convert the garb of the Gael into a quiet style or reduce it to the monotony of Anglo-Saxon evening clothes are contemptible and an affront to the nation."

Paying the Piper

Before we get swept away by this sartorial splendor, let us look at the price-tag. A plain outfit—jacket, kilt, sporran and hose made to measure—costs from £300; brogues another £50. The full dress outfit, with all trappings and trimmings, will be upwards of £500. It is possible to pay a great deal more than that.

Now we are all dressed up—and nowhere to go. Apart from Highland Balls, Highland Gatherings, clan society functions and the like, there are not many opportunities to wear full Highland dress. By day, in a Highland village, you might see three or four people in the costume of their ancestors—it could be precisely that, the indestructible kilt and sporran that grandfather handed down. In the cities, a few kilts get an airing at weddings or at the Kirk on Sundays. Pipe bands and the military are the outfitters' best customers. Scots still thrill to the swing of the kilt and the skirl of the pipes as a Highland regiment goes by. But for most people clan devotion is an affair of the heart, not a matter of dressing up. Financially the garb of old Gael is beyond the reach of ordinary folk and for every enthusiast you see being measured for a Montrose doublet or Prince Charlie coatee there will be two or three going in for the "quiet style"; the dinner jacket or trews (trousers) in the most restrained tartan the catalog has to offer.

FOOD AND DRINK

A Farmhouse Cuisine

If you have spent time in England, Wales or Ireland before coming to Scotland you will not find much about the Scottish cuisine which is excitingly different. This is especially so if you eat and drink in grand hotels and gourmet restaurants: they offer the same sort of international fare as their equivalents all over Europe.

But there are differences. Porridge, shortbread, haggis, malt whisky, Scotch broth, finnan haddie . . . a moment's reflection calls to mind several important items which are exclusively Scottish.

Scotland is more of a home-cooking, home-baking country than most. History and geography shaped her cuisine. She was for centuries a peasant, parochial land, a region of villages and towns rather than cities. Smalltown society thrived on neighborly visits—which meant tea parties, sewing bees and the like. They introduced the competitive element into the baking of bread, scones, biscuits, baps (soft round rolls), bannocks (griddle cakes), malt loaves, shortbreads, gingerbreads, pancakes, oatcakes and other flour-and-sugar-based concoctions. Hence the old nickname for Scotland: the "Land o' Cakes."

Her agriculture produced oats, barley and potatoes. Dr. Johnson's *Dictionary* tells us that oats are "a grain which in England is given to horses, but in Scotland supports the people"—hence porridge, the dish which supplied the roughage in a frugal diet. Many Scots still prefer porridge to packaged cornflakes at breakfast, and traditionalists season it with salt.

Others, and most visitors, make it more palatable by adding cream, sugar, syrup or nutmeg.

Oatmeal is also an ingredient in some meat and fish dishes and in desserts. Scots maintain that a herring rolled in oatmeal provides all the nourishment and vitamins the human body needs: the perfectly-balanced meal.

So much for oats. As to barley, the rippling fields of grain which add such color to Lowland landscapes are nearly all destined for the maltings, to make whisky. When Robert Burns wrote of whisky he used expressions like "John Barleycorn" and the "barley bree." ("Bree" is brew or broth.)

Potatoes still loom large in Scottish diets, and Scotch seed potatoes are exported all over Europe. "Come awa' in tae your tatties," a mother tells her child—"tatties" being potatoes and potatoes meaning lunch. You may find the same kind of double meaning when, for example, your landlady goes to the butcher for her "beef"—which covers all kinds of meat—and uses the word "meat" to describe all kinds of food.

Potatoes in Scotland are the bed on which various dishes lie. Strangers imagine the Scots eat haggis six days a week, but the typical everyday dish in an ordinary household is "mince and tatties"—ground beef and mashed potatoes.

The French Connection

If you have occasion to go to the butcher yourself, note that while the cuts are much the same as elsewhere the names are sometimes different. A leg of pork or lamb is a "gigot" (pronounced "jigget"). The best steak is "fillet" *(filet de boeuf)*. At dinner your fillet or gigot will appear on an "ashet" (an oval dish, from the French *assiette*). These expressions, hardly comprehended outside Scotland, pay a tribute to the nation which, in the days of Mary Queen of Scots, first introduced the Scots to the refinements of gastronomy. Wine, too, has a long history as a bond between the two countries—with many famous cellars deep beneath Scottish castles nursing rare French vintages.

Soups

Cold winters and a simple life made the Scots a nation of soup-drinkers. Gardening in the domestic plot is a tradition, as in England, but where the English gardener grows flowers his Scottish counterpart tends to cultivate useful vegetables and sometimes herbs. Cabbages, leeks, beans and peas enrich the soups of Scotland. The national soup is Scotch broth, a thick peppery soup with a mutton base to which onions, leeks, grated carrots and pearl barley are added. More venerable, and a favorite with hoteliers, is cock-a-leekie, made from chicken broth and numerous vegetables. In hotels and restaurants a whole range of consommés and bisques of fish, seafood, pheasant, ptarmigan and wild duck is developing.

Fish

Despite complaints that the European Economic Community has condemned Scotland's fishing industry to a slow death, some of the world's best saltwater fish is landed daily at Scottish ports, to make its way to most towns and cities within a few hours.

In Scottish fish shops the most popular items are haddock, cod and mackerel, which are sold fresh or smoked. The well-known native specialties, finnan haddie (haddock) and Arbroath smokies (smoked haddock) are readily available, as are the Loch Fyne kippers (kippered herring) which many Scots enjoy—and many hotels offer—for breakfast. These days the herring are fewer than formerly, but if you like fresh fish the herring rolled in oatmeal is worth seeking.

Among freshwater fish, salmon and salmon trout appear on most restaurant menus as grilled steaks or cold with mayonnaise or (the fashion of the 1980s) en croûte. Trout farms flourish in many districts and the grilled brown trout is a common item on the menu. Scampi have become another popular dish: at city take-out restaurants and pub lunches scampi-and-chips threaten to supplant the traditional fish-and-chips.

Considering their availability in Scottish waters, lobster, crab and scallops are not always easy to get hold of except in the more expensive restaurants and the larger coastal fishmongers. Oysters, once common, are now a rarity but in specialist seafood restaurants you may be offered Musselburgh pie, beefsteak and oysters in a pie-dish, a gastronomic treat. Eels abound in Scottish rivers, but people are suspicious of them (they are, after all, rather bony). It may be said that the Scots are down-to-earth and conservative about their fish recipes; but that the quality and freshness of the fish you will eat are beyond reproach.

Meats

They used to say that Scotland had the best meat and the worst butchers. It is probably true of the meat, no longer true of the butchers.

When you observe how greatly in Scotland the sheep outnumber the people, you would suppose that mutton and lamb were the staple meat diet. So it used to be, but nowadays the Scots prefer beef (but not veal) and pork. The Aberdeen-Angus steak is in a class by itself. At railway buffets you may buy it in a bread sandwich, like a hamburger. Best ground beef is the filling for a variety of pies, bridies (with suet and onions in pastry) and casseroles and it may be served as a snack meal in the form of collops or Scotch egg (a boiled egg wrapped in sausage meat). The cuts are familiar to all, but New World descriptions such as T-bone and tenderloin are not used.

At breakfast or high tea (see below) the Scots are fond of grilled bacon or grilled sausage with fried potatoes and perhaps mushrooms. The traditional Scottish sausage, by the way, which you may still be offered, is a flat disc of sausage-meat, pork or beef, sliced on a machine; several times the diameter of the English "banger" which is steadily replacing it.

The Mysterious Haggis

Subject of much facetious comment abroad, haggis may be bought at the butcher's or, if you want to send it home, in a sealed can at some superior grocery stores. You are not likely to come across it at table unless you ask for it, or unless it happens to be Burns Night, January 25. Some visitors are a little nervous about haggis because it contains all the bits of a sheep that cooks usually throw away and because it is stitched up in the stomach bag of a sheep (or should be: these days they often use plastic bags). But a good haggis is hot and savory, nourishing and distinctively flavored; excellent when accompanied by the traditional "tatties" and "bashed neeps" (mashed swede or turnip)—and even better when it has a generous portion of "gravy" poured over it, for that is a coy term for a glass of whisky. Some food stores offer vegetarian haggis!

Game

Scots keep up the old custom of shooting for the pot and various game birds, notably pheasant, partridge and grouse, give the housewife room for culinary maneuver in their seasons. In and out of season you will find the birds on restaurant menus, either roasted or incorporated in game pies and pâtés. Hare and venison are also treated according to well-tried recipes. The latter, with its classy overtones of royal stag-hunts and the like, is now the raw material with which many a hotel and restaurant chef makes a declaration of his abilities—with the aid of vegetables, red wine, redcurrant preserve, rosemary, thyme and garlic.

Desserts

Some Scots pretend to regard puddings and sweets as a decadent English habit. How then do they get their sugar intake, which World Health Organization statistics show to be the highest of all the nations? The answer is in the many kinds of bakemeats to which the "Land o' Cakes" has long been addicted. You see them in all their glory, not in smart hotels and fashionable restaurants but in humble teashops and in family-run hotels and guest-houses where early-evening "high tea" is served instead of mid-evening dinner. (Some establishments serve both.) At high tea you will sit down to one hot dish, perhaps fish or a mixed grill, and will follow it with masses of cakes and scones, not forgetting the peculiarly Scottish "black bun" (pastry top and bottom, currants, candied peel, apples, nuts, cloves and ginger inside) and a pot or two of strong tea to help them down.

Despite the diehards, a dessert course in Scotland may be the most imaginative part of the meal. Here cream and oatmeal again come into their own. Scottish honey (exceptionally sweet) and whisky-based liqueurs are involved. Desserts in some restaurants make the most of the local fruits such as strawberries and raspberries. The sunshine and adequate rainfall in the Lowlands around Blairgowrie in Strathmore have made it the EEC's largest soft-fruit growing area.

The diehard, ignoring all that, rounds off his meal with cheese and biscuits. In restaurant and supermarket, French and English cheese are always on hand, as are numerous so-called regional Scottish cheeses. These include Cheddar varieties from mainland Scotland, and Dunlop from the islands of Arran, Orkney or Islay. Lanark Blue is another favorite specialty cheese and there is also a good range of soft cheeses.

The "Taste of Scotland"

Now independently run, Taste of Scotland was started by the Scottish Tourist Board in 1973 to encourage the upgrading of standards of food in Scottish hotels and restaurants. Since 1983 the scheme has publicized its own selection of hotels and restaurants, large and small, which specialize in local foods. These places offer menus, both modern and traditional, prepared with care and imagination, to demostrate that Scotland has culinary standards equal to the best in Europe. Look for a "soup tureen" symbol in participating places. Certainly it is a desirable goal—and the huge majority of places within the scheme reflect these aims. (Indeed, some of Scotland's finest establishments are members.) Beware, however, of the very occasional rogue participant, the enterprising southerner perhaps, who uses the scheme to introduce, by way of a few Scottish names, a note of spurious authenticity into ordinary fare.

Drinking

The Scot's staple drink is tea, but coffee of variable quality is always available. In another sense the staple drink is whisky (note spelling—only the Irish stuff is "whiskey") but brewing as well as distilling brought prosperity to many Scottish towns and Scots ale and lager are sold all over Britain. "Hawf and hawf," a dram of whisky and a half-pint of beer, is the Glasgow tipple, a somewhat lethal one.

Scottish entrepreneurs, two centuries ago, formed English tastes in port and sherry—drinks the Scots themselves have never been crazy about. There are old traditions of wine-drinking, particularly claret, but ordinary Scots hold that there is something slightly effeminate about wine; nonetheless many pubs sell wine by the glass.

All pubs and hotel bars, as you might expect, serve an immense variety of whiskies. In some areas, notably Grampian and the western isles, locally-produced "malts" of a more refined and longer-matured character are preferred to ordinary "blended" whiskies. We deal more fully with this subject in our Grampian chapter.

Once more tightly controlled than elsewhere, drinking in Scotland is now quite promiscuous (English liquor licensing laws have only very recently caught up with the liberal Scots.) Subject to local licensing approval, the publican may sell liquor from 11 A.M. to 11 P.M. daily.

There are no liquor stores in Scotland. The nearest equivalents are the wine merchant's or the off-licence, which are found in all towns and many villages. Either there or at a supermarket you may buy drinks, both alcoholic and non-alcoholic, on weekdays.

Where to Eat and Drink

Ideas of café society or family outings to restaurants are alien to the Scots. In Glasgow, Edinburgh and Aberdeen there are a few expensive restaurants where you may eat a gourmet meal and dance in the evenings; perhaps even see a floor show; but nothing on the scale of London for sophistication or price.

Department stores and bakery shops in cities and towns often have their own restaurants and cafeterias, not always permitted to sell alcohol, and while the food may be run-of-the-mill the places themselves are clean and cheap. High streets abound with cafés and coffee-bars: some good, some quite disgusting. Country places often go in for old-fashioned tea rooms with waitress service; generally good value.

Non-Scottish restaurants proliferate. In Glasgow and Edinburgh the home-grown establishment is hard to find among the Italian restaurants,

French bistros, American-style hamburger joints, Indian and Pakistani restaurants, Chinese restaurants, and eating places of flavors as unlikely as Turkish and Norwegian. Even in the lonely Highlands the signs "tandoori" and "takeaway" are not unknown. Such places generally stay open later than Scottish restaurants and the Scots have become enthusiastic patrons of them.

Don't Be Late for Lunch!

Except in first-class hotels you will not find it easy to get breakfast before about 8 unless you make prior arrangements for it. Most cafés and some hotel restaurants serve morning coffee/tea and snacks from 10.30 until lunchtime—which may be 12 noon in country places, 12.30 in the towns. They are open again about 3.30 for tea or coffee and light meals—relics of the "afternoon tea" habit which you may associate with the British way of life but which is dying out.

High tea (see *Desserts*, p.72) is available in most cafés and medium-priced restaurants, as well as most guesthouses and modest hotels, from about 5.30 P.M. It takes the place of dinner and is useful if you have other plans for the evening—though high tea is regarded as a somewhat provincial habit and you will probably come across it in all its lavish glory in some outlandish place where there is not all that much to do in the evenings anyway. In city hotels and restaurants the international dinner hour, 8 P.M. onwards, is increasingly observed.

The more prestigious restaurants in Glasgow and Edinburgh open for only four hours a day, 8 to midnight.

It is worth noting that many of Scotland's multitudinous pubs have smartened themselves up, no longer look askance at unaccompanied ladies and have diversified into basket-meal, bar-lunch, shepherd's-supper and similar amenities. Such meals are generally inexpensive and a good bet for the passing traveler. Scottish pubs however do tend to be small, crowded and noisy with conversation.

SPORTS IN SCOTLAND

Pleasures and Pastimes

It has been argued that golf came to Scotland from Holland. But all the historical evidence points to Scotland being the cradle, if not the birthplace, of the game. Citizens of St. Andrews were playing golf on the town links (public land) as far back as the 15th century; and bishops of St. Andrews were encouraging them at it in spite of laws which prohibited the game. The Stuart kings wanted their subjects to practice archery instead.

In 1754 the first association of players, the Gentlemen Golfers of Edinburgh, moved to the breezy links of St. Andrews, which in due course (1834) became the Royal & Ancient Golf Club. Maximizing the available space, golfers played nine holes out and the same nine holes back. Thus the number of holes on a golf course was fixed for all time.

The Old Course at St. Andrews coped with further congestion when a huge influx of people turned up, anxious to learn the new game. The peculiar "double greens" were devised. Exclusive to St. Andrews, they have been mystifying strangers ever since.

As time went by the manufacture and export of golf balls became the principal industry of that corner of Fife, the Royal & Ancient became the game's ruling body (as it still is) and year after year the Open Championship to determine the world's best golfer was held on the Old Course.

Scotland is now a land-mass entirely surrounded by golf courses; and packed with them too. The Gleneagles hotel boasts three 18-hole courses of its own. Every town and village has its course and its club. Celebrated courses—Carnoustie, Muirfield, Royal Troon, Turnberry and others—attract international championships in their turn.

Golf in Scotland is quite a plebeian game, whereas in England it is a distinctly middle-class pastime. A round on a Scottish municipal course costs very little and the Scottish clubs, apart from a few pretentious places modeled on the English fashion, demand only modest subscriptions.

Snow Business

A few climbing enthusiasts were skiing in Scotland in the early years of this century, but the big expansion took place in the early 1960s with the development of Aviemore and the slopes on nearby Cairngorm. This remains the largest development and, amid furious opposition from conservationists, its continuing expansion will mean the destruction of the fragile Arctic environment of the heart of the Cairngorms.

Other centers have arisen at Glencoe, Glenshee and a smaller development at the Lecht. Work has started to develop the high Aonach Mor near Fort William, while corries near Dalwhinnie on the A9 are also set to cater to this blossoming sport. Ben Wyvis behind Strathpeffer is also under consideration. Outside visitors to the area may be puzzled by the fierce emotions aroused by promoters and conservationists over this marginal activity amid the patchy snow-cover of Scotland's hills—with snows falling as late as February in some years and melting by April. However, its champions maintain that skiing is an important job provider.

The Roaring Game

The winter game is curling, a uniquely Scottish invention, now exported to other countries, particularly Canada and Switzerland. Curling has increased in popularity of late and a number of towns have indoor rinks, so the "roaring game"—so-called from the humming of the stones in motion—may be played all the year round. But ideally it is an outdoor spectacle. About once in ten years sustained frosty weather produces thick ice on big shallow lochs and then a Grand Match takes place, North of Scotland against South. Hundreds of players and thousands of curling stones—polished, one-handled ovals of granite—occupy the ice; and the fun is more important than the result. The big mass-curling venues are Loch Leven near Kinross and the Lake of Menteith near Aberfoyle.

A winter game confined to the Highlands, and to two sharply-defined areas of the Highlands at that, is shinty. To the uninitiated it looks like a mixture of football and hockey, a brutal conflict between two teams of young men whose principal qualifications are brawn and energy. But devotees insist that shinty has its finer points.

Insignificant villages like Newtonmore and Kingussie are the Giants and Dodgers of this game. It will be a lasting experience if, while traveling on Speyside in early spring, you happen on those villages when they are battling it out for the annual trophy, the Camanachd Cup.

"Fitba' Daft"

The mass spectator sports are professional football (the Association game, or "soccer" in England) and amateur rugby. The professional game, which Scotland claims to have invented, rouses extraordinary passions and is the Scotsman's favorite topic of conversation. Moralists say the Scots lost religion and found football. The uninterested say that Scots are "fitba' daft"—football crazy.

Besides football, there are racecourses (for flat racing) at Ayr, Hamilton, Musselburgh and Lanark and over jumps at Perth and Kelso. Sailing and yachting are naturally popular and most forms of watersport are taught and practised at coastal towns and on inland lochs.

Licensed to Kill

Fish, game and deer, the three ingredients of Scotland's renowned field-sports tradition, are carefully controlled; and of course you cannot own or use a gun without a license. Fishing, shooting and deer-stalking are expensive hobbies. Since World War II there has been a sad falling-off in the numbers of shooting tenancies and angling "beats" on which impecunious Highland lairds so heavily depended for an income. The parties you see on the moors these days are either the laird and a few friends or else a syndicate of businessmen, frequently Germans or Belgians, on a costly sporting vacation package.

Most rivers and lochs teem with salmon and trout, but the poacher risks a stiff fine. In the Border country, along the Tweed, they used to say that a man would be hanged for taking a salmon but not for killing his mother-in-law. Occasionally you may hear of a stretch of water where the fishing is free to all: one such is the "town water" of Peebles. Angling is popular, however, and some country bus services seem to be designed more to get the fisherman to his beat than to get shoppers and commuters into town.

From the time when Queen Victoria and her Scotophile consort Prince Albert began spending their summers at Balmoral, the Highlands became a sporting Mecca for the princes, potentates and politicians who went north to visit her. In late Victorian and Edwardian days vast quantities of deer, game birds and assorted wildlife were slaughtered. The annual massacre of the fauna does not go on to the same extent now, but dates like the "Glorious Twelfth"—August 12, when grouse-shooting begins— are still hallowed. Highland estates have arrangements with New York restaurants, the beaters and the guns are out at dawn that day, the first few brace of grouse are rushed to the nearest airport and charter jets fly them across the Atlantic. They are on the menu for lunch. Some Scots consider this stunt the height of vulgarity; the gourmet does not look at grouse until it has been hung for a week or two.

Fox-hunting in Scotland is chiefly confined to the southern countryside and to the winter and early spring. It is a more democratic pursuit in Scotland than in England but as a feature of rural life it is declining. The tide of Scottish opinion generally seems to be running against blood sports.

Gathering of the Clans

If you look good in the kilt, here is your big chance: the Highland Games, more properly called Highland Gatherings, which add such brilliance and color to the Scottish summer. But beware of getting too deeply involved. The Games have become commercialized and the rates charged for meals and accommodations at the venues betray a rapacity one does not usually associate with Highland hospitality. So-called Highland Games also take place on a professional basis in the cities and mining towns of the central belt, where the Highland tradition is imported.

Long ago a Highland Gathering was simply an assembly of clansfolk, called by the chief in some convenient valley or glen. It was his opportunity to inspect their weapons, advise them about their affairs and confirm their loyalties; and to set tests enabling him to choose the most skilled and strongest, perhaps as bodyguards. He could also select the best dancers and musicians to increase his prestige. Thus Highland games are a unique mix of sport and music.

In course of time friendly neighborhood clans joined in and the games were put on a more systematic footing. Typical activities, displays of manhood with the raw materials most readily available, were tugs-o'-war, hammer throwing, shot putting, caber-tossing and mountain racing.

Most events at a Highland Gathering have some story behind them. Sword-dancing goes back to King Malcolm who in 1054 slew a chief of Macbeth and, crossing the swords of victor and vanquished on the ground, danced a victory jig over them. The steps and posture of the Highland fling—arms raised and fingers pointed, like antlers—are said to imitate the movements of a rutting stag. Mountain racing—up to the summit and back—was included in the program of the first Braemar Gathering at King Malcolm Canmore's request because of complaints that the royal messengers were too slow. The lore and legends of the Gatherings are as picturesque and confused as the Gatherings themselves where for long periods, you feel, only the Master of Ceremonies knows what is going on.

Highland Games are widespread throughout Scotland in the summer months. Local tourist information centers will advise on dates and places. The most famous of these gatherings takes place annually in Braemar in September in the presence of the Royal Family. Dunoon's Cowal Gathering claims the largest assembly of Highland music in its "March of 1000 Pipers." This annual outburst of tartanry and traditional Highland events throughout Scotland can be seen as an ironic victory for the Gael—a curious celebration of a culture and way of life which, though greatly changed, has survived politics, emigration, and centuries of exploitation by "Sassunachs"—both Lowland Scots and English alike.

EXPLORING
SCOTLAND

SCOTIA'S DARLING SEAT

Edinburgh

Aeons ago, a glacier started moving eastwards through what is now Lowland Scotland, scouring out a valley which became the Firth of Forth, hitting and flowing over the cones of volcanoes from an earlier era. One hard cone resisted. The glacier parted and flowed round it, leaving a diminishing trail of rubble behind. Thus, in the formation which geologists call crag and tail, the Castle rock and mile-long slope of the future Old Town of Edinburgh came into being.

The rock was one of the first inhabited places in Scotland, inhabited by the predecessors of those mixed and mysterious people we call the Picts. The Romans avoided the rock. They made for the river-ports of Cramond and Inveresk, six miles west and east respectively. After their departure, Edinburgh's history as a capital city began. Celtic chieftains made the rock their fortress. They knew it as Dun-Edin, a name which some have connected with the 7th-century Anglican king Edwin. But Dun-Edin probably means "the dun (fort) on the slope." In due course the Angles replaced the Celts and in the 10th century they were themselves replaced by the Scots. By that time Dun-Edin's name had been translated into Anglo-Saxon—Edinburgh.

St. Ninian is supposed to have preached Christianity there in the 5th century and St. Columba in the 6th (Inchcolm in the Firth of Forth is the "isle of Columba"). St. Cuthbert, a monk from Melrose, founded the first Christian church in the 7th century, perhaps on the spot where the cathedral church of St. Giles was afterwards built.

The saintly Margaret, consort of King Malcolm Canmore, lived and died (1093) on the Castle rock. She is credited with having introduced a little culture to the uncouth Scots. Her son David founded Holyrood Abbey a mile away at the foot of the slope and a small burgh called the Canongate grew up around it. From the Castle rock to Canongate and the palace of Holyroodhouse there now runs a sequence of streets called the Royal Mile.

By 1500 Edinburgh was a true capital city and proud of it. In 1596, when King James VI, faced with a riot, threatened to move palace and parliament to Linlithgow, the citizens capitulated at once. King James was shortly afterwards to forsake Edinburgh for London, where he became the first king of England and Scotland. With him some of Edinburgh's tawdry, noisy, insanitary and often violent glory departed. She was stripped of more pomp and ceremony 100 years later, when the Union with England required the disbanding of the old Scots parliament.

"Gardy-loo!"

Up to the middle of the 18th century Edinburgh had the appearance of a medieval city. Confined to the Royal Mile—a narrow street, but a spacious boulevard compared with the suffocating "wynds" and closes, alleyways and passageways, which sloped off it—and to the huddled tenements round the Castle at one end and the Canongate at the other, its citizens lived in what visitors from England and France considered dangerously overcrowded squalor. Nobles and peasantry rubbed shoulders. Fur-robed merchants and beggarly hucksters shared the same "turnpike" (spiral) stairs in the warrens of the buildings. At night the citizens emptied their chamber pots into the street and the cry of *"Gardez-l'eau!"* or "Gardy-loo!" ("Beware water") would be followed by a noxious discharge from a fourth or fifth floor. The Royal Mile's inhabitants multiplied so fast that there was no space for shops and the tradesmen operated from little wooden stalls which they closed up at night, like traveling showmen. "Luckenbooth" (locked booth) is a word you may come across in Edinburgh today.

When the harbor of Leith, two miles from Edinburgh, developed as a port for wines, fruits and spices from the Continent, the city's trade was greatly increased and the magistrates reserved certain areas for particular commodities. You can still walk through the Grassmarket, Fleshmarket Close and Fishmarket Close. Growing rich, the merchants took over and extended some of the tall tenements in the Royal Mile: for example Gladstone's Land in the Lawnmarket ("Land" means property and "Lawn" means linen), where the ceilings are painted with motifs of fruits-and-vegetables, the wares on which a 17th-century Mr. Gladstone founded his fortune.

In 1563, during the reign of Mary Queen of Scots, Edinburgh had established the first civic university in Scotland (those already in existence, Glasgow, Aberdeen and St. Andrews, had been founded by the church). Stone houses, dour little versions of French baronial châteaux, had made their appearance. The capital was a mixture of French fashions and grinding poverty, solemn churchmen and irreverent urchins. But in the 1600s the Kirk laid its reforming hand on Edinburgh. Plays, pageants and processions were banned, the raucous frivolity of the streets was eclipsed and people took to heavy drinking in taverns—which is the chief relaxation of some Edinburghers to this day. The cathedral of St. Giles on the Royal Mile became the High Kirk of Edinburgh.

King Charles II's restoration in 1660 promised a return to the good old merry-making days; and Charles put work in hand to make the Palace of Holyroodhouse a glittering royal residence. But his reign in Scotland was clouded by religious squabbles as the Presbyterian Covenanters reasserted their authority.

The Highest Buildings in the World

An 18th-century traveler to Edinburgh said its buildings were the highest in the world and that each stairway led to the rooms of 20 or 30 families. The city had expanded more upwards than outwards. It was still dark and dangerous at night. There was no water supply apart from one or two public wells.

A few fine buildings had appeared: George Heriot's Hospital (he was the royal jeweler and his hospital was a school for boys, as it still is); and a new Parliament Hall. The 1707 Union took national politics out of Edinburgh but the lawyers and bankers came into their own and Scottish literature and philosophy began to flourish. Edinburgh was approaching a golden age of the spirit, not courtly but aggressively cultural.

The New Town

In the 16th century, Edinburgh's smart set lived in the Cowgate, the street through which cattle had been let out to graze (200 years later the Cowgate was a slum). When a speculative builder put up George Square, which is now occupied by University buildings, fastidious citizens were quick to move there out of an Old Town susceptible to fire and plague. In 1762 an enterprising Lord Provost (in Scotland, a city mayor) started draining the swampland north of the Castle rock and over the next 40 years the New Town of Edinburgh took shape on rising ground beyond it.

The New Town, designed by a 27-year-old architect named James Craig and built with local stone, was one of the first examples of large-scale town planning in Britain. It had a gridiron pattern with squares at each end, and all the buildings were in the Georgian style, severe and elegant.

Street names complimented the royal House of Hanover. The main thoroughfare was George Street. Parallel with it ran Queen Street and Princes Street, named for His Majesty's wife and son. Between them were the narrower Rose Street and Thistle Street, for the emblems of England and Scotland. The two national patron saints, St. Andrew and St. George, gave their names to the flanking squares. (To avoid confusion with George Square, St. George's afterwards became Charlotte Square, another respectful nod in the direction of King George's consort.) The chief crosstown avenue was Hanover Street, named for the ruling dynasty, side by side with Frederick Street (the King's second son) and St. David's Street (the "sair sanct" King Scots).

The North Bridge connected the Old Town with the New, and the rubbish from the building operations was heaped up to form an "Earthen Mound," now The Mound, between Castle rock and Princes Street. The

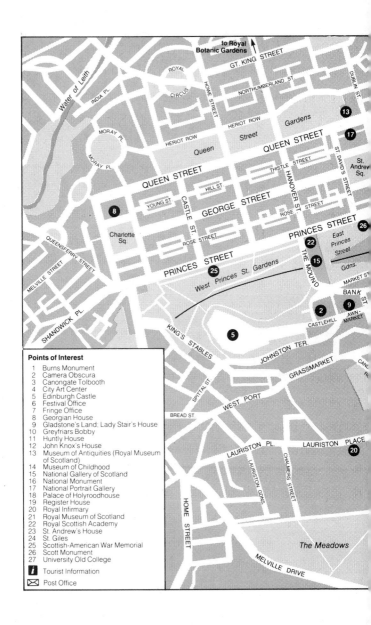

Points of Interest

1 Burns Monument
2 Camera Obscura
3 Canongate Tolbooth
4 City Art Center
5 Edinburgh Castle
6 Festival Office
7 Fringe Office
8 Georgian House
9 Gladstone's Land: Lady Stair's House
10 Greyfriars Bobby
11 Huntly House
12 John Knox's House
13 Museum of Antiquities (Royal Museum of Scotland)
14 Museum of Childhood
15 National Gallery of Scotland
16 National Monument
17 National Portrait Gallery
18 Palace of Holyroodhouse
19 Register House
20 Royal Infirmary
21 Royal Museum of Scotland
22 Royal Scottish Academy
23 St. Andrew's House
24 St. Giles
25 Scottish-American War Memorial
26 Scott Monument
27 University Old College

ℹ️ Tourist Information

✉️ Post Office

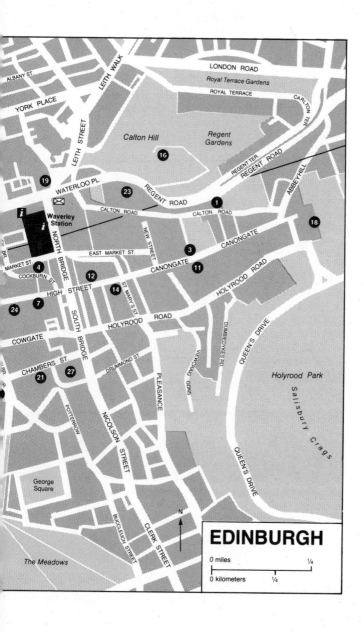

architect Robert Adam, then at the height of his powers, was involved in the designs but he died before he had had time to complete more than one street frontage in Charlotte Square.

The Old Town and the New Town represented two extremes of urban planning and social organization. Their juxtaposition and their magnificent natural situation, stepping down from the Castle on its rock to their footstool at the port of Leith, prompt many Scots to nominate Edinburgh the most beautiful city in the world.

Nowadays the New Town is as busy and congested as the Old, but it was not always so. At first the town council had to bribe traders to take shops in the New Town; and if you bought a house in Princes Street you could claim exemption from all city taxes!

A Piece of Nova Scotia

Edinburgh is a small city, there are around 500,000 inhabitants, with a dense concentration of tourist sights at its center. If you walk the Royal Mile, conscientiously studying them, you will need two or three days; but you will then have learned a great deal about the place they used to call the Athens of the North; a title that arose not as a result of its neo-classical splendor but because of its literary and academic life.

A bus will take you close to the Castle esplanade, where you are faced with a stiff climb on foot through the citadel to its highest point, 443 feet above sea level. Since the sea is only two miles away, you have a wonderful panorama of the Firth and the country beyond. Here (you can see the apex of the crag sticking through the floor) stands tiny St. Margaret's Chapel, built about 1090 by Malcolm Canmore's pious Queen; also the Scottish National War Memorial, an elaborate shrine for the fallen of the 1914–1918 war—Scotsmen, Scotswomen, even Scottish dogs and horses.

Outside, round the Palace Yard, are the historical apartments: Crown Room, containing the Scottish regalia of crown, scepter, sword of state and various orders of chivalry, and the diminutive Parliament Hall where medieval conferences of the Three Estates (monarch, nobles and common people) were held. A United Services museum tells the story of Scottish arms on sea and land.

Lower down you come to the Half-Moon Battery whose curving ramparts give Edinburgh Castle its distinctive appearance from miles away. In an ancient hall behind the battery stand Mons Meg and her huge cannonballs. The biggest gun in Europe when cast at Mons, Belgium in 1486, she was dragged from battle to battle but never, so far as is known, fired a shot in anger. The Battery's time gun, on the other hand, goes off with a bang every weekday at 1, causing Edinburghers to check their watches and visitors to jump out of their skins.

The Castle's steep cobbled passageways are thronged with visitors and soldiers of the garrison stationed here, sometimes a Highland regiment in the kilt, sometimes a Lowland regiment in trews (tartan trousers). Between July and September that stone-flagged parade ground in front of the citadel's drawbridge is obstructed by a grandstand, for this is where Edinburgh's famous military tattoo takes place during the International Festival.

The Castle esplanade is held to be part of the North American continent. In the 17th century when King Charles I wanted to create baronets

of Nova Scotia (New Scotland) constitutional law demanded that the ceremony be carried out on Nova Scotian soil; for which purpose the esplanade
was declared Nova Scotian territory.

The Royal Mile

Descending Castle hill, first of the streets which make up the Royal
Mile, observe Cannonball House with the round shot embedded in it. Tradition says it was fired by Bonnie Prince Charlie's men in 1745 when the
Jacobites occupied the town but the government troops remained in the
Castle. Stairs in the building opposite lead to the Edinburgh Camera Obscura, one of the most up-to-date, providing a telescopic perspective of
city and suburbs.

Next comes the Lawnmarket, and the first of the "closes," alleyways
leading off the Royal Mile, often with historical associations recalled in
their names or on information plaques, reminders of the famous folk—
David Hume, Robert Burns, James Boswell—who formerly lodged there.
Also on the lawnmarket is Gladstone's Land. This is a 17th-century tene-
ment easily recognizable from its arcaded front, the last survivor of a type
once common on the Royal Mile. A variety of tartan, souvenir and antique
shops may also delay progress. In Brodie's Close in the 1770s lived the
infamous Deacon Brodie, pillar of society by day and expert lock-picker
by night. R.L. Stevenson and W.E. Henley wrote a play about him and
he was the inspiration for Stevenson's *Jekyll and Hyde*.

After the Lawnmarket comes the High Street, the focus of daily life in
old Edinburgh. The Bank of Scotland, a few yards down Bank Street,
opened its doors in 1695. Where the street opens out to a square the Old
Tolbooth used to stand, the prison where the first scenes of Scott's *Heart
of Midlothian* are set. (When it was demolished in 1817, Scott took the
gates to his new house at Abbotsford.) The spot is marked with a Heart
of Midlothian set in colored stones in the roadway. Some older men spit
on it for luck as they pass.

Here too is the High Kirk of Edinburgh, the Gothic pile of St. Giles,
culminating in a stone crown 161 feet high. On the crown of St. Giles the
last stork in Scotland nested in 1416. The church has been here since at
least the 9th century—though the earliest work (Norman) is seen in the
central piers—but, having been three times Protestant and twice Roman
Catholic, it has seen changes, including brief elevation to cathedral status
on the orders of Charles II in 1633. A small brass plate let into the stones
of the square outside reads "I.K.1572"; the only indication of the grave
of John Knox, before whom all Scotland trembled. But in the Albany aisle,
inside the church, a bronze statue commemorates him. It was presented
in 1906 by "Scots at home, in Australia, in Canada and the United States."

Knox is sometimes remembered as a bullying, pig-headed Presbyterian
who loaded the Scots with the guilt and gloom which afflict some to this
day. But he was not against bishops, and not opposed to dancing. The stern
tyranny of Calvinism was imposed by the extremists who came after him.

A decorated stone pulpit opposite the City Chambers (seat of local government) just below St. Giles is the Mercat Cross. On royal occasions the
heralds make proclamations from it with due ceremony. The cross is modern, but part of its shaft is as old as the city.

Further down the High Street is another interesting survivor—John Knox House, said to be the only 15th-century dwelling in Scotland. Though there is doubt that the famous Reformer ever lived there, this interesting building still has its upper floor projecting galleries, once typical in the city. Look for a former owner's "marriage lintel" carved initials in the stone work. "J.M." was James Mossman, goldsmith to Mary, Queen of Scots.

The eastern extremity of the Old Town is below, at today's Jeffrey Street/St Mary's Gate crossroads. Here stood the Netherbow Port (Portgate). You will find it portrayed on a plaque outside the nearby Netherbow Theater. Beyond was the Canongate, literally the street of the canons—from Holyrood Abbey at the end of the Royal Mile. The Canongate was not only outside the town walls, it was an independent burgh with its own Tolbooth (civic center), still to be seen today. Opposite is 16th-century Huntly House, now the principal museum of local history, and there are other atmospherically restored 17th-century buildings in the vicinity, including the Canongate Kirk, with Adam Smith the economist, Robert Fergusson the poet and Robert Burn's "Clarinda" in its kirkyard.

The Official Royal Residence

The gates of the Palace of Holyroodhouse mark the end of the Royal Mile. The Palace grew from the guest house of the now-ruined abbey, though after the departure of the Scottish Royal Court for London it was for long unused and in decline. Today it is the offical residence of the Royal Family while in Scotland. The Queen's Park, in which the Palace stands, was formerly a Royal hunting forest. Now it is a public area of turf and small lochs gathered round Salisbury Crags and Arthur's Seat, a double-coned extinct volcano 823 feet high. There are footpaths to the top and a panoramic view indicator. A public road, the King's/Queen's Drive, three and a half miles long, encircles Edinburgh's inner-city mountain. You may see the Royal Company of Archers practicing with their longbows. They are the Queen's Bodyguard for Scotland, a corps of elderly respected citizens whose appearance in their bizarre uniforms has been likened to generals rolled in spinach.

When the royal family is not in residence (see *Practical Information*) you can walk freely around the palace and go inside for a conducted tour. The largely redecorated apartments recall the glamor and brutality of Stuart history—especially the little supper room where, in 1566, the Queen's private secretary David Rizzio was dragged out from behind her skirts and stabbed to death. Annexed to the main quadrangle are the Chapel Royal, where several Scottish monarchs were married, and the Royal Vault where others were buried among numerous very ancient and anonymous graves.

The Chapel Royal has fragments of the Abbey of Holyrood, built in the 12th century by King David I as a thank-offering for his deliverance from a rampaging stag when this area was a hunting marsh and forest; legend says that the holy rood (cross) appeared to him as a sign from Heaven above the stag's antlers. It is a common medieval legend, also attributed to St. Hubert and St. Eustache.

From David's time onwards Holyrood was gradually adopted as a royal residence. James IV was probably the first king to live there regularly. The palace as we see it now dates from between 1671 and 1677 and was chiefly the work of Sir William Bruce in the reign of Charles II.

The New Town

This was the vision of one of Edinburgh's most far-sighted civic leaders, Provost James Drummond, who, in the mid-18th century, saw the potential of the gently rising ground, due north of the Old Town, for a major development which would capture the spirit of Edinburgh's "Age of Enlightenment." He organized a competition, which was won by the young, unknown architect, James Craig. His gridiron design was subsequently carried out—though Craig himself did not actually design any of the buildings. The siting of the "New Town" on this broad ridge beyond the deep valley, formerly flooded for defensive purposes by the Nor' Loch, was a master stroke of town planning. The two towns were eventually linked by the North Bridge, 1772, and the Mound afterwards, while the deep valley became the New Town's residents' pleasure grounds, today's Princes Street Gardens.

When the New Town was planned, George Street was intended as the principal artery. Over the years commerce and fashion moved southward one block to Princes Street, a splendid thoroughfare, dead straight and nearly one mile long. Uniquely, it has shops on one side only, looking out over Princes Street Gardens (the swamp of pre-New Town days) to the Castle rock and Old Town skyline. A restaurant or café on the upper floor of a Princes Street department store is the place to be when the cavalcades and pipe bands go by. The Gardens, squirrel-haunted in spring and fall, have a secluded air despite the citizens who stroll in them, the Glasgow–Edinburgh railroad which cuts through them longitudinally and the traffic on The Mound which crosses them laterally. In summer, at a large open stage and auditorium, daily concerts and displays of Scottish country dancing are given.

What appears to be a Gothic cathedral spire chopped off and planted in the east of the Gardens is the Scott Monument; 200 feet high and 267 steps, the nation's tribute to Sir Walter and a fine viewpoint.

Also in East Princes Street Gardens you will find a monument to David Livingstone, whose African meeting with H.M. Stanley is part of Scots-American history. Eastward still, on the Calton Hill opposite St. Andrew's House and close to the incomplete Parthenon lookalike known as Edinburgh's Disgrace (it was intended for a National War Memorial in 1822 but the contributions did not come in), there is a monument to Abraham Lincoln and the Scottish-American dead of the Civil War. An impressive American monument to the Scottish soldiers of World War I stands in West Princes Street Gardens, among various memorials of Scottish and foreign alliances.

Princes Street shops no longer have a distinctly Edinburgh flavor. They include chain stores, dress shops, and shoe shops whose names are seen in every British city center. At the east end of the street are two important shopping arcades: the St. James Centre, rather tawdry, behind Register House, and the smart and stylish Waverley Market, bright with flags, fountains, waterfalls, kites, and patio cafés above the Waverley railroad station.

In George Street, more exclusive stores are found among banks and insurance offices. The pubs and howffs of George Street's canyon-like accompaniments, Rose Street and Thistle Street, have dwindled. Coffeebars, boutiques and cosmopolitan fast food outlets have taken their place, and in the few which remain the old clientele of drunken poets and crusaders for eccentric causes is heavily diluted with lawyers, journalists and bank tellers from offices round about.

In the middle of George Street, under the arcades of the Music Hall and Assembly Hall, you may see kilts and sporrans assembling in the evenings for a Highland Ball; the buildings are the venue for Edinburgh's most formal social occasions. At the east end of the street is St. Andrew Square and the city bus station behind it, for out-of-town and long-distance services. At the west end is Charlotte Square. Its north side is especially admired and architects come from all over the world to study its simplicity and perfect proportions. At No. 7 is the Georgian House, the National Trust for Scotland's recreation of plush New Town life. This square was a breeding-ground of talent, too: note the number of birthplace plaques. They include Earl Haig the field-marshal, J.Y. Simpson the pioneer of anesthetics and Alexander Graham Bell the inventor of the telephone.

On the Waterfront

Beyond the Old Town and the New, the city has plenty to offer a sightseer. The 74-acre Zoological Garden at Corstorphine ("Kor-*stor*-fin"), four miles west of the city, was one of the world's first open-planned zoos. Penguins are the specialty. The Royal Botanic Gardens (entrance in Howard Place, one and a half miles north of Princes Street) contain fine rose gardens, rock gardens and an arboretum. Inverleith House, to which the grounds formerly belonged, is a handsome centerpiece, with an exhibition inside devoted to natural history.

Further afield, the once-independent town and seaport of Leith, submerged by the expanding city and with its buildings roughly handled in places by Edinburgh's planners, enjoys a revival, with waterfront cafes and atmospheric pubs and an urban renewal program restoring some of its lost civic pride. Further east, in Edinburgh's own seaside resort, Portobello, a flavor of Victorian times remains in the sturdy villas — still redolent with scandal, perhaps, as Portobello has had to live with the tale that this is where respectable Edinburgh businessmen kept their mistresses!

In contrast, on the "upriver" extremity is Cramond, its exclusive reputation unsullied by such tittle-tattle. Little yachts and dinghies ride at moorings in the River Almond estuary and, nearby, you can enjoy a drink outside and watch the sunset. There is also a pleasant treelined river walk upstream which offers long-abandoned mill sites where water-power once produced ironwares.

You can also stroll over Arthur's Seat to discover Duddingston, once a brewing and weaving community, clustered by the attractive edges of its bird-speckled loch, or catch a bus to Hillend on the edge of the Pentland Hills, taking the chairlift (on the artificial ski slope) for magnificent city views. From Hillend, the energetic could stroll over to the hamlet of Swanston, with its white-washed thatched cottages associated with R.L. Stevenson.

Voyage of Discovery

Edinburgh and its suburbs are easy places to find one's way around in and the foregoing sketches of the principal sights only skim the surface of a district which the Greek poet might have linked with his homeland when he wrote: "Prick the stones with a needle and you discover the bones of heroes." We have not described the birthplace of Sir Arthur Conan Doyle in Picardy Place or the Royal Infirmary where he learned the inference-and-deduction techniques from Dr. Joseph Bell that he gave to his fictional investigator Sherlock Holmes. We have omitted the Dean Village, the curious complex of mills and tenements beside the Water of Leith under the city's busiest streets yet apparently remote from the world; and Greyfriars Bobby, the fountain in Candlemaker Row which commemorates the fidelity of a policeman's terrier dog; and the fine schools endowed by merchants of long ago—Daniel Stewart's, George Watson's, John Watson's, James Gillespie's, Donaldson's Hospital, Fettes and others—which add their spires and cupolas to the Edinburgh silhouette; and Edinburgh University with its great dome and Old Quadrangle long outgrown and its 16-story David Hume Tower; and the large Halls gifted by millionaire brewers McEwan and Usher, one for the University and one for music; and the castle of Craigmillar whose ruined walls could tell so much of the intrigues of Mary Queen of Scots; and the stately home of Lauriston in whose gardens you may watch a croquet tournament or a country-dance display . . . the multifarious attractions of the city beyond the Old Town and the New would take days to describe, much less visit.

The tourist season reaches its climax in the Edinburgh International Festival, the most complete cultural feast in Europe of music, drama, exhibitions and dance. The Festival was inaugurated in 1947 and it would be hard to name an artistic celebrity of the latter half of the 20th century who has not appeared at it. During the three weeks of this event, mid-August to early September, the city takes on a movement and brilliance worthy of its incomparable setting. Even if you are not culturally inclined or interested in the hundreds of Fringe entertainments which accompany and sometimes steal the limelight from the main events, you cannot help being uplifted by the color and cosmopolitan bustle of a Festival day and the marvelous floodlighting of a Festival night. Even provincial Scots invade the capital in their thousands to attend the military tattoo on the Castle esplanade or watch the last–night fireworks.

"Auld Reekie"

Finally, a word or two to explain Edinburgh's nickname: Auld Reekie. It means "Old Smoky," and was coined by a man of Fife who stood every morning on the opposite shore of the Forth and watched the fumes from 10,000 chimneys gathering into a pall above the towers and tenements of the capital. But Auld Reekie is no more. Today the city is a smoke-free zone and the old blackened buildings are gradually being sand blasted into something like their appearance when new. Nothing would more astonish a citizen of the past, time warped into the present, than the clear air and bright stonework of his native town.

PRACTICAL INFORMATION FOR EDINBURGH

GETTING INTO TOWN FROM THE AIRPORT. An airport bus connects Edinburgh airport with the city bus terminal at Waverley Bridge. Buses run regularly and journey time is around 25 minutes. One-way fare is £1.75. Taxi fare for the same trip is approximately £7.50.

HOTELS. Edinburgh has more than 300 hotels and guest houses, many very good, some not so good but nearly all an improvement on what they used to be; especially those in the lower price ranges. If you are simply looking for a night's lodging, and are motoring, you will easily find it along the approach roads to the city, at one of innumerable private houses which advertise Bed and Breakfast. You may expect to pay £7–£12 per head, rather more at Festival time.

If you arrive in Edinburgh without a place to stay, visit or telephone the Tourist Information and Accommodation Center, Waverley Market, 3 Princes Street EH1 1BQ (tel. 557 1700). If you arrive by air, contact the Information/Accommodation desk at Edinburgh airport (tel. 333 2167). Prefix numbers with code 031 if calling from outside Edinburgh.

Deluxe

Caledonian, west end of Princes Street (tel. 225 2433). 254 rooms with bath. Handsomely updated former railroad hotel retaining old dignity and elegance. Ornate, spacious rooms. Excellent location. Bright, lively restaurant offers good-value semi-buffet lunch.

Carlton Highland, North Bridge (tel. 556 7277). 207 rooms with bath. Close to the Royal Mile in the heart of the Old Town.

George, George Street (tel. 225 1251). 195 rooms with bath. An old favorite, in new guise. Spacious public areas, comfortable rooms. Very central. The *Chambertin* restaurant offers an interesting mix of Scottish and French dishes.

Prestonfield House, Priestfield Road (tel. 668 3346). 5 rooms, 4 with bath. Secluded situation 20 minutes from city center. Historic house, family portraits, tapestries, grotesque mouldings in Cupid Room. Notable international cuisine. Peacocks on lawns. Many interesting architectural features.

Roxburghe, Charlotte Square (tel. 225 3921). 76 rooms with bath. Restrained elegance to match the Georgian environment. Bedrooms are especially well-furnished and service is first-class.

Royal Scot, 111 Glasgow Road (tel. 334 9191). 252 rooms with bath. Halfway to airport. Bleak building, but voted Hotel of 1987 by American Express Travel.

Sheraton, Festival Square (tel. 229 9131). 263 rooms with bath. Opened in 1985, aims at the top of the market.

Expensive

Clarendon, Grosvenor Street (tel. 337 7033). 51 rooms with bath. In quiet Georgian terrace ten minutes from West End.

Donmaree, Mayfield Gardens (667 3641). 17 rooms, 14 with bath. Typical of numerous town-house hotels along southern approaches to Edinburgh. On main bus route. Favored by discriminating American visitors.

Howard, Great King Street (tel. 557 3500). 25 rooms with bath. High-class family hotel in quiet street of New Town.

Learmonth, Learmonth Terrace (tel. 343 2671). 51 rooms with bath. In tree-lined avenue only 5 minutes from West End. Bright and modern, lively at night. Bars, bistro and coffee lounge bring in the locals.

Moderate

Albany, 39–43 Albany St., (tel. 556 0397). 22 rooms with bath. Comfortable, with professional, friendly service in central location. Excellent value restaurant (M).

Bruntsfield, 69–74 Bruntsfield Place (tel. 229 1393). 52 rooms with bath. Two miles from center on bus route, south side. Pleasant outlook, reasonable standard of food and service.

Ellersly House, Ellersly Road (tel. 337 6888). 57 rooms with bath. High standard of service and cuisine, good big rooms, a pleasant suburban situation. Prices may increase sharply around Festival time.

Mount Royal, Princes Street (tel. 225 7161). 168 rooms, 150 with bath. Most modern hotel in city center, above department stores, good viewpoint for pageantry. Full range of amenities, but somewhat functional.

Nova, 5 Bruntsfield Crescent (tel. 447 6437). 11 rooms with bath. Its crow-stepped gables overlook a leafy cul-de-sac. Close to buses, minutes from center. Roomy apartments, modern decor, cheerful outlook. Food and drinks served to 11 P.M. Lavish "room service" breakfast.

Redholme House, 20 Colinton Road (tel. 447 2286). 17 rooms, 1 with bath—despite that, private facilities are good and general standards beyond reproach. Big saving on weekly rates.

Royal British, 20 Princes Street (tel. 556 4901). 77 rooms, 76 with bath. Old-established and reputable. Central, with old-fashioned standards.

Inexpensive

Ailsa Craig, 24 Royal Terrace (tel. 556 6055). 13 rooms, 6 with bath. Well-built, family-run, in heart of New Town.

Dean, Clarendon Crescent (tel. 332 0308). 12 rooms, 5 with bath. Close to Dean Bridge, 5 minutes' walk from center. Family-owned house in a Georgian terrace. Well-appointed, average cuisine.

Rothesay, Rothesay Place (tel. 225 4125). 40 rooms, 28 with bath. A successful transformation of elegant New Town buildings. Spacious and well-furnished.

West End, 35 Palmerston Place (tel. 225 3656). 8 rooms with bath. Spacious, comfortable, central, with Highland atmosphere and entertainment.

Guest Houses

Airlie, 29 Minto Street (tel. 667 3562). 15 rooms, 6 with bath. Large comfortable Victorian house on main south exit, with private parking and easy access to center.

Ashdene, 23 Fountainhall Road (tel. 667 6026). 5 rooms with bath. Spacious Victorian house in peaceful neighborhood.

Brig o'Doon Guest House, 262 Ferry Road (tel. 552 3953). 6 rooms. Friendly atmosphere, substantial breakfasts. Not a classy district, but handy for Botanic Gardens and exit to west.

Buchan, 3 Coates Gardens (tel. 337 1045). 10 rooms, 1 with bath. Former merchant's house near West End of city. Cheerful service, nourishing meals.

Dorstan, 7 Priestfield Road (tel. 667 6721). 14 rooms, 9 with bath. Serene atmosphere, tranquil surroundings.

International Guest House, 37 Mayfield Gardens (tel. 667 2511). 7 rooms with bath. Canadian proprietor. South side of city, 15 minutes by bus from center. Clean and comfortable.

Hostels

Universities and further-education colleges offer accommodations with (usually) cafeteria-style meals during vacation periods: March to April and June to September. A single room with breakfast and evening meal will cost from £13.50 to £20.15 per day, depending on establishment and season. Double rooms (there are few) approximately double. Enquiries to: The Principal Warden.

Carlyle Hall, East Suffolk Road (tel. 668 3377). 310 rooms. On south side, 2 miles from center. July–Sept. only.

Pollock Halls of Residence, Holyrood Park Road (tel. 667 1971). 1,600 rooms. Close to Commonwealth Swimming Pool and Queen's Park; 1 mile from center.

There is a Christian Alliance hostel with accommodation for about 35 at 14 Coates Crescent EH3 7AF (tel. 225 3608). Though designed primarily for single women, it will accept one or two married couples. Midnight curfew. Single room £11 bed and breakfast, subsequent nights £10; shared room £7–£11 per person. You don't have to be a C.A. member.

Self-Catering

Apartments may be rented through Frutin Travel Agency, 23–29 Great Junction Street, Leith EH6 5HX (tel. 554 0362); and Mackay's Agency, 30 Frederick Street EH2 2JR (tel. 225 3539).

HOW TO GET ABOUT. On foot. Edinburgh is a delightful city for walking in, and even when it is raining you will find all round the Royal Mile and New Town museums, exhibitions or libraries in which to take refuge. Many are free, some have cafeterias. In summer some institutions such as whisky distillers, breweries, the Northern Lighthouse Board, the Law Courts, the Scottish Record Office, the Scottish Poetry Library and the Post Office Philatelic Bureau open their doors to visitors at no charge. Consult the twice-monthly bulletin of events *The List,* 50p from stationers. There is a walkway along three miles of the Water of Leith, Edinburgh's diminutive river. Edinburgh is safer than most cities for walkers, but nevertheless it would be better to leave valuables behind. Escorted walking tours are organised by the *New Town Conservation Center* (tel. 556 7054), *Scottish Tourist Guides* (tel. 336 2560), the *National Trust for Scotland* (tel. 226 5922), and *Cadies* (tel. 225 6745).

By bus. Maroon and white Lothian Regional Transport buses cover city, suburbs and beyond from early till late. LRT (tel. 226 5087; 554 4494) run inexpensive city tours, half or full day tours further afield and have an interesting "Touristcard" scheme, giving some restaurant and admission price concessions as well as unlimited low-cost travel. Full information on services from The Ticket Centre, Waverley Bridge (tel. 226 5087).

Eastern Scottish green buses operate from St. Andrews Square Bus Station
(tel. 556 8464) and operate further afield. (They share the same bus stops
as LRT buses around the city.) Eastern Scottish Citylink, as its name suggests, links the main cities of Scotland and makes English connections (tel.
556 8464). Most buses are pay-as-you-enter and require the exact fare.
Keep a supply of 10p and 20p pieces handy. Drivers are helpful—
usually—and so are the locals waiting at the bus-stop!

By car. Central Edinburgh in peak times can be heavily congested, with
parking spaces a rarity. There are parking lots near the east and west ends
of Princes Street. Carry small change for windshield-display meter tickets.

By taxi. Taxis are black, custom-built and old-fashioned-looking. They
stand at strategically-sited ranks throughout central Edinburgh. You pay
around 80p a mile, plus 10% tip. Cruising taxis have their yellow rooftop
TAXI signs illuminated.

TOURIST INFORMATION. Tourist Accommodation and Information
Service, Waverley Market (tel. 557 2727) and Scottish Travel Center, 14
South St. Andrew Street EH2 2AZ; Citizen's Advice Bureau, 58 Dundas
Street EH3 6QZ (tel. 557 1500); American Consul, 3 Regent Terrace EH7
5BN (tel. 556 8315); British Airways, 32 Frederick Street EH2 2JR (tel.
225 2525); British Rail, Waverley Station EH1 1BB (tel. 556 2451).

MUSEUMS. We list here the principal museums and galleries of Edinburgh. You will likely be agreeably surprised at the modest charges—most
offer free admission.

Canongate Tolbooth, 163 Canongate. Houses "The People's Story"
which portrays the past life of ordinary city folk with displays and period
reconstructions. Open Mon.–Sat. 10–5 (June–Sept. 10–6; open Sun. during
Festival).

City Art Centre, 1–4 Market Street. Major exhibitions of fine and deco-
rative arts, also Scottish portraits and landscapes. Open Jun.–Sept., weekdays 10–6; Oct.–May, weekdays 10–5.

Huntly House, 142 Canongate. Principal museum of city history and
Edinburgh silver and glass. Open weekdays, Jun.–Sept. 10–6, Oct.–May
10–5; during Festival only, Sun. 2–5.

John Knox House, 45 High Street. Early example of stone-built town
house containing Knox items and Scottish Kirk relics. Open Apr.–Oct.,
weekdays 10–5; Nov.–Mar. 10–4.

Lady Stair's House, Lady Stair's Close, Lawnmarket. 17th-century
town house with relics of Burns, Scott, Stevenson. Open Jun.–Sept. 10–6,
Oct.–May 10–5; weekdays only.

Georgian House, 7 Charlotte Square. On the Adam side of the Square.
Fitted and furnished in the style of its period, 1760–1820. Open Apr.–Oct.,
weekdays 10–5, Sun. 2–5; Nov.–mid-Mar., Sat. 10–4.30, Sun. 2–4.30.
N.T.S.

Gladstone's Land, Lawnmarket. 17th-century merchant's house, appropriately furnished. Open Apr.–Oct., weekdays 10–5, Sun. 2–5; Nov., Sat.
10–4.30, Sun. 2–4.30. N.T.S.

Museum of Childhood, 38 High Street. The social history of children,
their dress, upbringing and toys through the centuries. "The noisiest museum in the world." Open weekdays, 10–6 Jun.–Sept., 10–5 Oct.–May.

National Gallery of Scotland, The Mound. European and British artists, 1300–1900. Lunchtime concerts in summer. Open weekdays 10–5, Sun. 2–5.

Royal Museum of Scotland, 1 Queen Street. Archeology, medieval and modern history. Some Celtic curiosities from pre-A.D. 1000. Open weekdays 10–5, Sun. 2–5.

National Portrait Gallery, 1 Queen Street (above Museum of Antiquities). Scottish portraitists and their famous and not-so-famous sitters. Open weekdays 10–5, Sun. 2–5; closed 12.30–1.30 Oct.–Mar.

Palace of Holyroodhouse. Official residence of Queen in Scotland. State apartments, tapestries, and portrait gallery with 100 Scottish monarchs, most looking strangely alike. Open Apr.–Oct. 9.30–5.15, Sun. 10.30–4.30; Nov.–Mar. 9.30–3.45, closed Sun. Occasionally closed, generally in May and early June, when royal visitors are in residence or when preparations in hand for royal visit.

Royal Botanic Garden, Inverleith Row. Exhibition hall for ecological displays. Open weekdays 9 to sunset, Sun. 11 to sunset.

Royal Scottish Academy, The Mound. Contemporary Scottish artists and periodical exhibitions. Open May–Jul. weekdays 10–6, Sun. 2–5.

Royal Museum of Scotland, Chambers Street. Ideal for a wet day. All kinds of working models of industry and science. Permanent displays of silver, ceramics, primitive arts, zoology. Open weekdays 10–5, Sun. 2–5.

Scotch Whisky Heritage Center, 358 Castlehill (top of Royal Mile). Opened 1988. An imaginative £2 million project providing a tour (in barrel railcar) of historical, topographical, and industrial landscapes associated with whisky production. Well-stocked malt whisky shop. Open Apr.–Oct., daily 9–7, Nov.–Mar., daily 9–5.

Scottish Gallery of Modern Art, John Watson's College, Belford Road. Impressive collection of contemporary painters and sculptors, avant-garde and pop art. Open weekdays 10–5 (or sunset); Sun. 2–5 (or sunset).

ENTERTAINMENT AND NIGHTLIFE. Except at Festival time, Aug.-Sept., nightlife is limited to pubs, discos and a few theaters and cinemas. Local newspapers give details. *The List,* twice monthly at bookstalls, is a comprehensive rundown of culture and entertainment in Edinburgh and Glasgow.

Theater and Music. The *Royal Lyceum* theater, Grindlay Street, offers straight plays and music shows. The *King's,* Leven Street, has occasional high-class opera but more often light opera and musicals with a sprinkling of conventional plays. Scottish symphony and chamber orchestras perform regularly in the *Usher Hall,* Lothian Road, and at the *Queen's Hall,* Clerk Street, which also has late-night jazz.

The *Playhouse,* Greenside Place, is mostly for rock and jazz concerts and occasional movies. The *Netherbow Arts Centre,* 43 High Street, and *Theatre Workshop,* 34 Hamilton Place, do more or less off-beat intimate drama and the well-known *Traverse* theater, West Bow, has built its reputation on avant-garde plays by young Scottish dramatists.

Movie Houses. *ABC,* Lothian Road, *Dominion,* Church Hill and *Odeon,* Clerk Street are three-in-one cinemas showing latest movies. *Filmhouse,* Lothian Road, shows classic and art movies—good value for film buffs. The *Caley,* also Lothian Road, has interesting late-night feature films. Edinburgh's original "little" cinema, the *Cameo,* still flourishes in Home Street.

Clubs and Discos. Lacking proper nightclubs, Edinburgh offers live music and jazz at *Platform One* (West End of Princes Street), *Kangaroo Club* (Easter Road), *The Venue* (Calton Road), *Gilded Balloon* (with restaurant), 209 Cowgate, and *The Amphitheatre,* Lothian Road. There are weekend discos in the bigger hotels. You may also hear jazz, blues and traditional music at *Basin Street,* Haymarket; the *Green Tree,* Cowgate; and at the *West End* (Palmerston Place) and *Learmonth* (Learmonth Terrace) hotels. *Outer Limits,* West Tollcross, is a disco complex with the best light show in town plus a roller disco, the only one in Edinburgh (*Coasters*); a reggae disco (*Bermuda Triangle*); and a club for "alternative" cognoscenti (*Hoochie-Coochie*).

Rumours in Lothian Road and *Buster Browns* in Market Street attract most out-of-town visitors. The former offers a cabaret of sorts, two or three evenings a week. *Annabel's,* Semple Street, is popular (especially with Oriental students), roomy and respectable and tourists have free membership. *Oscar's,* Shandwick Place, is likewise respectable, for over-23s.

Millionaires, Frederick Street, has sensible decor and a wide range of not-too-pricey cocktails—but don't mistake it for the tacky disco next door. *Cinderellas Rockerfellas,* St. Stephen Street, is big, plush and expensive for drinks. You may also eat there, at a price.

Fire Island, Princes Street, is essentially a gay club which discourages the merely curious. At *Sinatra's,* St. James Centre, which is dark and mysterious and bristles with tropical foliage, there is a thriving singles club twice a week (currently Mon. and Wed.).

Casinos. Gambling opportunities are strictly limited. Try *Casino Martell,* 7 Newington Road (tel. 667 7763). Blackjack, American roulette. Members only (membership is free but takes 48 hours to process).

THE EDINBURGH FESTIVAL. In 1947 Edinburgh inaugurated a three-week season that was to become world-famous as the Edinburgh International Festival of Music, Drama and Art. It now attracts the best in music, dance, theater, painting and sculpture from all over the globe. World celebrities throng Edinburgh's hotels, restaurants, theaters and concert halls during the three weeks mid-August to early September.

That is the Festival. Its once-tender offspring, the Festival Fringe, comprising a handful of enthusiastic students, has grown into a giant of more than 800 events that threatens to overshadow the Festival proper. Clowns, jugglers, musicians, mystery players, cabaret stars and horse-drawn caravanners . . . strolling players of many races and types fill Edinburgh's streets at Festival time, and even if some of the shows create no memorable experience for the audiences, at least admission is inexpensive and you don't have to stand in line (and the performers are obviously enjoying themselves). Some big names in TV got their initial break at the Edinburgh Fringe.

International film festivals, jazz festivals, and the Military Tattoo on the Castle esplanade run concurrently with the official Festival. There is also very often some important international or Commonwealth event contemporaneously at Edinburgh's great athletics stadium, Meadowbank, or the Commonwealth Swimming Pool.

Booking Details. The Festival takes place annually during a three-week period August 10 to September 1 or thereabouts. For a detailed program you can write two or three months in advance to the Festival Office, 21 Market Street, Edinburgh EH1 1DF (tel. 226 4001). Telephone bookings may also be made (225 5756).

Details of the International Film Festival are obtainable from Filmhouse, 88 Lothian Road, Edinburgh EH3 9BZ (tel. 228 6382). The Jazz Festival office is at Beauford House, 16 Dundas Street, Edinburgh EH3 6HZ; tickets from that office or from Adam Rooms, George Street, Edinburgh EH2 2PA. The Festival Fringe Society is in the Royal Mile Center, 170 High Street EH1 1QS (tel. 226 5257).

Remember that if you are phoning from outside Edinburgh (beyond about a 10-mile radius) you must prefix numbers with 031.

SHOPPING. Once an area of individualistic family shops, central Edinburgh is much like any other large British town, with well-known department stores—Marks & Spencer, Littlewood's, British Home Stores, John Menzies—prominently sited on Princes Street. Prestigious London fashion-and-fabric houses—Debenhams, Laura Ashley, Liberty's—are also represented on Princes Street and George Street. Central Edinburgh's main shopping mall, the Waverley Market, is just off Princes Street, close to Waverley train station. It also has a major tourist information center. A popular shopping rendezvous on Princes Street is the old-established quality house of Jenners, opposite Scott Monument. Fraser's at the west end, is similar but cheaper.

The Edinburgh Book Shop and Waterstone's, both George Street, and Bauermeister, George IV Bridge, are good for maps, magazines etc. Kinloch Anderson and Forsyth, both in the Royal Mile, and Romanes & Paterson and The Scotch House, both on Princes Street, specialize in tartan goods.

Antique shops are dotted about. Those of the Royal Mile and its neighborhood do good business in the tourist season, but in and around the Hanover Street–Thistle Street–Queen Street intersections there are more discriminating and expensive antiques businesses. Souvenirs proliferate on Princes Street and down the Royal Mile, and in the Canongate and Lawnmarket (at opposite ends of the High Street) you will see kiltmakers, bagpipe makers and other traditional Highland industries. The leading name in Highland dress and accessories is Geoffrey (Highland Crafts), 57–9 High Street (near John Knox House). Recommended for Scottish jewelry are Joseph Bonnar, 72 Thistle Street; and Modern Movement, 56 St. Stephen Street.

The greatest concentration of art and craft shops is also in the Royal Mile, though they are scattered across both Old Town and New. Galleries with exhibitions are attached to some of them. You may be directed to the somewhat expensive Scottish Craft Centre at 140 Canongate, but on the way you will pass several shops offering better buys in crafted pottery, glass, woven fabrics, etc. The Bruntsfield and Morningside districts, on the south side, are also good for attractive and superior shops handling craftwork, quality furniture, glassware, etc.

DINING OUT. As befits a capital city and tourist metropolis, the range of restaurants in Edinburgh is very wide. In recent years, joining the Italian, French, Chinese, Indian and other expected nationalities have been some unusual (for Scotland) culinary themes: for example, Armenian, Mexican, Japanese—so that considered overall, Edinburgh certainly offers dining out with an international flavor, as you would expect of a city hosting an International Festival. However, in common with many other cities, the restaurant trade is subject to fads and fashions and, in short, can be changeable. On-the-spot information and personal recommendations can help, as there are quite wide variations of standards of quality and value.

Deluxe

Prestonfield House, Priestfield Road (tel. 668 3346). Excellent dining surrounded by family portraits and old silver. Open on Sunday with a limited menu. (See under *Hotels.*)

Expensive

Consort, 136 George Street (tel. 225 6254). Adjunct of Roxburghe hotel. Pleasing layout, tends to be crowded and hot at lunchtime.

Cosmo's, 58 Castle Street (tel. 226 6743). One of the better Italian restaurants. Good for pheasant, guinea and other fowl.

Cousteau's, 47 Hill Street Lane (tel. 226 3355). Varied menu, large à la carte selection, particularly fish. Evenings only, closed Sun.

L'Alliance, 7 Merchant Street (tel. 225 2002). Brasserie. Businessmen's lunches. Refined French wines.

L'Auberge, 56 St. Mary Street (tel. 556 5888). French restaurant. Tourist menu (lunch time) and gastronomic menu.

Martin's, 70 Rose Street Lane North (tel. 225 3106). Quiet backwater off Princes Street. Modest layout but a delicate and varied cuisine. Oysters, snails, game, salmon, traditional dishes. Outstanding quality.

The Vintner's Room, The Vaults, 87 Giles Street (tel. 554 6767). Outstanding French cuisine in historic setting.

Vito's, 55 Frederick Street (tel. 225 5052). Neat basketwork decor and highly professional Italian cooking; intimate atmosphere.

Moderate

Alp-Horn, 167 Rose Street (tel. 225 4787). Immaculate Swiss restaurant, interesting veal and venison recipes. Swiss muzak.

Bar Italia, 100 Lothian Road (tel. 229 0451). Good pasta and gateaux. Open to a late hour, when young Italian waiters may give impromptu floor show.

Bar Napoli, 75 Hanover Street (tel. 225 2600). Pasta, pizzas, and excellent steaks predominate on a menu which is a compendium of the cuisines of various nations, handled with professional Italian flair. Extraordinarily cheap for a light lunch; more expensive evening *à la carte,* when 100 dishes are offered. Central, but a slightly garish entrance; inside, bright and efficient.

Le Bouzy, 22 Brougham Place (tel. 229 0869). Small intimate French restaurant, advance booking essential.

Get Stuffed, 192 Rose Street (tel. 225 2208). Celebrated for heavy eating. "The best and biggest steaks in town."

Kalpna, St. Patrick's Square (tel. 667 9890). Immaculate, friendly

Indian restaurant with first-class vegetable curries and interesting desserts.

Lancers, 5 Hamilton Place (tel. 332 3444). Classic Bengali and North Indian dishes, top-rated in *U.K. Good Curry Guide.* Advisable to book.

Le Marché Noir, Eyre Place (tel. 558 1608). A pleasant little place. Mainly French cuisine with seafood emphasis. Impressive wine list.

Palumbo, 40 Bruntsfield Place (tel. 229 5025). Rather small and sometimes crowded. Traditional Scottish and Spanish cuisine.

Sik Tek Fok, 97 Hanover Street (tel. 225 7938). Cantonese decor. Try the roast duck.

Skipper's, la Dock Place, Leith (tel. 554 1018). Enterprising small bistro, imaginative seafood cuisine. Rather out of the way, but large clientele obviously finds journey worthwhile.

Tinelli's, 139 Easter Road (tel. 652 1932). Best value in Italian restaurants, though located in a shabby district.

Inexpensive

Chan Richard Tong Sang, 12 Cadzow Place (tel. 661 3369). Mandarin Chinese restaurant.

Cornerstone Cafe, St. John's Church, west end of Princes Street (tel. 229 4541). Developed out of a Festival-season snack bar. It's unlicensed, clean, friendly, and deals mainly in wholefoods. Very reasonable prices. Open daytime only.

Dragon Pearl, 20 Union Place (tel. 556 4547). Authentic and satisfying Chinese cuisine behind unattractive facade.

Edinburgh Wine Bar, 110 Hanover Street (tel. 220 1208). A generous and satisfying array of salad dishes, predominantly vegetarian, brightens this aggressively stark and dingy room. Variety of unmemorable wines. Busy with business people at lunchtime.

Fat Sam's, 56 Fountainbridge (tel. 228 3111). Not the place for a quiet *tête-à-tête,* but it's good for generous and inexpensive Italo-American cuisine. Stays open till all hours. Crowded most evenings, best to reserve a table.

Helios Fountain, 7 Grassmarket (tel. 229 7884). Bright vegetarian/wholefood restaurant and "alternative" shop. Open 10–6; later in Aug.

Lady Nairne, Willowbrae Road (tel. 661 3396). On eastern approaches, 2 miles from center. Pleasant and bright for drinks and meals, easy parking.

New York Steam Packet, 31 North Rose Street Lane (tel. 225 4663). Cheerful, lively at night; convivial atmosphere, more than a hamburger joint.

Rake's, South St. David Street (tel. 556 6375). Regency-style wine bar with cheap and generous food. Hot dishes really hot. A mixed clientele.

Verandah, 17 Dalry Road (tel. 337 5828). Another Indian/Bengali restaurant—some say the best. Open seven days a week.

Viva Mexico, 10 Anchor Close (tel. 226 5145). Heart of Old Town. Authentic Mexican dishes, beers, atmosphere.

Waterfront, 1–C Dock Place (tel. 554 7427). Like *Skipper's,* a modish dockside bistro and wine bar. Blackboard menu advertises seafood. Handy for enterprising *Shore* art gallery.

PUBS. Edinburgh pubs are a study in themselves. In the eastern and northern districts of the city you will find some grim, inhospitable-looking places which proclaim that drinking, for the Scot, is no laughing matter. In the central and western districts many pubs have deliberately improved their old "spit-and-sawdust" images and in their lounge bars (as opposed to the public bars) you may find atmospheric revivals of the warm, oak-paneled, leather-chaired "howffs" of a more leisurely age. Pubs frequented by students are often highly-rated for their evening musical entertainments. At lunchtime a snack or bar lunch service is usual. On Saturday nights most city pubs are noisy and crowded and respectable citizens tend to avoid them. Opening and closing times vary, but 11 A.M. to 11 P.M. is normal. In the port of Leith, by old tradition, pubs open at 7.30 A.M. and, moving uptown, you could actually drink round the clock; but that requires local knowledge. Out of 400-odd city pubs we give a brief sampling:

Abbotsford, 3 Rose Street. Rendezvous of media people. A full restaurant service.

Allan Ramsay Tavern, 119 High Street. Has historic relics and associations with the 18th-century drinking clubs.

Bannerman's, 53–7 Niddry Street. Old-fashioned decor, log fires.

Deacon Brodie's, 435 Lawnmarket. Quaint and labyrinthine; attracts more tourists than locals.

Finsbury Park, 3 South St. Andrew Street. Cocktail bar and disco, frequented by young and footloose.

Trader Vic's, Victoria Street. Highly spoken of by beer-drinking students and aged whisky-bibbers.

Old Chain Pier, Trinity Crescent. Haunt of Newhaven longshoremen, formerly served ferry travelers on the Fife crossing.

Raffles, St. Stephen's Street. Clientele of young to middle-aged drinkers, attracted by wide range of beers including Budweiser, Schlitz and Cours.

Rose Street Brewery, 55 Rose Street. As a venerable gauntlet of pubs, the street has declined; but this place, which brews its own ale, maintains popularity with serious drinkers.

Royal Oak, Infirmary Street. Used by students. Sometimes offers folk/guitar and late sessions.

Scott's, 202 Rose Street. Another old tavern in a street full of them, this bar has long been under the direction of a stern and dictatorial proprietress and is noted for its refinement and respectability.

Smithies Alehouse, 47 Eyre Place. Between Edinburgh and Granton. Another pub for the connoisseur, with nostalgic Victoriana.

Starbank, 64 Laverockbank Road. In Newhaven, near Old Chain Pier. Typical waterfront tavern, perhaps the best for light meals and snacks.

Tilted Wig, 3 Cumberland Street. *Al fresco* drinking on patio behind narrow New Town thoroughfare.

Volunteer Arms, 237 Morningside Road. Gloomy atmosphere, sawdust on floor, but authentic Scottish character. Serves coffee all day (something unusual for an Edinburgh pub). Live music several nights a week. Locals call it **The Canny Man's.**

White Cockade, 55 Rose Street. Another long-established "howff" in Edinburgh's publand, once the haunt of poets and litterateurs.

White Horse, 266 Canongate. Small, usually overcrowded, but steeped in history. Dr. Johnson stayed here on first arrival in Edinburgh.

SCOTLAND'S HOME COUNTIES

Lothian

Taking the analogy of England's Home Counties, the counties immediately around London, the Lothian Region may be considered the Home Counties of Scotland. It is spread about the skirts of the capital city, Edinburgh, and consists of West Lothian (historically called Linlithgowshire from its principal town); East Lothian (Haddingtonshire); and Midlothian, which includes Edinburgh itself, a name familiar from Scott's novel *The Heart of Midlothian.*

The Region provides rich pickings for the historian. For 1,000 years Edinburgh has been Scotland's metropolis, even at periods when its castle was in English hands. How the stormy history of the Scots has been concentrated round this old gray citadel above the Firth of Forth may be seen from the battlefields and scarred fortresses strewn over the neighborhood.

In more peaceable times Lothian Region became a good address for aristocrats and rich merchants with interests in the political and commercial life of the capital. Hence the fine mansions in the countryside, the deer parks, the landscaping of gardens after the French fashion; and Lothian's fame as a seedplot of Lowland gentility.

Then, at the end of the 18th century, came the Industrial Revolution, the discovery of coalfields and the transformation of the upper Forth into a manufacturing base. Coalmines smudged many square miles of what was once idyllic scenery. Gentle streams in fairy glens—so the old writings describe them—steamed and stank with pollution. Rural mansions became colliery offices or the headquarters of papermaking companies.

However, it would be wrong to give the impression that Lothian Region is all satanic mills and smoke. Most of East Lothian is purely rural, the sort of place retired admirals live. Similarly, West Lothian and Midlothian have their black spots but a good deal of attractive country as well. And everywhere there is history, often more vivid when you stumble on it in council housing estates. As to smoke, it has been abolished. Today, tighter regulations and the decline of heavy industries have brought cleaner skies back to the workshops and playgrounds of Scotland's Home Counties. Anglers report that salmon and seatrout are once more making their way up Lothian streams which, within living memory, ran foul with industrial waste. And if you hear from your Lothian acquaintances the age-old valedictory "Lang may your lum (chimney) reek," that is a purely symbolic way of wishing you health.

The word Lothian may have something to do with lowland. The Region has no great hills to boast of. Upland areas of East Lothian reach 1,730 feet at the Lammer Law on the edge of Borders Region. Midlothian's Pentland Hills rise to 1,840 feet, which puts a breath of mountain air at the disposal of Edinburgh's suburbs. West Lothian has two clumps of hills of about 1,000 feet. But most of the Region is a coastal plain along the Forth as that river widens in its firth or sea-channel. The Forth is three miles wide at the western end of the Region, 25 miles wide at the eastern end.

It is also suggested that Lothian may mean "land of Lud"—the shadowy Dark-Age king whose name crops up here and there all over Britain; at Ludgate Hill in London, for instance. A stone coffin unearthed in 1861 at the foot of Traprain Law near Haddington was thought to contain Lud's bones.

Lothian Horizons

The obvious base for touring the Lothian countryside is Edinburgh. If you stand on an Edinburgh eminence—the castle ramparts, Arthur's Seat, Corstorphine hill—you can plan a few Lothian excursions without the aid of a map. If you leave Edinburgh by air from Turnhouse airport, eight miles from the city center on the Glasgow road, you will have a bird's-eye view of the landmarks along the Firth of Forth, including the famous rail and road bridges across the Narrows at Queensferry. If you go out by rail it will be either towards Glasgow via the Princes Street Gardens and West Lothian or towards Berwick-on-Tweed, past Holyroodhouse and the East Lothian barley fields.

The main roads exit to the west (A8, A9) for the motorways to Glasgow, Stirling and Perth; to the south (A701, A7 or A68) for the Borders Region and England; and to the east (A1) along the coast by the Great North Road to Berwick-on-Tweed. This last road was landscaped by Robert Stevenson, grandfather of R.L.S., and as you gaze back from it you see the hills closing over the city like curtains on a stage set with an improbably romantic backcloth.

West Lothian (A8, A9) starts with agriculture but grows industrialized as you progress westwards. Long ago it was the most thickly populated part of Scotland after Edinburgh herself. Even before the discovery of coal there was a considerable seaborne trade between the small Forth harbors and the Baltic countries. That trade and the coal industry have declined and you might get the impression that West Lothian consists mainly of disused mines and unsightly bings (cinder mounds). But the area has some pleasant hills and woodlands too.

Queen's Ferry and Roman Wall

Five miles from Edinburgh on the A90 to South Queensferry it is worth while turning right to visit the village of Cramond at the mouth of a glen where the Romans built a port and fished for oysters. If you felt energetic you could walk back to Granton along the seafront road (4 miles) or cross the River Almond and follow the path by the shore, through Dalmeny woods, to South Queensferry (5 miles).

At Cramond Brig (now on the M90) James V went a-wooing in disguise and was set upon by murderers. A farmworker, Jock Howieson, went to his aid, dressed his wounds and received as a reward the neighboring lands of Braehead, the condition being that whenever the monarch passed that way Jock and his descendants should offer a basin, a towel and clean water. For 450 years thereafter the Howiesons held Braehead. Queen Elizabeth II has paused there to receive the tribute and wash her hands.

The woods and policies of Dalmeny House border the M90 motorway. Trees were planted by princes and statesmen and are marked with plaques, most of them dated between 1890 and 1910 when the owner, the Earl of Rosebery, was prominent in British politics. The house is not remarkable but the park is famous for its drifts of snowdrops in early spring. Where Dalmeny park ends, South Queensferry begins, but the Rosebery's feudal village is Dalmeny (B9035), two miles inland. It is what used to be known as a model village, while its church has been described as the finest piece of Norman architecture in Scotland.

For South Queensferry, leave the M90 and continue on the A90. The burgh, wedged between hill and shore, has numerous 17th-century buildings whose grim high walls, tiny windows and turnpike stairs remind you of some corners of old Edinburgh. It also has some modern architectural monstrosities. The burgh takes its name from Margaret, Malcolm Canmore's Queen, who crossed at this point on her pilgrimages to Dunfermline Abbey. But the place has been a ferry port from the dawn of transport history.

You no longer wait hours or days for a fair wind across the Narrows of the Forth, as old-time travelers did. You have a choice of two bridges, each, in its time, the wonder of the civil engineering world.

The Forth Rail bridge, nine miles from Edinburgh's Waverley station, was designed by Benjamin Baker (who also built a tunnel under the Hudson River in New York) and opened in 1890. It is one-and-a-half miles long. Permission to walk across is sometimes granted to parties of railroad buffs by British Rail's traffic superintendent in Edinburgh. You really do need to walk to appreciate its massive size. A full-sized train could run inside its main tubular struts. It takes three years and 50 tons of paint to paint the bridge—"painting the Forth Bridge" is a household expression all over Britain, meaning no sooner have you finished a job than it is time to start again.

The Forth Road bridge, two miles upstream, was completed in 1964 to carry the M90 Edinburgh–Perth motorway. A walkway is provided for those who want to cross on foot. It was Scotland's first long-span suspension bridge, embodying many revolutionary features; but as a spectacle it is overshadowed by the bold cantilevers of the old Rail bridge.

West of South Queensferry (A904), the road skirts Hopetoun House, a large Adam mansion, seat of the Marquesses of Linlithgow. A detour (B903) drops down to the shore again at the odd-looking castle of Blackness, like a battleship thrusting its ram bow into the Forth. Further west is the formerly industrial town of Bo'ness, still smoke-blackened in a few parts by past industries such as mining, pottery and timber-milling (for pit-props). However, instead of decaying as these activities died out, Bo'ness smartened itself up, with an active heritage society, and is an interesting example of such renewal schemes. The Scottish Preservation Society, starting from scratch with tracks and buildings cannibalized from other parts of the Scottish railway network, have recreated the flavor of a typical Scottish branch-line (with steam trains). In pleasant parkland moments from the town, Kinneil Museum, next to the shell of 16th/17th-century Kinneil House, has interesting local pottery and tells the story of this once busy place.

Palace of the Stuarts

Four miles to the south, the chief town of West Lothian, Linlithgow, is dominated by the gaunt but gracious Linlithgow Palace, close to the main street, overlooking Linlithgow Loch. Though burned out in 1746—accidentally—by troops quartered there after the Jacobite rebellions, the Palace retains many interesting rooms and halls round its great quadrangle, in which stands a 16th-century fountain. The adjacent St. Michael's Parish Church, easily recognized by its much-debated modern metal spire, is the largest pre-Reformation church surviving in Scotland. South of the town, Beecraigs Country Park offers close-up views of farmed red deer and, among its many countryside attractions, has outstanding hilltop views of the Forth Valley and north to the Highland edge.

Other places of interest within easy reach of Linlithgow include the Union Canal—it passes through the town and there is a canal museum and canal-boat cruising. The "walkable" towpath leads over a well-preserved aqueduct; also within easy reach is Cairnapple Hill, an impressive prehistoric site with successive waves of cairn and monument builders from Neolithic to Bronze Age times.

Returning from Linlithgow to Edinburgh by the more direct A9 route (17 miles), you may detour again in the direction of the A904 to visit The Binns, an early 17th-century mansion uncharacteristically defenseless in design. Yet its creator, Sir Tam Dalyell ("Dee-ell"), was a general who recruited a famous regiment of cavalry, the Scots Greys, on that spot in 1681. In 1944, The Binns was taken into the care of the National Trust for Scotland, the first of many properties that the NTS was to acquire.

Although industrial in places, West Lothian certainly has its share of easy-access countryside. In addition to Beecraigs, there are also Polkemmet, and Almondell and Calderwood Country Parks, acting as a "green lung" to the extensive new housing developments around Livingston.

Midlothian

Quite a lot of Edinburgh's own county consists of the Pentland Hills where no roads go. Trains and automobiles heading for the southwest and

Carlisle travel under the Pentland ridges (A70, A701, A702). The A70, which ends up on the west coast at Ayr, starts with an up-hill-and-down-dale section affectionately known as the "Lang Whang" or long bootlace. From first impressions on Midlothian's other routes, you may think it offers only peripheral industrial parks and former mining towns. Even these communities have their own heritage, as you can discover at the Scottish Mining Museum at the Lady Victoria Colliery, Newtongrange. Elsewhere, some high-grade historic sites and countryside walks are on offer. 15th-century Rosslyn Chapel, moments from the village of Roslin, is Scotland's finest example of late medieval stone carving, its interior encrusted with intricately worked motifs. Nearby, in the mature woodlands of Roslin Glen, there is a variety of walks and nature interest. Romantically-ruined Crichton Castle is another site of great architectural interest. It is linked by a signposted walk, through attractive, rolling farmland, to nearby Borthwick Castle (now a hotel), where Mary, Queen of Scots "honeymooned" with Bothwell.

Locals will tell of such unpublicized points of interest as Sir Walter Scott's first house after his marriage, close to Lasswade, and also Thomas de Quincy's cottage (both private). Half-hidden in the woods and pasture, some handsome railway viaducts survive—the work of the infamous Sir Thomas Bouch, whose Tay Bridge collapsed in 1879. These works are part of a network of railway walkways on abandoned trackbeds.

East Lothian

"Ding doon Tantallon! Mak' a brig (bridge) to the Bass!"; a country proverb, scornfully applied to one who attempts a feat beyond his capabilities. Tantallon is one of the most impressive castle ruins in Scotland. It was built in the 14th century by the Douglases, a family almost as powerful as the King himself in southern Scotland. "Three sides of rock-like wall and one of wall-like rock," was how Hugh Miller the geologist described it. The wall-like rock is a sea-cliff of the East Lothian coastline (A198).

The Bass of the proverb is the Bass Rock, one and a half miles off Tantallon, a 300-foot clump of rock whitened with the multitudes of gannet (solan geese) which crowd the ledges. It is a favorite excursion of North Berwick holidaymakers.

Off-shore rocks and crumbling seafront fortresses line the bays and headlands of East Lothian. Since the 19th century they have also supported an almost unbroken chain of seaside resorts and golf courses. Golf and tourism owe their development to changes in the currents of the Forth (always a whimsical waterway) which brought sand sweeping in, silting up medieval harbors and creating beaches and dunes.

The chief resorts are North Berwick (A1 and A198 from Edinburgh) and Dunbar (A1). Both are small towns, the former created for golfers and commuters, the latter a fine old burgh with castle ruins and a harbor carved out of the red sandstone rock. From both places fishing boats go out after lobster, scampi and crab. In the old days Dunbar tackled bigger game. Relics of her whaling fleet are still scattered about the neighborhood in the shape of whalebone arches to garden paths and suchlike. Dunbar, incidentally, claims to have the best sunshine record in Scotland. But visitors from mild climates find this coast often cold and windy even in summer and on the hottest days a sea-fret or mist, locally called the "haar," can blot out the sun and lower the temperature by 20 degrees.

To Robert Burns in 1787 East Lothian was "the most glorious corn country I ever saw." Between coastal strip and hills is almost English-looking countryside. The fields are rich in barley and potatoes; the barley goes chiefly to make whisky and ale, the "red soil" potatoes are prized by growers all over Britain. This is the most prosperous farming country in Scotland, and the 18th-century landlords known as the Improvers were partly responsible for that. They brought the agricultural revolution to Scotland, draining and fertilizing the land, inventing or importing machinery and building groups of stone cottages for farmworkers. The landscape is therefore a patchwork of large prosperous farms and little villages which keep the communities together. Visit if you can Athelstaneford (B1347, off A1), Tyninghame ("Tinningum") (A198), Dirleton (A198) and Longniddry (A198) and the line of villages which are spaced out under the Lammermuir Hills on or near the B6355 and B6370 roads: Ormiston, Gifford, Garvald and Stenton.

A plaque opposite Gifford church commemorates a former clergyman, John Witherspoon (born 1723) who signed the American Declaration of Independence. His monument in Gifford churchyard has been renovated by the St. Andrew's Society of Philadelphia.

The strand between Tyninghame and Dunbar is part of the John Muir Country Park (access from A1). Dunbar-born John Muir (1838–1914) emigrated to the United States and formed the Sierra Club, which set up the Yosemite and Sequoia National Parks.

In Athelstaneford's churchyard the saltire, a flag with an X-shaped cross on a blue ground, always flies. The accompanying plaque explains how King Athelstan (895-940) was inspired to victory in battle by the appearance of a white cross in the blue sky—but there are several things wrong with the legend if, as is claimed, this was the origin of the Scottish national flag. Not the least is that Athelstan was a Saxon, fighting *against* the Scots. And the "X" or "decussate" cross was already associated with St. Andrew, Scotland's patron saint, who was supposed to have been martyred on it.

Devotees of war games may examine three genuine battlefields as they travel the A1 through East Lothian. Nearest to Edinburgh is Pinkie (1547) at Musselburgh, where English troops on the high ground and English warships in the Forth crushed a Scottish force and prompted the nation's leaders to send the five-year-old Mary Queen of Scots to France for safety. The next battlefield is Prestonpans (1745) near Tranent (roadside monument on A198), where Bonnie Prince Charlie's rebels overcame the government troops. The third is Dunbar (1650), where Cromwell defeated the Covenanters (roadside monument on A1 at Broxburn).

Apart from North Berwick and Dunbar, the most notable town of East Lothian is Haddington (A1), with outstanding Georgian architecture and a town house originally by William Adam. A street-plan on the town house wall outlines a town trail along the banks of the River Tyne (not Newcastle's Tyne) and round a hoary flat-towered church which, as a beacon of piety in more violent times, earned the name of "Lamp of Lothian." Among several celebrated sons and daughters Haddington claims Jane Welsh Carlyle, wife of Thomas Carlyle; Samuel Smiles (1812-1904), social reformer and author of the Victorian best-seller *Self-Help;* and John Knox.

Where East Lothian's cultivated fields rise to the bare back of the Lammermuir Hills the turf and heather, selectively cropped by agile Blackface sheep (watch out for them on the unfenced roads), reflect the variegated colors of the landscape. Trout streams gush through green valleys. The moors echo to the cries of lapwing, curlew, pheasant and grouse. On the B6355 and other unclassified roads some very wild country begins within half an hour's drive of the Edinburgh conurbation.

PRACTICAL INFORMATION FOR LOTHIAN

HOW TO GET THERE. By air. The main airport in Lothian is Edinburgh's Turnhouse. For details of the very frequent air services to Turnhouse, especially from London, see *Facts at Your Fingertips* page 10.

By train. Some London–Edinburgh expresses stop at Dunbar. From Edinburgh (Waverley) local trains run frequently to Prestonpans, Longniddry, Drem, North Berwick and Dunbar in East Lothian; and on Scotland's newest track to a variety of West Lothian destinations.

HOTELS AND RESTAURANTS. The environs of Edinburgh are thickly strewn with accommodations of all types, and on some routes in season it seems that every other cottage is offering bed and breakfast. Throughout the Region you will also find a considerable variety of restaurants, cafes and snack bars. Below we list some of the better places to stay and eat.

Bathgate (A899). *Golden Circle* (E), tel. 0506–53771. 75 rooms with bath. Modern executive-type hotel on edge of industrial region.

Bo'ness (A706). *Hollywood House* (I), 25 Grahamsdyke Road, (tel. 0506–823260). 3 rooms. Has received consistently favorable reports.

Bonnyrigg (off A7). *Dalhousie Castle* (L), tel. 0875–20153. 24 rooms with bath. Castle of 15th-century origin with later additions. Outstanding comfort and cuisine. Close by, at *Dalhousie Court* (M), mock-medieval banquets nightly in summer, with knockabout turns and impressive choir singing; mediocre food.

Cramond (off A90). **Restaurant.** *Cramond Inn* (E), tel. 031–336 2035. Whitewashed fishing inn on steep waterfront approach. Cramped at times, but cheerful service and sophisticated cuisine.

Dirleton (A198). *Open Arms* (E), tel. 062 085–241. 7 rooms with bath. Light, airy atmosphere, enterprising cooking with traditional Scots dishes.

Gifford (B6369). *Tweedale Arms* (E), tel. 062 081–240. 15 rooms with bath. Tastefully modernized 17th-century inn. *Goblin Ha'* (I), tel. 062 081–244. 8 rooms. Village inn, simple cuisine.

Gullane (A198). *Greywalls* (E) tel. 0620–842144. 24 rooms with bath. Mansion of character, cloistral atmosphere, *nouvelle cuisine.* Closed winter. *Mallard* (M), tel. 0620–843288. 20 rooms with bath. Efficiently run. Largely golfing and sporting clientele.

Restaurant. *La Potiniere* (I), tel. 0620–843214. Extremely good, French-style table d'hôte and wine. Very small dining room. Early booking essential.

Haddington (A1). **Restaurant.** *Waterside* (I), Nungate, (tel. 062 082–5674). Swans drift past this old-style riverbank hostelry, where you enjoy substantial steaks, seafood crêpes and alcoholic desserts. Good wines sensibly priced.

Humbie (A6137). *Johnstounburn House* (L), tel. 087 533–696. 20 rooms with bath. Country house dating from 1625, appropriately furnished, set in mature lawns and gardens. Delightful atmosphere, courteous staff, over-elaborate food does not measure up to the gourmet's standards.

Linlithgow (A9). **Restaurant.** *Champany Inn* (M), tel. 0506–83 4532. Old-style low-built whitewashed farmhouse about 3 miles east of town. Steaks a specialty. Some interesting fruity desserts. Range of expensive wines. Slightly condescending proprietors. Praised (perhaps over-praised) by food writers.

Newbridge (off M8). **Restaurant.** *Norton Hall* (M), tel. 031–333 1275. Detached from main road by mile-long leafy drive. Lovely environment.

North Berwick (A198). *Marine* (L), tel. 0620–2406. 86 rooms with bath. Big rooms, club armchairs, high standards of former ages maintained. Fishing.

Ratho (B7030). **Restaurant.** *Bridge Inn* (I), tel. 031–333 1320. Cozy little eating place, some would say claustrophobic, beside hump-backed canal bridge. Thronged with wedding guests most Saturdays—the couple get married on a barge alongside, and go for a cruise. Excellent cuisine, some plain and some unusually sophisticated dishes. Try Canal Mud, the chocolate dessert specialty. A somewhat mixed clientele.

South Queensferry (A90). *Hawes Inn* (M), tel. 031–331 1990. 6 rooms. Historic ferry inn featured in R.L. Stevenson's *Kidnapped.* Low beams.

Uphall (A899). *Houston House* (L), tel. 0506–85 3831. 30 rooms with bath. Executive-class establishment in own extensive grounds.

HOW TO GET ABOUT. By bus. There are buses between all towns on all main routes, but country districts are not so well served though there is scarcely a village without some sort of bus or minibus service, though for the most part you are likely to have to wait a few hours for these services.

By car. The major car-rental firms have desks at Turnhouse airport. Elsewhere in the Region (outside Edinburgh) you may rent a self-drive automobile from Style Chauffeur Drive, Uphall, Broxburn (tel. 0506–85 3553) or Fairway Tours, Roseberry Place, Gullane (tel. 0620–84 2349);

or from numerous garages in the country towns whose advertisements you will see in local newspapers. Unlimited-mileage rates per day range widely according to size of vehicle, with off-season reductions from October to April.

There are rarely parking problems in the towns and villages of the Region, except on main streets on Saturday mornings and in coastal resorts in July and August.

TOURIST INFORMATION. The Tourist Information Centre above Waverley Market is the main city information source. In addition, there are at least nine other "TIC's" open in season, of which Dunbar (Town House), North Berwick (Quality Street), Falkirk (High Street) and Linlithgow (Burgh Halls) stay open all year. They operate the Book-A-Bed-Ahead scheme as well as offering a local accommodation booking service.

FISHING. The Lothians are not one of Scotland's main game fishing areas, but the river Tyne, which flows through Haddington, followed by the Esk and the Almond, offer sport. Tackle dealers in Edinburgh can advise and all Tourist Information Centres also carry information. There is a good range of reservoirs offering bank or boat fishing. These include Gladhouse and Rosebery (near Temple), Glencorse (by Penicuik), Clubbiedean and Bonaly (near Colinton, Edinburgh), Crosswood (West Calder), Harlaw and Threipmuir (Balerno), Whiteadder, Hopes and Donnolly (near Gifford) and, finally, Linlithgow Loch. Information from Lothian Water Department, 55 Buckstone Terrace, Edinburgh. Prices from about £2 (bank).

GOLF. There are 23 golf courses in Edinburgh and about 40 in the rest of the Region, many of them sited among the dunes and headlands of the Firth of Forth shore. Of championship courses that periodically host the British Open and other important tournaments, Muirfield (A198 near Gullane) is the most exclusive. You will pay £12 a day and will not be allowed there without an introduction from a member or a letter from your own golf club secretary. All other courses welcome casual visitors, the only formality being payment of a fee of about £3 a round, £5 a day. Bar and restaurant facilities are usually available; at more exclusive places you are expected to dress semi-formally (men in jacket and tie) in the clubhouse.

HISTORIC HOUSES AND GARDENS. This region was home to many courtly and aristocratic families and has the castles and mansions to prove it. A feature of country districts is the tower house with cone-capped turrets, crow-stepped gables and perhaps a "doocot" or pigeon-house. The gardens are at their best in spring.

The Binns, Linlithgow (off A904). Early 17th-century country house, a tasteful blend of styles. Interesting plasterwork. Historical relics. Open May–Sept., daily except Fri., 2–5. Park 10–7 daily.

Crichton Castle, near Pathhead (A68). The impressive ruins date mainly from the 15th–17th centuries, though the keep is earlier. The elaborate arcaded range with diamond-faceted stonework is of particular note. Open Apr.–Sept., Mon.–Sat., 9.30–7, Sun. 2–7; Oct.–Mar., Sat. 9.30–4; Sun. 2–4.

Dalmeny House, South Queensferry (off A90). Large house set in fine park and containing Rothschild collection of 18th-century French furniture, tapestries, clocks etc. History of Rosebery family. Open May–Sept., Sun.–Thur., 2–5.30.

Hopetoun House, South Queensferry (on A904). Imposing Adam mansion buried in huge park. State rooms, family relics, stables, museum. Open May–Sept., daily, 11–5.

Lennoxlove, Haddington (B6369). Turreted country house, part of it dating from 15th century, in large park. Valuable paintings. Relics of Mary, Queen of Scots, and of Lennox family—including "La Belle Stuart," the model for Britannia on British coinage; and of Dukes of Hamilton, who own the property. Open April–Sept., Wed., Sat., Sun., 2–5; or by
appointment.

Linlithgow Palace, Linlithgow town center. Mixture of Gothic and Renaissance with 13th-century traces. Birthplace of Mary Queen of Scots. Open Apr.–Sept., weekdays 9.30–7, Sun. 2–7; Oct.–Mar., weekdays 9.30–4, Sun. 2–4.

Preston Mill, East Linton (B1407). Highly photogenic pantiled water-mill, restored to working order. Craftwork. Agricultural museum. Historic dovecote nearby. Open Apr.–Sept., weekdays 10–1 and 2–5, Sun. 2–5; Oct., weekdays 10–1 and 2–4.30, Sun. 2–4.30; Nov., Sat. 10–12.30 and 2–4.30, Sun. 2–4.30.

Tantallon Castle, North Berwick (A198). Splendid sandstone stronghold (14th century) on cliff edge. Open Apr.–Sept., weekdays 9.30–7, Sun. 2–7; Oct.–Mar., weekdays 9.30–4, Sun. 2–4.

MUSEUMS. Butterfly Farm, Dalkeith (off A7, five miles south of Edinburgh). Masses of rare butterflies in a charming tropical setting. Open Apr.–Oct. weekdays 10–6, Sun. 10–5.30.

Canal Museum, Linlithgow. History and uses of Edinburgh–Glasgow canal. Opportunity for canal trip in replica steamboat. Open Apr.–Sept., Sat. and Sun. only, 2–5.

Lifeboat House, Dunbar (off A1). A working establishment with models of early lifeboats. Open May–Sept., 2–5, weekdays only.

Museum of Flight, East Fortune, North Berwick (B1347). Pioneer aircraft and space rockets on an airfield from which transatlantic airships were launched. Open 10–4, Jul. and Aug.

Myreton Motor Museum, Aberlady (off A198). Old vehicles and relics of road transport history. Open May–Oct., daily, 10–6; Nov.–Apr., daily 10–5. Check if possible (tel. 087 57–288): curator tends to vary routine.

Scottish Mining Museum, Lady Victoria Colliery, Newtongrange (A7). Preserved former coal mine featuring giant steam winding engine and other artifacts, plus tableaux and displays recalling mining life. Further material at Prestongrange, near Musselburgh. Open all year (closed Mon.), Tues.–Fri., 10–4.30, Sat.–Sun. 12–5.

SONG OF THE TWEED

Borders

The Borders Region is the heartland of minstrelsy, ballad and folklore, much of it arisen from murky deeds of the past. It is the homeland of Sir Walter Scott, of the tweed suit and cashmere sweater, of medieval abbeys and hints of Elfland, of the lordly Tweed and its salmon and of the descendants of the raiders and reivers (cattle thieves) who harried England.

A general term for the area is Tweeddale. The Region embraces the whole 100-mile course of the Tweed, third river of Scotland, and most of its tributaries. By mill chimneys and peel fortresses and woodland luxuriant with game birds and stately homes, in a series of fast-rushing torrents and dark serpentine pools, the rivers flow through the history of two nations.

At different times the Region has been in English hands, just as slices of northern England, when things were going well for the Scots, have been in Scottish hands. Berwick-on-Tweed ("Berrick") was six times a Scottish town and seven times an English one in the period 1200 to 1600. Though the Border is no physical barrier—no customs or checkpoints for example—the Scottish Borders Tourist Board takes great pains to point out that Scotland begins straightaway, with different shopping hours, dialect, stock in local bakeries—even the Scots' £1 note—and all the other subtle ways in which visitors are made to feel that they have arrived in a different country.

All the main routes from London to Edinburgh traverse the Region. There are no commercial airports but from any point in the Borders you can be at the check-in desks of Edinburgh or Newcastle-upon-Tyne airports in about an hour. The eastern side of the Region is a rocky sea-coast in which tiny fishing villages are embedded. The hinterland of undulating pastures, woods and valleys is enclosed within three lonely groups of hills: Cheviot (highest point 2,676 feet) to the south; Tweedsmuir (2,700 feet) to the west; and Lammermuir (1,700 feet) to the north.

The towns are overgrown villages. The principal centers of Hawick, Galashiels, Melrose, Jedburgh, Selkirk and Peebles do not muster 50,000 inhabitants among them. About the same number are spread through innumerable hamlets, so the valley slopes have quite a lived-in look. There is a plan to open out some of the compact little towns which cluster along the middle Tweed, to promote industry and increase the population by 25,000. If it comes about, sheep will still outnumber human beings by 30 to one.

Sheep and clear streams, ideal for washing wool, gave the Borders its tweed and knitwear industries. The Scotch wool, however, is now considered too coarse for quality products and most of the raw material is imported.

Borderers preserve their isolation from their neighbors and are fiercely proud of their traditions. Civic rivalries are sublimated in local flower-shows, festivals and sporting encounters, especially rugby football. A Hawick–Selkirk clash is a Homeric struggle, but the communities sink their differences to make common cause against the rest of Scotland and England. They think it is a disgrace if a great rugby center like Melrose (2,000 inhabitants) or Jedburgh (4,000) fails to get players into the international team.

Tweedsmuir, Lyne and Manor

"From Berwick to the Bield" used to be proverbial in the Borders—from the mouth to the source of the Tweed; in other words the length and breadth of the land. We start at the Bield, though you won't find it on the map. It was one of four "howffs"—inns and resting-places for carters and carriers and their pack-donkeys—which once decorated the desolate landscape of Tweedsmuir. Only one, the Crook Inn, midway between Moffat and Peebles, survives.

Robert Burns and a later poet, Thomas Campbell, were habitués of the howffs. Campbell told of his first visit to the Bield. Soon after he had gone to bed the young girl of the house knocked on the door and, entering, stood before him in her nightie, a candle in her hand. "Please, sir, could ye tak' a neebor (neighbor) into your bed?"

"With all my heart," cried the gallant young poet, springing up to make room for her.

"Thank ye, sir. It's the Moffat carrier just come in soaking wat (wet) and we've nowhere tae put him."

Exit the lovely girl and enter a huge reeking hulk of a man.

The A701 road from Moffat climbs steadily northwards out of the town and runs past the Devil's Beeftub, at the head of a long green valley (actually in Dumfries and Galloway). This glacial feature is a huge steep amphitheater, formerly used by cattle reivers to hide their beasts. (View from a convenient parking lot). A little further on, in this high, windy sheep-cropped rough grassland, the hills patched with blocks of alien forestry, a roadside notice-board advertises the source of the River Tweed, flowing northeastwards—it is simply a bowl of marshy fields. Westwards, on the other side of the divide, are burns (streams) running west to the Clyde. Within a mile of the Tweed's beginnings, and probably of more interest that the subleties of local geography, is the lonely enterprise of the Border Collie and Sheepdog Centre, giving demonstrations of sheepdog handling.

Off the A701 and on the B712, you can visit the mature wooded walks of Dawyck Botanic Garden—wonderful in a late spring flourish of rhododendrons. It is an outstation of the Royal Botanic Garden in Edinburgh. Further on is Stobo Kirk. Originally built in the 12th century, though rebuilt in the 16th century, some Norman features survive. There are also some interesting monuments from the 12th–16th centuries.

Before it reaches Peebles, the Tweed, already a powerful river, is swollen by two streams, Lyne Water and Manor Water, rippling down from beautiful tranquil vales. Each is worth the detour. A couple of miles up the Lyne, muse on the vanity of human ambitions at the ruins of Drochil Castle. James, Earl of Morton, all-powerful in 16th-century Scotland during the minority of King James VI, built Drochil as a luxurious home. He introduced his last batch of political victims to a new toy from France, the horrible instrument of torture known as the Maiden; a species of crude and primitive guillotine with a formidable triangular blade that was dropped onto, or hammered into, the neck of the victim. But, suddenly he fell from power, was judged "art and part" in the murder of the King's father—and was himself the first to be beheaded by the grisly machine. Drochil, never inhabited, fell to ruins. The Maiden, good as new, is now in the National Museum of Antiquities in Edinburgh.

Along the Manor Water a road (unclassified) passes the Black Dwarf's cottage, where Sir Walter Scott met the misshapen eccentric who became the central character of his novel *The Black Dwarf.* The road ends after three miles at Macbeth's Castle, a heap of stones which has nothing to do with Macbeth. Excellent touring country, excellent highways and byways, plenty of accommodations and short distances between towns make motoring and sightseeing painless enough; but in this land of ancient ways and hill-paths the walker, cyclist and horse-rider have distinct advantages.

The Old Roads

Roman and pre-Roman routes, now grassed over, intersect the Tweed at several points. The Girthgate, a pilgrims' way from Edinburgh to Melrose Abbey, is intertwined with the A68 highway from Soutra Hill southwards. The old drove road from Traquair (B709), called for some obscure reason The Paddy Slacks, threading glen and moorland to Ettrick Forest and the banks of the Yarrow Water, has been incorporated in a Border Walk of 60 miles from Galashiels to Moffat. (Note that "Water" in southern Scotland means a river, not, as in the English Lake District, a lake.)

However, the route that will interest walkers most is the Southern Upland Way, Scotland's "official" east–west route, running 112 miles from coast to coast (Portpatrick in Galloway to Cockburnspath in Berwickshire), a switchback route against the grain and the natural contours of the rolling hills. Moffat, St. Mary's Loch, Traquair, and the Eildons are just a few of the places on the signposted route.

Local tourist information offices provide leaflets on country and town walks in their localities. The Regional Council's Countryside Ranger (council offices, Newtown St. Boswells) operates a program of guided walks; historical, scenic and naturalist. New roads are being driven through the hills of the Ettrick and Yarrow districts, opening up once inaccessible moors and fishing lochs to the motorist.

"Peebles for Pleesure"

The catchphrase, adopted as a tourist slogan, came from a native of upper Tweeddale who spent his holiday in Paris. The life of the French capital was all right in its way, he reported, "but gie me Peebles for pleesure."

Judging by its bustling streets—even on Sundays—Peebles still gives "pleesure" to locals and day-visitors from Edinburgh alike. With domed, wooded hills all around, and a broad river set in parkland within moments of the town center, Peebles has the further advantage of a good selection of country-style shops. Look, in particular, for its authentically old-fashioned "proper" ironmongers! A pleasant riverside walk leads upstream to Neidpath Castle, perched on a bluff above the Tweed waters.

Here begins the "wool run." Peebles was in the woolen business in the 1780s. The big name is Ballantyne. You can tour Ballantyne's mill in March Street and buy cashmere knitwear at their mill shop. (Mill shops all over the Borders keep ordinary shopping hours, usually 9–5 Monday to Friday, and a shorter day on Saturday.) As you travel on down the A72 road, which clings to the straights and sweeping bends of the Tweed, you soon come to more mill chimneys at Innerleithen and Walkerburn. The gaunt mid-Victorian buildings, so alien to the pastoral valley, have now settled into the landscape and begin to be valued as items of industrial archeology. Tweedvale mill at Walkerburn, still on the A72, houses both a tweed shop and the Scottish Museum of Wool Textiles.

The name "tweed" for cloth came about by accident. The original material, made up of strands of colored wool twisted together in a subtle combination of shades, was "twill" or "tweel." A London wholesaler misread the label on the samples which a Hawick firm sent him and asked for more "tweed." Seeing his chance to capitalize on the name of a river already famous through the poems and novels of Sir Walter Scott, the Hawick manufacturer didn't bother to correct him.

From Innerleithen, which once had pretensions to spa status, two charming hill routes go off, one right and one left, into the Ettrick Forest and the Moorfoot Hills respectively (both B709). They are Highland passes in miniature, well-stocked with sheep, flowery in summer. You may identify a few of the plants which used to provide dyes for the wool: yellow lichen (it produced a rich brown color), redcurrant and waterlily (chocolate brown), heather and broom (green), apple and bracken root (yellow), dandelion (magenta), bedstraw and bramble (red) . . . a wide range of natural juices, all now replaced by synthetic dyes.

The Twinset Towns

18 miles from Peebles, the Tweedside road reaches Galashiels (locally shortened to Gala) which, along with nearby Selkirk and Melrose and the

more distant town of Hawick, constitutes the tweed and twinset metropolis. The Scottish College of Textiles, established 1909, is at Gala (visitors by appointment). There are retail shops at the tweed mills in Bank Close and Huddersfield Street, Gala; at the Abbey mill, Melrose; and at the Tanneries, Mill Street and Walter Turnbull's, Dunsdale Road, in Selkirk.

Hawick, 12 miles south of the Tweed, most grim and introverted-looking of Border towns, is the important center for the classic sweater, the fully-fashioned cardigan, the plain-knit cashmere twinset . . . everything that goes with a tweed jacket or skirt, including, nowadays, the underwear and warm-ribbed tights. There are 25 knitwear firms in Hawick, including notable names like Pringle, Peter Scott, Lyle & Scott and Braemar. You will find half a dozen mill shops for individual customers and you can tour the mills at Peter Scott's, Wilson & Glenny's and Trowmill Weavers. The frequency of mill tours depends on the season and the demand.

Most of the Border towns have retained a strong sense of community—even Peebles, which has found itself greatly to the taste of "country-set" incomers from the south. Kelso, Melrose, Jedburgh, Selkirk and the others seem sure of their identity. Kelso has an almost Continental air, with its wide main square and sturdy civic buildings clustered around. Jedburgh, for long on the path of invading armies, is now on the path of coach tours and other visitors, offering them a historic town trail as well as an abbey, which in Border terms is well-preserved. Jedburgh Abbey Visitor Centre is an obligatory starting point for any visitor seeking to understand the role of these long-abandoned religious communities in the life and development of the area.

Selkirk—home of the Selkirk Bannock, a fruity scone-like accompaniment to afternoon tea—is another small, neat town going about the Borders mill business. Melrose seems more demure, just as neat and attractive, but perhaps with a wider choice of tea-shops, as well as a poignant survivor of the closed "Waverley Route" railway line in the form of the Melrose Station Craft Centre. This craft complex also has historical and model railway displays.

The identity of these Borders towns is reinforced annually at the major celebrations of the "Common Ridings." Either based on ancient incidents (such as a local victory over English raiders) or a ride-out to mark the town boundaries, these are grand and emotional occasions, taken seriously by the townsfolk. Selkirk's Common Riding is claimed to be the largest mounted gathering in Europe.

The Wizard of the North

Two miles from Melrose (B6360 road) stand the gates of Abbotsford, home of Sir Walter Scott and still in the hands of female descendants, the Maxwell-Scotts. This most-visited of Scottish literary landmarks was a damp farmhouse called Clartyhole when Scott bought it in 1811. In the course of writing nearly all his Waverley novels there, Scott changed its name and turned it into a pseudo-monastic, pseudo-baronial hall. The art critic John Ruskin described Abbotsford as "the most incongruous pile that gentlemanly modernism ever devised."

It is striking but rather ignobly sited. Inside, you can see many curios and souvenirs of Scottish history which Scott, magpie-like, picked up wherever he went. Here, in 1832, he died on what his son-in-law and biographer John Gibson Lockhart described as "a beautiful day, so warm that every window was wide open and so perfectly still that the sound most delicious to his ears, the gentle ripple of the Tweed over its pebbles, was distinctly audible as we knelt round the bed."

The neighborhood bristles with Scott memorabilia and busts. From the parking area on a bend above the Tweed (B6356), pause at the sign "Scott's View" to admire the convolutions of the Tweed—pause as the horses of his funeral cortège are said to have paused when they came to the viewpoint he loved. Leaving Galashiels by the A6091 road to Melrose, you will pass the wall-tablet which tells how the poet, brought home from Italy to die, "sprang up with a cry of delight" at that spot as his carriage came at last within sight of the Tweed. When you visit Dryburgh Abbey, a mile or so beyond Scott's View, have a look at his ornate tomb, open to the winds in a ruined chapel.

They called Scott the "wizard of the north" for his skill in weaving plots, but he was not the only one in these parts. Melrose Abbey is believed to contain the remains (unmarked) of Michael Scot, a 12th-century necromancer famous in the courts of Europe. Retiring to Scotland he was plagued by a devil who kept asking for work. To keep him out of mischief Michael told him to split the Eildon ("Eeldon") hill in three. He did it overnight and the triple peaks are there to prove it. Avid for further employment, the devil was given other seemingly impossible tasks and performed them in no time at all. Finally his master sent him to the mouth of the Tweed to spin ropes out of sand; a job on which, as far as we know, he is still working.

Here, too, under the Eildon tree at the foot of the Rhymer's Glen (close to Abbotsford, a stone marks the spot), sat Thomas of Ercildoune when the Queen of Elfland snatched him away and kept him for seven years; or so the ballad says. She returned him to the same spot as True Thomas, a poet endowed with the dubious gift of being unable to tell a lie. Students of Thomas's writings have discovered prophecies of important events like the Battle of Bannockburn and the Union of England and Scotland; clearest of all was the destiny of the local landowning family:

"Tide, tide what may betide,
Haig shall be Haig of Bemersyde."

In 1921 a grateful nation bestowed the Bemersyde ("Beemer-") estate on the war leader Field-Marshal Earl Haig and thus the prophecy was fulfilled. (He was an adopted child, only distantly related to the Bemersyde Haigs.)

The Holy Places

Thomas the Rhymer was alive and the Haigs were newly settled on the banks of the Tweed when David King of Scots, the "sair sanct," (see *Scottish History* chapter) built four large abbeys at Melrose, Dryburgh and Kelso on the Tweed and at Jedburgh close to its tributary the Teviot ("Tee-viot"). They were meant to be colonies for monks from France and Yorkshire and perhaps David saw them as oases of sanctuary in the war-torn border lands. If so, he was mistaken. Fate decreed that for 400 years these wonderful buildings should know no peace. They were hammered down and built up again and fought over as though they were military strongpoints; and their present dilapidated appearance proclaims the turbulence of their history.

Melrose Abbey in the middle of the market town of that name was an imposing pile in its day. It is still impressive: a red sandstone shell with slender windows in the Perpendicular style and some delicate tracery and carved capitals, carefully maintained. "If thou would'st view fair Melrose aright / Go visit it in the pale moonlight," says Scott in *The Lay of the Last Minstrel,* and so many of his fans took the advice literally that a sleepless custodian begged him to rewrite the lines.

Melrose, like the other three Abbeys, was destroyed by English troops under the Earl of Hertford. They laid waste to much of the south of Scotland under the orders of King Henry VIII of England. This episode, known as the "rough wooing," was an attempt by the English king to fulfil his territorial ambitions by persuading the Scots that his child, Prince Harry, should marry Scotland's own infant Mary, Queen of Scots. Her father King James V had just died, leaving a power vacuum. The Scots did not think the marriage was a good idea and hid their young queen.

Four miles out of Melrose, after descending from Scott's View (B6356), you come to Dryburgh ("Drybra") Abbey, perfect in beauty and tranquility in a loop of the Tweed. The river is about 80 yards wide by this time, halfway from source to mouth, but shallow enough in summer for anglers in waterproof trousers to wade across. From here to Berwick-on-Tweed the salmon beats are contiguous and in the quiet reaches a good deal of poaching goes on, in and out of season.

Dryburgh's extensive ruins once housed Premonstratensian canons from Normandy. The abbey suffered from English raids until, like Melrose, it was abandoned in 1544. The style is Transitional, a mingling of rounded Romanesque and pointed Early English. The side chapel where the Haig and Scott families lie buried is lofty and pillared, detached from the main buildings. Dryburgh in its heyday must have been an epic poem in sculpted stone. It has Bemersyde park and house on one side, Dryburgh Abbey hotel hidden in woodland on the other.

Jedburgh Abbey (A68, 13 miles from Melrose), in a town center of hilly streets and chilly breezes, undercut by the swift Jed Water, dates from 1138. The story of its role in the development of the religious and economic life of the Borders is told in a well laid-out interpretive center. Later on part of it became Jedburgh's parish church. The square tower still stands and the south-side windows, of unusual Transitional design, run in three tiers along the empty nave. Enough survives to confirm that the complex was justly renowned for its graceful arcades and exquisite stone carvings.

Kelso Abbey (A699, 14 miles from Melrose), tall and slim with little rounded turrets, must have looked reassuringly fortress-like when in 1128 the Benedictines from Picardy moved in. The Tweed crossing at Kelso was important to both sides in the Border wars, however, and the abbey was much knocked about by armies advancing to or retreating from each other's countries. The last monks and the townsfolk who had taken refuge with them died leaping from the turrets on to the English pikes and spears in 1545, after which the structure was reduced to its present fragmentary—but highly atmospheric—state.

The four abbeys of Tweeddale, battered and decayed as they are, represent the finest flowering of Scottish ecclesiastical architecture.

The Lower Tweed

The Tweedside roads (A69, A698) through Kelso and Coldstream sweep with a river through parkland and game preserve and past romantic redstone gorges. Close to Kelso, where Sir Walter Scott went to school, stands the palatial mansion of Floors Castle on the "floors" or flat terraces of the Tweed bank opposite the barely-visible ruins of Roxburgh ("Roxbra") Castle. Ancestral home of the Dukes of Roxburghe (note the different spelling!), it was conceived in 1718 by Sir John Vanbrugh, arch exponent of massive Baroque architecture, and afterwards given mock-Tudor touches by W.H. Playfair in the 19th century. A holly tree in the deerpark marks the place where King James II was killed in 1460 by a cannon which "brak in the shooting."

Of nearby Roxburgh Castle very little has survived. Of the once-important town of Roxburgh not a trace remains. It stood at the confluence of Teviot and Tweed; it was one of Scotland's four principal burghs with Edinburgh, Stirling and Berwick; it minted coins; it was a royal residence and the birthplace of King Alexander III . . . but diligent search reveals only a few grass-grown mounds.

Three miles above Coldstream the England-Scotland border comes down from the hills and runs beside the Tweed for the rest of its journey to the sea. Coldstream, once, like Gretna, a marriage place for runaway couples from the south (a plaque on the former bridge toll house recalls this), is celebrated in military history. In 1659 General Monck raised a regiment of foot guards here on behalf of his exiled monarch Charles II. As the Coldstream Guards they have become a corps d'elite in the British Army.

This stretch of the Tweed is lined with dignified houses and gardens including The Hirsel, home of the former Prime Minister, Lord Home. A complex of farmyard buildings now serves as craft center and museum and there are interesting walks in the extensive grounds. If you are not in a hurry, stay with Scotland when the A698 for Berwick crosses into England at Coldstream bridge. Explore the network of peaceful high-hedged lanes, visit Ladykirk—a church which James IV built in gratitude for a safe passage across the Tweed before there were any bridges—and note the place-name of Upsettlington, appropriate for a bitterly-contested frontierland. Your route will discover enchanting glimpses of the now-majestic river in its corridor of greenery and red rocks. You can cross again into England at the Chain bridge (officially the Union bridge) on a minor road (unclassified) which only farm tractors seem to use.

"O, Flodden Field"

Sir Walter Scott claimed that when he stood on the Eildon hills he could see 43 places famed in ballad and war. Among them must have been Flodden in the Cheviot foothills, three miles into England from Coldstream bridge. There on an autumn evening in 1513 a Scottish army was outgeneralled and routed and its king (James IV), his son and most of his knights were slain. When Bannockburn is mentioned, says the Scottish writer Andrew Lang, the English remain calm; but Flodden has the bitterness of unavailing grief for Scots to this day. It inspired the best-known of bagpipe laments, always played at Scottish military funerals, from the song *The Flowers o' the Forest* by the 18th-century Jean Elliot of Minto House near Hawick.

A memorial on the site is dedicated "To the Brave of Both Nations." Most moving of epitaphs, perhaps, is the simple inscription on a monument in the center of Selkirk: "O, Flodden Field." Selkirk sent 100 young men to the battle and only one came home.

Quiet Flows the Tweed

Through a flat fertile country, the Tweed, shaken free of the hills at last, flows to the sea. North and west the Borders' most rich acres are spread, sprinkled with farms and hamlets. This is the Merse, a word which may mean "marsh" or "march" (boundary). Two rough trout streams come galloping into this quiet land from the heights of Lammermuir: the Blackadder and the Whiteadder ("Whittadder"). Above the Whiteadder near Abbey St. Bathans, six miles from Duns (B6355), stands the only Pictish "broch" (beehive hut) in southern Scotland.

Salmon are netted commercially along the last 10-mile windings of the Tweed. Between mid-February and mid-September you may see men watching the waters from ladders along the banks, and boats towing nets into midstream to trap the fish as they swim in from the North Sea. Powerful sporting interests have in recent years been a factor in the industry's decline. But many escape to travel the whole length of the river and provide sport for anglers even in the moorland fastnesses where our journey began.

Bone of Contention

Berwick-on-Tweed is in England although it lies north of the Tweed and gives its name to a Scottish county, Berwickshire. Scots say the town should belong to Scotland but opinion polls among the citizens show a decided preference for remaining English. Regularly claimed and occupied by one nation or the other, Berwick in the 16th century was declared a "free burgh" and mentioned separately in Acts of Parliament: "England, Scotland, Ireland and our town of Berwick-on-Tweed." The situation lasted until 1885 and some inhabitants will tell you that they are still at war with Russia, not having ratified the treaty which ended the Crimean War of 1853–55.

Four bridges span the Tweed estuary at Berwick: a new bypass bridge for traffic on the A1 highway; the ancient 15-arched structure built for King James VI and I about 1620; the Royal Tweed bridge of 1928 which carries the Great North Road (A1) into Scotland; and the Royal Border railroad bridge, a high viaduct of 28 arches, built in 1847 and inscribed at the Berwick station end: "The Final Act of Union."

The Great North Road

Though the town of Berwick can be bypassed, its extraordinary surviving Elizabethan fortifications alone make a visit worthwhile—even if it is not in Scotland! About two miles north of its outskirts is today's Border on the A1. Inland and close to the Berwick-Duns road (A6105) lies the battlefield of Halidon Hill, where in 1333 the English bowmen expertly dismantled the old-fashioned Scottish spear-ring (or schiltron) in a disastrous encounter—perhaps the worst of Scotland's many. Happening in an uncertain period soon after the death of Robert the Bruce, the nation was subsequently ruled by a puppet-king who swore allegiance to King Edward III of England. He garrisoned its castles with English troops and Scotland's independence was lost for almost a century.

If you are drawn to the seascapes on the A1 you may want to turn aside to inspect the fishing villages which are wedged like swallows' nests wherever the outfall of a torrent splits the cliffs. Burnmouth is typical, a precipitous half-mile from the main road. Eyemouth comes next, a major Scottish fishing port. Its river, the Eye Water, is canalized with quays and boatyards like a Mediterranean harbor. In bygone days this was the smugglers' haven and it is said that more people lived under the rocks than on top of them. (If you go looking for the caverns, beware rising tides.)

The fisheries museum at Eyemouth, opened in 1981, commemorates the centenary of a terrible disaster. Struck by a sudden squall, the Eyemouth fishing fleet was wrecked within sight of watchers on the shore and half Eyemouth's children were left fatherless.

The tiny village of St. Abbs is very popular with divers, who can explore an undersea voluntary nature reserve here. St. Abb's Head, lying to the west along this spectacularly rocky coastline, is a National Nature Reserve owned by the NTS and jointly managed by the Scottish Wildlife Trust. They run a visitor center (signposted by Northfield Farm, where visitors should park). The walk to the lighthouse, perched on the edge of the 250-ft. cliffs, is very worthwhile for the spectacle of enormous numbers of seabirds—kittiwakes, guillemots and razorbills stacked in rows on the rocky shelves—making this wildlife assemblage one of the most impressive and easily seen anywhere in Scotland.

A cliff path but no road goes on three miles to Fast Castle. The building grew out of a clump of stack rocks with a perilous high shelf to the mainland. Once impregnable, it has now surrendered to wind and weather and for an idea of what it was once like you must go to Scott's *Bride of Lammermoor,* the story Donizetti used for his opera *Lucia di Lammermoor.*

The last seagirt outpost before the coastal route passes into Lothian Region is Cove—toy breakwater, toy cottages, a toy boat or two. Until recently, a tunnel through the rock was its only link with the village of Cockburnspath ("Cobunspath" or "Copath") on the A1 above. Now a stony track goes dizzily down. Round the corner, by contrast, at Pease Bay there is a huge caravan park.

Local diesel trains and expresses from London to Edinburgh follow the A1, running a few miles inland north of Eyemouth to cross a shoulder of Lammermuir. By road or rail it is about an hour from Berwick-on-Tweed to Edinburgh.

"Jethart's Here!"

If you come to Scotland by train you are bound to arrive by way of Berwick in the east or Carlisle in the west. By road you have a choice of a dozen routes. Apart from the A1 there are first-class main roads over Tweedsmuir (A701, Moffat to Edinburgh); through the knitwear towns (A7, Carlisle to Edinburgh); and from Coldstream (A697) and Jedburgh

(A68). These last two roads combine near Lauder and continue to Edinburgh as the A68.

The A68 has much to recommend it. If you are heading for Edinburgh from the south, it is 30 miles shorter than the A1. It offers a dramatic introduction to Scotland at the summit of Carter Bar on the lonely Cheviots. It crosses the once-famous hunting chase of Jedforest—of which only one tree remains, the tottering Capon Oak near the roadside one mile south of Jedburgh; and it allows you to see something of Jedburgh itself, an archetypal Borders town.

In the Border wars Jedburgh was noted for stout hearts and thick staves—the Jethart staffs, wielded by brawny townsfolk to the battle-cry of "Jethart's here!" Proverbial also in Scotland was "Jethart justice," a sort of lynch law which consisted in hanging the prisoner first and trying him afterwards.

In 1566 Mary Queen of Scots stayed for a month at the grim fortified dwelling called Queen Mary's House, and scandalized the citizens by riding to Hermitage Castle and back in one day—a round trip of some 50 miles—to comfort her sick lover the Earl of Bothwell. Relics of the Queen are shown in the house. In the Canongate, Blackhills Close and Abbey Close are some tall narrow buildings, exotic to English eyes, which at different periods gave lodging to Robert Burns, Bonnie Prince Charlie and the poet Wordsworth and his sister.

Queen of the Gypsies

12 miles northeast of Jedburgh and eight from Kelso lies a remote village with two claims to notoriety. It is the northern terminus of the Pennine Way, the 250-mile footpath along the backbone of England that originates in Derbyshire's Peak District and which descends with the Border Fence to within a few hundred yards of the village; and it is the capital of Scotland's gypsies.

The gypsy clan called Faas were at Kirk Yetholm for centuries. Ordinary travelers learned not to go near the place. You can still see the Gypsy Palace (a humble cottage) and a street called Gypsy Row. Here the Romany kings and queens were crowned and held court until 1883 when the last "Queen," Esther Faa Blyth, died. The place is quiet and respectable today but it is easy to imagine it as a lawless frontier outpost, a long way from nowhere.

Lauderdale

Leaving Jedburgh by the A68 for Edinburgh, having maybe browsed and booked your accommodations ahead at the Scottish Tourist Board's large information center, your next landmark is the Tweed crossing at Leaderfoot, a network of bridges including a many-arched high railroad viaduct, now disused. The old Roman road, Dere Street, came this way from Corstopitum (Corbridge) on Hadrian's Wall and went on to Cramond on the Firth of Forth. The camps and stations of the route have been well excavated and most of the finds are in Edinburgh's Museum of Antiquities. But it is worth while going a mile down the Melrose road from Leaderfoot to see the block of stone at Newstead marked "Trimontium"—"of three peaks," the legionaries' name for the Eildon hills.

The next village as you continue north on the A68 into Lauderdale, valley of the Leader, is Earlston, birthplace of Thomas the Rhymer. Then comes Lauder, nominally a royal burgh, actually a village, where King James III's lords hanged his favorites from the river bridge in 1482. Lauderk Kirk is of unusual cruciform type; Thirlestane Castle (with its integral Border Country Life Museum) is nearby. After Lauder you climb to a saddle of the Lammermuir hills at 1,200 feet and descend into Lothian Region.

The Moorland Trails

Given time and clear weather you might choose more roundabout routes through the Region. The countryside is uniformly picturesque and endlessly varied. There is exhilarating moorland in the Ettrick Forest (from which the trees vanished long ago), south and west of Selkirk; also between Gordon Arms, where Scott took a last farewell of James Hogg the "Ettrick Shepherd," and Traquair and Borthwick (B709, B7007); also on the bleak unfenced roads (beware of sheep!) which rise to the sources of the Lammermuir burns north of Duns (B6355) and Longformacus ("Longfor-make-us") (unclassified).

PRACTICAL INFORMATION FOR BORDERS

HOW TO GET THERE. By train. Fast trains from London to Edinburgh often stop at Berwick-upon-Tweed, adjacent to the Border country. Rail cutbacks in the 1960s left the Borders all but rail-less. The main stations are, in the east, Berwick-upon-Tweed, and in the west, Carlisle, from where there are bus services—ironically called "The Borders Rail Link"— to the main Border towns.

By bus. From larger centers within Scotland, particularly Edinburgh, several companies run many day and half-day bus tours through the Border country. On the various routes between Edinburgh and Newcastle-upon-Tyne, buses pass through Berwick, Coldstream, Kelso and Jedburgh. There are also frequent services between Edinburgh and the towns of the middle and upper Tweed: Melrose, Galashiels, Selkirk and Peebles.

HOTELS AND RESTAURANTS. Borders Region is a great tourist area and as such is reasonably well-served with a range of hotels from budget to luxury. A further advantage is its proximity to Edinburgh, giving the attractive option of a Borders base for city exploration.

Blythe Bridge (A701). **Restaurant.** *The Old Mill* (M), tel. 0721–52220. Festooned in horse brasses and similar rustic bric-a-brac. Good fresh food. Busy at weekends.

Cockburnspath (A1). **Restaurant.** *Cockburnspath Hotel* (I), tel. 036 83–217. Unpretentious stop on A1 highway for a bar lunch. Excellent fresh fish.

Coldstream (A697). **Restaurant.** *Collingwood Arms* (M), tel. 0890–2424. Over Coldstream Bridge, technically a few miles into England. First-class menu and service.

Dryburgh Abbey *see* St. Boswells.

Ettrick Bridge (B7009). *Ettrickshaws* (E), tel. 0750–52229. 6 rooms with bath. Waterside Victorian mansion. Both hotel and restaurant commended in international reports. French *Routiers* "Casserole" award-winner in 1985.

Gattonside (B6360). **Restaurant.** *Hoebridge* (M), tel. 089 682–3082. Walk across footbridge from Melrose or take minor road from Leaderfoot. Authentic Italian flavor. "Best ice-cream since Venice," a customer says.

Hawick (A7). *Kirklands* (M), tel. 0450–72263. 6 rooms, 3 with bath. Commended in foreign tourist guides. *Elm House* (M), tel. 0450–72866. 15 rooms, 11 with bath. In town center. High standards, low rates.

Kelso (A699). *Sunlaws House* (L), tel. 0573–5331. 14 rooms with bath. Restful old house, library bar, daily change of menu, a celebrity chef. Run by the Duke of Roxburghe.

Melrose (A6091). *Burts* (M), tel. 089 682–2285. 21 rooms, 18 with bath. Cozy 18th-century inn, very obliging owners. *George & Abbotsford* (M), tel. 089 682–2308. 34 rooms, 30 with bath. Ancient High Street hostelry successfully modernized.
Restaurant. *Marmion's Brasserie* (M), Buccleuch Street, tel. 089 682–2245. Outstanding country-style cuisine.

Peebles (A72). *Peebles Hydro* (M), tel. 0721–20602. 139 rooms with bath. Two miles from town near Tweed bank. Heated pool, sauna, sports facilities. Popular conference center.
Restaurant. *Park* (M), Innerleithen Road, tel. 0721–20451. Superior Scots cuisine, trout- and seafood-based.

St. Boswells (B6356). *Dryburgh Abbey* (M), tel. 0835–22261. 29 rooms, 21 with bath. Bogus baronial, but very civilized. Fine gardens next to abbey in bend of Tweed. Excellent restaurant, very handy for lunch.

St. Mary's Loch (A708). *Tibbie Shiels Inn* (I), tel. 0750–42231. 6 rooms, no private baths. Historic fishing/drovers' inn set between two lochs. Fishing, sailing. Has several times changed hands and lost its old informal charm. Junior staff still good-natured.

Selkirk (A708). *Philipburn House* (E), tel. 0750–20747. 16 rooms with bath. 18th-century house on site of battlefield at junction of rivers. Wide range of amenities, including tree houses for children. The *restaurant* is noted—for effort, perhaps, rather than achievement.

Tweedsmuir (A701). *Crook Inn* (E), tel. 089 97–272. 8 rooms, 6 with bath. Renovated 17th-century "howff." Outlook bleak but spacious, cozy inside. Reservation advised for overnights—there is no other hotel for miles around.

Walkerburn (A72). *Tweed Valley* (E), tel. 089 687–636. 16 rooms with bath. Edwardian country house in peaceful setting. Traditional Scottish food. Log fires and superb views.

HOW TO GET ABOUT. By bus. Country people depend on buses and services are therefore quite comprehensive, especially on Saturdays and market days; reduced services operate on Sundays. Most isolated villages have their bus connections with some main-route town at least once or twice a week. The Tweedside roads described in the first half of the chapter are also busy bus routes and you could travel downriver from Peebles to Coldstream in a day, stopping off at one or two places on the way.

By car. This is excellent motoring country, though strangers should beware the surprising ups-and-downs and sharp bends, even on the major roads. Self-drive automobiles are available from D.S. Dalgleish & Son, Galashiels (tel. 0896–4767) and Hawick (tel. 0450–76028); and Smith's Motor Services, Elcho Street, Peebles (tel. 0721–20217). The last-named company also provides chauffeured automobiles for renting by the day or longer.

TOURIST INFORMATION. There are Tourist Board information centers for visitors entering Scotland by road at Jedburgh (A68) and Southwaite (Cumbria, M6). Local information centers with book-ahead facilities are at Coldstream, Eyemouth, Galashiels, Hawick, Kelso, Melrose, Peebles, and Selkirk; open Apr.–Oct.

FISHING. The chief fishing rivers are the Tweed, Teviot, Ettrick and Whiteadder, but every hill-stream has brown trout and sometimes salmon too. On the Tweed the salmon season runs February through November. The heaviest hauls come with the fall run (September and October) when salmon of 20–25 pounds are caught.

Most beats are strictly preserved or very expensive but on the Tweed at Peebles and certain stretches of the Teviot the visiting angler can buy a permit quite cheaply. Trout fishings are mostly in the hands of local angling associations who welcome casual visitors. Many hotels offer trout fishing. Fishing-tackle shops provide information and issue the permits. The trout season is effectively April to September. Dry fly on June, July or August evenings achieves the best results.

For the stillwater fisherman many lochs and reservoirs are stocked and managed by district angling societies. The best are St. Mary's Loch (A708), Coldingham (A1107) and Lindean (B6360). Sea-angling is offered at Eyemouth, weekends only. For a boat and boatman, contact Eyemouth Sea Angling Club. Whitefish angling off the rocks is free everywhere all the year round.

GOLF. There are 17 golf courses in the Region, most of them in attractive surroundings. Galashiels, Hawick, Kelso, Minto, Peebles and West Linton all have 18-hole courses. Golf is not a costly game in Scotland and at smaller courses you pay about £1 a day, perhaps a little more on Sat.

and Sun. (Where the steward is not full time, put your money in the trust box.)

Drinks and meals, or at least sandwiches, are available at clubhouses. Peebles municipal course is the only one with caddy cars for hire. At Peebles you pay £4 for the day or £2.50 a round; £6 and £4 at weekends.

HISTORIC HOUSES AND GARDENS. The following are but a few of Border properties open through the summer. Many more open periodically, details being advertised in the local press and in shop windows. Entrance, where charged, is usually £1 or less, most of which goes to charity.

Abbotsford, on the Tweed near Melrose (B6360). Mementos of Sir Walter Scott and many historic relics. Open mid.-Mar.–Oct., weekdays 10–5, Sun. 2–5.

Ayton Castle, Ayton (A1). Pseudo-baronial pile in red sandstone. Occupied. Open Sun. 2–5 or by appointment.

Bowhill, near Selkirk (A708). Grandiose mansion dating from 1812 and the home of Dukes of Buccleuch. Extravagant furnishings and fine pictures. Woodland play area for children. Pony-trekking. Park and playground open May–Aug.; house July–Aug., weekdays except Fri., 12–5; Sun. 2–6.

Dawyck, on the Tweed near Peebles (B712). Choice collection of trees and shrubs, gathered over 300 years. Herons and deer. Open daily Apr.–Sept., 12–5.

Floors Castle, near Kelso (B6089). Great 18th-century mansion with Victorian embellishments. Impressive maze under construction. Valuable paintings. Garden center. Open May–Sept., daily except Fri., Sat., 11–5.30.

The Hirsel, near Coldstream (A697). Ancestral home of Earls of Home. Colorful gardens and birds. Estate interpretation center. House not open but you may walk in the gardens any time. Box for charitable donations.

Manderston, near Duns (A6105). Much-lived-in Edwardian mansion. Rooms, kitchens, stables, dairy etc. open to parties by appointment. No entrance charge. Open mid-May–mid-Sept., Sun. and Thurs. only, 2–5.30.

Mellerstain House, near Gordon (A6089). One of the finest creations of Robert Adam. Outstanding furnishings and pictures of his era (late 18th century). Beautiful gardens. Open May–Sept., daily except Sat., 12.30–4.30.

Neidpath Castle, on the Tweed near Peebles (A72). Splendid situation, 14th-century tower. Open Easter–mid-Oct., weekdays 10–1, 2–6, Sun. 1–6.

Priorwood, Melrose (A6091). Priorwood adjoins Melrose Abbey and is enclosed in walls of architectural distinction. The Georgian house is a National Trust center and shop. Open Apr., Nov., Dec., weekdays 10–1, 2–5.30; May–June and Oct., weekdays 10–5.30, Sun. 1.30–5.30; July–Sept., weekdays 10–6, Sun. 1.30–5.30.

Thirlestane Castle, Lauder (A697). Ancestral home of Maitlands, notorious in Scottish history. Contains *Border Country Life* museum (see below).

Traquair House, near the Tweed at Innerleithen (B709). Claims to be the oldest house continuously inhabited in Scotland. Furnishings reflect

10 centuries of domestic life. Brewhouse and craft workshops. Open Easter–early Oct., daily 1.30–5.30—in July–mid-Sept., 10.30–5.30.

MUSEUMS. There are museums all over Borders Region, often attached to public libraries, and where admission is free. We include the following because they illustrate particular aspects of regional life.

Border Country Life Museum, Thirlestane Castle, Lauder (A697). Splendid evocation of monastic, farming and wildlife history. A tour of Thirlestane Castle, the pseudo-baronial "great house," is offered. Museum opens mid-May–June and Sept., Wed. and Sun. 2–5; July–Aug., daily except Fri., 2–5.

Castle Jail, Jedburgh (A68). Local lockup, but a model of prison reform when opened in the 1820s. Open Apr.–Sept., Mon.–Sat., 10–12, 1–5., Sun. 1–5.

Coldstream Museum, Coldstream (A697). Local crafts and curios, history of Coldstream Guards. Open May–Sept., daily except Mon., 2–5, Sat. 10–1.

The Cornice Museum of Ornamental Plasterwork, Peebles (A72). Unique displays of plaster casting and ornamental work and largest surviving collection of "masters" in Scotland. Visitors can try plastering for themselves! Open April, May, Oct., 10–12, 2–4; June–Sept. 10–1, 2–5.

Eyemouth Museum, Eyemouth (A1107). Story of a fishing port. Tapestry depicts disaster of 1881. Open Easter–Oct. 10–6.30, Sun. 2–5.30.

Halliwell's House, Selkirk (A7). Award-winning display of local crafts, notably shoe-making, in renovated terrace of 18th-century cottages. Open Apr.–Oct., weekdays 10–5, Sun. 2–5.

Jedburgh Abbey Visitor Centre, Jedburgh (off A68). Visitor route, panoramic outlooks, tearoom and shop. Open Easter–Sept., Mon.–Sat., 9.30–7, Sun. 2–7; Oct.–Mar., Mon.–Sat., 9.30–4, Sun. 2–4.

Jim Clark Memorial Room, Duns (A6105). Jim Clark was motor-racing champion of the world (died 1968); trophies and cups (including the *Indianapolis 500*); also personal items. Open Apr.–Sept., Mon.–Sat. 10–6, Sun.2–6.

Kelso Museum, Kelso (A698). Portrait of past life of Kelso as market town, tanning industry center. Opening hours linked to tourist information center on ground floor. Basically, Easter–Oct., Mon.–Sat., 10–12, 1–6, Sun. 2–6.

Melrose Motor Museum, Melrose (off A68). Private collection of vehicles, mainly 1900s–1960s. Also memorabilia, street signs, toy car displays, shop. Open mid-May–mid-Oct., daily 10.30–5.30.

Scottish Wool Textiles Museum, Walkerburn (A72). History of Borders woolen industries, old machinery, spinning and weaving demonstrations. Open Mon.–Fri., 10–5; in summer months also Sat., 11–4 and Sun. 12–4.

Wilton Lodge, Hawick (A7). Social, industrial and archeological history of town. Handsome building in parkland on Teviot bank. Open Apr.–Oct., Mon.–Sat. 10–5, Sun. 2–5, in winter months by appointment.

SCOTLAND'S DEEP SOUTHWEST

Dumfries and Galloway

This Region was for many years neglected by tourism. It lies away from the major England–Scotland routes and travelers to Glasgow and Edinburgh have usually been more concerned with getting to their destinations than with turning aside to explore it. One historic line of communication does pass through it: the road from Carlisle to Stranraer and Cairn Ryan, two harbors which offer the shortest sea crossings, 40 and 35 miles respectively, between the United Kingdom and Ireland.

Of the rich pre-history of this Region very little of substance remains. Scotland's first settlers, about 4000 B.C., had villages on Luce Bay and beside the banks of the River Annan; flint implements, now in museums, have been recovered. There are small chambered cairns of the Neolithic period (2000 B.C.) at Cairnholy near Gatehouse of Fleet and at Windy Edge near Langholm. The sites of "crannogs," lake villages on stilts, have been identified on the lochs of Milton near Crocketford, Carlingwark near Castle Douglas and the Castle at Lochmaben. They have rotted away but you can still see the low, brushwood-covered isles on which they were built.

In the second century A.D., the important Roman camp of Blatum Bulgium stood at Burnswark in Annandale. The name means "Flour Bags" and presumably it was a grain stockpile. But afterwards a thoughtless Duke of Buccleuch took the stones away to build walls; and Birrens, as the place is now called, has only a mound and a hollow to show for its Roman past.

The large decorated Celtic cross (7th century) of Ruthwell near Annan was also destroyed. The shaft, pieced together again, now stands inside the parish church.

The Region's outstanding ancient building was a small church built about 410 at Whithorn, south of Wigtown, by Ninian, Scotland's senior saint (c.360–432). A replacement for his original cell on the "Isle" of Whithorn three miles away, it became a mandatory shrine for Scottish royalty. But current excavations are possibly locating Ninian's real "Candida Casa" (White House) in the peaceful little town of Whithorn. Visit the museum and visitor center for the latest discoveries.

The prevailing mild southwesterlies and the warming influence of the Gulf Stream encourage gardens to flourish throughout Galloway. Though today a little off the beaten track, the region played its part in Scotland's story. Caerlaverock, Threave, Cardoness and Castle Kennedy are symbols of Scots–English struggles and wars between kings and unruly barons. The principal abbeys, Lincluden, Dundrennan, Luce and Sweetheart have also known moments of turbulent history. No building, however, attracts more attention than the blacksmith's shop at Gretna Green on the Cumbrian border with its tales of marriages between eloping English couples.

There are no large towns. Dumfries ("Dum-freess") has fewer than 30,000 inhabitants and Stranraer, the next largest, only 10,000. The Dumfries district is split by the valleys of three rivers, the Nith, Annan and Esk. Their courses reach back into the Borders and Strathclyde hills and their sources are lost in the lonely lochs of Tweedsmuir and Lowther.

West of Dumfries the land is called Galloway. In these parts mild temperatures, copious rainfall, well-drained hills and shelter from northerly winds favor arable and dairy farms. The black rough-haired Galloway pony is not so common now and on the pastures the belted Galloway cattle—black with white belly-bands—are giving way to heavier imported stock like the Charollais. But cattle-raising, agriculture and forestry are still the traditional industries. There are shiny silo towers but very few factory chimneys.

The central districts cover the old county of Kirkcudbright ("Kircoobry"), commonly called the Stewartry because from early times it was governed by a Steward directly answerable to the King. For more than 200 years the Steward was a Maxwell, a name you will often come across. The Maxwelton Braes of *Annie Laurie* rise above the Cairn valley north of Dumfries.

The Glen Trool National Forest Park occupies a large area in the middle of Galloway. Here the scenery is of Highland character. Large lochs appear in unexpected places and many of them have been harnessed for hydroelectric schemes. The Queen's Way from New Galloway to Newton Stewart is a beautiful drive.

Coastal areas are pleasantly pastoral. The coastline is deeply indented with sandy or muddy river mouths on the southern shore and low cliffs on the western. There is a network of minor roads which encourage leisurely exploration—but watch out for cows en route to their dairy! One of Scotland's most exhilarating coast drives is the 18 miles from Gatehouse of Fleet to Newton Stewart.

Old-time occupations—farming and smuggling—were portrayed in the novels of S.R. Crocket (1860-1914), who was born at Balmaghie near Castle Douglas. His sentimentality is mawkish to modern readers but *The Raiders* and *The Lilac Sunbonnet* were extremely popular in their day. Scott's *Redgauntlet* and *Guy Mannering* are both set in the Region and his character "Old Mortality" (Robert Paterson, 1715–1801) is buried at Caerlaverock. R.L. Stevenson's *The Master of Ballantrae* (actually a picture of Borgue near Kirkcudbright rather than Ballantrae) illustrates the deep-dyed conservatism of Galloway folk.

Thomas Carlyle was born at Ecclefechan, J.M. Barrie went to school at Dumfries Academy and Robert Burns lived, died and was buried in the same town. James Clerk-Maxwell the 19th-century physicist was brought up near Corsock and Thomas Telford the 19th-century engineer was born near Langholm. Inhabitants of Eskdale have made much in recent years of the fact that Neil Armstrong, the first man on the moon, claims a local ancestry. Galloway's hero is Alexander Murray (1775–1813), archetypal "lad o' pairts". A humble shepherd lad, he became a famous scholar and Professor of Oriental Languages at Edinburgh University. His memorial obelisk, a stiff 10-minute climb from the Queen's Way near Newton Stewart, commands sensational views.

Marriage à la Mode

Traveling along the A74 from Carlisle, over the border in England, to Glasgow, the first village in Scotland you reach is Gretna, a junction of routes among the marshes at the head of the Solway Firth. For 200 years it was the goal of eloping couples from England who could take advantage of Scots law and marry by simply making a declaration before a witness— such as the village blacksmith. After 1939 such marriages were made illegal, but young English and foreign couples continued to flock to Gretna Green because in Scotland you could marry without parental consent at 16 while in England and most Continental countries the age was 21. Today at the Old Blacksmith's, one of two smithies at Gretna Green, mock ceremonies are performed daily as entertainment for bus parties.

Dumfries

From Gretna via the small town of Annan, where the River Annan checks its headlong rush from the uplands and winds soberly to the sea, it is 24 miles to Dumfries (A75). Like Annan it is an estuary town, seven miles from the sea, spread over the bends of the canal-like River Nith; a busy agricultural center with traffic congestion on market days.

Dumfries became a royal burgh 700 years ago. The foundation of its Greyfriars monastery off Buccleuch Street near the river bank dates back almost as far. It was there in 1306 that Robert the Bruce, pressing for recognition as Scotland's rightful king, stabbed his rival John Comyn. As Bruce fled with his supporters, one Roger Kirkpatrick turned back and drove his dagger again into the dying man "to mak siccar" (make sure). The Dumfries Kirkpatricks have ever since borne a bloody hand with a dagger for their coat-of-arms with the motto: "I mak siccar."

In the 1870s, the playwright J.M. Barrie spent his childhood in Victoria Terrace, Dumfries, and attended Dumfries Academy. The garden of Moat

Brae House is supposed to have been the playground which inspired his boyish dreams of Peter Pan. In his memoirs Barrie wrote of running to the street corner to doff his cap to the literary giant of the age, Thomas Carlyle. "I dare say I paid this homage 50 times, but never was there any response."

Dumfries's real lion is Robert Burns. His last and most lyrical songs and poems were written while he lived in and near the town. Burns gave up his third unsuccessful farming venture at Ellisland, six miles upstream on the Nith, in 1791. *Tam o' Shanter, Of A' the Airts, Jo Anderson my Jo* and *Auld Lang Syne* belong to that period. He and his wife Jean Armour took a house in the Wee Vennel, afterwards moving to what is now called Burns Street. For the first time in his life Burns had a steady salaried job. He was a customs officer at the port of Dumfries. Here he wrote, among scores of songs, *Ae Fond Kiss, Duncan Gray, The Lea Rig* and— possibly the most perfect of 18th-century love-poems— *O, wert Thou in the Cauld Blast.*

To the doctor who attended him on his deathbed in 1796 he described himself as "a poor pigeon not worth the plucking." He was only 37. The cause of death has been variously diagnosed as rheumatic fever, endocarditis and a diseased nervous system. Many such details of the poet's life can be learned in the Robert Burns Centre, a major visitor center attractively sited on the banks of the River Nith in Dumfries. The premises, a converted 18th-century mill, contain an exhibition and informative displays on the life of Burns in Dumfries. This is just one of the features on the Burns Heritage Trail around Ayrshire and Galloway. Look for signposting.

Dumfries has many Burns relics in its civic museum, which is a converted 18th-century windmill. The house in the Wee Vennel (now Bank Street) is not visitable. The house in Burns Street, formerly Mill Vennel, where Burns died is the poet's official museum. You may visit the Globe tavern, his regular "howff" in the last years, and the mausoleum in St. Michael's churchyard where he is buried. His farm at Ellisland has been transformed into a showcase of agricultural methods of Burns's time and is open to the public.

Between Nith and Solway

South of Dumfries, where the Nith widens to the mudflats of the Solway Firth, a number of castles resistant to the "crumbling touch of Time" dot the shoreline. Caerlaverock, noble in decay, islanded in a lake-like moat, in the 13th century was the Maxwells' proudest stronghold. King Edward I of England took it with battering-rams and catapults in 1300. The Covenanters accomplished its ruin in the wars of 1639–40. "Old Mortality," who crops up everywhere in the moss-grown corners of Scotland, is buried in Caerlaverock churchyard.

Caerlaverock is also associated with nature conservation as the coastal flats and marshes are an important wildfowl wintering ground. The Caerlaverock National Nature Reserve offers extremely comfortable birdwatching in a variety of hides, as well as a visitor center with a large picture window and birds floating past!

On the A710, looping west of Dumfries, there is a concentration of attractions around the village of New Abbey, including Sweetheart Abbey, its great, roofless, red sandstone church looming over the village. It was founded in 1273 by Devorgilla, a descendant of the ancient lords of Galloway who married John Balliol (founder of Balliol College, Oxford) and gave birth to the more historic John Balliol, puppet king of Scotland before Bruce. The lady also built Dumfries's first bridge, precursor of the 15th-century "Old Bridge" which pedestrians use to this day, and the Greyfriars monastery. Within walking distance of Sweetheart Abbey is the New Abbey Corn Mill, a preserved example of a building once vital in every local community. This fascinating building has been fully restored. A little beyond the village is Shambellie House, a museum of costume housed in a Victorian mansion in Scots Baronial style.

Further along the A710, near Kirkbean, is the charming garden of Arbigland, its primulas, oriental garden and stream-side walks sheltered from the sea winds by tall trees. Arbigland was the birthplace of John Paul ("I have not yet begun to fight") Jones, the gardener's boy who became an American citizen and is sometimes called the founder of the U.S. Navy, while Kirkbean was the birthplace of Dr. Craik, personal physician to George Washington. One wonders if the two ever met.

For several weeks in 1778 in the *U.S.S. Ranger,* the first ship to wear the Stars and Stripes, Jones bombarded ports and harried shipping in the Solway Firth and Irish Sea in pursuance of orders to "distress the enemies of the United States." The propaganda effect was considerable: not for 100 years had any foreign vessel dared attack a British coast.

Jones, who died in Paris in 1792, is commemorated with a plaque on his birthplace, a font in Kirkbean church presented by the U.S. Navy in 1945; and a museum at Kirkcudbright's 16th-century Tolbooth, the jail where he was once imprisoned.

Castle Douglas to Newton Stewart

Castle Douglas takes its name from a 14th-century castle called Threave, a stronghold of the Black Douglas on an island in the River Dee. So powerful was this medieval warrior-lord that King James II had to bring an army to Threave in 1455 to teach him a lesson; an occasion on which the "bombard" (cannon) was first used in Scotland. You can see one of the cannon-balls, 17 inches in diameter, in the Dumfries Burgh museum. Modern Threave, three miles south of the ruined castle, is a showplace of rhododendrons and rock plants. This is where the National Trust for Scotland trains its gardeners. The watery neighborhood is a great place for greylag geese.

Threave's river, the Dee, flows down from Loch Ken and the Water of Ken, an elaborate system of hydroelectric reservoirs and barrages; down from New Galloway, population 300, the smallest royal burgh for miles around; and down from Carsphairn among Galloway's highest and wildest hills. This was the country of the Macadams, of whom John Loudon Macadam (1756–1836), inventor of carriageable roads, was the most distinguished son. Tradition says the family were MacGregors, a name proscribed by law after the Jacobite risings, and that John's grandfather called himself Macadam because none could deny that all men were "sons of Adam." It is a coincidence that the other pioneer of road engineering, Thomas Telford, was born in the same region at about the same date (1757). Telford was a shepherd lad from Eskdale.

The Dee meets the sea at Kirkcudbright (A711), chief town of the Stewartry and best-looking of Galloway burghs—at least when the tide is in. As in all Solway estuaries there is a lot of mud about at low water. Kirkcudbright is an 18th-century town of unpretentious houses, some of them color-washed and roofed with the blue slates of the district. The Tolbooth is a good example of 16th–17th-century public building with a plain facade and an outside stairway. The slender Mercat Cross in front of it dates from 1610. Witches were tried there. The last witch to be burned was one Elspeth McEwen in 1698, but as recently as 1805 a Jean Maxwell was convicted of witchcraft at Kirkcudbright and sentenced to a year's hard labor.

Kirkcudbright's L-shaped main street is full of craft and antique shops. The castle, called Maclellan's Castle, is the shell of a once-elaborate castellated mansion dating from the early 17th century.

Below the town, on the shores of the estuary, you will see herons. For centuries there has been a heronry on St. Mary's Isle in the bay. There are priory ruins too on this small island; and some years ago the Canadian government decided to set up a monument at the site of a demolished house. It was the home of Lord Selkirk, who helped establish the Red River colony, afterwards Winnipeg, in 1817.

A few miles east (A711) stands ruined Dundrennan Abbey, founded 1142, where Mary Queen of Scots spent her last night in Scotland. At Port Mary, a mile away, you can see the stone from which she stepped into the boat which took her to England and delivered her to the mercy of her cousin Queen Elizabeth I: the spot where she left Scotland never to return.

From Kirkcudbright bridge, the A755/A75 leads west to Gatehouse of Fleet, Creetown and Newton Stewart, three insignificant townships situated among quiet waters. Cardoness Castle (15th century) south of Gatehouse, overlooking Fleet Bay, has associations with the "Young Lochinvar" of the well-known poem; as has Rusco Castle, a few miles northwest. Only fragments survive of these formerly important towers of the Gordons of Lochinvar.

St. Ninian's Chapel

Newton Stewart, largest of the three townships, is an obvious touring center for Galloway's far west. South of the town, the A746 winds above the shores of Wigtown Bay on a promontory called The Machars—an area of gentle rolling farmlands, yellow gorse hedgerows, rich grazings for dairy cattle and a number of stony prehistoric sites. Wigtown is another royal burgh in name, a sleepy village by nature. Both in the churchyard and on the mudflats of the shore are memorials to the Wigtown Martyrs, two women tied to stakes and left to drown in the incoming tide during the anti-Covenant witch-hunts of 1685. Much of Galloway's history is linked with Border feuds; but even more with the ferocity of the Killing Times. Wigtown, like several other places in the Region, is dominated by a hill-top Covenanters' Monument, a reminder of the old persecutions.

The A746 was a pilgrim's way and a royal route. It ends at Isle of Whithorn (which is not in fact quite an island), a place which early Scottish kings and barons sought to visit at least once in their lives, as Moslems seek to visit Mecca. The pilgrimage was often prescribed as a penance, but these pleasant shores impose no penance today. The goal was St. Ninian's chapel, the 4th-century cell of Scotland's premier saint. Some pilgrims made for Whithorn village and others for the sandspit "isle." Both places claimed to be the site of the original "Candida Casa" of the saint. As you approach Whithorn's 12th-century priory, observe the royal arms of pre-1707 Scotland (that is, Scotland before the Union with England) carved and painted above the arch of the Pend (covered way).

Newton Stewart to Stranraer

The abbeys of Galloway, like the castles, have all been scarred and beaten down, but are nowadays oases of tranquility once more, carefully maintained and surrounded by lawns. Luce Abbey near Glenluce beside the Water of Luce and close to the A75 belongs to the 12th century; Carscreuch Castle, three miles northeast on an unclassified road, to the 17th. From Glenluce you cross a neck of water-meadows and pools which just saves the Rhinns of Galloway from being an island; and then you are at Stranraer.

Ferry ports, designed to speed the traveler away in one direction or another, are rarely worth visiting on their own account. Stranraer is an exception. Having been in existence long before steamer piers and customs sheds were thought of, it has a life of its own. "Bluidy" Claverhouse, scourge of the Covenanters in the Killing Times, made his headquarters at the 16th-century castle in the middle of the town. Another "castle," on the waterfront, bears the curious name of North West. It was built by Rear-admiral Sir John Ross (1777–1856), explorer of the Canadian Arctic and born four miles away at Inch. The "castle" is now a hotel.

The ferry port for Ireland used to be Portpatrick, now a neat little holiday village on the western side of the Rhinns, 12 miles nearer the Irish ports. But the harbor proved too exposed and when regular ferry schedules were introduced the port of Stranraer, well sheltered at the head of its sealoch, was chosen. More recently a rival ferry company has developed Cairn Ryan, halfway down the loch, as an alternative ferry station.

You may find some Irish money in your small change in the Stranraer and Cairn Ryan districts: check your money before you leave, because the Irish coins and notes will not be accepted elsewhere in Scotland; note also that the Irish pound (punt) is worth slightly less than its British equivalent.

The Rhinns

Stranraer is the doorway to the T-shaped peninsula of the Rhinns of Galloway, which appear to have been stuck on to the mainland as an afterthought. The Rhinns are a bright patchwork of cultivated land with quiet open roads and calm little villages. Sandhead (A716), where a battle once took place between Scots and Picts, nestles at one end of the eight-mile-long sands of Luce. Among Kirkmadrine's chapel ruins, two miles from Sandhead, early Christian inscribed stones are preserved, hinting at a possible saintly settlement as old as St. Ninian's.

Climate and soil have produced tender vegetation like that of Kintyre and the southwest of Ireland. A Galloway landowner, Lord Stair, demonstrated the agricultural potential of the area in 1770 when he planted the grand gardens at Castle Kennedy near Stranraer (A75). They have since been matched by brilliant displays at Ardwell House south of Sandhead (A716) and Logan Botanic Gardens near Port Logan (B7065), where cabbage palms and other delicate species flourish in Scotland's mildest climate. At Port Logan itself, in the small tidal basin, there is a fishpond to which cod and other saltwater fish have been attracted for 200 years to feed out of visitors' hands.

Run on another four miles from Port Logan to see the sculpted stones in the churchyard of Kirkmaiden, the most southerly parish in Scotland (not to be confused with Kirkmadrine above). The greatest continuous distance in mainland Scotland, 280 miles in a straight line, is the proverbial "Maiden Kirk to John o' Groats"—the extreme southwest to the extreme northeast.

Heart of the Stewartry

The road for Glasgow (A77) goes north from Stranraer along a coastline which offers fine views in clear weather of Northern Ireland and the hills and isles of the Firth of Clyde. This road links up with Girvan, Ayr and the Clyde coastal towns, described in our Strathclyde chapter.

To return to Dumfries from Stranraer you must take the A75 again at least as far as Newton Stewart. This once-peaceful route is sometimes heavily trafficked with commercial vehicles for the Irish ferries. But from Newton Stewart you may strike northeast along the A712 for New Galloway, passing through part of the Glen Trool National Forest Park. Glen Trool itself lies north again, beyond the ridges of Galloway's highest hills; accessible on unclassified roads from the A714.

Scenically, the A712 is one of the Region's best roads, reminiscent in parts of the Highlands; although the large-scale afforestations on the hills and the hydroelectric dams on the lochs give the landscape more of a man-made look. These areas are well furnished with picnic places and marked nature trails, but they are among the least-frequented districts in southern Scotland. All the way to Dumfries the nearest thing you will see to a town will be a tightly-knit little cluster of cottages here and there.

East of New Galloway on the A712 an unfenced road (B794) goes south, bounding down a valley with a little stream called the Urr Water. Follow this stream through its wooded length and you will pass close to the Mote, or Motte, of Urr, an important Norman fortification. Continue through Dalbeattie, another old-fashioned little burgh, and you will reach the coast again on a typical Solway inlet (reeds, weeds and mud) near Palnackie. The 15th-century tower of Orchardton, one mile south, is circular: a unique feature for Galloway. Across the water you look towards Kippford and see the yachts and the cocktail terrace of the hotel: a sophisticated oasis in a land of rustic seclusion.

A remarkable open-air display of stone sculptures can be seen on the hillside above Shawhead (off the A75 soon after it joins the A712 to take you the final 10 miles to Dumfries). The sculptures were placed there by the local landowner, Sir William Keswick, in the 1950s and include a head by Rodin and two large groups of figures by Henry Moore.

Drumlanrig

From Dumfries there are several roads to Glasgow and Edinburgh. They follow the dales, climbing out to surmount the masses of overlapping hill ranges which separate the English border from the Forth–Clyde valley.

The A76 goes via Thornhill, a place to which, to borrow the words which the Scottish judge Lord Cockburn used of another town of the Region nearly 200 years ago, "decent characters with moderate purses might retire for quiet comfort." Chief among the stately homes with which the village is ringed is Drumlanrig Castle, a square-built, turreted, shocking-pink 17th-century palace, elegantly planted on well-manicured parkland beside the River Nith.

Happy the owner, you might imagine, who could choose such an idyllic spot and maintain such a handsome pile. But gruesome tales are told of Drumlanrig. Its builder, the first Duke of Queensberry, lived there for one night and fled. In the 18th century an idiot heir of the Queensberrys escaped from his tower prison, seized a kitchen-maid and boiled her alive in the supper cauldron. In the park are the ruins of a much older castle called Tibber's, badly knocked about by Bruce in 1311.

The inventor of the bicycle in 1842 came from Keir, two miles west of Thornhill. He was Kirkpatrick MacMillan (1813-1878), locally known as "Daft Pate." On his prototype velocipede he raced the mailcoach to Glasgow; but unluckily knocked a child down while traveling at the dangerous speed of nine miles an hour.

Grey Mare's Tail

From Thornhill the A702 goes by the Dalveen pass, an awesome defile to Elvanfoot in Strathclyde Region; and so to Edinburgh or Glasgow. The A701 is an equally fine road with dramatic changes of scenery. Moffat, 20 miles from Dumfries, sits in a bowl of the hills where several torrents splash down to form the Annan River. Roughly halfway between Carlisle and Edinburgh, this comfortable-looking small town, with its exceptionally pretty public park, makes a good touring center for the southern uplands of Scotland. Its original *raison d'être* is expressed by the statue of a ram in the square at the end of its broad main street.

At Moffat House in 1759 the literary impostor James "Ossian" MacPherson produced the Gaelic epic poems which brought him into conflict with Dr. Johnson. The road-builder John Loudon Macadam is buried in Moffat kirkyard. Robert Burns and James Boswell both came to Moffat to seek relief from their digestive troubles.

The place has a spa air, and was indeed at one period regarded as Scotland's answer to Bath, Cheltenham and other English watering-places. Other Scottish springs have been claimed as the "St. Ronan's Well" of Scott's novel of that name—but it is most likely that he had Moffat in mind. From chalybeate waters discovered in the 1780s miraculous cures of scurvy and scrofula were reported. Baths, hotels and a *kurhaus* sprang up, but suddenly Moffat's fame subsided. Possibly invalids found the remedy worse than their diseases: the taste of the waters was officially likened to "rotten eggs beaten up in the scourings of a foul gun."

Or maybe the gold rush trampled fashionable hypochondria out of existence. In 1863 a nugget containing seven grains of pure gold was exhibited in the window of Moffat's Black Bull hotel; it had been found in the Moffat Water. Prospectors, professional and amateur, descended on the town. Miners with their picks and sieves trekked down from Fife to pan the hill-burns. Quantities of yellow-grained rock were brought in. But geological analysis destroyed all dreams: the pure gold was pure iron pyrites, fool's gold. (20 miles away at Wanlockhead and Leadhills gold has been found, though in uneconomical amounts.)

However, these high settlements are also associated with another mineral. Lead was mined in the Wanlockhead/Leadhills area as early as Roman times. By the 18th century it was an important industry. Many items of this industrial heritage remain and the mining story is told in a museum. Trips into a lead mine are also available. The two villages also have the distinctions of founding the oldest subscription libraries in Britain and formerly having the highest railway line. On the wild road to Selkirk (A708) a 220-foot cataract called the Grey Mare's Tail streams down. The short path to the cascade is treacherous in wet weather, but after heavy rain a close-up view is impressive. Heed warnings at the information kiosk on the site.

Ecclefechan

The plain two-storied house where Carlyle was born stands on the main A74 (Glasgow-Carlisle road) in Ecclefechan village, nine miles north of Gretna Green. No historic site in Scotland could be more accessible, but it has the distinction of being the least-visited of all the National Trust for Scotland's properties.

Thomas Carlyle (1795-1881) is thought of, if at all, as the sage of Chelsea in London, and indeed his years of distinction were spent at 5 Cheyne Row in Chelsea. But before his *History of the French Revolution* and *Frederick the Great* established him as one of the most influential of the 19th-century philosopher-historians, he lived penuriously at Craigenputtock in the Cairn valley (B729) north of Dumfries; and before that he taught at Annan Academy (A75). In 1837 a young American admirer, Ralph Waldo Emerson, came to see him at Craigenputtock. "I found the house amid desolate heathery hills," Emerson recalled, "where the lonely scholar nourished his mighty heart . . . tall and gaunt with a cliff-like brow, holding his extraordinary powers of conversation in easy command. . . . "

Langholm

Cross the empty moorland routes of the B725 and the A709 from Ecclefechan or take the main A7 Edinburgh road from Carlisle and you arrive at Langholm, a little metropolis of the dales, strung out along the Esk River. Langholm is called the "Muckle (big) Toon"—surely for its length, certainly not for its size. But this tiny Eskdale community supports woollen mills and tweed shops; a golf course, two bowling greens and a cricket ground, all delightfully situated by the rippling mountain river; and a great Scottish rugby football team. There are four hotels, much patronized by trout fishermen.

The Langholm Monument, commemorating locally-born General John Malcolm, crowns the 1,200-foot Whita Hill above the village and is a focal point of the Langholm Common Riding, held annually on the last Friday in July: one of those picturesque Borders cavalcades which patrol the parish boundaries.

In Borders history, Langholm was the stamping-ground of Johnny Armstrong, a 16th-century desperado whose dubious activities are celebrated in popular ballads. From the Armstrongs, a name distributed throughout Eskdale, sprang the family of Neil Armstrong, the first man on the moon. When he came to be sworn a freeman of the burgh in 1972 the local mill wove a special Moon tartan for him.

Scotland's major modern poet, Hugh MacDiarmid, was born in Langholm in 1892, the son of the local postman. As was the case with Burns at Dumfries, this poet is too recently dead to be thought much of in his native town.

The main road for Edinburgh (A7), an appetizer for the romantic scenery you will feast on in the Highlands, climbs through an ever-narrowing gorge and crosses the watershed at a historic travelers' rest, the Mosspaul Inn, at around 1,600 feet. By following the Esk from Langholm on the B709 you come, after seven miles, to Westerkirk, birthplace of Thomas Telford the "Colossus of Roads." Continuing on B709 through lonely dales full of color you come to Eskdalemuir. This insignificant hamlet boasts an observatory, a meteorological station, a Tibetan center and a vast golden-roofed Buddhist temple.

Liddesdale (B6357) is another south–north thread tying England to Scotland. Ruined forts and peel towers dot the harsh landscape of the "Debatable Lands." One of them (B6399) is Hermitage Castle, a 13th-century Douglas stronghold with a long and cruel history. It still looks menacing. Newcomers to Scotland who make Hermitage their first stop will get a vivid taste of something they will get used to as they travel on: the influence of history on the landscape. In few countries of Europe has a stormy past left more indelible marks on the present.

PRACTICAL INFORMATION FOR DUMFRIES AND GALLOWAY

HOW TO GET THERE. By train. Two main inter-city railroads pass through the eastern part of the Region: Carlisle to Glasgow via Annan, Dumfries and Kirkconnel; and Carlisle to Glasgow via Lockerbie. These are the routes by which you enter the Region from London (Euston), Birmingham or Manchester. From London to Dumfries takes 5½ hours. Another railroad links Stranraer with Glasgow; on this line there are no intermediate stations in the Region.

By boat. *Sealink,* Sea Terminal, Larne, Northern Ireland (tel. 0574–73616), operate ferry services for passengers and vehicles between Larne and Stranraer, voyage time 2¼ hours; *P. & O. European Ferries,* The Harbour, Cairn Ryan (tel. 05812–276) between Cairn Ryan and Larne, voyage time 2 hours. There are up to 10 crossings a day in the tourist season.

By air. Nearest airports are actually outside the Region: Prestwick (55 miles from Stranraer) and Glasgow (82 miles).

By car. Main routes from Carlisle (Cumbria) pass through the Region on their way to Glasgow and Edinburgh. The main east–west road is the A75, Carlisle–Dumfries–Gatehouse of Fleet–Stranraer. From Newton Stewart and Stranraer in the far west there are main roads (A714 and A77) to the Clyde coast and Glasgow. Dumfries is 33 miles from Carlisle, 73 from Edinburgh, 74 from Glasgow, and 69 from Stranraer.

HOTELS AND RESTAURANTS. The Region is relatively inexpensive for accommodations and food. Standards are adequate but luxurious hotels are few. However, guest-houses have improved in recent years. Of the many restaurants in the hotels and inns on the touring routes, those we have listed below have all received good reports.

Annan (A75). *Queensberry Arms* (E), tel. 046 12–2024. 27 rooms, 24 with bath. Old-fashioned town-center inn, above average for food.

Auchencairn (off A711). **Restaurant.** *Balcary Bay* (M), tel. 055 664–217. On seashore south of Dalbeattie. Local beef, seafood, Scottish specialties. Accommodation available, 14 rooms, 12 with bath/shower.

Canonbie (A7). **Restaurant.** *Riverside Inn* (M), tel. 054 15–295. A pleasant backwater off main touring route. Trout and salmon locally caught. Home-grown vegetables. Inexpensive bar lunch.

Dumfries (A75). *Cairndale* (M), English Street (tel. 0387–54111). 60 rooms with bath. In town center. Pleasant atmosphere, excellent meals. *Station* (M), 49 Lover's Walk (tel. 0387–54316). 32 rooms, 30 with bath. A grand Victorian hotel which is a "Taste of Scotland" member.

Gatehouse of Fleet (A75). *Murray Arms* (E), tel. 055 74–207. 13 rooms with bath. Typical main-street coaching inn, expensively restored. Here, it is said, Robert Burns wrote *Scots Wha Ha'e.* Old-fashioned rooms but first-class service and imaginative cuisine. *Cally Palace* (M), tel. 055 74–341. 63 rooms with bath. Splendid Palladian house in parkland, high standard of amenities, many outdoor attractions on site. Traditional Scottish and Continental cuisine. For all its *mondaine* air, this place is warm and hospitable and has extensive leisure facilities.

Kirkcudbright (A711). *Selkirk Arms* (M), tel. 0557–30402. 16 rooms, 11 with bath/shower. Robert Burns scratched the "Selkirk Grace" on its window-panes.

Langholm (A7). *Holmwood House* (I), tel. 0541–80211. 7 rooms, 2 with bath. Exceptionally good cooking and baking; local produce, fish and steaks.

Mochrum (off A714). **Restaurant.** *Greenmantle* (M), tel. 098 87–357. Also a peaceful bed-and-breakfast stop; 7 rooms, 6 with bath/shower.

Moffat (A701). *Beechwood Country House* (M), tel. 0683–20210. 7 rooms with bath. All-round excellence in attractive surroundings. *Hartfell House* (I), tel. 0683–20153. 9 rooms. Large suburban house in small park. Chef is a "Taste of Scotland" enthusiast.

Newton Stewart (A75). *Kirroughtree House* (L), tel. 0671–2141. 22 rooms with bath. Lovely house in landscaped gardens, loaded with rich furnishings. Children, pets and wild parties understandably frowned on. Elaborate cuisine.

Port William (A747). *Corsemalzie House* (E), tel. 098 886–254. 15 rooms with bath. Peaceful country house; "Taste of Scotland" member.

Portpatrick (A75). *Knockinaam Lodge* (L), tel. 077 681–471. 10 rooms with bath. Victorian country house set in 30 acres with lawns sloping to beach. New owners (1987) have achieved accolade for restaurant, where formality rules—i.e., jacket and tie.

Rockcliffe (off A710). *Baron's Craig* (E), tel. 055 663–225. 27 rooms, 20 with bath. On coast south of Dalbeattie near lively yachting center. A large 19th-century house of character in spacious grounds.

Sandyhills (A710). **Restaurant.** *Granary* (I), tel. 038 778–663. On coast road west of Dumfries. Excellent home-cooked kitchen-garden produce. Home-made puddings in lieu of ubiquitous "sweet trolley." Bar lunch good value, but nothing exciting about the wine list.

Stranraer (A77). *North West Castle* (M), tel. 0776–4413. 77 rooms with bath. Historic house with Arctic exploration connections, hence the name. High standard of comfort and amenities. Curling holidays offered.

Whithorn, Isle of (A750). **Restaurant.** *Queen's Arms,* (I), tel. 098 85–369. An old inn on remote but popular harbor. Fish, lobster, Galloway beef, regional cheeses. "Taste of Scotland" member.

HOW TO GET ABOUT. By car. Communications through the Region are swift: long, fast stretches of roadway, few towns. You can hire a self-drive automobile from *Burgess Motor Services,* North Strand Street, Stranraer (tel. 0776–2451) or *Godfrey Davis Europcar,* Rosefield Mills, Dumfries (tel. 0387–56393).

By bus. The bus network is comprehensive and in summer there are many excursions on offer, both daily and for longer periods, from the Bus Station, Whitesands, Dumfries.

TOURIST INFORMATION. The local centers, open daily, Apr.–Sept., are: Castle Douglas, Dalbeattie, Dumfries, Gatehouse of Fleet, Gretna, Kirkcudbright, Langholm, Moffat, Newton Stewart and Stranraer. They operate booking services for local accommodations. Opening hours can vary (and change frequently) so for accurate information check notice on door of information center.

The Information Center, Dashwood Square, Newton Stewart, is open daily: 9.30–6, Apr.–Jun. and Sept.; 9.30–8, Jul.–Aug.; and 10–4, Oct. The National Information Center at Port Rodie, Stranraer, is open daily 10–6.30, Jun.–Sept.; weekdays 10–5 and Sun. 10–4, May and Oct.; and weekdays 10–5, Nov.–Apr. The offices sometimes close for an hour at lunchtime. The National Trust for Scotland operates an information service at Threave Gardens, open daily 9.30–7, Apr.–Oct. At Carsphairn on the A713 there is a tourist information noticeboard.

For visitors heading toward the Region on the M6 in England there is an Information Bureau at Southwaite (Cumbria), 8 miles south of Carlisle.

FISHING. The rivers of the Region, especially the Annan, Cairn, Cree, Esk, Nith and Urr, are very good for salmon, sea trout and brown trout. Hotels at Beattock (A74), Canonbie (A7), Gatehouse of Fleet, Moffat, New Galloway and Newton Stewart have their neighboring beats and offer fishing to non-residents for £3 or so per day, £6 or so if hire of boat is involved. The small lochs and reservoirs of Galloway's highlands are stocked with brown trout. The Newton Stewart Angling Association, Arthur Street, Newton Stewart, controls many of them and issues daily and weekly permits. Permits for fishing the Water of Ken and large Clatteringshaws Loch may be obtained from the Ken Bridge Hotel, New Galloway (A712). The average rate for permits is £2.50 per day.

North and south of New Galloway the natural and artificial loch and river systems attract pike, perch and roach anglers. For coarse fishing permits, about £1 per day; contact hotels, grocery store or post office at New Galloway.

The Solway Firth is good for cod, bass and flatfish. Kippford (off A710), Kirkcudbright (A711), Port William (A747), Portpatrick (A77) and parts of Loch Ryan near Stranraer (A77) are becoming sea angling centers of a casual and informal nature: go down to the harbor and ask the first weatherbeaten sea-dog you meet! Tackle, bait and boats are always available Jun.–Sept. at Isle of Whithorn where there are good rock marks and sheltered waters. Boatwork generally is for experts: the coast is notorious for reefs, strong tidal streams and shifting sands.

GOLF. The Golf Coast (see Strathclyde chapter) ends north of this Region, but Stranraer and the Rhinns of Galloway have their courses, as do most towns along the south shore from Wigtown (A714) to Annan (A75). Dumfries has two courses with the usual amenities, around £3.50 per day, book in advance if possible. Moffat (A701) and Thornhill (A76) have attractive 18-hole courses. Elsewhere golf courses are nine-hole or nonexistent.

HISTORIC HOUSES AND GARDENS. Long ago, when the Maxwells and Douglases ruled the land from Annan Water to "bonnie Doon," a lengthy chapter might have been written on the once-formidable stately homes of Dumfries and Galloway. But the medieval castles are now empty shells, and, sad to say, the Region is no longer rich in living, visitable properties.

Drumlanrig Castle, Thornhill (A76, 4 miles north). Imposing house and grounds. Notable collection of paintings, furniture, plate. One silver chandelier weighs 120 pounds. Open May–Aug., weekdays (closed Fri. in May and June), 1.30–4.15 (11–4.15 in Aug.); Sun. 2–5.15.

Ellisland Farm, Holywood, Dumfries (A76, 7 miles north). The farm Burns rented 1788–91. House and granary sympathetically restored. Open at all reasonable times. Groups phone 0387–74426 in advance.

Castle Kennedy Gardens, Stranraer (A75, 4 miles east). Nationally famous garden with rhododendrons, azaleas, magnolias and many tender species. "Monkey Puzzle Avenue" one of the longest in Scotland. Open Apr.–Sept., daily 10–5.

Maclellan's Castle, Kirkcudbright (A711). Atmospheric ruin of a great Jacobean house. Open Apr.–Sept., weekdays 9.30–7, Sun. 2–7; Oct.–Mar., weekdays 9.30–4, Sun. 2–4.

If great houses are few, the gardens of the flowery southwest—and public parks—are rich and colorful. **Threave** near Castle Douglas is where the National Trust for Scotland trains its gardeners. The house, a pseudo-baronial extravaganza, is a school where soil science and plant genetics are taught; it has a two-way student exchange link with Longwood Gardens in Pennsylvania. There are rose gardens, rock gardens and heather and woodland gardens laid out in 65 acres. A Visitor Center has interpretative displays. Gardens open daily 9–sunset, glasshouses daily 9–5; Visitor Center Apr.–Oct., daily 9–6; tearoom Apr.–Oct., daily 10–5.

Other gardens frequently open are the **Meadowsweet Herb Garden,** Soulseat, Castle Kennedy and **Glenwhan Garden,** Dunraggit; **Arbigland,** Kirkbean (A710), where John Paul Jones worked as a boy; **Ardwell House,** Stranraer (off A716), and **Lochinch,** Stranraer (A75), two splendid azalea and rhododendron gardens best seen in late May and early June; **Galloway House,** Garlieston (B7004 south of Wigtown), with fine trees and shrubs round a severely classical mid-18th-century house. Finally, **Logan Botanic Garden** near Port Logan is an outstation of the Royal Botanic Garden in Edinburgh and contains many warm temperate plant species. Open Apr.–Sept., daily, 10–5.

MUSEUMS. Several towns and rural centers in Galloway and Dumfries Region have interesting local museums and art exhibitions. The following selection should be of general interest.

Burns' House, Burns Street, Dumfries (A756). The house where Robert Burns died in 1796. Period furnishings and relics of the poet. Open Apr.–Sept., weekdays 10–1 and 2–7, Sun. 2–7; Oct.–Mar., Tues.–Sat. 10–12 and 2–5.

Carlyle's Birthplace, Ecclefechan (A74). A neat cottage appropriately furnished. Manuscripts and relics of the historian. Open Apr.–Oct., weekdays 12.30–5 or by appointment (tel. 057 63–666). N.T.S.

Creetown Gem Rock Museum, Creetown (A75). Wide-ranging collection of gems and minerals including fascinating "fluorescing" display. Also gemstone cutting workshop. Open daily, Easter–Sept., 9.30–7; Oct.–Easter, 9.30–5.

Deer Museum, Clatteringshaws (A712 west of New Galloway). A Forestry Commission display covering red deer, wild goats and other regional fauna. Nearby is a reconstructed Romano-British homestead. A short woodland walk away is a memorial stone recalling a Bruce victory in the Scots Wars of Independence. Museum open Apr.–Sept., daily, 10–6.

Famous Old Blacksmith's Shop, Gretna Green (A74). Marriage registers, documents relating to elopements, a collection of horse-drawn carriages. Open Apr.–Oct., daily, 9 in morn. to 10 at night.

Maxwelton House Museum, Moniaive (B729). Pageant of domestic life from 14th century. Birthplace of Annie Laurie. Open May–Sept., Wed., Thurs., and last Sun. of month, 2–5.

Museum of Scottish Lead Mining, Goldscaur Row, Wanlockhead (B797). Indoor museum with wide range of mining artifacts and displays. Also outdoor trail past beam engines, mine sites, smelt mill and other sites of activity. Excursions into mine-shaft also available. Open Apr.–Oct., daily, 11–4. Mine tours 11–3.30.

Newton Stewart Museum, York Road, Newton Stewart (A75). Life of the town and Machars district down the ages. Reconstructed forge, kitchens, laundry, schoolroom. A recent and growing museum. Open Apr.–Sept., weekdays only, 2–5.30, July–Sept., also Sun. 2–5.

Samye-Ling Tibetan Centre, Eskdalemuir (B709). Oldest Tibetan study-and-meditation center in western world, located among lonely, damp, and muddy pastures. A magnificent golden-roof Buddhist temple is steadily assuming Kinkaju-like proportions. Visitors made welcome to craft workshops and study sessions. No smoking. A small donation is appropriate. Open daily 9–12.30, 1.30–6 and 6.30–8, but choose a dry day.

Stewartry Museum, St. Mary Street, Kirkcudbright (A711). Historical material including John Paul Jones relics. Open Apr.–Oct., weekdays, 10–1 and 2–4.

Whithorn Priory and Museum, Whithorn (A746). Medieval ruins, early Christian crosses and carvings, large-scale excavations in progress, also additional displays following successful dig to uncover remains of first Scottish church. Open Apr.–Sept., weekdays 9.30–7, Sun. 2–7; Oct.–Mar., weekdays 9.30–4, Sun. 2–4.

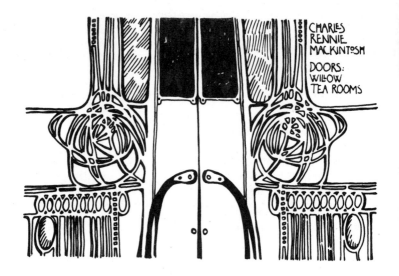

CHARLES
RENNIE
MACKINTOSH

DOORS:
WILLOW
TEA ROOMS

HEARTLAND OF INDUSTRY

Glasgow

"Surely they're not going to slide that great ship into that trout stream?" a guest at the launching of the 80,000 ton *Queen Elizabeth* was heard to say. The workaday part of the Clyde, before it enters the Firth (which we describe in the Strathclyde chapter), is remarkable for its extreme narrowness. The double line of navigational buoys marks a channel only a few hundred yards wide and the buoys look gigantic. This part of the Clyde was once a sandy salmon river, shallow enough to wade across. Glasgow put it to work by making a canal out of it, to bring the tobacco and sugar clippers into the heart of the city and begin an era of prosperity. Hence the saying: "Glasgow made the Clyde and the Clyde made Glasgow."

In Glasgow, the river presents a dismal foreshore to its Firth, with no hint of the stunning scenery on which it is to open. Here are Clydebank, Renfrew, Govan, with Dumbarton, Port Glasgow and Greenock in the widening estuary, all formerly playing their part in this major Scottish shipbuilding workshop, now greatly in decline. Where the communities once rang with the riveters' hammers, the talk now is of "diversification" and "urban renewal"—of which the recent Glasgow Garden Festival was just one symbol. The old days have gone for good. For five and a half years in World War II the five miles below Glasgow called Clydeside built and repaired 13 ships every day. But things are quieter now.

Where the docks, basins and slipways congregate round the black and sluggish river, two centuries of war and commerce, adventure and exploration have begun. James Watt of Greenock solved the problems of steam propulsion in 1765. Henry Bell in 1812 offered Scotland the world's first steamship service in his three-horsepower *Comet,* every lawful day (that was, not Sundays) from Glasgow to Greenock. There is an obelisk to Henry Bell near Bowling (A82) and the timbers from his *Comet* paddlewheeler, eventually wrecked in the Firth of Lorne, are laid in the floor of the Queen's Hotel at Helensburgh (A814). The ship's flywheel stands in Helensburgh's Hermitage Park.

Glasgow's dockland was a cradle of disaffection in periods of economic depression. In the early 1930s the legend of "Red Clydeside" was born and the district returned Communist members to the Westminster parliament. But Clydeside has now turned to the "sunrise" industries, such as electronics, in hopes of economic salvation. Historic yards which built battleships and liners for the maritime nations of the world have diversified, not always successfully, into special jobs for gas and oil seabed exploration. Within the city of Glasgow itself, many of the former quays and docks have gone—developments such as the Scottish Exhibition Centre take their place.

No Mean City

Glasgow, with nearly a million inhabitants, is the biggest city in Scotland and the third biggest (after London and Birmingham) in Britain. Writers of earlier periods, even up to the late 18th century, rarely failed to admire her neat, well-paved streets and well-built houses and the way the salmon leapt up the rapids of the crystal-clear Clyde on their passage through the city. Later the picture changed. The river was dredged and deepened. Industry crowded its banks. A large influx of peasants from Ireland and the Highlands did not settle down too happily. Scandals arose in public affairs, slum districts spread out from the lower waterfronts, dirt and soot (made worse by the steady drizzling rain which Glasgow knows so well) painted layers of ugliness on an urban scene which had become a chaotic mass of unplanned streets and factories.

Until fairly recently Glasgow has been a byword for civic corruption, petty gangsterdom and abysmal squalor. If you have read the novel *No Mean City* by Alexander MacArthur (who ended up taking poison and throwing himself in the Clyde) or seen the ballet *Miracle in the Gorbals,* you will already have a picture of Glasgow which you might have recognized as you walked her streets any time in the first half of this century.

Things are different now. There are black spots. There are some areas of inner and outer urban deprivation, some skylines of factory chimneys and concrete cooling towers and shabby high-rise apartment blocks; some waste ground and blank walls frescoed with aerosol. But you can walk through the infamous Gorbals and wonder when you are coming to the Gorbals and your lasting impression of that quarter may be of the graceful suspension bridge over the Clyde, the fine Victorian facades of Carlton Place and the gardens which slope to the river.

Glasgow has 260 parks and areas of public gardens, more per head of population than any other European city. She extends over 16 hills (at least, there are 16 Hill Streets in different areas) and she throws 15 bridges over the Clyde, not counting those above Rutherglen, outside the main downtown area.

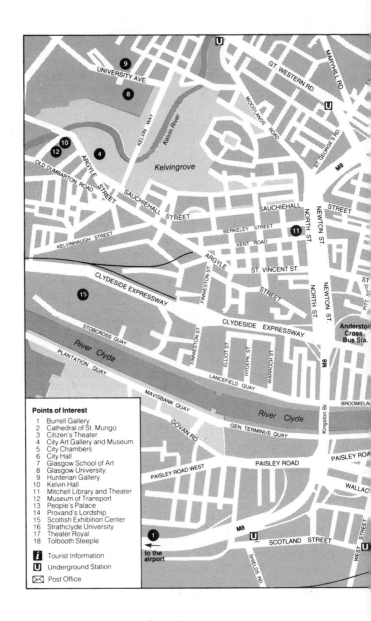

Points of Interest

1   Burrell Gallery
2   Cathedral of St. Mungo
3   Citizen's Theater
4   City Art Gallery and Museum
5   City Chambers
6   City Hall
7   Glasgow School of Art
8   Glasgow University
9   Hunterian Gallery
10 Kelvin Hall
11 Mitchell Library and Theater
12 Museum of Transport
13 People's Palace
14 Provand's Lordship
15 Scottish Exhibition Center
16 Strathclyde University
17 Theater Royal
18 Tolbooth Steeple

i Tourist Information
U Underground Station
✉ Post Office

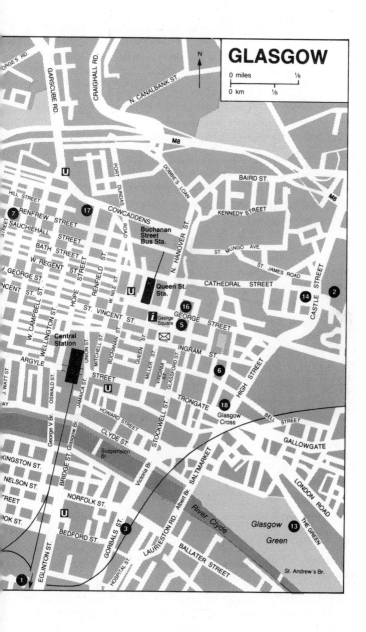

River of Glasgow

Since we came in on the river, let us continue upstream through the heart of the city. No boat can take us, unless we are among those dozens of rowing-club members who ruffle the surface night and morning. No paddle-steamer will carry us "doon the watter" from the Broomielaw landing-stage as once it did: new bridges prevent ships coming into town. But promenades and walkways are pushing among derelict warehouses and one day it will be possible to walk the Clyde on either bank from Renfrew Castle to Rutherglen and beyond.

Near Old Kilpatrick (A814), 11 miles from the city center, the Erskine road bridge (toll) replaces a fond old landmark, the Erskine ferry. The next road crossing, going upstream, is the Clyde tunnel; actually it's two tunnels, one for northbound and one for southbound traffic.

Renfrew and Govan, just above the tunnel, are the first of the shipyard complexes. For all their cheap and dingy housing they are ancient settlements. Renfrew is the cradle of the royal house of Stuart: Walter the Steward acquired his first Scottish lands there in the 13th century. The Inchinnan church, one mile west of the town center, stands on 800-year-old foundations and in the churchyard there are Celtic stones, tombs of the crusading Templars and several "mortsafes"—iron cages built over graves to deter body-snatchers. Govan's kirkyard too has Celtic crosses and monuments. Here the numerous bridges of central Glasgow begin. You can see Glasgow University—founded 1451, not here but in the High Street farther east—on the more respectable north side, above large buildings which include the city art gallery and museum, and Kelvin Hall, the largest covered arena in Scotland. Round them flows the Kelvin River through the park called Kelvingrove, down to the Clyde. In 1967 salmon reappeared in the Kelvin, giving hopes that antipollution measures were succeeding; but the environmentalists still have a lot of work on their hands.

If the river is not too clean, at least it flows fast, swerving among gentle hills. You may walk its banks for four miles without more than a distant glimpse of buildings, passing through Glasgow's botanic gardens. The large palm-house, Kibble Palace, once did duty as an assembly hall where Disraeli and Gladstone, 19th-century Prime Ministers, delivered their election addresses to the Scottish nation.

Near the Kelvin's confluence with the Clyde is a system of crescents and terraces which would not look out of place in the New Town of Edinburgh.

Charles Rennie Mackintosh

If we leave the Clyde and climb through those terraces we shall soon be within sight of Renfrew Street, which runs parallel with a famous thoroughfare, now partly pedestrianized, called Sauchiehall Street.

Cultural tourists and architectural students in Glasgow give Renfrew Street a high priority. There stands the prestigious Glasgow School of Art, the creation of Glasgow-born Charles Rennie Mackintosh. The building incorporates the Mackintosh Library. Like the Adam brothers 150 years before him, Mackintosh also designed the furniture and interior decor for his buildings, to make them one harmonious whole.

When he died in 1928 his name was scarcely known, least of all in Scotland. Now he is confirmed as a distinguished innovator in art and architecture. Other examples of Mackintosh buildings and decor in Glasgow, all visitable, include the church at Queen's Cross (now the Charles Rennie Mackintosh Society headquarters), the former *Glasgow Herald* and *Daily Record* buildings at Mitchell Street and Renfrew Lane, the Ruchill church hall off Maryhill Road, the Ingram Street tearoom on Miller Street and the Willow Tearoom on Sauchiehall Street (now a hotel and a gift shop/café respectively), and Scotland Street school off Shields Road. Notable examples of his private houses include Windyhill and Mosside at Kilmacolm (A761) and Redclyffe in Balgrayhill Road.

The Merchant City

Glasgow has a long tradition of commerce and entrepreneurial flair. Seemingly saddled with an unsavory image by the 1970s, the city drew on its resources of pride and enterprise, in spite of an unfavorable economic climate, to build itself a new reputation and a new environment for resident and visitor alike.

It turned to its legacy of Victorian (and older) buildings and preserved or cleaned up those which had escaped the developers' mistakes of the 1960s. The symbol of this renewal is the area south of George Square, down as far as Argyle Street. This is known as the Merchant City, a name recalling some of Glasgow's early businessmen: the tobacco barons, who made their fortunes trading with the Americas.

From being a run-down, faded grid of streets with old warehousing and almost no residents, the Merchant City has been turned into a wide-awake community of small businesses and interesting shops, cafes, restaurants and also, importantly, people who live locally. All this has been done while preserving the integrity of the city environment. Buzzing and buoyant, this is the face of Glasgow which has confounded its critics.

"Dear Old Glasgow Toon"

We may continue along a riverside path to Rutherglen Bridge and on through Motherwell and Wishaw, the steel and coal towns. But it is not tourist country. Though we shall meet the Clyde again in more salubrious surroundings, for the present our route takes us uptown from Glasgow Green into the crisscross pattern of streets which constitutes the commercial, shopping and historic nucleus of "dear old Glasgow toon."

The Glasgow comedian Will Fyffe had a song in which those words occurred. And Glasgow is indeed dear to her inhabitants. Like some other ugly cities, the redeeming features of Glasgow are the warmth, cheerfulness and wry humor of the citizens and their love for their town, with all its faults. Once you have penetrated the accent, Glaswegians are the wittiest and most outgoing of all Scots. They do not sneer at culture either. Glasgow has one of the best civic collections of European paintings in Britain.

The Burrell art treasures, the nation's finest private collection and gathered by a magpie millionaire, were given to Glasgow in 1945. In 1983 a specially-built gallery in Pollok Park, three miles south of the city center and imaginatively set in a woodland framework, was completed and opened by the Queen. The collection is especially rich in medieval tapestries, stained-glass and furniture, as well as Oriental ceramics and European pictures. The Burrell Gallery was chosen as Britain's "Museum of the Year" in 1985. Glasgow is also the headquarters of the Scottish Opera and Scottish Ballet Companies and the Scottish National Orchestra. The renaissance continues, and the city has been chosen as European City of Culture for 1990.

Historic Glasgow

Glasgow's original settlement was around the Cathedral and High Street area. In the 18th-century economic expansion, this medieval center was to some extent left out in the cold as the emphasis swung westward. The merchants built grand houses, and developed warehousing and manufacturing centers on the rural grazings (recalled in surviving names such as Goosedubs). These were the original "dear green places" referred to in the meaning of the name Glasgow. But traces of old Glasgow still remain: beyond the Tolbooth steeple (1626) and modern Mercat Cross at the intersection called Glasgow Cross, you come to the High Street and the Old College, original site of Glasgow University, today reduced to a couple of plaques outside a railroad freight yard. But if you visit the present University in Kelvingrove, have a look at the porter's lodge which is built with stones from the original foundation.

In Castle Street, a continuation of the High Street, stands the house called Provand's Lordship. Built in 1471, it is probably Glasgow's oldest dwelling and it is believed that Kings James II and IV and Mary Queen of Scots lodged there at various times. It was a church house attached to Glasgow Cathedral and inhabited by a prebendary of Provand, the old name for the parish of Barlanark. Northwards again, near the disused Monkland Canal (off B806) stands Provan Hall (also 15th century), twin buildings on a courtyard, once the country retreat of the same prebendary. Both houses are open to the public.

Opposite Provand's Lordship you see the Cathedral, the only large Scottish church apart from St. Magnus Cathedral in Orkney to have survived the Reformation intact. It is dedicated to Glasgow's patron saint, Mungo (sometimes also known as St. Kentigern) and is said to stand on the site where that wandering monk built his humble chapel on the banks of the Molendinar Burn: the beginnings of Glasgow. The chapel has gone, the Molendinar is piped underground, the plain Gothic 12th- to 14th-century Cathedral itself has lost its main bell-tower and undergone changes for the worse . . . but the crypt, consecrated in 1197, adorned now with murals of the legends of St. Mungo, is worth a visit.

Castle Street and the High Street may well be the oldest thoroughfares in Scotland. A document refers to the existence in 540 of this route between Clyde and St. Mungo's chapel, a pathway known as the "King's Highway."

Glasgow's civic arms originate in a typical St. Mungo legend. The King of Strathclyde gave his wife a ring which she was rash enough to present to an admirer. The King obtained it by a ruse and threw it in the Clyde, then asked his wife what she had done with it. In her distress the Queen went to her confessor, St. Mungo, and asked his advice. He instructed her to fish in the river and—surprise!—the first salmon she landed had the

ring in its jaws. If you study the Glasgow coat-of-arms you will see that
the supporters are three salmon, one with a ring in its mouth.

Let Glasgow Flourish!

Inheriting the flair and confidence of the 18th-century developers, the
Victorians built yet more ebullient public buildings and laid out areas such
as George Square, with its magnificent City Chambers in sumptuous Italian Renaissance style. Major shopping streets—probably the most varied
in Scotland—lie to the south and west.

Central Glasgow, starting from George Square (with Queen Street Station nearby) is, in fact, best discovered on foot, not just for its shops but
for its architectural gems. However, it means looking at eye-level at shop-
windows and at the same time into the sky for some of the architectural
features—such as the dome of the Merchants' House, with its golden sailing ship, or the impressive spire of Hutchesons' Hall, west of Scotland
headquarters for the National Trust for Scotland.

In Virginia Street you should look for the former tobacco exchange or
auction house, now well-disguised as part of an antiques complex, while
two blocks eastwards you will find the impressive colonnaded facade of
the former Royal Exchange, now Stirling's Library. (On the subject of libraries, you should note that Glasgow's Mitchell Library, financed by another tobacco lord, is Europe's largest public reference library.)

Modern commerce is represented by the magnificent Glasgow Stock Exchange, which its Victorian architect designed in Venetian Gothic style.
All of these buildings, which add so much to the dignified aspect of "downtown" Glasgow, are only minutes from George Square, the center of the
city. So also are shopping streets such as Buchanan Street, Sauchiehall
Street and Argyle Street, all at least partly pedestrianized.

"A Dear Green Place"

"All Glasgow needs," said an architectural pundit, "is a bath and a little
loving care." She is getting her bath; even the Clyde is getting a bath and
one day we shall see riverside drives comparable to those along the Seine
in Paris and the Danube in Budapest; glass-canopied river boats are already promised. One day Glasgow may be again the "dear green place"
which the word is supposed to mean.

The city aspires to be a tourist center, having now acquired what she
has long lacked, some first-class city-center hotels. She is ringed with
splendid scenery and has always been a wonderful starting point for day
trips: Loch Lomond half an hour; Clyde coast 40 minutes; Trossachs 50
minutes.

If you still feel that Glasgow is not for you, remember that the best
urban expressway in Britain soars across the city and you may traverse
the whole conurbation east to west without meeting a stop light.

PRACTICAL INFORMATION FOR GLASGOW

GETTING INTO TOWN FROM THE AIRPORTS. A frequent express coach service links Glasgow airport with all major bus and rail termini in the city. From the airport to Buchanan Street bus station takes 25 minutes and costs £1. There are also bus and rail services several times a day between Prestwick international airport and central Glasgow. (For timetables contact the Anderston Cross bus station or Buchanan Street Travel Center.) The bus fare for the 33-mile journey (70 minutes) is £3 by Citylink, £7 by airport bus. Taxis are available from both airports. Expect to pay around £7 from Glasgow airport and £30 from Prestwick.

Remember that in general the service buses, such as Citylink and city transport, are far cheaper than other forms of transport.

HOTELS. The city is now better equipped with hotels of all categories than it has ever been—but that is not saying much. Glasgow was historically a very poor oasis for the traveler. Nonetheless there are now some big city-center hotels of both expensive and moderate character and some good and reasonable small hotels and guest-houses in the suburbs, with easy transportation into town. A feature of Glasgow's hotels is the excellent breakfasts, normally included in the price of the room. All the larger hotels have restaurants which are open to non-residents.

When calling from outside Glasgow, prefix numbers with the code 041.

Deluxe

Albany, Bothwell Street (tel. 248 2656). 254 rooms with bath. Glasgow's newest hotel, centrally situated. Its two restaurants are highly praised.

Burnside, East Kilbride Road (tel. 634 1276). 16 rooms, 8 with bath. Some distance from center, but highly rated for all round quality.

Crest, 377 Argyle Street (tel. 248 2355). 121 rooms with bath. New construction on main shopping thoroughfare. Traditional Scottish and vegetarian options in restaurant.

Holiday Inn, Argyle Street (tel. 226 5577). 296 rooms with bath. Another city-center innovation of the most up-to-date kind. Has French restaurant, coffee shop and terrace buffet.

Hospitality Inn and Convention Centre, 36 Cambridge Street (tel. 332 2311). 316 rooms with bath. This place, the largest hotel in Scotland, is centrally located. Single occupancy costs little more than half double.

One Devonshire Gardens, off Great Western Road (tel. 339 2001). 8 elegant apartments with bath in fine town mansion. Sumptuous meals. Dinner, costing £35 or so with superior wine, may consist of inhouse pheasant terrine, globe artichokes, salmon and lobster cream and magnificent fillet steaks.

Moderate

Beacons, 7 Park Terrace (tel. 332 9438). 36 rooms with bath. Quiet and dignified hotel overlooking rustic Kelvingrove Park yet close to main downtown area.

Central, Gordon Street (tel. 221 9680). 219 rooms, 167 with bath. Typical Victorian railroad hotel with thick carpets, mob-capped chambermaids and ample rooms from another era. Its *Entresol* restaurant is a noteworthy rendezvous for breakfast, lunch and dinner.

Ingram, 201 Ingram Street (tel. 248 4401). 90 rooms with bath. In a city center street restricted for space. Business people crowd its public rooms. A friendly, well-run place.

Kirklee, 11 Kensington Gate (tel. 334 5555). 11 rooms with bath. Quiet district near University. Owners take a real pride.

Pond, Great Western Road (tel. 334 8161). 137 rooms with bath. The pond it overlooks is no Loch Lomond but it is well sited for heading that way.

Sherbrooke Castle, Sherbrooke Avenue (tel. 427 4227). 9 rooms with bath. Old-established and very respectable. Close to western parklands. Not a real castle.

Tinto Firs, 470 Kilmarnock Road (tel. 637 2353). 27 rooms with bath. More country-house than city style, on park-like south side but handy for center. Good reports of food and room furnishings.

Wickets, 52 Fortrose Street (tel. 334 9334). 9 rooms, 5 with bath. Good reports of this small establishment in a quiet neighborhood; elegant furnishings and impressive range of amenities.

Inexpensive

Crookston, 90 Crookston Road (tel. 882 6142). 23 rooms, 10 with bath. Quiet atmosphere. Food writers have praised generous cuisine.

Hazelcourt, 232 Renfrew Street (tel. 332 7737). 9 rooms. Better-than-average rooms, friendly staff, but best to eat out.

Marie Stuart, 46 Queen Mary Avenue (tel. 424 3939). 31 rooms, 9 with bath. Excellent service, popular bar.

Queen's Park, 10 Balvicar Drive (tel. 423 1123). 30 rooms, 18 with bath. Good all-round standard, flexible meal hours.

Smith's, 963 Sauchiehall Street (tel. 339 6363). 26 rooms. Not highly rated for food but otherwise comfortable and conveniently situated. No evening meals.

Guest Houses

Belle Vue Guest House, 163 Hamilton Road (tel. 778 1077). 12 rooms, 1 with bath. Rather out of the way but reasonable value for modest price.

Chez Nous Guest House, 33 Hillhead Street (tel. 334 2977). 18 rooms. Attentive staff, imaginative menu, meals until 9.30 P.M. (many guest houses serve only high tea in evenings).

McLays Guest House, 268 Renfrew Street (tel. 332 4796). 38 rooms, 15 with bath. Family-run, friendly guest house in central position.

Student Halls of Residence

Accommodations at around £11.50 to £19.50 per night bed and breakfast per person are offered at the city's educational establishments during vacation periods, usually a month at Easter and three months in summer. Single and double rooms are available. No lunches, but dinner may be taken for an extra £6 to £8. Rooms are bright and modern, but bathroom facilities must be shared. Applications are made to the Warden of each establishment.

Baird, Clyde and Forbes Halls, University of Strathclyde, 73 Rottenrow East (tel. 552 4400). 417 rooms. In city center. Three separate halls, 2 open all year.

College Hostel, Jordanhill College, 76 Southbrae Drive (tel. 959 1232). 172 rooms. Apr., July–Sept. only.

Dalrymple Hall, Glasgow University, 22 Belhaven Terrace West (tel. 339 5271). 133 rooms. Easter and summer.

Queen Margaret Hall, Glasgow University, 55 Bellshaugh Road (tel. 334 2192). 345 rooms, nearly all single. Meals highly rated. Easter and June–Sept.

Wolfson Hall, Maryhill Road (tel. 946 5252). 231 rooms. Easter and July–Sept.

Glasgow University has other accommodations in west and central locations, including the self-catering **Maclay Hall.** For information contact the Accommodation Office, 52 Hillhead Street, Glasgow G12 8QJ (tel. 334 3020).

Youth Hostels

The **Scottish Youth Hostels Association,** 10 Woodlands Terrace (off Uddington Road), Glasgow G3 6DD (tel. 332 3004) offers hostel accommodation in various parts of the city and suburbs at £3 to £5.50 per night.

HOW TO GET ABOUT. By bus. Glasgow and suburbs are served by a comprehensive network of city buses, fares averaging 10p–15p per mile. Short journeys to outer suburbs begin at Anderston Cross (tel. 248 7432) and Buchanan Street (tel. 332 7133) bus stations. The former serves west and south, the latter north and east. Buses for Glasgow airport leave from both stations. Day and half-day tours in and around Glasgow on city buses start from St. Enoch Square.

By subway. Glasgow's Underground (subway), built when Victoria was Queen, was completely modernized and reopened in 1979. It consists of a circle embracing the city center and going under the Clyde. Two of its 15 stations give access to British Rail stations: Queen Street on the east and Partick on the west. Fares average 20p between stations.

There are surface rail connections between central Glasgow and the suburbs with very frequent commuter services. Queen Street station serves five routes to west, north and east; Central station nine routes to west and south. A bus service links the two stations.

By taxi. Glasgow's taxis are like London's and Edinburgh's; black and old-fashioned-looking with yellow TAXI signs on their high roofs. When the TAXI light is on the vehicle is available for hire. Taxis cruise the city and there are ranks at all rail and bus stations and in the principal squares. Fares for one adult passenger are 80p for the first mile and 60p thereafter (90p outside city boundary, e.g. to airport), with a 15p per mile surcharge between midnight and 6 A.M. Additional passengers pay 10p each, however short or long the journey.

By car. Unlike Edinburgh, Glasgow is well organized for the motorist. The trans-city expressway has removed much through traffic and parking is easy in most central districts except around George Square, where it is controlled and parking meters are extensively used. There are multi-story parks open 24 hours a day at Anderston Cross, Cambridge Street,

George Street, Mitchell Street, Port Dundas Road and Waterloo Street; and many short-term carparks.

By boat. New Clyde bridges have sealed off central Glasgow's river from all but light craft. In summer there are down-river cruises from Stobcross Quay.

TOURIST INFORMATION. Head Post Office, George Square (tel. 242 4545). Canadian Consulate, 195 West George Street (tel. 204 1373). (The American Consulate is in Edinburgh.) Customs & Excise, 21 India Street (tel. 221 3828). British Airways, 66 Gordon Street (tel. 332 9666). British Rail passenger enquiries and sleeper reservations (tel. 204 2844, 24-hour service).

The principal Information Bureau is at 35–39 St. Vincent Place, tel. 227 4880. Guidebooks, maps, calendars of events and timetables are supplied. You may book accommodations here for Glasgow or other parts of Scotland. Open Jun.–Sept. weekdays 9–9, Sun. 2–9, Oct.–May weekdays only, 9–5.

Remember that if you are calling a Glasgow number from anywhere outside the Glasgow area you must prefix it with the Glasgow code 041.

MUSEUMS. Burrell Gallery, Pollok Park. New building housing famous arts and crafts collection. Open weekdays 10–5, Sun. 2–5.

City Art Gallery and Museum, Kelvingrove. Magnificent fine arts collection, notable displays of silver, jewelry, ceramics, arms and armor. Open weekdays 10–5, Sun. 2–5.

Haggs Castle, 100 St. Andrew's Drive. Museum of social history, emphasis on children at work and play through the centuries. Activities for young visitors. Open weekdays 10–5, Sun. 2–5.

Hunterian Museum, Glasgow University, 82 Hillhead Street. Geology, archeology. Incorporates *Art Gallery* (Rembrandt, Chardin, Whistler) and Charles Rennie Mackintosh House (interiors and art works from the designer's Glasgow home). Open weekdays 9.30–5, Sat. 9.30–1; Mackintosh House closed lunchtime.

Museum of Transport, Kelvin Hall, Dumbarton Road. Trains, buses, bicycles, streetcars, horse-drawn vehicles and model ships. Old subway station. History of Scottish automobile industry. Open weekdays 10–5, Sun. 2–5.

People's Palace, Glasgow Green. A 100-year-old city museum illustrating textiles and shipbuilding, feminist movement, landmarks of Glasgow's political and cultural history. Open weekdays 10–5, Sun. 2–5.

Pollok House, 2060 Pollokshaws Road. An Adam mansion in parkland, housing important fine arts. Open weekdays 10–5, Sun. 2–5.

Springburn Museum, Ayr Street. Local museum recalling Springburn's days as world's largest loco building center. Open Mon.–Fri. 10.30–5, Sat. 10–1, Sun. 2–5.

Third Eye Centre, 350 Sauchiehall Street. Continuous exhibitions and music recitals, concerts etc. Open Tues.–Sat. 10–5.30, Sun. 2–5.30.

ENTERTAINMENT AND NIGHTLIFE. Theaters. Glasgow is home to the Scottish Opera, the Scottish Ballet and the Scottish National Orchestra. There are winter and spring performances in the *City Hall* and the *Theatre Royal* (which a leading music critic has described as "the most enchanting opera theater in the United Kingdom"). The huge *Kelvin Hall* stages promenade concerts in June, noted for their informality and the enthusiasm of a young audience. The B.B.C. Scottish Symphony Orchestra plays in the *Henry Wood Hall,* Claremont Street.

There are other theaters: the *King's* for light entertainment and musicals; the *Drama Centre,* 126 Ingram Street, for esoteric modern plays; the *Mitchell* at the Mitchell Library, straight plays; the *Tron,* drama and light jazz; and, most prestigious, the *Glasgow Citizen's Theatre* in the Gorbals, which has a reputation for serious and experimental drama.

Movies, Dancing, Discos. The city has a good choice of cinemas. The big ones are the *ABC Centre* and *Scala Centre* in Sauchiehall Street. Three large cinemas in Renfield Street are the *Odeon Centre, Regent* and *Classic.* At 97 Eglinton Street is the *Coliseum.* The *Glasgow Film Theatre* on Rose Street and the *Grosvenor* off Great Western Road specialize in Continental and avant-garde movies.

For jazz and rock go to *Blackfriars,* Bell Street, and *Riverside Club,* Fox Street. (See also *Pubs.*) Among currently popular nightclubs and discos are *Cleopatra's,* Belmont Lane, Kelvinbridge; *Pzazz,* Royal Exchange Square; *Panama Jax,* Custom House Quay; *Cotton Club,* Scott Street; and *Sub Club,* Jamaica Street.

SHOPPING. The trend is toward large covered shopping malls with fountains and glass-walled elevators. *Princess Square* (between Argyle and Buchanan Streets) is the most chic and modern, with specialty shops on three levels and a café complex above. The *St. Enoch Centre* is the latest of Glasgow's new generation of shopping malls which have improved the city's image over the last few years. Bargain hunters throng the adjacent *Paddy's Market,* but the main attraction is still the adventure of visiting the Barras, Glasgow's premiere market.

Sauchiehall Street (pedestrianized) has two superior arcades, of which the *Savoy Centre* (north side) is the seedier. Buchanan Street and Argyle Street (partly pedestrianized) contain the major chain stores.

Uptown, the best shopping areas are Hillhead and Kelvinbridge, which includes a selection of small commercial art galleries. The *De Courcy's Arcade,* off Byre's Road, features a number of small antique shops.

DINING OUT. A big and increasing number of restaurants offer cuisines of all the nations. Don't disdain the shopping arcade cafés (see above) for lunch and afternoon tea; or the pubs for cheap bar lunches.

Deluxe

Four Seasons, Albany Hotel, Bothwell Street (tel. 248 2656). Continental and Scottish cuisine. Impressive layout and discreet atmosphere. Dancing.

Rogano, 11 Exchange Place (tel. 248 4055). An old favorite of Glasgow's diners-out. Specializes in French dishes and elaborate seafood.

Expensive

La Bonne Auberge, 7a Park Terrace (tel. 332 3520). Quiet surroundings and discriminating French menu.

Buttery, 652 Argyle Street (tel. 221 8188). Near Holiday Inn. Dignified and formal. Downstairs, *Belfry,* also (E), has background jazz.

Colonial, 25 High Street (tel. 552 1923). Simple appearance near the Merchant City, but a faultless cuisine in Scottish, quasi-*nouvelle* style. Impressive wine list kicks off with £147-a-bottle claret; some bizarre and exciting dishes.

Fountain, 2 Woodside Crescent (tel. 332 6396). Distinguished *pot au feu,* tournedos, coquilles. Dinner-dance Thurs., Fri., Sat. Does business lunches, and has a budget bistro.

Moderate

Babbity Bowster, 16–18 Blackfriars Street (tel. 552 5055). Typical of "new breed" of Glasgow's restaurants. International cuisine.

Boston Pizza, 18 Gibson Street (tel. 339 7195). Vivacious Italian ambiance, Neapolitan and international cuisine, original cocktails, good cheap house wines.

Fouquet's, 7 Renfield Street (tel. 226 4958). Imaginative Franco-Scottish cuisine, big wine list. Cellar atmosphere, brickwork and mosaics. Incorporates reputable wine bar.

Moussaka House, 36 Kelvingrove Street (tel. 332 2510). Greek and other Continental food with suitable music and decor. Open till midnight, also Sun. evenings.

Peking Inn, 191 Hope Street (tel. 332 8971). Pastel decor, Peking and Cantonese cooking. Over 100 dishes.

Rotunda North, 28 Tunnel Street (tel. 204 1238). On Clyde bank, near Exhibition Center. Own parking lot. Imaginative restoration of old fort. Four levels comprise wine bar, pizzeria, French restaurant (expensive at night), and roof cocktail bar with panoramic views of river and Festival site.

Sloan's, Argyll Arcade (tel. 221 8917). Sturdy British cuisine among unique decor of etched glass and Victorian mahogany panelling.

La Taverna, 7a Lansdowne Crescent (tel. 339 7128). Fairly sophisticated Continental cuisine, drinkable Italian wines. Open late, including Sun.

Ubiquitous Chip, 12 Ashton Lane (tel. 334 5007). Good fish and seafood, roedeer steaks, lamb. Sub-tropical decor.

Inexpensive

Arnott's, Sauchiehall Street Centre (tel. 332 6833). Department store, offering elegant service for morning coffee, lunch, tea and scones, and high tea.

Change at Jamaica, Clyde Place (tel. 429 4422). Just south of river, under railway bridge. Clean modern decor, big menu features a little of everything. A late-night haven, usually closes around 5 A.M.

Cul-de-Sac Crêperie, Ashton Lane (tel. 334 4749). Candlelight, accordionist, nimble French waiters, snails.

Inn on the Green, Glasgow Green (tel. 554 0165). Neat little place with cheerful atmosphere and its own art gallery.

Lucky Star, 92 Sauchiehall Street (tel. 332 6265). Big and unpretentious with good Chinese food from extensive menu; open late, closed Sun.

Pollok House, Pollok Country Park (tel. 632 0274). Recommended alternative to crowded cafeteria at nearby Burrell Art Collection.

Warehouse Café, 61 Glassford Street (tel. 552 4181). Above trendy fashion store. Light bright atmosphere, young clientele. Tasty meals and snacks.

Willow Tea Room, 217 Sauchiehall Street (tel. 332 0521). Originally designed by Charles Rennie Mackintosh. Coffee, light lunches and afternoon tea.

PUBS. Nowhere is the changing face of Glasgow better reflected than in its public houses. The city's drinking scene has undergone a revolution over the past few years, and a great many city pubs can now be confidently recommended to visitors. The welcome change is largely due to two main developments—the liberalization of Scotland's drinking laws, and the redevelopment of large areas of the city which simply wiped out many of Glasgow's seedier drinking holes.

Bonham's Wine Bar, Byres Road. Opens 10 A.M. to serve coffee and croissants. Live jazz most evenings.

Caskies, 79 St. Vincent Street; also at corner of Sauchiehall and West Campbell Streets. Latest development of upmarket hotel-restaurant entrepreneurs. Not only wide range of local and imported beers but also ice cream, coffee, soups and snacks.

Chimmy Chungas, 499 Great Western Road. Lively, noisy, high-energy establishment. Mexican food.

De Quincey's, 71 Renfield Street. Unobstrusive pub with beautiful interior reminiscent of high days of Empire, *circa* 1900.

Drawing Room, 214 Clyde Street. A "brasserie," something new for the city. Opens for breakfast—another novelty. Live jazz in evenings.

Halt Bar, 160 Woodlands Road. Noted for an atmosphere all its own, despite uninspiring decor. Live entertainment nightly.

Pot Still, 154 Hope Street. A "must" for malt whisky connoisseurs, but don't wear jeans or they won't serve you.

Rock Garden, Queen Street. Impressive list of draught beers. Decor is based on 1950s memorabilia.

Wall Street Exchequer, 59 Dumbarton Road. A short stroll from the Kelvingrove Museum and Art Gallery. Somber interior but spacious and authentic old Glasgow. Bar lunch is excellent value; food served all day.

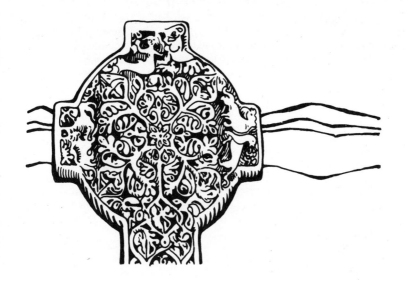

A COAT OF MANY COLORS

Strathclyde

Those grand solitudes you see when you fly in to Glasgow airport or Prestwick, that jigsaw puzzle of firths and straits and interlocking islands: that is Strathclyde. There must be some mistake, you feel. Is not Strathclyde the most densely-populated Region in Scotland? Yes, it contains more inhabitants than all the other regions of Scotland put together. But it also contains large areas of no population at all.

Strathclyde wears a coat of many colors. Every aspect of Scottish life, character and scenery is to be found here: the crofting and small farms of Clyde estuary islands such as Arran (itself often called Scotland in miniature), the Highland hills of Argyll, the rich green dairy pastures of Ayrshire with its traditional resorts, the Upper Clyde Valley, and, further east, the industrial heartlands of the central belt of Scotland.

Historically, Strathclyde embraces two of the four ancient kingdoms into which Scotland was once divided: a territory called Strathclyde, maintained by the original Britons in cooperation with their kinfolk of Cumbria (England) and Wales, a land they had to defend against Picts from the Highlands and Scots from Ireland; and Dalriada, afterwards Argyll, the kingdom established by those same colonizing Scots. It is only 13 miles across the sea from the Mull of Kintyre in Strathclyde to Torr Head in Antrim, Northern Ireland. The place-names of Strathclyde commemorate many Irish saints—eight of them on the island of Bute alone—and they have left their stones and ruined chapels in many rural places.

Glasgow, once proclaimed the second city of the British Empire, has shrunk a little but she still sprawls over the middle belt of the Region. Her river, the Clyde, its waters drawn from the heart of the Southern Uplands, has become a wide river and Scotland's industrial gateway to the world for 200 years. Northwards, ancient glaciers cut deep channels and fjords: the sea-lochs which take you deep into Highland glens and mountains. The southern shores are smooth, prolific with greenery and dotted with white houses and small towns: commuter country, the yachting-and-golfing enclave.

Though the mountains of Argyll can trap rain-clouds, the mild southwesterlies and the Gulf Stream ensure that one of the great glories of this part of Strathclyde is its range of gardens growing tender plants. In March and April the turreted country houses are immersed in drifts of daffodils, while palmettoes and eucalyptus trees grow in sheltered places. If the Scots of this western lochland could live on scenery they would be rich indeed. Instead, Strathclyde is one of the most deprived regions in the European Economic Community.

This is the country of Scott's *The Abbot* (which describes Cathcart Castle and the battleground of Langside, afterwards swallowed up by Glasgow); of the humorous tales of the coasting skipper "Para Handy," told by Neil Munro; of the fast-moving novel *Kidnapped* by Robert Louis Stevenson; of James Boswell the biographer and David Livingstone the explorer; of James Watt and Henry Bell and William Symington and many other pioneers of the industrial revolution; and above all of Robert Burns the national poet.

Strathclyde's offshore islands, like those of Highland and Islands Region, are barriers against the Atlantic. They include the geological freak of Staffa and the holy isle of Iona, burial place of Celtic kings. They also include away-from-it-all corners which rock stars, politicians, actresses and north-country industrialists have made their own. Fingers of mainland can easily be mistaken for islands, so tenuous is their grasp. The narrowness of the Kintyre peninsula, for example, is suggested at one point by the place name Tarbert (one of several in Scotland), indicating a place where boats may be carried across from one stretch of water to another. Yet this long finger of land continues south for another 40 miles to Campbeltown and the Mull of Kintyre, famous in song—by which time Kintyre is no longer Highland, but instead green and fertile, raising dairy cattle to serve its local creameries.

Embedded in the islets and landlocked channels of the Firth of Lorne, a tiny road link with Seil island is quite properly known as the "Bridge over the Atlantic."

South from Glencoe

For no particular reason, most round-Scotland tourists go counterclockwise, up the east coast and down the west. They enter Strathclyde by Glencoe, most romantic of Highland passes. In this chapter we shall do the same, passing first through the mainland districts north of Glasgow, then into the southwestern areas and finally into the islands.

South from Glencoe, the A82 is a fast winding road over the Black Mount to Tyndrum, thence by winding valleys to Crianlarich and down the full length of Loch Lomond (see *Central Region* chapter); and so to

Glasgow. Many Glaswegians make the 150-mile round trip on winter weekends to sample the rudimentary—but improving—winter-sports facilities in the Glencoe area.

Near Kingshouse Hotel at the top of Glencoe a minor road (unclassified) meanders away through savage Glen Etive to the head of Loch Etive where, if you had a boat, you could sail 20 miles through the loneliest country to the sea at Connel Ferry near Oban (A85). In the other direction, from Taynuilt (A85), you can do this trip in summer on a regular small-boat service—as Wordsworth and his sister Dorothy did early in the 19th century. They loved it.

Oban

We reach Oban by turning right off the A82 at Tyndrum and following the A85 which, beyond Dalmally, is gradually squeezed between the head of Loch Awe and the shoulders of Ben Cruachan. Note the Cruachan Dam Visitor Centre on the left, before you reach the narrow Pass of Brander. Another spectacular route is the A828 from Ballachulish, coasting Loch Linnhe and crossing Loch Etive at Connel on a bridge built for trains.

Oban, most lively of West Highland mainland resorts, faces a bewildering tangle of isles in the Firth of Lorne. It is a great yachting port—for the experienced!—as well as a ferry port for the islands and a collection point for cargoes of shellfish. With its russet-stone, white-painted houses it has a venerable air, but most buildings were the result of an influx of early-20th-century vacationers. Much older are two nearby castles. Dunnollie Castle, an ivy-clad ruinous shell, stands on a headland, beyond the breezy promenade and before the resort's sandy beach. This was once a MacDougall stronghold, as was 13th-century Dunstaffnage Castle, in a better state of preservation 3 miles north of Oban. It stands above the shore, a strategic site which controlled the sea lanes of the Firth of Lorn and Sound of Mull and gives superb views of Argyll's hills, especially Ben Cruachan.

The Roman Coliseum lookalike on the hill above the town is no antiquity. It was the unfinished masterwork of a 19th-century Oban banker named MacCaig and is known as "MacCaig's Folly." He went bankrupt trying to immortalize himself with that grandiose temple and simultaneously provide work for distressed fishermen. The portholed shell on the hill symbolizes more than one set of wrecked hopes.

Campbell Country

All this is Campbell country. The Campbell's war-cry is "Cruachan!", the name of a mountain above the A85 near Loch Awe. The great seat of the Campbell chiefs, currently the Dukes of Argyll, is at Inveraray near the head of Loch Fyne at the end of the A819, a roundabout route from Oban. Inveraray Castle is a smart place with a self-satisfied air, dominating a well-disciplined town. Here Dr. Johnson was entertained in 1773 and here, as Boswell tells, the celebrated lexicographer first tasted Scotch whisky. At the castle you can inspect items which successive Dukes of Argyll have salvaged from the Tobermory galleon, a vessel from the Spanish Armada which sank (legend says it was blown up by a daring Scot) in the Sound of Mull near Tobermory. The turmoil of the years round Inveraray is introduced into Scott's *The Legend of Montrose,* Robert Louis Stevenson's *Kidnapped* and Neil Munro's *John Splendid.*

Going from the neat little town of Inveraray back towards Glasgow or the Clyde estuary, the choice of routes is limited by the lengths of the glacier-gouged fjord-like sea lochs. Loch Fyne or Loch Long are dramatic examples of this interplay of high ground and salt sea.

The key to road travel in the area is the A83 over the high pass called the Rest and Be Thankful. Eastwards, from the head of Loch Long, the distant jagged profile of The Cobbler catches the eye, not the highest but the most spectacular of the hills often described as the "Arrochar Alps." (By a map-maker's convention, The Cobbler is sometimes marked as Ben Arthur, but never referred to by this name.)

Another interesting way in or out of this pleasing area of Argyll is through Cowal. This broad peninsula, defined by Lochs Fyne and Long, hangs claw-like, reaching for the island of Bute. Cowal is swathed in the Argyll Forest Park, the Forestry Commission's first state forest, while the profile of the hills known as "Argyll's Bowling Green" are wedged between Lochs Goil and Long. South towards Dunoon, the Younger Botanic Garden at Benmore features a Sierra redwood avenue. Dunoon has a ferry service, short-cutting the Glasgow journey time.

Do not be fooled into thinking that these sleepy hamlets and quiet hills are a backwater. The U.S. sailors in the streets of Dunoon and the black, creeping submarines in the Gare Loch and the Holy Loch are a reminder that the landscapes shelter a nuclear arsenal.

Mull of Kintyre

We retrace our steps, as you often must if you are to give this labyrinthine land of Argyll its due, and go south again from Inveraray to the peninsula of Kintyre (A83), which is 70 miles long. First stop is Crarae Lodge, the horticulturist's challenge to the myriad wild flowers which Nature has assembled on the shores of Loch Fyne. Crarae's exotic blooms and shrubs, notably azaleas, at their best in June, help explain why rich English landowners for two centuries have sought Scottish gardeners. The setting, under hills on the loch shore, complements the floral display.

Kintyre's chief town is Campbeltown but long before you arrive there the intrusive sea-lochs have almost cut through the peninsula. The nine-mile neck of land at Lochgilphead (A83) was severed by the Crinan Canal, surveyed by James Watt around 1793, built by John Rennie and in use by 1801. The Crinan area is famous not just for its picturesque canal but also its wealth of prehistoric monuments, cairns, standing stones, medieval carved grave-slabs and—on a high, bare rock overlooking the Crinan levels—Dunadd Fort, the ancient capital of Dalriada, an early kingdom from which Celtic Scotland sprang.

The main A83 is a fast road down the west side of Kintyre, giving superb sea-glittering views of the silhouetted hills of the island of Jura, and also little Gigha, closer to the coast. The east-side road is the narrower and winding B843, giving a summer-only ferry connection with Arran at Claonaig. Either way, you reach Campbeltown, a well-stocked town, complete with palm trees by the harbor and famed for its whisky and its local cheeses.

From Campbeltown, the B843 and a disused railroad cross to Machrihanish on the west side of the peninsula. This was a historic railroad, narrow gauge, unusual for Scotland, only six miles long but grandiloquently known as the "Railway of the Atlantic." It was detached from the nearest mainline station by 100 miles and up to 1932, when the last train ran, the small resort and golfing center of Machrihanish could boast itself the westernmost railroad station in Britain.

Minor roads from the B842 south of Campbeltown lead down to the Mull of Kintyre. Sunsets are spectacular here. (Park well above the lighthouse and stroll on to the moorland nearby.) The coast of Antrim in Northern Ireland and Rathlin Island where Bruce shared a cave with the spider seem only a jump away.

If you return north by the west-coast road (A83) up Kintyre you will find at Tayinloan a small ferryboat which serves Gigha ("Gee-aa") three miles away; an isle whose owner at Achamore House created famous subtropical gardens.

Bute and Arran

On the sea-route from Kintyre to Glasgow lie two easily accessible islands folded in the arms of the Argyll mainland. Arran, bold and shapely with several summits of 2,500 feet and glens with steep torrents rushing seawards on all sides, is the sort of place where city-dwellers aspire to own holiday cottages—and many do. Lamlash, Brodick and Lochranza are vacation resorts too and Brodick Castle is one of the commanding stately homes of the west.

Bute also has its aristocratic establishments: Mount Stuart, ancestral home of the Marquesses of Bute; and Kames Castle, which competes with Dunvegan (Skye, Highland and Islands) and Traquair (Borders) for the title of oldest continuously-inhabited house in Scotland. Bute is undulating and pastoral, a stopover for migratory geese and other wildfowl and a vacation isle with a long history. The early Stuart kings, 600 years ago, relaxed at Rothesay Castle. One of them made his eldest son Duke of Rothesay, a title still borne by the Prince of Wales, the monarch's eldest son. These old Firth of Clyde castles give the heir to the throne no fewer than three out of his five titles. He is Duke of Rothesay. He is Earl of Carrick, from Robert the Bruce's Carrick Castle whose ruins you can see on the west side of Loch Goil near Lochgoilhead. And he is Baron Renfrew, from the castle in the ancient burgh of Renfrew, close to Glasgow, which was the feudal citadel of Walter the Steward, progenitor of the Stuart dynasty.

A traditional Glasgow treat used to be to go "doon the watter" on holiday—a fleet of steamers plied from the Broomielaw, the city center quay, to a variety of Clyde coast resorts. The last of them, the *Waverley,* the oldest paddle-steamer afloat, was under threat of withdrawal in 1988.

Rothesay town presents a facade of hotels and boardinghouses to its bay—traditional establishments ever waiting for the return of the old "doon the watter" days. If you walk across the island you will pass silent lochs, hedgerows loaded with autumn fruits; and, two miles from Rothesay, the cottage called Woodend in which Edmund Kean the English tragedian, satiated with London's acclaim, found in 1826 his "loophole of retreat."

Bute's scenic wonder is the Kyles, a narrow strait between the mainland and the island's northern corner. This strip of water, forming a Y-shape with Loch Rhidon, is one of the most popular and favored yachting grounds anywhere in the Firth of Clyde. Two lifelike pinnacles, the "Maids of Bute," have been painted up to look like real female figures. One charming little port of call is Tighnabruaich, the archetypal lochside village, on the mainland shore. Until recently it was virtually inaccessible by land, but now there is a road (A886) from Strachur on Loch Fyne.

If you have an automobile on Bute, then note the "back door" Rhubodach–Colintraive ferry, returning you to Cowal after a five minute crossing.

Firth of Clyde

Shipping entering the Firth of Clyde has Arran and Bute on one side and the coastal towns of Ardrossan, Largs, Fairlie and Wemyss Bay ("Weems") on the other—all, except Fairlie, giving ferry connections across the Clyde: Ardrossan–Brodick (Arran), Largs–Millport (Great Cumbrae), Wemyss Bay–Rothesay (Bute). Largs annually celebrates with a festival a Viking defeat by the Scots in 1263. The island town of Millport has a marine biology station and a kirkyard with the tomb of the 19th-century minister James Adam who used to pray for "the Great and Little Cumbraes and adjacent islands of Britain and Ireland."

The gentle air of this stretch of the Firth, for many years an innocent playground, is now mocked by the expanding NATO base and deepwater harbor works at Fairlie; by the nuclear power station of Hunterston near Largs; and by the Polaris nuclear-submarine base in Holy Loch above Dunoon on the opposite shore. It is said that the loch took its name from a consignment of earth from the Holy Land, destined for the foundations of Glasgow cathedral but sunk off Dunoon in the wreck of the ship which carried it.

Sailing higher up the Firth, shipping for Glasgow turns east at the Cloch lighthouse. The Cloch is the first, or last, of a dead-straight line of lightships and lighthouses down the British and Irish coasts which lead from the Bay of Biscay to the narrows of the Clyde. The Cloch stands beside the A78, which runs from Gourock to Wemyss Bay, and is visitable.

Here the Firth is two miles wide. On the north bank stands Dunoon with all the trappings of a seaside resort—pier, promenade, gardens, theater, cinemas, bowling greens, golf courses—but little of noise or stridency except on days of the Cowal Highland Gathering (annually, end of August) when upwards of 150 pipe bands compete for trophies. The town is an excellent touring center with many opportunities for bus and boat excursions, the most popular Clyde resort after Rothesay.

On Castle Hill, see the monument to "Highland Mary," whom Robert Burns loved and lost. Some of his most poignant lyrics were written in memory of this girl, who died in 1786, soon after they had parted, vowing to be ever faithful.

Dunoon Castle, now a heap of ruins, was once the principal Campbell residence. In 1646 that clan which has so much blood on its hands treacherously murdered a glenful of Lamonts against whom they had some grudge. The then Earl of Argyll, the Campbell chief, hanged 36 Lamont clansmen from one tree in Dunoon and shot or stabbed the rest.

Helensburgh

Sailing up the Firth or motoring along the south shore (A8) towards Glasgow we see Loch Long tapering away beyond Dunoon; maybe an oil-tanker inward or outward bound, to or from the terminal at Finnart, to which oil is piped across Scotland from the North Sea. The model residential town of Helensburgh lays a gridiron pattern on the hill-slope. It is something of a cultural shock, to embark in a gloomy cavern of a Glasgow station and ride with the commuters, arriving within the half hour at this sparkling burgh which resembles a segment of Georgian Edinburgh transported to the western mountains. This is one of Glasgow's superior satellite towns. James Logie Baird, the television pioneer, was born here; Henry Bell of *Comet* fame was provost (mayor).

Helensburgh was also the birthplace of the stage and screen stars Jack Buchanan and Deborah Kerr, and is the site of Charles Rennie Mackintosh's most impressive work, the Hill House in Upper Colquhoun Street. "Here is your house," wrote Mackintosh when he handed it over to the Glasgow publisher Walter Blackie. "It is not an Italian villa, an English mansion, a Swiss chalet or a Scots castle. It is a dwelling house." The Hill House came into the care of the National Trust for Scotland in 1982.

Directly opposite Helensburgh is the very different and grimly industrial town of Greenock; and between them the Firth widens to provide the great anchorage called (from a long shoal in the fairway) the "Tail o' the Bank." Veterans of World War II might perhaps recall that this was the place where thousands of overseas servicemen and women had their first sight of wartime Britain.

The next landmark on the northern shore after Helensburgh is the Rock of Dumbarton with its memories of William Wallace and Mary Queen of Scots. Then comes Old Kilpatrick where the Antonine Wall ended and the Forth-Clyde canal came to the sea. And here we approach the gates of the Clyde river and the confines of Glasgow, which we deal with in our Glasgow chapter.

Glasgow to Hamilton

We have to travel some 25 miles up the Clyde to see anything resembling those crystal founts and bosky arbors the old writers saw. By Rutherglen, Cambuslang and Bothwell the Clyde pours through a seemingly endless corridor of housing estates, steelworks and coalmining villages. Road-works and repairs have erased all traces of the battle of Bothwell Brig (between Royalists and Covenanters in 1679). Next door to Bothwell (A74, Glasgow–Carlisle) is the cotton and coalmining village of Blantyre (A776). It was here, in 1813, that David Livingstone was born, and here that he went to school and started work at ten, in a cotton-mill. Self-sacrificing parents and sisters scraped to send him to Glasgow University. In 1840, as doctor and missionary, he went to Africa and in the course of the next 17 years crossed that continent twice, making important geographical discoveries. On a third trek he disappeared, to be found in 1871 by the Anglo-American journalist H.M. Stanley. He declined to come home.

Five miles from Blantyre is the new town of East Kilbride (A749). It is one of three new towns in Strathclyde Region, the others being Irvine on the Clyde coast (A71) and Cumbernauld (M80, Glasgow–Stirling). They were established in the 1950s to take pressure off the decaying hearts of Glasgow and Clydeside. Some say they prosper only at the expense of older communities, but Cumbernauld alone has attracted 55 English and 29 foreign businesses, something the tired old industrial centers round Glasgow could not have done. Having now grown to their fixed limits, the new towns have achieved a social balance and one-quarter of their houses are privately owned—a high proportion by Scottish standards. But the Scots call them "polo-mint cities" on account of their innumerable traffic circles.

Hamilton (A74) is the next place upstream on the Clyde. The Mausoleum, burial-place of the Dukes of Hamilton, faces the river, looking like a large classical beehive. The caretaker does not fail to astonish you with the acoustics: his voice echoes like the sound of military bands and massed choirs. But even more extraordinary is the restored hunting lodge of Chatelherault ("Shatlerro"). A one-room-deep facade, this extraordinary Adam building was conceived as a glorified neo-classical dog-kennel, and as a suitably impressive closure of an avenue-view which once led up from the Dukes of Hamilton's nearby Palace.

The great Hamilton Palace, built on the profits of coal and undermined by coal workings, had to be pulled down earlier this century. One of its smaller rooms contained the whole of the Beckford Library, 15,000 rare volumes collected by the eccentric early 19th century Romantic, builder of impossible follies and author of *Vathek*. Being hard up, the Duke auctioned it in 1882 and was disgusted with the mere £400,000 ($2 million at that time) it fetched.

Hamilton to Lanark

Upstream again, Cambusnethan Priory (A72) is a hotel where today medieval banquets are served. It was owned by Sir James Craig the industrialist, who covered this landscape with steel strip- and rolling-mills. Here the Clyde begins to look like the sylvan stream the old-timers praised. Soft-fruit gardens and apple orchards and red sandstone bridges decorate the banks. Near Crossford on the Nethan Water the ruin of Craignethan Castle recalls Scott's novel *Old Mortality,* in which he fictionalized it as Tillietudlem Castle. After her escape from Loch Leven (Tayside), Mary Queen of Scots took refuge there.

The most interesting town on the upper Clyde is Lanark (A73), an old-established community on the edge of the hills of Clydesdale, of which Tinto Hill is the local landmark. The Falls of Clyde, set in wooded river-gorge scenery, are a short distance south; natural beauties commemorated in verse by Wordsworth, Coleridge and others and painted by Turner. Lanark is a proud market and fruit-growing town with the oldest race course in Scotland. The town also celebrates some traditional pagan ceremonies, of which Lanimer Day early in June is the most elaborate, and lays claim to memories of the Scottish freedom-fighter William Wallace. He came from Elderslie near Paisley, but at St. Kentigern's church in Lanark he married a Lanark girl and a building in Castlegate has the inscription: "Here stood the house of William Wallace who in Lanark in 1297 first drew sword to free his native land." The first to revolt against English occupation, he slew the English sheriff of Clydesdale.

New Deals for Weavers

"New towns" are not all that new. In 1797 a mill-owner named David Dale built one. It consisted of a textile mill and barracks for workers, one mile south of Lanark. He called it New Lanark. He envisaged a company estate on which employees would live as one happy family. His son-in-law and successor, Robert Owen, sometimes known as the father of the cooperative movement, took paternalism a few steps farther by introducing free health and education schemes. His ultra-progressive notions, such as reducing the working day to 12 hours and declining to employ children under 10, got him into trouble with fellow mill-owners. Nonetheless, New Lanark flourished until 1824, by which time Owen was involved with wider philanthropies. He afterwards started the first free-thinking commune in America.

New Lanark, mills, school and houses, survived into the present century intact and overlooked in the green wooded Clyde gorge, where the "linns" or falls had originally provided water power for its now-silent mills. Today, this remarkable survivor is a World Heritage Site.

Clydesmuir

The Clyde's early course is among the open dales and the amiable hills of Tinto and Lowther. You see the broad shallows of the infant river when you come north to Glasgow by road (A74) or rail from Carlisle. Early travel writers placed the river's source in the broad uplands close to the source of the Tweed—the romantic Scots like to think of their great southern rivers as starting from a common source! However, the truth is more prosaic; as a glance at a modern map will reveal, the longest feeder of Clyde's waters runs from the Daer ("Daar") reservoir.

Alps of Strathclyde

West of the stripling Clyde lies another Strathclyde landmass: the districts historically known as Cunninghame, Carrick and Kyle. This is an area of rolling moorland and rippling streams, scarred here and there with coal-mining villages and peat bogs.

Road passes through gaps in the hills are often dramatic, none more so than the B797 and/or B7040 from the A74 Glasgow–Carlisle road. It takes you across the Lowther hills from Abington or Elvanfoot to Sanquhar ("Sankar") in Dumfries and Galloway. In about six miles it climbs, with many ups and downs, to nearly 1,600 feet. Incredibly, a railroad went this way in the 1930s and the blue-and-white railcar with its weekend loads of walkers and climbers gave the landscape the appearance of a scene in the Swiss Alps. The summit station, Wanlockhead (just inside Dumfries and Galloway Region), was the highest in the British Isles. The village, at 1,380 feet, is still Scotland's highest, and its neighbor Leadhills the second highest at 1,355—both are Southern Upland places, paradoxically, and not Highland.

These twin villages, with the regional boundary between them, make a miniature mountain kingdom, remote from other realms. Gold and lead were once mined and you may visit the old workings. At Leadhills (population a few hundred) Allan Ramsay the elder, poet and dramatist, was born in 1686 and William Symington, pioneer of steam navigation, in 1763. If that were not enough fame for one village, Leadhills has the highest golf course in Britain and the grave of Scotland's longest-lived person: John Taylor, died aged 137.

Green Lowther, a hill above Wanlockhead (2,403 feet), has a future as a winter-sports center.

Sanquhar puts us on the A76, a fast road back to Strathclyde Region and the coastal resorts of the Firth of Clyde. We pass Kirkconnell and then New Cumnock and the Afton Water, which recalls Robert Burns's *Sweet Afton;* then Auchinleck ("Affleck"), family home of Boswell, visited by Dr. Johnson; then Mauchline, renowned for lace. Now we are in the Burns country, conveniently laid out for tourists around the seaside resort of Ayr (A70) and the international airport of Prestwick, the most important in Scotland.

Burns Country

English children know that Burns is a good minor poet. Scottish children know that he is Shakespeare, Dante, Rabelais, Mozart and Karl Marx rolled into one. As time goes by it seems that the Scots have it more nearly right. As poet and humanist, Robert Burns increases in stature. When you plunge into the Burns country, as plunge you must, do not forget that he is held in extreme reverence by Scots of all degrees. They may argue about Sir Walter Scott and Bonnie Prince Charlie; there is no disputing the merits of Burns.

His birthplace, Alloway, is now a respectable, leafy suburb of Ayr, and a concentration of places associated with him can be found here. These include: his birthplace, Burns Cottage (and adjacent museum); a short drive away, the major Land o' Burns Centre; a few moments' walk away the Auld Kirk of Alloway (where Tam o' Shanter saw the witches!); opposite is the Burns Monument amid peaceful gardens stretching down to the waters of the Doon and the picturesque "Brig o' Doon" (Bridge of Doon), over which Tam escaped from the above-mentioned witches, by then in hot pursuit. There are plenty of opportunities for buying souvenirs and for picking up a Burns Heritage Trail leaflet as a guide to further sites.

Ayr (A77, five miles from Prestwick, Glasgow–Stranraer railroad) has a Burns statue, a Tam o' Shanter Museum, in what was a brew house in Burns' time, the Auld Kirk where he was baptized, the Auld Brig "where twa wheelbarrows tremble when they meet" and, four miles away on the A713, the farm at Mount Oliphant where he was brought up.

Kirkoswald, on the A77 near Maybole, has the graves of Souter Johnnie and Tam o' Shanter, two of Burns's best-loved characters, and in the garden of Souter Johnnie's museum-cottage you will see effigies of them, and of various other worthies immortalized by Burns. Tarbolton (B744) has the Bachelors' Club of which Burns was first president; it is now a museum maintained by the National Trust for Scotland. Mauchline (A76) has Burns's first married home, graves of his children and friends in the kirkyard, Poosie Nansie's tavern (his favorite "howff," still open) and the National Burns Memorial.

Two of the farms he failed to make a living at, Mossgiel and Lochlea, are near Mauchline. At Irvine (A78) on the coast road north of Ayr is the house he lodged at and the Burns Club museum. For the southern parts of the Burns Heritage Trail see the chapter on Dumfries and Galloway Region.

One word of warning: call him Robert, Robin, Robbie, Rob or Rab—but never Bobbie.

The Golf Coast

Between Ayr and West Kilbride along the coast road there are 20 golf courses, one for every mile. South of Ayr as far as Girvan (A719, A77) they are hardly less numerous. This curving shoreline of the Firth of Clyde, flat with dunes and interspersed with bold headlands, is commonly called the Golf Coast. At Turnberry the railroad company built one of Scotland's finest hotels specifically for golfers. Turnberry, (A719) to the south of Ayr, and Royal Troon, (B746) on a slender peninsula to the north, are among golf's major international championship venues.

It might be called the Castle Coast. On Turnberry's cliff-top in a now ruined castle, Robert the Bruce is believed to have been born. At Dunure a few miles north (A719) some medieval land-grabbers named Kennedy encouraged the local abbot to make over his castle by, says the chronicler, "rosting him in sope." Roasting in soup and similar ploys secured to the Kennedys a large slice of southwestern Strathclyde which they fortified with a string of coastal castles. In many places only ruined towers survive, but one place has blossomed. This is Culzean ("Cullane") off the A719 four miles north of Turnberry.

Culzean Castle

The Kennedys prospered and were ennobled: their present-day representative is the Marquess of Ailsa. The 11th Earl was born and raised in America and had quite a good address: 1, Broadway, New York City. The troubles of 1776 drove him back to the land of his fathers, where he found himself heir to the seagirt fortress of Culzean which the celebrated architect Robert Adam was transforming into a civilized family house. Adam worked on Culzean, inside and out, even on follies in the gardens and neo-classical farm steadings, until 1792 when he died.

Culzean Castle today, despite being difficult to get at without an automobile, is the most-visited of all National Trust for Scotland properties. Its unique oval staircase leads to an oval dome and then to . . . well, not exactly an Oval Office but an oval presidential suite nonetheless. It's a penthouse apartment presented to President (then General) Dwight D. Eisenhower in 1947 as a mark of Scotland's gratitude to a great war leader. The President stayed once or twice at Culzean and his relations still do occasionally. Between visits it is used by the N.T.S. for official hospitality. Approach is by way of rooms evoking the atmosphere of World War II: mementoes of Glenn Miller, Winston Churchill, Vera Lynn and other personalities of the epoch all help create a suitably 1940s mood.

Culzean's "home farm," more pleasing architecturally than the Castle itself, is built round an octagonal courtyard where barns, stabling and swine pens have been upgraded into historical tableaux, educational displays and a restaurant. There is a country park with deer. The garden shrubberies reflect the essential mildness of this coast, though some visitors, meeting the full force of a westerly gale, might be inclined to think otherwise. Culzean's perpendicular sea-cliff offers views across the Firth of Clyde to Arran and the Irish coast. Not a stone's-throw away, it seems, the pinnacle of Ailsa Craig rears from mid-channel. It is halfway along the sea route from Greenock to Belfast and was known of old as "Paddy's Milestone." From Girvan (A77), excursion motorboats go to Ailsa Craig in summer, a round trip of 25 miles.

Roads to Glasgow

From Ayr northwards the roads are drawn into Glasgow like spokes to a hub. The pleasantest is the longest, all round the Clyde coast (A78). After Greenock it is dull, but you have the compensation of Argyll's shifting panorama across the water. If you are in a hurry the M8 will take you from Greenock across Glasgow to Edinburgh or (M74, A74) to Carlisle.

An exceptionally pretty village called Eaglesham straggles along the B764 under bleak Fenwick Moor, an alternative to the main A77 Ayr–Kilmarnock–Glasgow road. Eaglesham has Covenanting memories in its kirkyard but the cottages make up a perfect late 18th-century planned village of the type devised by landowners desperate to tempt workers back to the land. Eaglesham also has the bizarre distinction of being the site where in 1941 Rudolf Hess, the German vice-fuehrer, landed in his bid to secure a peace agreement with Britain.

Paisley

Another route from the Golf Coast (A737) comes into Glasgow by Paisley, a place not often dwelled on in guidebooks though if your taste is towards the urban, rather than the rural, then this town offers plenty of gritty character. It is associated with the "Paisley pattern"—in shape a palm shoot, an ancient Babylonian fertility symbol brought in via Kashmir! Paisley introduced new weaving techniques and its decorated woollen shawls became internationally recognized. The full story is told in the Paisley Museum and Art Gallery, with its world-famous shawl collection. Paisley's town-center 12th-century abbey is also famous and there are trails through the mill heritage, including Sma' Shot Cottages, a refurbished artisan's house. The thread manufacturers Coats were the town's benefactors, their name recalled in various public buildings and, unusually, an observatory open to visitors.

Isles of Strathclyde—Mull

There are scores of islands in Strathclyde Region, a continuation of the groups we deal with in the Highland and Islands chapter. Many are fragments of rock and bars of sand and others have only a seasonal population of fishermen or cattle. For practical purposes there are six Inner Hebridean isles in the Strathclyde Region worth visiting: Mull, Coll and Tiree west of Oban; and Colonsay, Jura and Islay west of Kintyre; plus two islets, Staffa and Iona.

These isles are microcosms of Scotland. Each has its jagged cliffs or tongues of rock, its smiling sands and fertile pastures, its grim and ghostly fortress and its tale of clan outrage or mythical beast. None is more microcosmic than Mull, a large island by Inner Hebridean standards and much penetrated by the Atlantic billows.

This is the largest of the islands of the region. The pace of life is gentle, the roads are narrow and tortuous and not designed for heavy vehicles. (Beware pilgrim coaches to Iona in summer: they can cause delays on the southside routes.) The big car-ferry from Oban takes 40 minutes. The small, cheaper one from Lochaline cannot cope with all the holiday traffic. This should not deter you from touring Mull by automobile (and once you are there you really need one) but it does mean that you cannot hope to combine a ferry crossing with an island circuit in the same day. Try to spend at least two nights on Mull.

The chief town, Tobermory ("Well of Mary"), is a fishing village. In the strait which divides it from Calve Island the pride of the Spanish Armada went down in 1588, allegedly with rich treasure on board. But despite many costly salvage operations down the centuries very little gold has been recovered. Other sights around the northwest shore include Aros Castle, from which the Lords of the Isles once exacted a toll from passing ships; and the beautiful white-sand beach of Calgary, near the village whose emigrants founded a great Canadian city. Loch na Keal, which gives Mull a narrow waist, has been called the finest sea-loch in Scotland. On the east shore, don't miss two impressive castles, Duart and Torosay.

Boats take you in summer from Fionnphort (A849) to Staffa and Iona; and a passenger ferry links Oskamull (B8073) with Ulva, the islet of Thomas Campbell's poem *Lord Ullin's daughter*.

Staffa and Iona

Staffa consists entirely of basalt pillars stacked on a rock shelf; the very name means "isle of staves." Strangely this geological freak was unknown to the world until, in 1772, the English naturalist Sir Joseph Banks found it the hard way—he ran aground on it—while on a voyage to Iceland. The grotto on Staffa, known to locals as the "musical cave," and to the rest of the world as Fingal's Cave, was visited by several 19th-century romantics. John Keats wrote: "For solemnity and grandeur it far surpasses the finest cathedral." Mendelssohn said: "What a wonder is Fingal's Cave! this vast cathedral of the seas with its dark lapping waters within and the brightness of the gleaming waves outside!" They were two who were lucky enough to land—the ocean swell and slippery rocks can sometimes make landings impossible. Here Mendelssohn was inspired to write his *Hebrides* concert piece, which ended up as the overture *Fingal's Cave*. But it was not for this reason that it was called the "musical cave," rather for the strange Aeolian-harp effect of the wind through the basalt pillars.

Of Iona, Dr. Johnson said it all when he wrote the passage beginning: "We were now treading that illustrious Island which was once the luminary of the Caledonian regions. . . . " St. Columba chose Iona for his monastery in 563 and from it his monks carried Christianity throughout northern England and Scotland. Many Dark Age kings, 48 of them Scottish, are buried on this sacred islet; and many carved slabs commemorate clan chiefs. The present cathedral dates chiefly from the 15th and 16th centuries but fine decorated crosses from earlier periods stand round it. Of some interest to American visitors is the plot set aside for 19 victims of the *Guy Mannering*, shipwrecked in 1865. They were American sailors and the then American consul in Glasgow, the novelist Bret Harte, persuaded the Duke of Argyll to give them burial and a monument in the island graveyard.

Coll and Tiree

Both Coll and Tiree are low-lying and exposed, an inadequate barrier for Mull against the Atlantic. Coll has pastureland and silver sands. Tiree, so flat that it was known to the Gaels as "the kingdom less tall than the waves," claims to be the sunniest spot in the west. The inhabitants of both islands are crofters (smallholders) but the boat from Oban brings mainland families for their vacations and if you talk to them you will hear that they would not dream of taking a holiday elsewhere.

Jura and Islay

Jura lies south again and runs roughly parallel with the coast of Kintyre, only about four miles away. Its twin conical peaks, the Paps of Jura, are a landmark for sailors. The island's deer population greatly outnumbers its inhabitants. There is only one small settlement, one hotel and one main road. Separated by a deep strait, ferry-linked Islay ("Eye-la") bustles by comparison, busy with whisky distilling, with good roads and direct air connections to Glasgow. It is flat and green, much frequented by Glasgow people, some of whom have been known to go over merely to play golf. Among the coastal villages are 12 hotels. Even so, you will always find peace and solitude if you want it.

Colonsay

While not the largest or most important of Strathclyde islands, Colonsay represents the culmination of island charms. It has cliffs and moors, small stone walls, lochans full of waterlilies, woods embosomed in rhododendrons and sand-dunes infested with rabbits. Wild goats are seen in the north (A870 beyond Colonsay House) and on Oronsay, an islet which hangs from Colonsay's southern tip on a sand-spit.

Colonsay, west of Jura and south of Mull, is one of the very finest of the Hebrides. Fertile and welcoming, it offers an extraordinary diversity of landscape in a small area: moors, fields, ancient Hebridean woodland, cliffs, sandy bays and Colonsay House's colorful gardens. A scattering of ancient monuments, from a ruined chapel near Balnahard to the remains of a 15th-century priory on Oronsay, suggest a Celtic priestly occupation. There is a hotel on Colonsay and some self-catering accommodations in island cottages and at Colonsay House. You may take a car but not a caravan and ride a bicycle but not pitch a tent!

PRACTICAL INFORMATION FOR STRATHCLYDE

HOW TO GET THERE. By air. There are daily flights from Glasgow airport to and from Campbeltown, Islay and Tiree; and helicopter links with Rothesay, Lochgilphead and Oban.

By train. If coming from England it is best to travel into Glasgow and then come out again! The Strathclyde region has a very good suburban network co-ordinated by the Greater Glasgow Passenger Transport Executive (GGPTE for short!). Glasgow's Central station—the terminus for trains from south of the border—basically serves the area to the south and northwest of the Clyde, and to the southeast and west of the city through suburban services. Glasgow's Queen Street Station is the starting point for trains to Oban, Fort William and Mallaig, on the West Highland Line, and for Scottish services to Stirling, Perth and Inverness, and also for the express shuttle to Edinburgh.

There is a bus link between Central and Queen Street Stations. Note: services are greatly reduced on Sundays.

By bus. Long-distance coaches day and night connect London (Victoria), Coventry (Corley Service Station) and Birmingham (St. Chadsway) in England with Abington, Motherwell, Cumbernauld, Airdrie and Hamilton in Strathclyde. This is by far the cheapest way of traveling in Scotland. Excellent and inexpensive buses run very frequent services between Glasgow's Anderston Cross and Buchanan Street bus stations and most towns of the Region.

HOTELS AND RESTAURANTS. Accommodations range from château-style hotels to modest inns. Fresh local produce at very reasonable prices is a feature of many country places.

Abbotsinch (M8). *Excelsior* (E), tel. 041–887 1212. 290 rooms with bath. One of the best British airport hotels and right next to the check-in desk. Discreet bars, average restaurant.

Ayr (A77). *Chestnuts* (M), 52 Racecourse Road (tel. 0292–264393). 14 rooms, 11 with bath. Suburban villa, family-owned and run. Well-equipped and comfortable. Lavish table, good bar food.

Restaurant. *Fouters Bistro* (M), Academy Street (tel. 0292–261391). Interesting French-style cooking using Scottish produce.

Bute, Isle of (A844) *Palmyra* (I), 12 Ardbeg Road, Rothesay (tel. 0700–2929). 6 rooms with bath. Substantial private house on seafront. Very low rates suggest modest service and amenities, but in fact it outclasses many a hotel.

Campbeltown (A83). *Royal* (M), Main Street (tel. 0586–52017). 16 rooms, 12 with bath. Impeccable service, one of the best lunch or dinner stops in the west.

Colonsay, Isle of. *Isle of Colonsay* (E), tel. 095 12–316. 11 rooms, 8 with bath/shower. 18th-century inn on beautiful Hebridean island. Outstanding cuisine, using local ingredients, in relaxed setting.

Dunlop (A735). *Struther Farmhouse* (I), tel. 0560–84946. 6 rooms. Genuine old farmhouse, genuine Scots country cuisine, not at all primitive and really inexpensive.

Helensburgh (A814). *Upper Ericstane Guest House* (I), 7 West Montrose Street (tel. 0436–4922). 3 rooms—you will be one of the family in this quietly located Victorian villa. No lunch served, but a splendid dinner.

Kentallen (A828). *Ardsheal House* (L), tel. 063 17–4227. 13 rooms, 10 with bath. Famed for comfort and cuisine. *Holly Tree* (M), tel. 063 17–4292. 12 rooms with bath. Converted railroad station; superb views, outstanding cuisine and friendly service.

Kilmarnock (A77). **Restaurant.** *The Artful Dodger* (M), St. Marnock Place (tel. 0563–37995). Bar lunches and suppers; dining room with à la carte menu; pizza restaurant.

Kilmory (Isle of Arran, A841). **Restaurant.** *The Lagg* (M), tel. 077 087–255. Old coaching inn; sophisticated cuisine—good trout and scampi.

Knipoch (A816 near Oban). *Knipoch Hotel* (E), tel. 085 26–251. 22 rooms with bath. Great views over Loch Feochan. Gracious living at its Scottish best.

Langbank (B789 off M8). *Gleddoch House* (E), tel. 047 554–711. 33 rooms with bath. House of dignity and exclusive character on south Clyde shore, 18 miles from Glasgow. Fine views across Clyde; large lawns and gardens.

Lochaweside (B845). *Taychreggan* (E), tel. 086 63–211. 16 rooms, 15 with bath. Old drovers' inn on lochside, enlarged and carefully modernized.

Luing, Isle of (off B8003). **Restaurant.** *Longhouse Buttery* (M), tel. 085 24–209. Cross bridge over Atlantic and take a ferry for gourmet lunch or early dinner. Last ferry back 10 P.M.

Mull, Isle of (A849). Restaurant. *Ardfenaig House* (M), Bunessan (tel. 068 17–210). Formal dinner, men wear tie. (Off B8035.)

Port Appin (off A828). *The Airds* (E), tel. 063 173–236. 15 rooms with bath. Old ferry inn, haven of serenity under majestic Morven skyline. Salmon, venison, hare, seafood—and that's only the bar lunch!

Stewarton (B769). *Chapeltoun House* (L), tel. 0560–82696. 7 rooms with bath. Secluded mansion house with views. Spacious rooms, superb cuisine.

Tarbert (Loch Fyne, A8015). *Stonefield Castle* (E), tel. 088 02–836. 33 rooms with bath. Baronial house of charm and character on Loch Fyne. Generous amenities. *West Loch* (M), tel. 088 02–283. 6 rooms, 2 with bath. Family run. Home cooking.

Tiroran (Isle of Mull, A848). *Tiroran House* (E), tel. 068 15–232. 9 rooms with bath. Candlelit cuisine in enchanting country house.

Troon (A749). *Sun Court* (E), tel. 0292–312727. 20 rooms, 18 with bath. Mansion overlooking golf course and sea. Chiefly a sporting clientele.

Turnberry (A77). *Turnberry Hotel* (L), tel. 065 53–202. 128 rooms with bath. Scenic outlook from famous golfing hotel. Expensive international menu.

HOW TO GET ABOUT. By boat. Western Ferries, 16 Woodside Crescent, Glasgow G3 7UT (tel. 041–332 9766) operate a trans-Clyde ferry between Gourock (A8) and Hunter's Quay (A815).

The principal ferry operator is Caledonian MacBrayne, The Pier, Gourock PA13 1QP (tel. 0475–33755) with car and passenger services on weekdays as follows.

From Oban: to Lochboisdale (South Uist), Castlebay (Barra), Craignure (Mull), Coll, Tiree, Colonsay and Lismore. *From Tayinloan* (Kintyre, A83): to Gigha. *From Kennacraig* (Kintyre, A83): to Port Ellen and Port Askaig (both Islay) and Feolin (Jura). *From Wemyss Bay* (A78): to Rothesay (Bute). *From Largs* (A78): to Millport (Great Cumbrae). *From Ardrossan* (A78): to Brodick (Arran). *From Claonaig* (Kintyre, B842): to Lochranza (Arran), May–Sept. only. *From Colintraive* (B8000): to Rhubodach (Bute). *From Fionnphort* (Mull, A840): to Iona, no automobiles. *From Lochaline* (B849): to Fishnish (Mull, B8035). *From Gourock* (A8): to Dunoon (A815) and Kilcreggan (B833).

There are numerous small-boat excursions in summer between mainland vacation resorts and off-lying islands.

By bus. The main bus station in the Region is on Buchanan Street, Glasgow, with services to all parts of Scotland and many day excursions and longer tours.

By train. Both Central and Queen Street mainline stations have Blue Trains to Helensburgh and Balloch (Loch Lomond), as well as to outlying towns including Lanark, Cumbernauld, Kilmalcolm and Milngavie.

By car. The M8 is a great boon to motorists going to, from or across Glasgow, but driving in the city and its satellite towns can be slow and depressing; and signposting is not clear. In the countryside the roads are good, with some fine fast stretches to south and west and some twisting and at weekends heavily-trafficked sections to the north. Fish trucks from Oban and other ports are a hazard; car-and-caravan drivers an irritation in summer.

There are many car-rental firms in Glasgow and all the well-known operators are represented at the airports of Glasgow and Prestwick as well as in many of the smaller towns.

TOURIST INFORMATION. You will find tourist information offices at Abington, Ayr, Balloch, Biggar, Bowmore, Brodick, Campbeltown, Culzean, Cumnock, Dalmellington, Darvel, Dunoon, Girvan, Glasgow, Gourock, Greenock, Hamilton (service area on M74 northbound), Helensburgh, Inveraray, Lanark, Largs, Lesmahagow, Lochgilphead, Mauchline, Millport, Motherwell, New Cumnock, Newmilns, Oban, Paisley, Prestwick, Rothesay, Tarbert (Loch Fyne), Tarbet (Loch Lomond), Tobermory and Troon. In Glasgow (St. Vincent Place, tel. 227 4880) the office is open all year round, usually 9–6; and in summer months on weekday evenings also and Sun. afternoons. Smaller offices keep shorter hours. At all tourist information centers you may obtain accommodations locally or "book-a-bed-ahead."

FISHING. In northern and western districts most hotels offer free fishing to guests for salmon, sea trout, rainbow and brown trout. Loch Awe southwest of Dalmally (A819 and B840), the River Awe and lochans of the area are particularly good: permits around £15 per day from Inverawe Fisheries, Taynuilt (A85), or the Chief Forester, Dalavich, Taynuilt. The Clyde above Glasgow is noted for brown trout and grayling—tackle dealers in Edinburgh, Glasgow and Clyde towns will provide permits for about £1 per day or £5 the season. The Loch Lomond Angling Improvement Association, Ballindalloch Farm Cottages, Balfron G63 0RQ, issues permits for salmon and brown trout fishing in various parts of Loch Lomond, as do the hotels at Luss and Ardlui (both A82 lochside road). There is good trout fishing in the lochs and burns of Mull: contact Tobermory Angling Association, c/o Brown's Shop, Tobermory, or the Western Isles Hotel, Tobermory. On Bute the Glenburn Hotel, Rothesay, can arrange fishing for island and adjoining mainland lochs at about £5 per day.

Coarse fishing for pike, perch and grayling is popular in the Glasgow and Greenock areas and farther south in rivers, canals, lochs and reservoirs. Spring and fall are best. Contact tackle shops or hotels in the areas or apply to British Waterways Board, Applecross Street, Glasgow, who issue permits at nominal cost.

There is good sea-angling (facilities provided) from Port Charlotte (Islay), Salen and Tobermory (Mull), and the Coll Hotel (Coll). Local hotels supply boats and tackle. Fishing from pier-end or from boats locally available is a major pastime on the Clyde coast at Girvan, Ayr, Prestwick, Troon and Ardrossan (all on or near A78/A77); also in villages of Bute and Arran. The long, deep Loch Fyne, with depths of 600 feet even at the head of the loch, is fine sea-angling ground and you can hire boats on the quays of Tarbert (A8015) and Inveraray (A83). Elsewhere on Loch Fyne it is hard to launch a boat on account of the rugged coastline.

GOLF. Notable among Glasgow's 20-odd golf courses are Haggs Castle, Cathcart Castle, Cawdor (Bishopbriggs) and Pollok (men only). Visitors require introductions through member or home club secretary. Fees around £5 per day. Every town and many villages of southern Strathclyde have golf courses, the greatest concentration being around Glasgow and on both sides of the Clyde coast. There are few courses in northern Strathclyde. Among the islands there are three on Bute, seven on Arran, two on Mull, one on Tiree, one on Islay and one on Colonsay.

The small town of Troon (B746) has five courses. Among Scotland's famous championship courses are Royal Troon, Turnberry and Old Prestwick. You must have an introduction to them and will pay up to £18 per day. At most other clubs and all municipal courses you can play without formality for a maximum of £3.50 per day.

HISTORIC HOUSES AND GARDENS. Of the many historic houses and castles found in Strathclyde Region, the following are particularly noteworthy and well worth visiting.

Brodick Castle, Brodick, Isle of Arran (A841). Long, severe, island cita-del of ducal families, formerly Hamilton and now Montrose. Sporting prints. Silver and porcelain from William Beckford's amazing collection. Open 1–3 Apr. and May–Sept., daily 1–5; rest of Apr. and 1–15 Oct., Mon., Wed., Sat. 1–5; gardens all year, 9.30–sunset. N.T.S.

Castle Sween, 15 miles southwest of Lochgilphead, Argyll. Certainly not a stately home, this atmospheric 12th-century ruin by the rocky edge of the sea is of interest as Scotland's oldest stone castle on the mainland. Open all reasonable times.

Culzean Castle, Maybole (A719). Large, castellated mansion on 150-foot headland. Medieval tower, Robert Adam additions. Farm complex also styled by Adam. Woodland, lake, picnic areas. Open 1–10 Apr. and May–Aug., daily 10–6; 11–30 Apr. and Sept.–Oct., daily 12–5. Country Park all year, daily 9–sunset. N.T.S.

Dean Castle, Dean Road, Kilmarnock (A77). Castle dates from 14th–15th centuries, with period furnishings, medieval musical instru-ments. Open May–Sept., Mon.–Fri. 2–5, Sat. and Sun. 10–5.

Duart Castle, near Craignure, Isle of Mull (B8035). This grim seat of the MacLean chiefs has commanded the entrance to the Firth of Lorne for 600 years. Furnishings reflect the clan's changing fortunes. One room devoted to history of Boy Scout movement—Lord MacLean was Chief Scout of the Commonwealth in the 1960s. Open May–Sept., daily, 10.30–6.

The Hill House, Upper Colquhoun Street, Helensburgh (A874). Splen-did art deco suburban château, Charles Rennie Mackintosh's greatest work. Open daily 1–5. N.T.S.

Inveraray Castle, Inveraray (A83). Four-square, conical-towered home of Duke of Argyll, chief of Campbell clan. Tapestries, armor, 18th-century furniture. Open Jul.–Aug., weekdays 10–6, Sun. 1–6; Apr.–Jun. and Sept., weekdays except Fri., 10–1 and 2–6, Sun. 1–6.

Iona, off Isle of Mull (A849). Monastery, abbey, ancient graves and monuments. Restored chapel of St. Oran (1080). Shops open 10–4.30 daily. Boat service from Fionnphort.

Kelburn Castle, near Fairlie (A78). Ancestral home of the earls of Glas-gow. House not open, but the park has entertainments and cafés amid fine natural scenery. Open mid-Apr.–mid-Sept., daily 10–6.

Torosay Castle, Mull (B8035). Scottish Baronial style, friendly and idio-syncratic, plus beautiful Italian gardens with statue walk. Miniature rail-road to/from Craignure Pier (1¼ miles). Open Apr.–Oct.

Mild, moist air and sunlight reflected off deeply winding lochs contrib-ute to the wonderful displays of azaleas, rhododendrons, fuchsias, camel-lias and other blooms in Strathclyde not seen much in Britain outside botanical gardens. Of the properties listed above, Brodick Castle has Hi-malayan, Chinese and Burmese plants, vast shrubberies, and 250-year-old formal gardens; and Culzean Castle has formal and walled gardens, as well as spring flowers in the woods.

Many gardens are open to the public on only one or two days a year—usually a Saturday or Sunday. For details, see advertisements in local newspapers or posters in shop windows etc. The following, which you will find open most days in summer, are of special note: **Achamore House,** Gigha (ferry from Tayinloan, A83); **Achnacloich,** Connel, near Oban

(A85); **Adruaine,** A816, south of Oban; **An Cala,** Easdale (B844 south of Oban); **Ardanaiseig,** Kilchrenan, Loch Awe (B845); **Ardchattan,** North Connel (off A828); **Crarae,** Loch Fyne (A83); **Stonefield Castle,** Tarbert (A83); **Strone,** Cairndow (off A83); and **Torosay Castle,** Craignure, Mull (B8035).

MUSEUMS. Auchindrain, near Inveraray (A83). Communal tenancy farm township with surviving 18th/19th-century buildings. Displays and folk museum. Open Apr.–May and Sept., daily except Sat. 11–4; June–Aug., daily 10–5.

Bonawe Iron Furnace, near Taynuilt, 12 miles east of Oban (A85). Restored remains of 18th-century charcoal furnace plus associated buildings. This iron-smelting industry devastated Highland woods in the 18th century. Open Apr.–Sept., Mon.–Sat. 9.30–7, Sun. 2–7.

Burns' Cottage and Museum, Alloway, Ayr (B7024). Birthplace of poet, with large collection of books, letters, manuscript poems. Open June–Aug. daily 9–7; May and Oct., weekdays 10–5, Sun. 2–5; winter, daily except Sun. 10–4.

Coats Observatory, Oakshaw Street, Paisley (A737). Well-designed building and scientific instruments gifted to local Philosophical Society, 1880, by cotton-thread tycoon Thomas Coats. Stained glass commemorates astronomers. Small planetarium. Open Mon.–Fri. 2–5, Sat. 10–1 and 2–5.

Combined Operations Museum, Cherry Park, Inveraray (A83). History of *the* chief amphibious base, 1939–45. Mementoes of war leaders involved include those of Patton (U.S.A.) and Macready (Canada). Open weekdays 10–6, Sun. 1–6.

David Livingstone Center, Blantyre (A776). Birthplace and elaborate national memorial with relics of explorer's diaries and instruments. Open weekdays 10–6, Sun. 2–6.

Gasworks Museum, Biggar (A702). Perhaps Scotland's most unusual monument and certainly her only preserved town gasworks, closed in 1973. Nostalgic gassy smells! Open July–early Sept., Mon.–Sat. 2–5, Sun. 11–5.

Gladstone Court, Biggar (A702). A museum-street with shops, bank, school etc. illustrating country life of last century. Open Apr.–Oct., weekdays 10–5, Sun. 2–5. Closes for lunch.

Museum and Art Gallery, High Street, Paisley (A737). Paisley shawls, Scottish artists, and fine contemporary ceramics. Open weekdays 10–5.

New Lanark Counting House, Lanark (A73). Interpretative display on innovations of David Dale and Robert Owen between 1797 and 1824. Open on request; village open all times.

BATTLEFIELDS AND BONNIE BANKS

Central

Stand on a high point of Central Region—there are several, but Stirling Castle rock is as good as any—and you will survey the whole Region, from the impressive "Arrochar Alps" beyond Loch Lomond, to the tip of the Forth Rail Bridge. You will see Scotland coast-to-coast. This is where Scotland draws in her waist from the Clyde in the west to the Forth in the east. All the Lowland highways converge here and fan out again to the Highlands.

The Forth–Clyde belt, only 28 miles wide, was a cradle of Scottish industry, a forcing-house of that mechanical genius to which engineering science worldwide was indebted. On the Forth–Clyde canal in 1790 Patrick Miller demonstrated the first paddle-steamboat. Scotland's first iron ship, Sir John Robinson's *Vulcan* took to the Monklands Canal, 29 years later. Iron foundries on the Carron River had by that time built the heavy guns for Nelson's warships: hence the term carronade. In 1850 James "Paraffin" Young, extracting oil from locally-mined shale, showed how it could be burned in lamps. That led to the decline of mineral oil as a patent medicine in America—and to the founding of the Rockefeller fortunes.

Central Region is still to the fore in oil technology. It has the petroleum refinery of Grangemouth, with a pipeline to the west coast for American tankers; and a petrochemical industry that ranks among the top six in Europe.

But the Region is not all industry. As in Lothian and Strathclyde, wild scenery begins on the doorsteps of manufacturing towns and a sense of the past intrudes on the present. Stirling's braes (hilly streets) ascend to a 900-year-old citadel which—like that of Edinburgh, but smaller and neater—holds a military garrison and dominates a landscape. From the ramparts you can see seven battlefields, including Stirling Bridge and Bannockburn, scenes of victories by William Wallace and his successor Robert the Bruce; and Sheriffmuir and Falkirk, which belong to the history of the Jacobite rebellions.

Under Stirling's fortifications the River Forth, not yet a firth, meanders about the meadows, taking nine miles to do a journey of three as the crow flies. In former times, this looping river was a barrier to travel. Westwards, the river flats (called in Scots "Carselands"), now cultivated, were once marshy and dangerous. Eastwards the steep "scarp" face of the Ochil Hills rises while to the south, the Campsie Hills prevent direct access to Glasgow. All this means that Stirling Castle, in former times, was a strategic center of high importance, controlling routes into the Highlands.

Almost at your feet as you stroll round Stirling's battlements are Cambuskenneth Abbey where the Scottish Parliament once sat and the Gothic pencil of the Wallace Monument against the backcloth of the Ochil Hills. Look eastwards, far down the Forth estuary, where in good visibility, the top of the Forth Rail Bridge is just visible—almost 25 miles.

The Highland Line, the geological boundary which in olden times was a sociological one too, slices through the Region. You can see this boundary fault most clearly where it crosses the southern end of Loch Lomond. It goes through the loch's islands and away northeastwards through the knobbly back of Conic Hill (behind Balmaha) towards the Trossachs, conspicuous from Stirling Castle's ramparts.

The Romans' Antonine Wall crops out in several places on its march across Scotland's wasp waist. The Celts are represented in the curious Stone of Manaan at the village of Clackmannan: the sea god Manaan also gave his name to the Isle of Man. There are medieval strongholds at Dollar, Fintry and Doune, an ancient cathedral at Dunblane, a modern university at Bridge of Allan, elaborate gardens at Keir and Gargunnock, Highland Games at various centers in summer and plenty of lochs for fishing, boating and boat excursions.

Memories of Wallace and the Bruce abound, but Central Region's folk hero is Rob Roy MacGregor, the Highland freebooter whose real-life exploits were concerned with cattle-rustling on the approaches to the trysts (markets) of Falkirk and Stirling. The novels *Rob Roy* and *The Legend of Montrose,* both by Sir Walter Scott, are set in the Region and Scott's *Lady of the Lake,* a long narrative poem, is almost a step-by-step guide to the Trossachs. Numerous regional place-names are immortalized in songs by Robert Burns and others: *Allan Water, The Battle of Sheriffmuir, Bruce's Address Before Bannockburn* ("Scots Wha Ha'e"), *Bonnie Strathyre* and, of course, *Loch Lomond* ("Ye'll tak' the high road and I'll tak' the low road").

High road or low, there is a microcosm of Scottish scenery and history in this Region which clasps the Lowlands to the Highlands.

Stirling

As the meeting place of Scotland's motorway network from Edinburgh, Glasgow and the south, Stirling is the first Scottish town many visitors see. It is the tourist capital of the Region, a little Edinburgh with "crag-and-tail" foundations and a royal half-mile. Stirling's strategic position, commanding the lowest bridge on the Forth, was appreciated by the Stuart kings and they spent a lot of time at its castle—a fact which, together with the relics of freedom fighters in the neighborhood, has led some Scottish Nationalists to declare that should Scotland achieve independence again Stirling must be her capital city.

Earlier in this chapter we were on the ramparts, admiring the view. Take time to inspect this lovely Renaissance citadel of crow-stepped gables, stone carvings and twisted chimneys. The hammer-beamed Parliament Hall still whispers of dark 14th-century deeds, and across the courtyard the fine regimental museum of the Argyll & Sutherland Highlanders houses more recent battle memories. The royal palace, still inside the castle walls, was built by James V and the chapel beside it by James VI. Several kings and queens were born or crowned in these buildings. Mary Queen of Scots lived there in her infancy before she was sent to France. An embrasure on the battlements with the inscription "MR 1561" is still called Queen Mary's Lookout.

Going downhill from the esplanade you pass the National Trust for Scotland Visitor Centre, a garden, tearoom, bookshop and craftshop and an exhibition hall with a multiscreen theater showing historical films. On the right is Mar's Wark, the roofless ruin of a mansion which the Earl of Mar, premier earl of Scotland, put up in 1570. The building of slightly later date on the left, the Argyll Ludging ("ludging" was "lodging," a nobleman's town house), was for many years a military hospital and is now a youth hostel. Darnley's House at the foot of the street has an inscription: "Nursery of James VI and his son Prince Henry."

Before you descend to modern Stirling's shopping streets you pass the old Town House (City Hall), the Mercat Cross, where proclamations were made, and the parish church of the Holy Rude (rood, cross), a fine Gothic building dated 1414. Here King James VI was crowned at the age of one year; the presiding clergyman was John Knox.

Close by in Back Walk stands the gaunt 17th-century Cowane's Hospital, built as a refuge for the old. You can walk from here along the south side of the castle hill to the Smith Institute, the local museum and art gallery. As you start, note the square patch of ground beside the Dumbarton road (A811) called the King's Knot. It was once a garden of intricately intersecting paths and borders and dates from around 1628.

Across the Forth

Just north of the convolutions of the Forth, a river which seems reluctant to leave Stirling, you come to the Wallace Monument on a crag above a loop in the river. (Take Wallace Street and cross by Stirling Bridge, A9.) The tower has a good view from its 220-foot balcony and a sword alleged to be Wallace's is kept in a small museum.

Inside another loop of the river (take Shore Road—right, across the level-crossing) are the tower and ruins of Cambuskenneth Abbey, founded by the "sair sanct" King David I in 1147. It was briefly Scotland's House of Parliament 500 years ago. A tombstone marks the graves of James III (murdered after the battle of Sauchieburn, 1488) and of his queen, Margaret of Denmark.

The Battle of Bannockburn

English school pupils have their Battle of Hastings in 1066, Scottish pupils the Battle of Bannockburn in 1314. Though this most significant battle in Scotland's story is recalled in a well-equipped visitor center, the battle-site itself has vanished beneath houses and industrial developments. Every June 24 the Scottish National Party holds a rally here.

In the culmination of the Scottish Wars of Independence, Edward II of England had accepted a challenge to come north to relieve the besieged Stirling Castle. He wanted to finish off this impudent usurper Robert Bruce, who styled himself king of Scots. Before the battle, Bruce chose ground which he knew well—undulating grasslands with thick woods, above the marshy river. His forces numbered about 5000 spearman with some archers, plus 500 light cavalry. They faced Edward's 2–3,000 heavy, mounted knights, with 15,000 archers and spearmen. Bruce had dug pits in soft ground, planted spikes and felled trees across tracks, all to ensure that the cumbersome cavalry could not be deployed effectively.

On Sunday June 23, 1314, battle was joined, initially after the English Sir Henry de Bohun had recognized Bruce, leveled his lance and charged him single-handedly, in full view of both armies. Bruce unchivalrously split his skull with his battle-axe. In the ensuing mêlée, the English horse were hampered in the pits and traps, then skewered on Scottish spears. By nightfall the English knights had suffered heavy losses.

Edward moved to lower ground, seeking water for men and horses. The ground here was not only marshy, but confined by the Bannockburn which flowed into the looping Forth. Next morning, the Scots advanced slowly with a wall of spears, forcing the English knights into an increasingly narrow space between Bannockburn and main river. The English spearmen were trapped behind their own milling heavy horsemen. The English archers, so often to be the bane of the Scots' spear-ring, were also ineffectual. King Edward retreated from the field, his knights falling back and fighting bravely to protect him. The Scots camp followers appeared on the scene, increasing the panic in the English forces. The impossible had happened. An inferior force of mainly foot-soldiers had defeated a superior mounted army.

The full story is told in the fascinating Bannockburn Heritage Centre with an audio-visual presentation, a breathtaking panoramic painting of the battle and a "Kingdom of the Scots" Exhibition.

The strategic center of the year 1314 has become a strategic center of motorways. Bannockburn is the point at which the M80 from Glasgow meets the M9 from Edinburgh and continues (as the M9) to Dunblane. Though set in a most unpicturesque landscape it is a tourist metropolis with, apart from the Visitor Centre, the large King Robert hotel, a restaurant and a major National Trust for Scotland information center and shop, open throughout the summer season.

The somber majesty of Bannockburn, its panoply and glitter, are a loud shout for Scotland. One cannot help contrasting it with that other great

battleground just across the English border, Flodden, where the victory
went to the other side and where the commemoration is a simple stone:
"To the Brave of *Both* Nations." But then, Flodden did not lead to Scotland's independence.

Ironworks and Roman Camps

Five Scottish Regions surround Central Region. Journeying towards
them in turn, the first route is along the M9 motorway, or the accompanying A9, into Lothian Region (Edinburgh 37 miles). The horizons are lined
with hills and with the shining lattice-work and flaming towers of Grangemouth oil port, but the immediate surroundings are heavily industrialized
as you negotiate the coalmining and iron-founding sprawl of Stenhouse-
muir, Larbert and Camelon. Scotland's Arthurian students link the last-
named place with Camelot, a theory which the density of factories makes
impossible to disprove from evidence on the ground. It is no easier to re-
construct the past in Falkirk, though the place has a history. It was the
chief Scottish market for sheep and cattle, which were driven down from
the Highland fastnesses before the railways took over the transportation
of livestock. Bonnie Prince Charlie slept the night at a shop in the main
street before the battle of Falkirk (1746); and not long afterwards the Duke
of Cumberland, commander of the Government forces, also stayed there
in the "Great Ludging"—a room above a bootmaker's shop. The Jacobites
were retreating towards their doom on Culloden Moor and Prince Charlie
claimed the victory in this rearguard action; but Major James Wolfe (afterwards of Quebec), a down-to-earth officer of the opposing side, wrote:
"'Twas not a battle for neither side would fight."

Three miles north of Falkirk the famous Carron Ironworks were established in 1760. To serve their needs brickworks and coal mines began to
proliferate. The Carron Company in its prosperous days made every con-
ceivable cast-iron object, from guns and bridge girders to fireplaces and
kitchen pots.

Two miles east of Falkirk the Antonine Wall crosses the A9. It comes
from the Forth shore near Bo'ness (Lothian), enters the grounds of Callen-
dar House and then runs more or less parallel with the Forth-Clyde canal
to Old Kirkpatrick below Glasgow. Most of the interesting finds in the
Wall were made between 1769 and 1790, when the waterway was being
excavated and people came from miles around to see the miracle of ships
sailing through dry land. Now both canal and Wall are done for, killed
by the march of science. You can pick up a leaflet at the Falkirk museum
which shows where Roman remains are still visible. The most conspicuous
of its 20 forts is Rough Castle, a mound of earth near Bonnybridge, six
miles west of Falkirk on the A803. It is cared for by the National Trust
for Scotland.

"Look Aboot Ye"

Crossing the Forth at Stirling and turning east on the A91 towards Fife
Region you enter the district of Clackmannan. Before regionalization, it
was the smallest county in the British Isles. It was once thickly forested.
Robert the Bruce lost a glove there while hunting and sent his lieutenant
back to find it. "Go to a path near Clackmannan village," he instructed

him, "and look aboot ye." The road is called Lookabootye Brae to this day and tourism has adopted the slogan, advising "Look aboot ye" as you travel the small burghs, old and new, rustic and industrial, threaded along the hillfoot road under the ridge of the frowning Ochils.

Menstrie, Alva and Tillicoultry are nothing much to look at from the main road, but among these villages the back streets are worth investigating. Menstrie has a 17th-century fortress, the birthplace and property of Sir William Alexander who founded the Canadian colony of Nova Scotia. Behind Alva and Tillicoultry two charming little glens climb up waterfalls into clefts in the hills. A road and a mile-long footpath beside it goes up from Dollar to Castle Campbell, a former residence of the Clan Campbell chiefs. Perched on a crag above the meeting of two streams, the castle is like a woodcut in a Gothic novel. The streams are called Care and Sorrow, the fortress was originally Castle Gloom and Dollar itself was once spelled Dolour; yet the scene, though romantic, is not at all melancholy. Legend says the names were bestowed by a noblewoman kept captive there, but the likelier explanation would be some punning reference or corruption of forgotten Gaelic names.

Dollar has a peaceful early 19th-century air and some handsome buildings of that period, notably Dollar Academy, founded 1818 and built by Playfair. Now it is a fairly prestigious school for girls and boys. From here you pass on to the Yetts of Muckhart ("yetts" are gates; we are back to another old drove road) and the Rumbling Bridge beneath which the Devon River tumbles noisily in an echoing gorge. To stay in Central Region you now turn southwest on the A977 for Clackmannan village, Alloa and the riverside road (A907) to Stirling.

South of the Hillfoots

The immediate area east of Stirling and north of the Forth is sometimes overlooked by visitors anxious for the scenic delights of the Trossachs on the other side of Stirling. It is backed by the impressive edge of the Ochil Hills, ancient lava flows which butt against the softer coal-bearing rocks of the Forth Valley. Early exploitation of these mineral resources ensured the development of various communities along or close to the river. Kincardine on Forth has an interesting selection of carved gravestones in its local kirkyard, showing local artisans' tools. There is a preserved beam engine (used to pump out mines) now standing in a greenfield site near Sauchie.

The largest town, Alloa, is also workaday and of interest to industrial heritage enthusiasts. It has, for example, the last surviving glass cone in Scotland, a brick structure used in glassmaking. Perhaps the most pleasant memorial to those early industrial days is Gartmorn Dam, signed from north of Alloa. The Earl of Mar, who commanded so ineffectually at the Battle of Sheriffmuir (*see* page 185) owned extensive coal-mining interests here and built a dam to run water-powered pumps. The mines have long gone, but Gartmorn Dam survives as a pleasant stretch of water, complete with Countryside Ranger Service, flocks of wildfowl and outstanding views of the Ochil Hills to the north. (Incidentally the Jacobite earl's progressive interest in industry and improvements disproves the common view of the Jacobites as a movement which wanted to turn the clock back to old times.)

Finally, good views can be had of this area from the summit of Dumyat ("Dum-*eye*-at"), the prominent "end-bump" of the Ochils—reach it by a short walk from a back road behind the Wallace Monument. Near the little top is a ruined fort—no more than rings of stones—said to be of Pictish date (Dumyat = Dun Maeatae, i.e., the fort of the Maeatae, a local Pictish tribe).

Dunblane

Our third route from Stirling is also a short one. The north road (A9) soon passes into Tayside Region. Along with the M9 motorway it leads to Bridge of Allan and Dunblane, four and eight miles respectively from Stirling.

They are two suburban-looking towns, mainly populated by commuters and retired people, pleasantly spread out on the banks of Allan Water, which Burns celebrated in song. Near Bridge of Allan in a fine waterside situation stands Stirling University, one of the newest and most progressive in Scotland. Its MacRobert Centre, open to non-students, offers jazz concerts, debates, avant-garde theater and films.

Dunblane is noted for its hydropathic establishment, a spa center built in the 19th century. There are quite a number of these centers in various Scottish towns, all dating from the days when the vogue for Scottish air and mountain water led some doctors to consider them a wonder cure for every complaint. Like most of the "hydros," Dunblane's is now a hotel.

In the middle of the town stand the partly-restored ruins of a large cathedral. King David, the "sair sanct", built the existing structure on the site of St. Blane's little eighth-century cell. Dunblane cathedral is contemporary with the Border abbeys but more mixed in its architecture, part Early English and part Norman. The 19th-century art critic John Ruskin said of it: "I know nothing so perfect in its simplicity and so beautiful, as far as it reaches, in all the Gothic with which I am acquainted." Restoration over the past century has been sensitive on the whole. Dunblane ceased to be a cathedral, as did most others in Scotland, at the time of the Reformation in the mid-16th century.

The moorland east of Dunblane, sloping up to the ridge of the Ochil Hills, is the site of the battle of Sheriffmuir (1715) at which Government troops scattered the Earl of Mar's Jacobites and destroyed the hopes of the Old Pretender, Bonnie Prince Charlie's father. The site is marked with the so-called Gathering Stone (for gathering the clans) near the unclassified Wallace Stones road, two miles from Dunblane. A turning to the right would bring you down steeply among forested slopes and small reservoirs into Bridge of Allan again.

Rob Roy's Native Heath

The most heavily-trafficked road out of Stirling in the summer months is the A84 to Callander and Lochearnhead. It is a section of the main highway between Edinburgh and the western Highlands, and near Fort William it joins up with the old Road to the Isles.

The first town is Doune, feudal seat of that "Bonnie Earl o' Moray" who was treacherously slain near Aberdour in 1570. The incident inspired one of Scotland's best-loved ballads:

"O lang will his lady
Look o'er the Castle Doune
Ere she sees the Earl o' Moray
Come sounding through the toon. . . ."

For every person who nowadays visits Doune to climb the massive walls and descend to the reeking dungeons of the stronghold for a glimpse of the harsh life of long ago, there must be a score whose destination is the Doune Motor Museum, a collection of automobiles ancient and modern, the lifelong labor of love of the late J.C. Sword.

After Doune you follow the Teith River to Callander, a well-built town-let with a broad main street thronged in the season with visitors. It is the base for the Trossachs, which we shall come to presently, and it disputes with Pitlochry the claim to have more hotels per head of population than any town in Britain. Local walks include the Roman Camp Walk, on the left before you reach the town center. The nearby Roman Camp Hotel on a peaceful riverside site was a former hunting lodge of the Dukes of Perth. On the right the Bracklinn Falls are signed, and the car park here can also be a starting point for exploring the woodlands of the Callander Crags behind the town. Callander, like Pitlochry, justifiably describes itself as a Gateway to the Highlands.

Northward through Strathyre with the newly-afforested Braes of Balquhidder sweeping up to the west, the road struggles to disentangle itself from rock and torrent and overhanging rowan, oak and birch. Two serpentine lochs spill down the glen, and it is fascinating after rain to watch the stream racing beneath you in a succession of rapids and water-falls.

"My name is MacGregor," says Rob Roy in Scott's novel, "and my foot is on my native heath". These rough ravines and the heather-covered wilderness from which they radiate are his native heath. Rob and his wife and two sons are said to lie under some stone slabs in Balquhidder ("Balhwidder") churchyard, the turning on the left after you pass through Strathyre; but the quaint carvings of weapons and animals suggest that the stones are a good deal older than those characters whose exploits belong to the early 18th century. Tales of Rob Roy MacGregor, a man of great physical strength and courageous energy, tend to romanticize him. He was a kind of throwback—a Highlander who stood for old values and a way of life which Lowland authorities could not tolerate or understand.

Across the watershed you arrive at Lochearnhead, a water-sports center on Loch Earn. Local hotels offer sailing lessons, canoeing, fishing, water skiing and suchlike. The A85 climbs spectacular Glen Ogle (which Queen Victoria likened to the Khyber Pass) then gives a fine view of the Ben Lawers range from the top before descending to the Killin road junction at Lix Toll. Fanciful writers link it to LIX—the 59th Roman legion! The road then turns west along Glen Dochart, shadowed by Ben More, to reach Crianlarich.

This is an important T-junction for tourists. The A82 from Glasgow comes in, having traveled the full 23-mile length of Loch Lomond, one of Strathclyde Region's famous routes. It, and the road from Lochearn-head, now continue northwest for Glencoe and Fort William in the Highlands.

On this historic route trodden by Romans and Picts, cattle drovers and cattle thieves, you must have an automobile or be a hardy walker. The railroad from Stirling to Crianlarich which used to accompany the highway has been closed down; although its continuation from Crianlarich to north and west was mercifully reprieved. The serenely remote vale from Crianlarich to Tyndrum has the strange distinction of being the only valley in Britain with two mainline railroads through it: Glasgow–Crianlarich–Oban and Glasgow–Crianlarich–Fort William.

Near Crianlarich and even more conspicuously at Tyndrau, another junction a little to the west, it is not just road and rail links which are important. You will see another aspect of Scottish recreation. These are just two of the places on the West Highland Way, an "unofficial" long-distance footpath which runs from the outskirts of Glasgow to Fort William, by way of Loch Lomond and Glencoe. Its presence explains the number of pained-looking earnest walkers trudging around.

For energetic tourists with time on their hands there are rewarding walks round the quiet riverine lochs of Lubnaig and Voil. To the summits of neighboring mountains it is usually quite a long walk, and proper equipment is essential. Three miles north of Callander on the A84, an iron bridge crosses the river and, beyond the disused railroad, a fairly obvious route intermittently marked with a footpath leads in about 3 miles to the top of Ben Ledi (2,873 feet), a magnificent viewpoint from which in clear weather you can see Arthur's Seat in Edinburgh and Goat Fell on the island of Arran, two places 80 miles apart. From Lochearnhead an unclassified road goes along the south shore of Loch Earn past Ardvorlich House, and by the gray slopes of Ben Vorlich (3,224 feet) with equally dramatic views of the approaches to the Highlands.

The Trossachs

The popular road to the Trossachs from anywhere in the east of Scotland is via Callander on the A84, the road we have just traveled. One mile north of that town the A821, rather bumpy and narrow for its summer traffic, goes off to the left and almost at once you are coasting Loch Vennachar, the first of the Trossachs lochs. From here on the most comprehensive guide is Sir Walter Scott's poem *The Lady of the Lake:* it mentions every little bridge and farmhouse. Various engineering schemes of the Glasgow Water Department have rendered some of the topography out of date.

Loch Vennachar gives way to the beautiful little Loch Achray, shrouded in woodland; and Loch Achray leads on to the principal loch, Loch Katrine (pronounced "Kattrin"), where the road ends. Wandering byways in this area will take you to the smaller and more isolated Trossachs lochs: Arklet, Chon and Ard.

It is hard to describe the Trossachs or to account for their peculiar charm. They combine the wildness of the Highlands with the prolific vegetation of an old Lowland forest. Their open ground is a dense mat of bracken and heather, their woodland is of silver birch, dwarf oak and hazel which fasten their roots into every crevice of the rocks and stop short on the very brink of the lochs. The most colorful season is the fall, particularly October when the visitors have departed and the hares, deer and game birds have taken over. But the district is rich in color from early spring onwards with the variegated greens of the leaves and the grays and blues of the crags gradually yielding to the browns and purples of bracken and heather, soft and bright as an old tartan.

In rainy weather the Trossachs are a sponge and the water which filters through the rocks comes out so pure and clear that the lochs are like sheets of crystal glass. When Glasgow folk, who draw their water from this area, want distilled water for their automobile batteries they simply get it from the kitchen tap.

Throughout the summer the steamboat *Sir Walter Scott* plies between the Steamer Pier, one mile from the Trossachs hotel on the A821, and the hamlet of Stronachlachar, seven miles away near the head of Loch Katrine. You can also reach Stronachlachar by the minor B829 from Aberfoyle. Another tiny road continues beyond Stronachlachar and beside Loch Arklet for five miles to Inversnaid on Loch Lomond, where the landing-stage is a port of call for summer steamboats from Balmaha and Balloch (Strathclyde Region).

Though there is a range of forest tracks and trails, for many people the easiest way to glimpse the Trossachs's splendor is to walk from the main car park along the north bank of Loch Katrine. This is on a well-surfaced road, owned by Strathclyde Water Board and closed to traffic, except for pedestrians and cyclists.

Place-names and topographical features commemorate Rob Roy, whose stamping ground this was. His supposed cave is close to Inversnaid on Loch Lomond. The old Highland word for a roughneck marauder like Rob Roy was "cateran," and that is said to be how Loch Katrine got its name. When you take a walk and find the going tough, think how it was in this brigand country when Rob was an outlaw—when, as Scott says, "there was no mode of issuing from the Trossachs except by a sort of ladder composed of the branches of roots and trees."

An area of 45,000 acres covering most of the Trossachs, the two high hills of Ben Lomond and Ben Venue and a stretch of Loch Lomond's eastern shore has been designated the Queen Elizabeth Forest Park.

Aberfoyle

When motoring for pleasure you can hardly go wrong on the scenic drives in the Trossachs. The lanes are narrow, with passing places; sometimes they end abruptly and you have to turn back. But to delay or retrace your steps is no hardship in this fresh, picturesque and varied landscape.

In the Pass of Achray, between Lochs Achray and Katrine, the A821 turns south for Aberfoyle. Old inhabitants can remember when this seven-mile road was the "Duke's Drive" and no automobiles were allowed on it. Busloads of vacationers from Glasgow had to walk or travel in horse-drawn wagonettes. But now the Duke's Drive is a fine skyline route, snaking up to 800 feet and down again with panoramas of all the Trossachs lakes. Three miles from Aberfoyle, near the David Marshall wildlife park (hillpaths and picnic lodge) you may detour round the Achray Forest Drive (toll road, pay as you enter with two 50p pieces) and relax on a loch shore among the birds and beasts of the forest.

Aberfoyle village is popular with pony-trekkers. If you are only passing through, the focal point of interest is the local inn, with its supposed relics of the brawl in *Rob Roy,* when Bailie Nicol Jarvie of Glasgow set the Hielandman's kilt on fire with a red-hot poker.

Here you are on the road for Stirling (A873). It runs level along a broad valley, rather humdrum after the Trossachs scenery. It skirts the Lake of Menteith, often described as the only "lake" in Scotland (there are others in fact) and a venue for an occasional Grand Match between curlers, Highlands against Lowlands, whenever winter frosts permit the ice to bear. At a priory on one of the two islands in the lake the five-year-old Mary Queen of Scots was taken for safe keeping after the battle of Pinkie (Lothian) in 1547—a foretaste of the island prisons of her later captivity.

The serene parkland around Blair Drummond, where you rejoin the A84, contains a range of exotic fauna in Scotland's Safari Park at Blair Drummond. This drive-through commercial concern offers entertainment of a gawking kind which modern conservation-oriented visitors may find distasteful. There are, however, lots of amusements for children.

It is now eight miles to Stirling, our starting-point. The roundtrip, Stirling–Callander–Trossachs–Aberfoyle–Stirling, is only 52 miles, so if you devote the day to it there is plenty of time for exploring byways.

Loch Lomond: the Eastern Shore

Our last Central Region route travels due west (A811) towards Strathclyde Region. A group of smooth rounded hills separates it from the Forth–Clyde valley where the Roman Wall, the canal and now the invisible oil pipeline from Grangemouth to Loch Long and the M80 to Glasgow run. The mini-massif has different names on its different sides: Fintry Hills, Campsie Fells, Kilsyth Hills. One minor road (B818) crosses them east to west and another (B822) north to south. They are relatively quiet alternatives to the arterial roads of the Region and not without charm. Northern slopes look towards the Highlands, southern slopes over the central-belt industrial conurbations.

Drymen ("Drimmen"), 23 miles from Stirling, is a pleasant-looking village built round an open square. The fast-flowing Endrick River runs close by, coming out of the Fintry Hills and heading for Loch Lomond. This is Buchanan country, as the name of the hotel tells us. Buchanan Castle stands aloof in its neighboring park. George Buchanan (1506-1582), scholar, poet and tutor to Mary Queen of Scots, was born at Killearn, two miles from Drymen.

At Drymen you are only three miles from Balmaha Pier on the east bank of Loch Lomond (B837); and Balmaha is one of the places offering loch cruising and island visiting. Beyond Balmaha a popular—and cul-de-sac—road runs on to Rowardennan (eight miles). On the way, there are many car parks and signposted walks to enjoy the magnificent woodland, loch and hill scenery.

The boundary between Central and Strathclyde Regions is an imaginary line down the middle of Loch Lomond. It divides a pattern of islands opposite Balmaha. They look like clumps of forest lifted from the Trossachs and dumped in the loch, and the steamboat threads its way through them. Most have Gaelic names, but note two little rocks which do not: St. Rosalind's and St. Winifred's. There is a sentimental tale attached to them. In the 1880s the great map-maker John Bartholomew took his girl friend, suitably chaperoned, for a sail. They picnicked on one of those tufts of greenery. Maybe they managed to maroon the chaperone on another—at all events, two islets were involved in the happy memories that came back to John Bartholomew years later when he drew up the new map of Loch Lomond. Discovering that the islets had no names, he named one for his girl friend and the other for the chaperone.

Note also Bucinch and Ceardoch. They are washed by the passing boats but their dense foliage and lack of a boat landing make a visit difficult. They belong to the National Trust for Scotland. Legend says Robert the Bruce planted Bucinch's yew trees to provide weapons for his bowmen. Legend and history have stuck their labels on all the isles of this little Lomond archipelago: this one has a ruined château, that one a ruined nunnery, this one was the scene of a massacre, that is the old burial ground of the MacGregor chiefs . . . to visit them you would have to hire a boat and that is best done from Luss or Inverbeg on the western shore (A82).

Here at Balmaha and all the way up the track to Rowardennan they are part of the embroidery of the loch, anchored for eternity in the shimmering water, calm and mystical like green stones in a Zen garden.

To reach Rowardennan with an automobile is no problem, but beyond that point you have to walk; and it is another 16 miles on the well-marked West Highland Way footpath through native oakwoods (look out for wild goats!) before Loch Lomond—barely a mile wide at Rowardennan—eventually tapers to a stream at Ardlui. But climb Ben Lomond if you can (3,192 feet, not a difficult walk from Rowardennan) and from its summit you will see the whole of Loch Lomond, its surface area larger than any other Scottish loch, stretching into the hills. At weekends there is a good deal of boating, skin-diving, fishing and rock-climbing going on; but somehow these activities never disturb the essential tranquility of the loch.

From Stirling to Balmaha by the direct A811 route and back by the more roundabout routes over the Campsie Hills would be a total journey of 70 miles. The boat trip from Balmaha Pier to Inversnaid and back takes nearly three hours.

PRACTICAL INFORMATION FOR CENTRAL

HOW TO GET THERE. By train. Mainline railroads connect Stirling with Edinburgh (intermediate stations at Larbert, Falkirk and Polmont); with Glasgow (intermediate station at Croy); with Carlisle; and with Perth (intermediate station at Dunblane). From London the best services are from King's Cross and run via Edinburgh, where it is usually necessary to change trains. The complete journey takes around 6 hours. Slower services from London Euston via the west coast line—because you must change stations at Glasgow. Motorail services (cars and passengers) run to Edinburgh. In the northwest of the Region there are rail connections from Tyndrum and Crianlarich to Glasgow in the south, Oban (Strathclyde) in the west and Fort William (Highland) in the north.

By car. Stirling is 37 miles from Edinburgh, 27 from Glasgow, and 35 from Perth. The M9 and M80 motorways from Edinburgh and Glasgow respectively pass one mile west of the town and continue to Dunblane; they are gradually being extended to Perth and Dundee.

By air. Airports for Central Region are Glasgow (M80, M8), 31 miles from Stirling; and Edinburgh (M9), 30 miles from Stirling.

HOTELS AND RESTAURANTS. Central Region's main touring bases are Stirling and Callander. There, and at small towns and villages throughout the Region, you will find a spread of tourist accommodations out of all proportion to the size of the communities. (The industrial towns are the exceptions.) Standards of inexpensive and medium-price establishments have improved in recent years and are still improving. The grand hotels, though few, were brought into existence by the rich "carriage trade" of the 19th century, when travel in Scotland was the fashion, and their services have not slipped. But you will also find many country hotels that can match them for comfort.

Like hotels, the restaurants of the touring districts are many and competitive, and continually improving. Regional country delicacies like loch trout, river salmon, mutton and venison are found regularly on modest menus, something extremely rare 20 years ago. The urban areas south and southwest of Stirling, in contrast, lack refinement in matters of eating and drinking. There you will find simple low-built pubs, often crowded and noisy, but serving substantial food at lunchtime (often eaten balanced on your knee, or at a shared table). Three heavy courses at one of these pubs will cost you all of £2 or £3.

Aberfoyle (A81). *Bailie Nicol Jarvie* (M), tel. 087 72–202. 37 rooms with bath. The wild men of Rob Roy's "clachan" (village) would not recognize their old drinking den on the fringe of the Trossachs, now enlarged and attractively modernized.
Restaurant. *Old Coachhouse* (M), tel. 087 72–535. Fishing net hangs on wall, but menu is cosmopolitan.

Airth (A900). *Airth Castle* (L), tel. 0324–83411. 23 rooms with bath, plus 24 in conference center. 14th-century castle with later additions. Gothic elements. Dungeon ballroom where visitors are put through country-dance paces. Ultra-modern sauna, solarium, games complex in stables. Smart lagoon pool. Every meal a banquet.

Blair Drummond (A873). **Restaurant.** *Broughton's Country Cottage* (M), tel. 0786–841897. Quite small (prior booking advisable). Prices are low for this category and the food and atmosphere are memorable.

Callander (A84). *Roman Camp* (E), Main Street (tel. 0877–30003). 14 rooms with bath. Former hunting lodge in beautiful, secluded grounds. Sophisticated cuisine in elegant and comfortable surroundings. *Dalgair House* (M), Main Street (tel. 0877–30283). 9 rooms with bath. Family-run, very hospitable. "Taste of Scotland" cuisine.
Restaurant. *Pip's Coffee House* (I), Ancaster Square (tel. 0877–30470). Good lunch stop. Wide choice of dishes, despite name.

Crianlarich (A82). *Allt-Chaorain House* (I), tel. 083 83–283. 9 rooms, 6 with bath. Lovely spacious country house on edge of moors. Log fires. Scottish cuisine.

Drymen (A81). *Buchanan Arms* (E), tel. 0360–60588. 35 rooms with bath. Imposing building, high standard of cuisine.

Dunblane (A9). *Cromlix House* (L), Kinbuck (tel. 0786–822125). 14 rooms with bath. Hoary old fortified house, noted for gracious and spacious living. Memorable soups and shellfish on dinner menu (but be prepared to spend £50 for two). *Dunblane Hydro* (E), tel. 0786–822551. 188 rooms with bath. Ample caravanserai of well-heeled hypochondriacs of long ago, today replaced by delegates of high-powered conferences. Beautiful situation. Elaborate venison, salmon and seafood dishes.

Fintry (B818). *Culcreuch Castle* (M), tel. 036 086–228. 6 rooms. In grounds of medieval castle, with fishing and boating. Old-fashioned cozy rooms, adequate cuisine. Bar and restaurant often crowded.

Killin (A827). *Ardeonaig* (M), tel. 056 72–400. 14 rooms with bath. Seven miles outside the village. One of the best hotels for miles around. Formal dress in restaurant.

Kippen (B822). *Cross Keys* (I), tel. 078 687–293. 3 rooms. Agreeable little pub under Fintry hills, well-managed in all departments.

Polmont (A9). *Inchyra Grange* (E), tel. 0324–711911. 31 rooms with bath. Solid stone country house, secluded but handy for motorway. Quiet luxury. Large wine cellar. Good bar meals. Leisure complex opened 1989.

Rowardennan (on unclassified road from Balmaha). *Rowardennan* (M), tel. 036 087–273. 11 rooms, 1 with bath. A homely, whitewashed inn at the ferry slip, halfway along Loch Lomond. Surprisingly sophisticated cuisine, attracts many visitors at weekends for drinks and lunches. Other times this is a place to unwind amid unforgettable scenery.

Stirling (A9). *Castle* (M), Castle Wynd (tel. 0786–72290). 6 rooms, 3 with bath. In 14th-century building; friendly and comfortable with good food. *Golden Lion* (M), King Street (tel. 0786–75351). 84 rooms, 50 with bath. Venerable staging post with much coming and going, but efficiently run. First-class cuisine. *Stirling University Hostel* (I), tel. 0786–73171. More than 1,000 rooms with basic facilities; available June–Sept. Pleasant surroundings.

Restaurant. *Heritage* (M), 16 Allan Park (tel. 0786–73660). Elegant, French-owned 18th-century establishment; fanlights and candles.

Thornhill (A873). **Restaurant.** *Lion and Unicorn* (M), tel. 0786 85–204. A place of real character.

Trossachs (A821). *Loch Achray* (I), tel. 087 76–229. 61 rooms, 28 with bath. Recently refurbished, now offering meals or beds in a magnificent situation beside the Duke's Drive.

HOW TO GET ABOUT. By car. The road network in the Central Region is excellent. Though it may sometimes be hard for the stranger to extricate himself from the industrial towns south of Stirling, traffic pressure on the narrow streets of the old burghs has been much relieved by the construction of the motorways. In July and August the roads west and northwest of Stirling are busy by Scottish standards, especially at weekends. On a fine Sunday afternoon you will find the minor roads in the Trossachs and Loch Lomond areas quite congested: they were built for a more leisurely age of touring.

Self-drive automobiles may be rented from *T.M. Templeton,* Whitehouse Road, Springkerse, Stirling (tel. 0786–63137).

By bus. The Region is well covered by public transport and details of all schedules on the routes we have described may be obtained from *Midland Scottish Omnibuses Ltd.,* Stirling (tel. 0786–73763). Highlights of the region may be seen on the many day excursions and longer tours organized between April and September from Glasgow and Edinburgh (contact Travel Center in these cities).

By boat. A scheduled boat service operates on Loch Lomond between Inversnaid, Balmaha and Balloch (Strathclyde). Daily cruises, Apr.–Sept., from Steamer Pier on Loch Katrine; steamer services operate from May–Sept.

TOURIST INFORMATION. Principal information centers are at Stirling (Dumbarton Road, tel. 0786–75019) and Callander (Leny Road, tel. 0877–30342). There you can "book-a-bed-ahead."

Stirling is open all year. Callander is open Apr.–Oct. District centers, open in summer, are at Aberfoyle, Dunblane, Killin, Stirling (Broad Street), Stirling (Pirnhill service area, M9), Tillicoultry and Tyndrum. Opening hours are usually weekdays, 10–6.

The Forestry Commission maintains a Forestry Information Service at Strathyre (A84), where there are also forest cabins to rent. Open Easter–mid-Oct.

FISHING. There is salmon fishing in the upper Forth, Teith and Devon rivers and in Loch Lomond (from Inversnaid hotel). Day or season permits may be obtained from or through local fishing-tackle shops. Sunday fishing is prohibited in most parts of the Region.

Sea trout and brown trout are fished in the Allan Water (permits from Stirling and Bridge of Allan tackle shops). The Lake of Menteith is stocked with brown and rainbow trout: fly fishing only, from boats at Lake of Menteith hotel, and rather expensive at around £18 per day. The Carron Valley reservoir in the Fintry Hills has brown trout; fly fishing from boat around £14 per day (permit from Director of Finance, Central Regional Council, Viewforth, Stirling). Two good inexpensive lochs for brown trout are Loch Achray in the Trossachs (£3 per day, permits from Loch Achray hotel, some pike, bream and perch also); and Banton Loch (£1 per day, permit from Kilsyth Fish Protection Association, 24 Kingston Flats, Kilsyth, or Colzium Service Station, Stirling Road, Kilsyth).

Hotels that offer fishing to residents in own grounds or nearby include Forest Hills, at Aberfoyle; Winnock, at Drymen; Inversnaid, at Inversnaid; Lake, at Port of Menteith; Loch Achray, at Trossachs; Glazertbank, at Lennoxtown; and Rosebank House, at Strathyre.

GOLF. As elsewhere in Scotland, every town and many a village has its nine- or 18-hole course. You can normally turn up and play a round without formality on payment of a fee of £3.50–£6 a day. Caddy cars, snack meals and drinks are usually available. The three smart clubs are at Dollar, Drymen (Buchanan Castle) and Dullatur. These clubs require an introduction from a member or a golf club secretary and do not welcome casual clothes in their lounge bars, or visitors at weekends.

HISTORIC HOUSES AND GARDENS. The northern parts of Central Region were too close to the predatory Highlanders to encourage much building of elegant houses or the laying out of woods and estates; while southern parts were completely overlaid by industry in the 19th century. Nonetheless, there are some attractive houses and gardens in the valleys of Forth and Teith, west of Stirling, but most are privately-owned and open on specified days only, in spring and summer. Consult local newspapers or information centers for details.

Ben Lawers Visitor Centre, by Killin (off A827). Audio-visual wildlife presentation, guided walks, access to mountain summit through a national nature reserve. Open Apr.–Sept., daily 11–4; June–Aug., daily 10–5. N.T.S.

Castle Campbell, Dollar (off A91). Formidable ruin approached by scenic footpath in wooded glen. Now impressively restored. Open Apr.–Sept., weekdays 9.30–7, Sun. 2–7; Oct.–Mar., weekdays 9.30–4 (closed Thur., Fri.), Sun. 2–4. N.T.S.

Doune Castle, Doune (A84). Ruins of a 14th-century stronghold, massive in decay. A descendant of the earls of Moray, who owned it, now has the **Doune Motor Museum** close by. Open Apr.–Oct., daily, 10–5.

Dunmore Pineapple, Airth (A900). Unique folly, country retreat of 18th-century noblewoman. You may rent it—apply National Trust for Scotland. Open daily 10–sunset (grounds only).

Gargunnock House, 6 miles from Stirling (A811). Entrance to the house itself is by written appointment only. The gardens are especially worth visiting and are normally open Apr.–Oct., Wed. only, 1–5.

Menstrie Castle, Castle Road, Menstrie (A91). 16th-century fortress almost completely modernized. Part is privately-occupied, but you can visit the Nova Scotia commemoration rooms with relics of Sir William Alexander (1567–1640) and the history of the colonial baronetcies. Open by appointment (tel. 0738–31296). N.T.S.

Stirling Castle (A9). Most graceful and dramatic of royal strongholds. Visitor center. Open Feb.–Mar. and Oct.–Dec., weekdays 9.30–5, Sun. 12.30–4; Apr.–Sept., weekdays 9.30–6, Sun. 10.30–5.30. N.T.S.

MUSEUMS. Bannockburn Heritage Centre, Bannockburn (A9). Information center, shop, audio-visual theater, murals, snack-bar, interpretative displays in a custom-built concrete edifice. Scotland's flamboyant tribute to her 14th-century freedom-fighters. Open daily, Apr.–Oct., 10–6.

Falkirk Museum, Orchard Street, Falkirk (A9). Social, industrial and archeological history of the district, including material on Antonine Wall. Open weekdays 10–12.30 and 1.30–5.

Glengoyne Distillery, near Killearn (A81). One of the most historic and picturesque of malt whisky distilleries, where ancient skills and techniques are displayed along with modern methods. Open Apr.–Oct., Mon.–Fri., 10–3; from mid-July–end Aug. the distillery is not in production.

Grangemouth Museum, Bo'ness Road, Grangemouth (A904). History of Forth-Clyde and Falkirk-Edinburgh canals. Open weekdays during library hours, currently 10–7.

MacRobert Arts Centre, 3 miles along road to Bridge of Allan, University of Stirling (A9). Enterprising exhibitions of many kinds in a lively cultural center. Open Jan.–May and Sept.–Dec., weekdays 11–5, Sun. 2–5.

Queen Elizabeth Forest Park Centre (A821). Interpretation center, and walks' starting point. Superb views. Open daily Apr.–Sept. 10–6.

Scottish Railway Preservation Society, Union Street, Bo'ness (off A904). Old trains, refurbished station. Steam trains run on rebuilt Bo'ness–Kinneil track. Visitor center, "Buffer Stop" café. Open Apr.–mid-Sept., Sat. and Sun., 12–5.

Smith Art Gallery and Museum, Albert Place, Stirling (A9). History of district; various temporary exhibitions. Undergoing renovation. Open 2–5.

Andrew Carnegie

KINGDOM OF THE PICTS

Fife

"Fareweel Scotland, I'm awa' to Fife," cried the fishwife of Newhaven, setting sail for the opposite shore of the Firth of Forth. It was all of six miles away but she expressed what many Lothian people used to feel: that Fife was a foreign place. Since her time, communications between Fife and the rest of Scotland have been made easier. There are the one and a half-mile-long Forth rail and road bridges to join her to the south, and the longer but less spectacular Tay rail and road bridges to the north. Travelers in a hurry to get across one or other of these bridges are out of Fife before they realize they are in it.

It is called the Kingdom of Fife. It is the only remaining kingdom of the seven into which Scotland fell when the Romans went home in the 4th century A.D. and the Picts moved in. That distinction was remembered when local government in Scotland was reorganized in 1973. Of all the county councils which put up arguments against merging with their neighbors to form Regions—and most of them did—only Fife won the day. Plans to divide her between Central and Tayside Regions were abandoned. She kept her kingdom intact and the eight Regions became nine. This tells us something about Fife folk: they are stubborn, even among Scots, and will go to greater lengths than most to preserve their independence.

Until recently, the main touring routes avoided Fife. The great northern highway from Edinburgh to Perth and Inverness (M90) now runs along its western borders. Its northern and southern limits are the Firths of Tay and Forth respectively; its eastern border is the open sea. Not surprisingly, fishing and seafaring have played a role in its history. At an earlier period a large population lived and worked in the small ports and harbors which form a continuous chain round its coasts. James V called Fife "a beggar's mantle fringed with gold."

That was before the exploitation of another kind of gold, black gold, began in the western parts of the Region. Coal from the West Fife coalfields provided the energy which got Scotland moving in the Industrial Revolution in the late 18th century. As in West Lothian across the Forth, this industry has now declined and you will see more disused pits than working ones. Fife's industrial hopes these days are pinned to 20th-century black gold—oil, petrochemicals and liquid gases from the North Sea. A large liquid-gas development at Moss Morran near Aberdour (A92) produces propane and butane for export to North America from the nearby Braefoot tanker terminal. Westward along the same shoreline, off the A895 road near Culross, the biggest power station in Great Britain (2,400 megawatts) pours its hot effluent into the Forth.

Around and About

The industrial corner of Fife, a depressed and depressing district, occupies only a small part of the Region. The rest is pleasant agricultural country, not sensational but never monotonous. And the whole Region is still ringed with those fishing villages which, weathered down by the centuries, have become antiques of domestic architecture.

At Castle Law near Abernethy (A913) you will find a pre-Roman hill fort. Pictish names are common and you may be shown the occasional Pictish stone built into the wall of a church or cottage. There is one at the gates of Upper Largo church (A915). In Dunfermline and St. Andrews, Fife has the two senior religious settlements in Scotland; and at Lindores and Balmerino near the Tay shore (A913) the ruins of two minor abbeys, greatly reduced.

There are no commercial airports in the Region. Fife people use either Edinburgh or Dundee. The main railroad from Edinburgh to the north, coming in by the Forth bridge, passes through the middle of the Region, where it divides in two, one track curving away to Perth for the old Highland line and the other going forward to the Tay bridge, Dundee and Aberdeen. There is also a branch line from the Forth bridge to Dunfermline and the mining towns of Cowdenbeath and Cardenden.

South to north through the Region, from Forth bridge to Tay bridge, is 40 miles, that is, about the same distance as the route west to east, from the M90 motorway to the promontory of Fife Ness.

The M90 cuts off a corner of the Region but the best road south to north through Fife is the A92, which takes in an old-fashioned little burgh called Cupar ("Cooper"), the "capital of the kingdom." The main west–east routes leave the M90 at different points for the coastal towns of the Forth (A911, A921); St. Andrews (A91); and the coastal villages of the Tay (A913).

West Fife

Coming off the Forth bridges by road or rail you plunge into a short stretch of uninspiring, rather tired-looking industry. On your left is the naval base of Rosyth, the Royal Navy's most junior home port, founded 1912. It ought to have been on the opposite shore, more convenient for Edinburgh and the south, but the Marquess of Linlithgow at Hopetoun House would not have it; and in those days the noble landowner's word was law. Rosyth has often been threatened with closure but it is now a refitting yard for nuclear submarines and its future seems assured.

On your right you glimpse the reverse side of the naval coin: the ship-breakers' yards at Inverkeithing, where famous old battleships were brought to end their days. The first of them were the surrendered units of Germany's High Seas fleet in 1919.

Dunfermline, five miles beyond the bridge going north, lifts her head proudly above a semi-industrial landscape scene round about. This was once the Royal Court of Scotland. Margaret, of the English royal house, married the Scottish King Malcolm Canmore. As Queen Margaret of Scotland, she worked to improve the local Celtic church, bringing her saintly Saxon influence to bear. Her church lies beneath today's Dunfermline Abbey, founded in 1128, 35 years after her death.

Malcolm and Margaret had a small palace at Dunfermline (you can see its remains inside the abbey walls) and both of them were buried there in 1093, the Queen having died of grief at hearing of her husband's death. Scottish monarchs, who had up to that date always gone to Iona for burial, were thereafter interred at Dunfermline. There are 15 royal graves in the abbey, including that of Robert the Bruce. But the place suffered in the English wars and at the hands of John Knox's reformers and what we see today is chiefly an early 19th-century renovation. Purists consider the stone lettering "Robert the Bruce" round the parapet of the tower to be in rather poor taste.

Dunfermline's modern "patron saint," the man most responsible for its air of comfortable self-satisfaction, is Andrew Carnegie. His birthplace (1835) was a small house, now a museum, in Moodie Street. His parents rented the attic. As a steel baron in the States, Carnegie wielded power that the old Scottish kings would have envied, but he never forgot Dunfermline. He created the Carnegie Trust (1903) which enabled his native town to enjoy social and educational amenities and he bought and gave to the town the beautiful private park through whose heavy locked gates he had hardly dared look as a child. Pittencrieff Glen is still open to the public and is probably the most lavishly-endowed public park in Britain.

Seven miles west of Dunfermline, just off the A985, the 17th-century burgh of Culross ("Coo-russ") nestles beside the Forth. Its cottages, wynds, miniature abbey, town house and palace are like scenes from an old engraving: hard to believe that Culross 350 years ago was a bustling seaport and a pioneer of the coal trade. The National Trust for Scotland saved Culross from decay, restoring its houses and preserving its bumpy cobbled lanes with their characteristic plainstanes, the strips of level paving reserved for local gentry. Culross is a three-dimensional social history of a vanished era.

Old Hills and New Towns

Rejoining the M90 in the direction of Perth you pass by Loch Leven and come to the next main road into Fife, the A911. Vincenzo Lunardi, the first aerial traveler in Britain, floating toward Fife in his balloon in

1785, wrote: "I saw huge hills which I took to be the Highlands." They were not. They were the Lomonds (nothing to do with Loch Lomond) which curve up from the Howe of Fife, the agricultural heart of the Region, to heights of about 1,700 feet. A bi-centenary plaque (1985) at Ceres (pronounced *See-reez*), near Cupar, marks the spot where Lunardi "revisited the earth."

As the Lomonds sink behind you in the west you approach some towns of fairly innocuous industry, a small complex of which Glenrothes is the center. Glenrothes is a startling intruder in this archetypal Lowland scene: a new town, developed since 1950 and originally designed to meet the housing needs of new colliery workers. But coalmining has declined and Glenrothes instead has attracted the trailblazers of Scotland's most important new industry, electronics. Most of its 35,000 inhabitants are employed in factories which manufacture computers, office machinery and rocket and satellite systems. Having seven universities within a 90-minute drive of its center, it has also become an exchange-and-mart of scientific research. Glenrothes boasts the Fife airport, for light aircraft only.

The neighboring communities at Leslie and Markinch depended on papermaking at mills powered by the streams which flow from the Lomond Hills. In Glenrothes, the Balbirnie Craft Centre—displaying jewelry, knitwear, pottery, furniture, and glass—is well worth a visit.

Following the A911 and its continuation A915 and A917 we come to the Firth of Forth, with views of Edinburgh 15 miles across the water, and enter the East Neuk ("new k") of Fife.

The East Neuk

The East Neuk of Fife (Neuk is Scots "corner") is usually taken to be the easternmost portion, which road travelers reach by way of the relatively undistinguished countryside (see page 202) beyond the Forth Bridge. From Lundin Links onwards the ambience changes: the farmlands and hedgerows seem prosperous, with the grainfields appreciating the East Neuk's high sunshine and low rainfall records. There are glittering southward sea-views across the Firth of Forth to the Lothians.

The main attractions lie in the string of coastal villages with medieval origins. In those days, Scotland traded across the North Sea and the Dutch influence still survives today in the East Neuk's architecture of red pantiles and crow-stepped gables. (One of the most significant imports was a strange game from Holland, called golf.) As well as these strong European trading links, the East Neuk, like many other parts of the east coast of Scotland, expanded with the development of sea fishing. This poignant story is told in Anstruther's Scottish Fisheries Museum.

The first place you come to is Largo, popular with the bucket-and-spade brigade. Here a juvenile delinquent named Alexander Selkirk grew up, terrorized the neighborhood and departed to sail the seas. In 1704, having quarrelled with his captain, Selkirk was put ashore on the isle of Juan Fernandez off the coast of Chile. Four years later a British privateer picked him up; his rescuers found him dressed in goatskins and surrounded by tame goats. Piratical adventures on the way home earned him a fortune and he returned to Largo so richly dressed that his mother did not know him. Daniel Defoe heard his story and out of it created the famous tale of *Robinson Crusoe*.

After Upper and Lower Largo come the twin communities of Elie and Earlsferry, popular with surfboard sailors, then St. Monans, Pittenweem, Anstruther and Crail, especially attractive with photogenic places. The boatyard of Miller of St. Monance has been building Fifies, traditional high-stemmed, broad-beamed, three-man fishing boats, for more than two centuries. At Pittenweem (meaning the place of the cave), with its active fishing fleet, you can walk up an alley from the harbor to find the cave-shrine of St. Fillan. Anstruther (locally called "Anster") is the site of a Fisheries Museum. Crail, oldest and most aristocratic of East Neuk burghs, was the place the fish merchants retired to and built cottages, pala-tial by local standards. The Devil came to the Isle of May, six miles off-shore, and threw a boulder at them. Half of it lies in the market-place and you can see his thumbprint on it.

Local history says that Crail once had the biggest fishmarket in Europe. Certainly the disproportionate size of the tolbooths (town halls) and mar-ket crosses in all these little harbors is significant; and so are the large hous-es and their doocots (dovecots, where pigeons were kept for winter meat) of the country round about. According to an old saying, the Fife landown-er's possessions amounted to "pickle (small) land, muckle (large) debt, a doocot and a lawsuit"—Fifers were great litigants. From somewhere around here in the 19th century came "Muck Andrew," a figure all too well known at the court of session in Edinburgh, for he was there year in year out until the law finally beggared him; and all for a trivial squabble with a neighbor over the ownership of a farmyard manure-heap.

"Little City, Worn and Gray"

From Crail to St. Andrews is only 10 miles but we shall return to the M90 turn-off and approach that cathedral city by the A91, along the crop-growing Howe of Fife ("howe" is hollow). The road passes through Auchtermuchty (something of a joke in pronunciation for the English, but locals call it "Muchty") and through Fife's capital city, the royal burgh of Cupar. Royal burghs abound in Fife, though they rarely look regal. The hard-up Stuart kings bestowed charters with suspicious generosity; it was a cheap way of supplementing the royal income.

Cupar is a venerable market center with something of a neo-classical air. More than 900 years ago it was the seat of those thanes (earls) of Fife who are mentioned in Shakespeare's *Macbeth*. A conspicuous landmark one mile south is the 16th-century castellated mansion of Scotstarvit. From the top of its five-storied tower you can see most of the Kingdom of Fife, including "St. Andrews by the northern sea . . . a little city, worn and gray."

That poem by Andrew Lang (1844-1912) expresses the affection that almost everyone who lives or studies there seems to feel. Possibly the most-visited town in Scotland after Edinburgh, though rather out of the way, St. Andrews is spread out above a wide bay, open to the northeast breezes. Its oldest monuments are the Celtic church ruins above the harbor; St. Rule's tower (1126); the castle (about 1200), the cathedral (dedicated 1318) and the West Port, the only original town gate in Scotland which is still in use.

St. Andrews came into prominence as the first bishopric of Scotland in the reign of Mary Queen of Scots. By that time the legend of St. Rule,

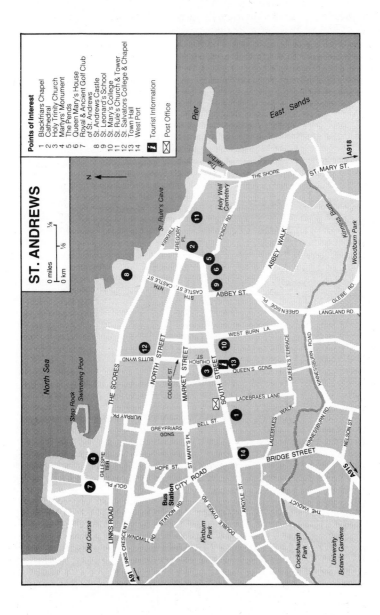

ST. ANDREWS

0 miles 1/8 1/4
0 km 1/8 1/4

N →

Points of Interest
1 Blackfriars Chapel
2 Cathedral
3 Holy Trinity Church
4 Marys Monument
5 The Pends
6 Queen Mary's House
7 Royal & Ancient Golf Club of St. Andrews
8 St. Andrews Castle
9 St. Leonard's School
10 St. Mary's College
11 St. Rule's Church & Tower
12 St. Salvators College & Chapel
13 Town Hall
14 West Port

i Tourist Information
⊠ Post Office

or St. Regulus, had taken root. Briefly, Regulus was a 7th-century Greek monk divinely inspired to steal some of St. Andrew's bones from Patras cathedral where the apostle had been martyred; and to take them on a journey. Led by dreams, Regulus ended up on the Fife coast and managed to convert the Pictish king to Christianity. There is some debate where, if anywhere, St. Andrew's bones lie: most of the skeleton is in Amalfi cathedral in Italy.

St. Andrews in plan is pure Middle Ages, three main streets converging on a cathedral. Like most of the town's ancient monuments the cathedral is impressive in its desolation—but this is no dusty museum-city. The streets are busy, the gray houses sparkle in the sun and the scene is brightened during the academic year by bicycling students in scarlet gowns.

The ghost of a "white lady" periodically moans from the cathedral ruins in the direction of the castle, which was also a bishop's palace in bygone days and now covers a grassy headland with its remaining stones. Here, during the Reformation, there were savage struggles between Catholic bishops and Protestant extremists. The Cardinal-bishop Beaton was murdered and his murderers occupied the palace, where they were joined by John Knox. In August 1547 some French galleys appeared in St. Andrews Bay and their gunfire broke down the walls. Knox and his companions were transported to France and Knox himself spent 18 months as a galley slave.

In those fights the delicate stonework of St. Andrews University was damaged. The oldest of the Scottish universities, founded 1411, it now consists of two fine old colleges in the middle of the town and some attractive modern buildings on the outskirts. A third old college (1512) has become the fashionable girls' school of St. Leonard's.

And so to golf. The Royal & Ancient Golf Club of St. Andrews is the ruling house of golf worldwide and the spiritual home of all who play or follow the game. Its clubhouse on the dunes—a building of some dignity, more like a town hall than a clubhouse—is a treasury of golfing relics but you may enter only by invitation. Anyone, on the other hand, can play on the four courses at St. Andrews, even the famous Old Course itself.

In the churchyard near St. Rule's tower and also on a wall tablet in Holy Trinity church you will see memorials to Tommy Morris. Tommy's father, old Tom, was the greatest golfer in the world—until his son reached the age of 17, won his first professional title and went round the Old Course in 47. That was when fairways were not mown and greens were cut with a hand-scythe. Next year, 1868, Tommy won the Open Championship and held the title for five years. Then he died, aged 24, unchallenged supremo of golf, whose like the game will never see again.

St. Andrews prospers on golf, golf schools and equipment. The manufacture of golf balls has been a local industry for more than 100 years. But it is also a popular seaside resort; and at the Lammas Fair, held in early August, half the population of East Fife seems to be in town.

The "Lang Toun"

Now we return to the Forth bridge to take the main route (A92, A914) through Fife, which accompanies the principal rail line to the Tay bridges. The first town is Inverkeithing, an ancient Royal burgh, but its period charm smothered by factory development. After the commuter suburb of

Dalgety Bay you pass through Aberdour with its "Silver Sands" and, offshore, the resting place of Sir Patrick Spens of ballad fame. (There is another local ballad association—the murder of "The Bonnie Earl of Moray"
took place west of the town at Donibristle.)

Aberdour, a family vacation resort on a small scale, at one period supported an artists' colony. Now there is a sailing school for beginners. From
Aberdour (and South Queensferry) boats ply to Incholm Island with its
well-preserved abbey buildings, including a church founded in the 12th
century. Inside its walls the earliest known Scottish fresco, a 13th-century
scene of priests in procession, was discovered.

Burntisland ("Burnt Island") comes next; a shipyard and a restored
tower house which Mary Queen of Scots used as a staging-post on her
journeys into Fife. Here her impetuous French admirer Chastelard propo-
sitioned her and was promptly beheaded for it. The incident taught Mary
how vulnerable a beautiful 19-year-old could be, even if she were a queen,
and prompted her to embark on the rash marriages which split the nation.

At the next coastal village, Kinghorn, a tablet beside the railroad commemorates Alexander III's fatal fall over the cliff. A short steep lane leads
down to the firm crystalline beach on which he landed.

Kirkcaldy ("Kirkawdy"), 15 miles from the Forth bridge, is the "Lang
Toun" (Long Town). Its main street measures four miles and somewhere
along it, according to an old tradition, St. Serf wrestled with the Devil.
"The Deil's dead, the Deil's dead / And buried in Kirkcaldy" goes the
children's song and some say it must have been the stench which killed
him. What with rotting flax for the linen industry and the Spanish cork
and Greenland whale oil used in the manufacture of linoleum, Kirkcaldy
used to have an aroma which strangers found hard to take. To inhabitants
who knew the old days, the fumes from the large Coal Board installations
at Seafield, one mile from the town, are mild and pleasant.

Kirkcaldy and Dunfermline, each with 50,000 inhabitants, are the largest towns in Fife Region. Kirkcaldy used to be the principal port, but her
shipping connections with numerous North Sea ports are virtually reduced
to a dilapidated sign above the harbor office announcing long-discontinued
passages to London. Some of the little angular streets and alleyways have
curious names. What, one wonders, was the origin of Prime Gilt Box
Street? The houses of Sailor's Walk have been restored by the National
Trust for Scotland with the usual pleasing result.

Where the High Street swings round into the Esplanade you will find
the birthplace of Adam Smith, pioneer economist and author of *The
Wealth of Nations*. At the old Burgh School there is a plaque recording
that both he and Robert Adam the architect were pupils there in the 1730s;
and that Thomas Carlyle the historian and essayist taught at the school
nearly 100 years later.

If you leave Kirkcaldy by the Dunfermline road (B925) you will pass
by two handsome public parks on left and right: Beveridge, gifted by the
local linoleum tycoon; and Raith, the old feudal demesne. Raith House
was formerly one of the many defensive strongholds of this coast, property
of that Shakespearian MacDuff who was urged to "Lay on!"

The Right Royal Burgh

Heading now for the Tay bridges we come to a crossroads and old
coaching station, the New Inn. (Fife is a land of historic intersections

marked with stagecoach houses.) At this point you should detour two miles to Falkland, another royal burgh of twisting streets and crooked stone houses.

Falkland is more royal than most royal burghs, for here stands the great courtyard palace of the Stuarts, one of the earliest examples in Britain of the French Renaissance style. Of the original not much remains. It belonged to the 12th century but was badly damaged by the English in 1377. The really imposing survivals, the gatehouse and flanking towers and the pit dungeon, were chiefly the work of James IV and James V, who were especially fond of Falkland. The most attractive feature is the south range of walls and chambers, rich with Renaissance buttresses and stone medallions and built for James V in 1539 by French masons. It has been described as the outstanding symbol of the "Auld Alliance" between Scotland and France.

Why build a palace here in the dangerous backwoods of the medieval Howe of Fife? It was primarily a hunting lodge, a center for such royal pleasures as hawking, archery, deer-slaying and pig-sticking in the Falkland Forest. It still has its "real" tennis court, like that at Hampton Court on the Thames near London; but no mementoes of the lions and performing seals which James V kept in a private zoo. In Falkland's beautiful walled garden, overlooked by turret windows, you may easily imagine yourself back at the solemn hour when James V on his deathbed pronounced the doom of the house of Stuart: "It cam' wi' a lass and it'll gang wi' a lass."

And all of this, palace and fortifications and garden, agreeable to the old Scottish fashion, is embedded in the heart of the burgh. Whatever else you miss in Fife, do not miss Falkland.

Northeast Fife

From the New Inn to the Tay bridge is 21 miles of undulating, cultivated country. The road and rail bridges, each two miles long, are low-built and workmanlike, lacking the photogenic appeal of their Forth counterparts; and lacking also the flimsy latticework of that notorious first Tay bridge, miracle of 19th-century technology, which collapsed in a storm in 1879 while a train was crossing it. Shortly before that, General Ulysses S. Grant was among the celebrities who had come to view it: a wall-tablet at Tayport, the old ferry station two miles east, recalls his visit. That bridge's replacement, built 1883-88, still carries the railroad to Dundee. The modern road bridge (1966) crosses the Firth a short distance downstream and delivers motorists into the heart of Dundee.

Newport and Tayport are firthside towns, residential suburbs of the Dundee conurbation of which they have close-up views. Near the bridge is a T-junction of interesting roads: first, the one we have traveled from Kirkcaldy; second, a 10-mile route to St. Andrews (A919) past the wild flats of Tentsmuir with its bird sanctuary, the Royal Air Force's strike command headquarters at Leuchars and the five-arched medieval bridge and ultra-modern paper mill at Guardbridge; third, a delightful winding route westward along the Firth, which here resembles a small inland sea, to the M90 and Perth.

On that unclassified but perfectly smooth and safe byroad you may inspect fragments of the 13th-century monastery at Balmerino ("Bal-merry-no"), the 14th-century Rothes fortress at Ballinbreich, and the ruins of the once-lordly red-sandstone abbey of Lindores, overthrown in 1559 by John Knox and his crusaders in an excess of reforming zeal. You encounter hardly any traffic. Fife, which began with a sprawl of industry, ends here in a landscape of rustic charm and tranquility. Newburgh, a royal burgh sunk in the decrepitude of old age, despite its name, is where you join the A913 road for the motorway and Perth and Dundee to the north, Edinburgh to the south.

PRACTICAL INFORMATION FOR FIFE

HOW TO GET THERE. By train. Fife Region is well served by British Rail (see beginning of chapter). There are passenger stations on the main London–Edinburgh–Dundee line at Aberdour, Burntisland, Kinghorn, Kirkcaldy, Markinch, Ladybank, Cupar and Leuchars; and at Dunfermline, Cowdenbeath, Lochgelly and Cardenden. It takes 5½ hours by fast train from London (King's Cross) to Kirkcaldy.

By bus. There are daily bus services between London (Victoria) and Coventry (Corley Service Station) in England and Dunfermline and Glenrothes in Fife. *Eastern Scottish Omnibuses,* St. Andrew Square, Edinburgh (tel. 556 8464—prefix 031 if dialling from outside Edinburgh), connect Edinburgh with the main Fife towns. From London to Dunfermline takes 11 hours, from Edinburgh to St. Andrews 90 minutes.

By car. Fife is accessible from the south by the Forth road bridge and from the north by the Tay road bridge. The Edinburgh–Perth motorway (M90) crosses the western side of the Region and from numerous points on it there are good main roads to Kirkcaldy, the "East Neuk," Dunfermline, Culross, Cupar, St. Andrews and Newburgh.

HOTELS AND RESTAURANTS. If you are staying in Fife the obvious base is St. Andrews, where you will find ample accommodations of all kinds, including vacation-time accommodations at a university hall of residence (tel. 0334–72281), single rooms from £13–£17.95 with meals. Other towns do not offer a wide range, but you will find hotels and guest-houses at Dunfermline and Kirkcaldy; and all the royal burghs have hotels or inns in the town or the neighborhood. Along the coastal strip and in the Howe of Fife between Strathmiglo and Cupar there are some superior country-house hotels and restaurants.

In Kirkcaldy, Dunfermline and West Fife towns in general, you will find Italian and Chinese restaurants, and cafés of all kinds. Bar lunches are becoming the rule in hotels large and small throughout the Region, while in seaside places the "carry oot" (to go) meal is an old tradition.

Anstruther (A921). **Restaurant.** *Cellar* (E), 24 East Green (tel. 0333–310378). Has been called the best seafood restaurant in Scotland. Catch is landed twice a day from the harbor a few yards away.

Ceres (B393). *Meldrums* (M), Main Street (tel. 0334–82286). 5 rooms, 4 with bath. Pleasingly unpretentious in a charming village.

Crail (A917). *Croma* (I), 33 Nethergate (tel. 0333–50239). 9 rooms, 4 with bath. Superior facilities for this modest price range. Dinner until 10 P.M.

Cupar (A91). **Restaurant.** *Ostler's Close* (E), 25 Bonnygate (tel. 0334–55574). Minuscule whitewashed cottage. Seafood and Continental dishes, good French house wine. Reasonable *à la carte* lunch.

Dunfermline (A823). *King Malcolm* (E), Wester Pitcorthie (tel. 0383–722611). 48 rooms with bath. Spacious hotel, popular with conference organizers, business executives. *Keavil House* (M–E), Crossford (tel. 0383–736258). 32 rooms with bath. Intimate, country-style hotel, triumphing over drab surroundings.

Falkland (A912). *Covenanter* (M), tel. 059 284–317. 13 rooms, 10 with bath. In historic center, close to Jacobean palace. Newly residential with warm, well-equipped rooms. Excellent restaurant with small but select menu—quails eggs, poached salmon. Among the very best in Fife.

Kinnesswood (B920). *Lomond* (M), tel. 059 284–253. 12 rooms, 6 with bath. On peaceful east shore of Loch Leven.

Kirkcaldy (A92). *Dunnikier House* (M), Dunnikier Way (tel. 0592–268393). 16 rooms with bath. A good-looking, well-organized hotel. *A la carte* dinner.

Largo (A915). *Crusoe* (I), 2 Main Street (tel. 0333–320759). 6 rooms, 3 with bath/shower. Seafood a specialty.

Lundin Links (A921) *Old Manor* (M), Leven Road (tel. 0333–320368). 19 rooms, 15 with bath. Handsome Victorian mansion overlooking Firth of Forth, with golf course next door. Excellent inhouse restaurant, not expensive, to which down-to-earth Fife people come for a satisfying meal without gastronomic frippery.

Newport-on-Tay (A914). *Sandford Hill* (E), at Wormit (tel. 0382–541802). 15 rooms, 13 with bath. Typical of several Fife country hotels that have been expensively modernized. Small rooms, labyrinthine passages, courtyard; even a wishing well. High-class cuisine attracts a discriminating clientele.

Peat Inn (B940). **Restaurant.** *Peat Inn* (E), tel. 0334 84–206. Old stagecoach change-house, much praised by food writers. Good for a leisurely sophisticated meal.

St. Andrews (A91). *Old Course* (L), tel. 0334–74371. 150 rooms, 146 with bath. Biggest hotel in St. Andrews with balcony views over Old Course. *Rusacks* (L), Pilmour Links (tel. 0334–74321). 50 rooms with bath. Golfers' rendezvous for 100 years. Organizes golf weeks and golf holiday packages. *Argyle Private Hotel* (I), North Street (tel. 0334–73387). 21 rooms, 13 with bath. Good amenities, reasonable rates. Bar.

Restaurants. *Brambles* (I), College Street (tel. 0334–75380). Charming restaurant and coffee-house. Wholefood. *Grange* (I), tel. 0334–72670. Old farmhouse-type building; excellent bar lunches individually prepared. Candlelit dinners; good selection of malt whiskies.

St. Michaels (A92). *Pinewoods* (M), tel. 0334–83 8262. 5 rooms with bath. Simple life in rural setting, but nothing primitive about furnishings or services and handy for St. Andrews.

Strathmiglo (A91). **Restaurant.** *Strathmiglo Inn* (M), tel. 033 76–252. A village inn since 1790s, sensitively restored and well managed. Useful lunch stop.

West Wemyss (off A955). **Restaurant.** *Belvedere* (E), tel. 0592–54167. Mock-baronial house among derelict mining cottages. Lobster, haddock, salmon, locally-landed mullet extremely good on a comprehensive menu. Snacks and light suppers in bogus "nautical" bar.

HOW TO GET ABOUT. By car. The Region is so small and has such good roads that if you are motoring you might well choose to make your base in Edinburgh, Perth or Dundee and cover Fife in the course of a few daily excursions. Conversely, you could take accommodations at St. Andrews or some other royal burgh of the Region, and explore the previous three cities along with Fife itself.

By train. The main Edinburgh–Dundee railroad has stations in Fife at Kirkcaldy, Markinch (for Glenrothes), Ladybank, Springfield, Cupar and Leuchars; with a loop from Markinch (southbound traffic only) to Carden-den and Dunfermline. Trains from Edinburgh to Perth and the Highlands also follow this route as far as Ladybank.

By bus. Dunfermline and Kirkcaldy are the chief centers of local buses and day or half-day touring coaches in Fife. In summer, there are also excursion buses from St. Andrews.

By boat. Daily trips May–Sept., weather permitting, from Anstruther to May Island. Contact Anstruther Pleasure Trips, 14 Dreelside, Anstru-ther (tel. 0333–310103). For the Aberdour–Inchcolm boat service contact Dougal Barrie, Hawkcraig House, Aberdour (tel. 0383–860335).

TOURIST INFORMATION. Well signposted in their respective towns are the year-round centers of Burntisland, Kirkcaldy, Leven and St. Andrews; and summer-only centers of Anstruther, Cupar, Dunfermline, Forth Bridge, Glenrothes and Crail.

FISHING. River and loch fishing is controlled by local angling associa-tions from whom permits may be obtained. Consult Eden Angling Associ-ation, Braehead, Cupar, for salmon and trout fishing on Eden River and Ceres Burn; and the Fishing Lodge, Lochore Country Park, Lochgelly, for trout fishing in the Ore Loch. At Tayport, St. Andrews, Pittenweem, Anstruther and Methil you may fish from hired boats or harbor walls. Mostly cod, flatfish and haddock. Local information from fishing-tackle shops and strategic hotels.

GOLF. Every golfer's ambition is to play at St. Andrews and once you are in Fife the ambition is easily realized. Old, New, Eden and Jubilee, the four St. Andrews courses, are open to visitors, the charges varying between £7 and £20 a round. For details of availability—there is sometimes a waiting list—contact the Secretary, Links Management Committee, Golf Place, St. Andrews (tel. 0334–75757). There are about 40 other courses in the burghs of Fife, from Tulliallan in the far west to Tayport on the Tay estuary. They have refreshment facilities and offer golf to the visitor by the round or the day.

HISTORIC HOUSES AND GARDENS. Houses grand and not-so-grand, public and private, are to be found all over the Region. Prime visiting is in spring and summer, when the flower gardens are looking their best (usually open Saturday and Sunday). Opening details can be found in local shop windows and the Scottish national and local press.

Falkland Palace, Falkland (A912). Seat of kings and childhood home of Mary Queen of Scots. Rare plants in gardens. Open Easter–Sept., daily 10–6; Oct., Sat. and Sun. 10–6. N.T.S.

Hill of Tarvit, Cupar (A916). Ancient mansion house remodeled in 1906 for a millionaire. Fine tapestries, paintings, furniture. Superb views. Open May–Sept., daily, 2–6; Apr. and Oct., Sat. and Sun. 2–6. Gardens and park open all year, 10 to sunset. N.T.S.

Kellie Castle, Pittenweem, 3 miles from town (A921). Tower house of the Siwards who came to Scotland in Macbeth's time. Carefully enlarged in 16th century and since 1875 restored by the well-known Lorimer family of Scottish architects. Good plasterwork, colorful garden. Open May–Sept., daily 2–6; Apr. and Oct., Sat. and Sun. 2–6. Gardens and grounds open daily, all year, 10–sunset. N.T.S.

Pittencrieff Park, Dunfermline (A823). Formal gardens, nature walks, aviary and animal center, maze, and romantic glen set in 76 acres on edge of town. Open all year during daylight hours.

St. Andrews Castle, St. Andrews (A91). Sprawling ruins of 13th-century fortress, former home of bishops. Bottle dungeon and secret passage. Open Apr.–Sept., weekdays 9.30–7, Sun. 2–7; Oct.–Mar., weekdays 9.30–4, Sun. 2–4.

MUSEUMS. Carnegie Birthplace Memorial, Moodie Street, Dunfermline (A823). Personal relics of the Scottish-American industrialist. Open Apr.–Oct., Mon.–Sat. 11–5 (Wed. until 8); Nov.–Mar., daily 2–4.

Crail Museum, Crail (A917). History and heritage of a once-notable fishing port. Open Easter week, June–Aug., Mon.–Sat. 10–12.30 and 2.30–5, Sun. 2.30–5; Apr., May and Sept., Sat., Sun. and Bank Holidays 2.30–5.

Fife Folk Museum, Ceres (B939). Domestic and agricultural life of long ago. Open Apr.–Oct., weekdays, except Tues., 2–5, Sun. 2.30–5.30.

John McDouall Stuart Museum, Rectory Lane, Dysart (A92 near Kirkcaldy). Relics and audiovisual presentation at birthplace of Australian explorer (1815–66). Open Jun.–Aug., daily 2–5.

Light Vessel and Scottish Fisheries Museum, on harbor front, Anstruther (A917). Illustrates aspects of Scotland's fishing industry: actual boats stripped down, an aquarium, logbooks of the Greenland whaling skippers, and other historical items. Open Apr.–Oct., weekdays 10–5.30, Sun. 2–5;

Nov.–Mar., weekdays 10–4.30, Sun. 2–4.30. Incorporates the old **North Carr Lightship,** on station 1938–1975, open May–mid-Sept.

Lochty Railway, Lochty Farm, west of Crail (B940). Steam railroad, standard gauge, a reconstruction of old Fife industrial lines. Operates mid-Jun.–Aug., 2–5. Sun. only.

St. Andrews Cathedral, St. Andrews. Ruins of the largest church in Scotland. Displays of Celtic and medieval monuments, pottery, glass. Open Apr.–Sept., weekdays 9.30–7, Sun. 2–7; Oct.–Mar., weekdays 9.30–4, Sun. 2–4.

The Town House, Culross (off A985). One of several 17th-century dwelling houses in this "museum burgh" with painted ceilings and audio-visual historical program. Open May–Sept., daily 11–1 and 2–5; or by appointment (contact National Trust for Scotland's regional representative, tel. 031–336 2157). N.T.S.

LANDSCAPE IN ROSE AND GRAY

Tayside

On a world scale of rivers, the Tay is a trickle; 119 miles long from source to mouth. But it is Scotland's longest river and it pours a greater volume of water into the sea than any river in Britain.

The land drained by the Tay and all its lochs, streams and tributaries is Tayside Region. Its western border is Rannoch station, a desolate outpost of the West Highland railroad, 17 miles from the nearest village. Its boundary with Highland Region runs north through otherwise roadless tracts of the Forest of Atholl, crossing the Great North Road (A9) by the Boar of Badenoch and Sow of Atholl hills and the 1,506-foot Drumochter pass, the highest point reached by trains on British railroads.

Across the headwaters of four torrents in four long secluded glens—Esk, Prosen, Clova and Isla—the boundary descends to the terracotta-colored cliffs of Angus, turns south to the seaport of Dundee, carves a hunk of territory out of Kinross-shire south of Perth and makes its way westward again, enclosing the sinuous lochs and wooded valleys of the south-central Highlands.

The Highland Line cuts across Tayside Region, with some lonely mountain country on one side of it and some fertile stock-breeding and market-gardening districts on the other.

Tayside Region has two cities, large by Scottish standards: Dundee and Perth. It has the oldest Scottish capital at Scone ("Scoon"), where Dark-Age kings were crowned on what was popularly thought to be Jacob's pillow—the Stone of Destiny, which now lies under the coronation throne in Westminster Abbey, London. Legend says that Scotland received her national flower, the thistle, from this Region. In 990, before the battle of Luncarty near Perth, a barefooted Dane trod on one and gave early warning of a surprise attack. Legend also affirms that the gnarled yew tree in Fortingall churchyard is the oldest tree in Britain; that Pontius Pilate, offspring of a Roman centurion and a local girl, was born under it; that the sculpted stones of Meigle lined the grave of Guinevere, King Arthur's faithless queen; that the bones of St. Columba who brought Christianity to Scotland lie under Dunkeld cathedral. . . .

It is hardly surprising that Tayside is a region of legend. It has the antiquities and folk memories to sustain them. It seems to have been one of the first Scottish areas to be settled by Mesolithic man, around 6000 B.C. In several places now known only to the golden eagle and the mountain hare are to be found the prehistoric stone circles, hill forts and flint implements of a sizeable population.

The Romans established a presence in Strathearn and Strathmore—the vale of the River Earn, and the Great Vale which leads from Perth towards Aberdeen. Pictish remains are too numerous to list; you will come across them everywhere. Of especial note are the souterrains (sunken shelters) of Ardestie and Carlungie near the A92 road two miles north of Monifeith.

An early Pictish king set up his capital near Forteviot, southwest of Perth (B9112) and soon afterwards Scone became the political, and Dunkeld the spiritual, centers of Pictland. The word Pict means "painted" (the Picts tattooed themselves). And studying the rich decoration and complicated draughtsmanship of Tayside's Pictish stones, you realize what great pictorial artists they were.

Christianity came with the Irish monks; and the first churches, Abernethy, Dunkeld and Brechin, were built on their cells. The Tayside-Irish connection is venerable. The round towers of Abernethy and Brechin, unique in mainland Scotland, are an old Irish ecclesiastical feature. In more recent times, Dundee's shipyards attracted hosts of immigrant Irishmen.

Outside Dundee and Perth, the towns of the Region are either small holiday resorts or small agricultural centers. As you tour them you will see one huge medieval abbey (Arbroath); a dozen castles, including the showpieces of Blair and Glamis; a pink sandstone coastline ribboned with firm sands; a winter playground in Glenshee; numerous Munros—mountains of more than 3,000 feet, named for the Scottish geographer who classified every 3,000-foot-plus summit in Scotland; and the birthplaces or graves of a few celebrities, from Sir J. M. Barrie the playwright to William MacGonagall, the "world's worst poet."

Sir Walter Scott used the Region's scenery and folktales in his novels *Waverley, The Antiquary, The Abbot* and *The Fair Maid of Perth.* The moorland west of Loch Tay is featured in R. L. Stevenson's novel *Kidnapped.*

The Region is both cooler and drier than most parts of Scotland. It enjoys plenty of sunshine, winter and summer, but the coast is notorious for cold winds.

Kinross to Perth

Traveling north from the Forth bridges you enter Tayside Region at Kinross, once an important stopover for stagecoach passengers, as its two hotels with their stabling and haylofts indicate. Kinross's back gardens are washed by Loch Leven, renowned among anglers for its strain of pink-bellied trout. In summer you can take a boat trip round the castled island, 20 minutes each way, from which Mary, Queen of Scots made a daring escape in 1568, having exerted her powerful charms on her jailer's impressionable son.

If you are on the M90 motorway, avoiding the small towns of this district, you will ride high over Glenfarg. But if you are not in a hurry it is worth your while to tackle the tortuous route through the wooded gorge to the flat meadows of the River Earn. At its foot you could turn right for Abernethy (A913) and its round tower.

The Earn is a central river of Tayside, as is the Tay, and they meet near Abernethy. Upstream, Strathearn is rich in prehistoric and Roman remains. Forteviot (B935) was once a metropolis of Fortrenn, the Pictish kingdom. Two miles away, across the A9, are the mounds of a Roman station and a stretch of Roman road. Much history is still buried under the road as you approach Perth, for centuries the lowest crossing-place on the Tay.

At first glance this ancient foundation appears to consist of railroad yards, distilleries and dyeworks. But Perth is a civilized place. It is the "Fair City"; and a seaport, though only just. Below its trio of bridges, the Tay becomes a navigable waterway, above it is famous for salmon and local pearls. The flood levels of two centuries are marked on the arches and it is for good reasons that the open parklands north and south of a compact city center are called the "Inches"—islands. Two Perth bridges were built and washed away before the present mainroad bridge, built in 1771, at last provided a safe exit from downtown Perth's rectilinear streets.

Battle of the Clans

The Inches, with their massive beech and chestnut trees, now enclose golf courses and cricket grounds. Games of a more murderous kind were played in 1396, when Robert III decided to settle once and for all the quarrels between the Clans Chattan and Kay. He staged a mass trial by combat, a pitched battle between 30 champions from each side. In the specially-built wooden enclosure ringed with an invited audience of noblemen and women on the North Inch it must have been something like a Roman circus. The fight went on all day until the last Kay escaped the 11 surviving and desperately-wounded Chattans by diving into the Tay. The Clan Chattan had arrived that morning one short but a Perth man, Hal o' the Wynd, volunteered to make up the number. It was said that he had no idea who was fighting whom, that he committed mayhem on both sides and that he came out without a scratch. Scott tells the story in *The Fair Maid of Perth*.

Nothing now survives of the Blackfriars monastery from which King Robert watched the battle of the clans. It was one of four great Perth monasteries of the middle ages. Visiting kings took to lodging at Blackfriars amid "sweet arbours and soft flower-beds" after the royal castle on Tay bank collapsed in the spate (flood) of 1210. Forty years after the clan fight, James I was assassinated there by a party of courtiers led by his uncle the Earl of Atholl. This was the occasion of the well-known tale of Catherine Douglas—"Kate Bargate"—the brave lady-in-waiting who used her own arm as a padlock for the door in an effort to give His Majesty time to escape.

Pearls, Policies, and Port Wine

Perth, once Scotland's capital, is an overgrown market town with bustling streets and carriageways congested with motorists. The County Buildings in Tay Street occupy the site of the Gowrie conspiracy, a mysterious event in Scottish history concerning a plot to kidnap King James VI in 1600. Perth's most historic spot, the Fair Maid's house (see below) on the site of the vanished Blackfriars monastery, is now an attractive little gallery which exhibits the work of Scotland's most promising young craftspeople.

Some of Perth's little shops seem to belong to the countryside; and in the countryside round about you find the urban factories and offices which have made Perth an international capital of investment and insurance (a fifth of Britain's automobile policies are processed in Perth); of dyeing and dry-cleaning; of port wine and whisky.

The big name in port is Sandeman's, a firm whose founder established the first connections between Britain and Oporto (Portugal) in 1765. Two famous brands, Bell's and Dewar's, represent the whisky trade. Their Perth origins go back nearly two centuries and the polite rivalry between the first Bell and the first Dewar, two devout churchmen, is anecdotal in Perth. Example: on their way together to a meeting of church elders they stopped off for a drink. Bell: "What will ye have, Dewar?"—Dewar: "I'll have a Bell's. It wouldna do tae go tae the meeting smelling o' strong drink."

All these successful businessmen were benefactors to their town. The schools, libraries and public parks of Perth, like those of Dunfermline, give the city an air of distinction and prosperity.

The Fair Maid

A walk of one and a half miles takes in the best of Perth. Start at the Fair Maid's house in Curfew Row, just opposite Perth bridge on the edge of the North Inch. The young lady so renowned for her gentle beauty was Catharine Glover; her father a glover by trade. By way of George Street you come to St. John's, most historic of Perth's churches. Eight of the oldest bells in Britain are in its carillon, having been spared when other treasures were thrown down by Protestant extremists after John Knox's sermon there on 11th May 1559, when he challenged the Catholic regent, mother of Mary, Queen of Scots.

Off the High Street, near St. John's, the old vennels (French *venelle* meaning a funnel or narrow passageway) are worth exploring. A diagram of them is on the wall of Fountain Close at the end of South Street. Two famous inns of different character are in this quarter of Perth: the Salutation, looking much as it did when Bonnie Prince Charlie sought lodgings;

and the more stately Royal George hotel, renowned for its breakfasts in a land of substantial breakfasts.

Around the northern end of George Street lies the classical Perth of terraced streets and crescents. You might inspect Barossa Place and Atholl Crescent and then look at Rose Terrace where John Ruskin the 19th-century art pundit lived when young and met the girl he disastrously married. Another handsome terrace is Marshall Place, which faces the South Inch, with a stone-crowned church (like St. Giles's in Edinburgh) at one end and a well-proportioned rotunda at the other. This latter building, called the Round House, was for years part of the town's water-works and is now the city's tourist information center: ideally suited to the panoramic displays and audiovisual presentations which you can see when you call there.

Jute, Jam, and Journalism

Cross the Tay by Perth's Victoria bridge and turn sharp right and you are on the A85 to Dundee (22 miles). The sights of the route are at either end of this fast road: first a pretty stretch of the Tay under wooded crags on which the hill of Kinnoul juts out (take the signposted road off Gowrie Street for the summit and fine views of the Firth of Tay and of the labyrinthine motorway interchange on the opposite shore); and at the other end a dramatic prospect of the open firth and the two Tay bridges (see the chapter on Fife Region).

In between the A85 traverses the Carse (alluvial valley) of Gowrie, a district which made Dundee a great place for raspberry jam. The fruit gardens nowadays extend north to Blairgowrie and Coupar Angus and in the season, June and July, motorists are invited to stop and pick their own strawberries and raspberries, paying a nominal price for them.

Now the road enters Dundee, which is more than many guidebooks do, for Scotland's fourth city has somehow acquired a reputation of being unworthy of tourists' attention. It is at first sight a rather shabby industrial complex; though the redeveloped city center, with throughways leading straight to the Tay bridge tollgates, has brightened it up. Much Scottish history is written into the grim stonework of old Dundee. The place has been a royal burgh since 1190. William Wallace the patriot attended Dundee Grammar School and about 1465 the historian Hector Boece ("Boethius") was born there. It has associations with the Covenanters, the Cromwellians and both Pretenders. A plaque on St. Paul's cathedral in the High Street records that on the site where Dundee Castle used to stand, Wallace "struck the first blow for Scottish independence" in 1288 (though he must have been a mere boy, the tale still makes an attractive legend); and that Adam Duncan, famous admiral and victor of Camperdown in 1797, lived next door.

Admiral Duncan's son bought Camperdown Park (off Kingsway, the city ring route) and built a great mansion, Camperdown House. Nearly a century later another rich Dundonian, the industrialist Sir James Caird, bought Caird Park close by, where the gaunt, four-gabled, six-storied tower of 16th-century Mains of Fintry Castle stands. These two beautiful areas of greenery are now public parks.

The city has had its economic ups and downs. Through an early connection with Calcutta, citizens made fortunes in the jute and indigo trade.

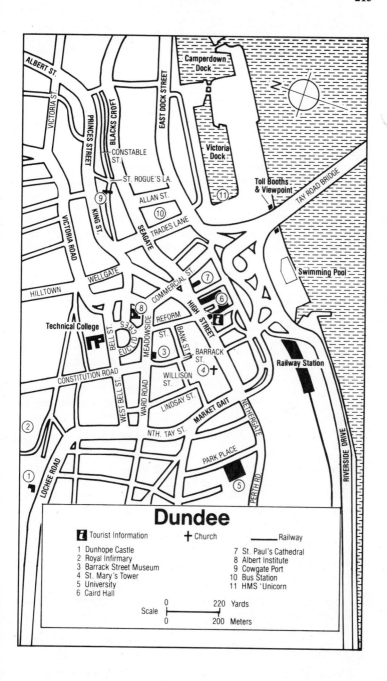

Dundee

🅸 Tourist Information	✝ Church	──── Railway

1 Dunhope Castle	7 St. Paul's Cathedral
2 Royal Infirmary	8 Albert Institute
3 Barrack Street Museum	9 Cowgate Port
4 St. Mary's Tower	10 Bus Station
5 University	11 HMS 'Unicorn
6 Caird Hall	

Scale

0	220	Yards
0	200	Meters

Dundee shipyards specialized in tough vessels for whaling and Polar exploration. The soft fruit poured in, and it also became a center for the manufacture of jam and marmalade. Valentine's of Dundee were pioneers of the picture-postcard industry, and from the 1870s onwards—when the education laws made schooling compulsory and literacy almost universal—Dundee's publishers issued torrents of cheap weekly papers, a large number of which are still going strong. The business of Dundee was encapsulated in the slogan "Jute, jam and journalism."

Once, Dundee had a reputation as a center of radical politics—it even had communists on its council! Many entrepreneurs elbowed their way to civic power and honors—hence the former name "City of Dreadful Knights." Within recent years all of this has been swept aside. Now Dundee is "City of Discovery"—Captain Scott's polar exploration vessel, the Royal Research Ship *Discovery,* has come home to its birthplace. (It was built in Dundee, as the local shipbuilders had experience in constructing specially strong hulls for the local whaling industry, which fished in icepack waters.) R.R.S. *Discovery* has become the focal point in a redevelopment between the road and rail bridges called Discovery Quay. The £45 million tourism and leisure development, due for completion in 1991, celebrates Dundee's heritage. Also in the dock nearby is H.M.S. *Unicorn* of 1824, the oldest naval ship afloat.

The jute and jam industries employed many women. In former times the female population greatly outnumbered the male and by some mysterious natural law standards of feminine beauty rose. Dundee has the most beautiful girls in Scotland, as Nottingham, for similar reasons connected with the lace and tobacco industries, has in England.

Dundee University, with its almost rustic campus, is set in the city's heart, at the west end of Nethergate. Also in Nethergate is the 15th-century Old Steeple, massive yet stylish, once an umbrella for no fewer than four churches. The East Port off the Cowgate is the only remaining covered port (gate) of the old city walls. Here, the reforming preacher George Wishart delivered a sermon in 1544 to the plague-stricken inhabitants.

As you leave the east end of the city, rejoining the A972 ring road, a perfect Scottish-baronial fortress-house rises above the roofs of bungalows. Grim and workaday, with the vertical proportions of some Aberdeenshire castles but none of their frivolities, Claypotts was built for defense, not for show. It originally belonged to the Grahams of Claverhouse ("Clavers") and that cruel Jacobite general ironically known as "Bonnie Dundee." It subsequently belonged to the Douglases, a loyal but consistently unlucky clan, and then to the Earls of Home, the well-known Borders family. Today, it is in the hands of Scotland's Historic Buildings and Monuments Department.

The view from Dundee is tremendous. Like Athens, the city drops from a hill and spreads out along a broad waterfront. The summit, Law Hill (571 feet), offers a wonderful panorama of Tayside and Fife Regions, including the inland sea of the Firth of Tay and the strips of coastline bending north and south as the estuary opens to the North Sea.

The Sandstone Coast

If it were the Mediterranean they would call it the Vermilion Coast or the Costa Rosa or something of that sort. It is the pink sandstone littoral which curves away northward by the cold sea. The A92, from Dundee to Aberdeen, hugs it closely.

Beyond the championship golf course of Carnoustie (A930), lying among the dunes, is Arbroath, 17 miles from Dundee. Here the characteristic scenery of Scotland's northeastern shores begins: blunt cliffs, ragged watch-towers and castles. Arbroath recalls that poetic line "a rose-red city half as old as time," for the sandstone arches, pillars and cloisters of an abbey founded by William the Lion in 1178 still dominate several acres, with a tangle of narrow streets and cottages clustered round them for protection.

In 1320 Abbot Linton of Arbroath drew up on behalf of Robert the Bruce a letter to Pope John XXII in Rome, affirming Scotland's rights to independence: the Declaration of Arbroath. Before he received it, the Pope had frequently condemned the Scots for their rebellious behavior and refused to acknowledge their own sovereignty. However the Scots' Declaration also contained a promise to fight in the Crusades. This pleased the Pope and he immediately ceased his fulminations against them!

During the building of the Bell Rock Lighthouse (see below), to make offshore communications easier, a tower was built by the sea. Now disused, it houses the Arbroath Signal Tower Museum, which tells the story of the town (including fishing, flax and, oddly enough, the manufacture of lawnmowers) and the Bell Rock light itself.

Arbroath has a flourishing fishmarket. In side streets which lead to it you may enter the little kiln-sheds where haddock are turned into "smokies," the local delicacy. Try a smoky with your high tea at 6 P.M., a meal of cakes and scones and one hot dish for which it might have been invented.

"Down Sank the Bell"

In the Abbey's great sea-facing rose window, the "Round O of Arbroath," monks of the middle ages kept a bonfire burning to light the fishermen home. They also placed a bell on the Inchcape Rock, 12 miles offshore, which thereafter became the Bell Rock. It lay athwart the tracks of vessels making in or out of the Firths of Tay and Forth and was the subject of a legend (and a popular recitation-piece by Robert Southey: "Down sank the Bell with a gurgling sound . . . ") about a pirate who cut the Bell and later drove his ship on the rock for want of the warning signal.

More than 70 ships were wrecked on this coast in the great storms of December 1799. When the Commissioners of Northern Lighthouses were appointed, their first priority was a light-tower on the Bell Rock; a job they entrusted to their new engineer, Robert Stevenson, grandfather of R. L. Stevenson. He began work in 1807 and completed the 115-foot tower in 1811. Robert Stevenson's ingenuity ensured that his men were able to work every minute the tides allowed—up to seven hours. He soon had a temporary beacon erected, then made into permanent accommodation for his work-force. Faced with tasks of unprecedented difficulty, Stevenson invented solutions to his problems as he went along: underwater cement, lifting appliances, a method of dovetailing masonry for an immovable foundation. The Bell Rock tower was a prototype for semi-submerged buildings the world over and its beam, flashing red and white, was the first two-color light in the mariner's almanac.

Stevenson's tower is still there, just as he built it. Only the lantern has been modernized and made more powerful. In summer, weather permitting, Arbroath boatmen run trips round the Bell Rock. The lighthouse itself is unmanned and hence not visitable. A program of automation has been carried out on many lights in recent years. (There are about 30 manned lighthouses round Scotland's coasts which you may visit. Afternoon, up to sunset, is the preferred time. It is best to phone the head keeper in advance: see under Lighthouses in the telephone directories.)

Montrose

Between the headlands of the Angus coastline are crescents of sand firm and expansive enough for an attack on the world's land-speed record. Tourist propaganda describes Lunan Bay and Montrose Bay as bracing— meaning that they are cursed with icy winds. But on a calm summer day there are no more desirable bathing beaches. At other times, wise holiday-makers wrap up well and engage in energetic activities.

Behind a four-mile sweep of sand, between two river mouths, South Esk and North Esk, stands Montrose, four-square on its promontory. The A92 enters by a structure of startling ugliness, a sort of art-deco suspension bridge made of concrete. The South Esk is tidal and behind the town it widens to several square miles of mudflats, covered at high water. This Montrose Basin is an important feeding and wintering ground for wildfowl and waders. It is a nature reserve with a visitor center and hides, and is wardened by the Scottish Wildlife Trust.

Montrose is a plain, handsome, unpretentious town: as long ago as 1684 local regulations prohibited the use of any building material except sandstone. In the Town House in 1773 the gentry entertained Dr. Johnson and his biographer James Boswell as they passed through on their Highland jaunt. Robert Burns was in Montrose in 1787 and Queen Victoria in 1848. One of Scotland's best-known modern poets, Hugh MacDiarmid, worked as a cub reporter on a Montrose newspaper in the 1920s.

From town center to beach is a long trek, with only the splendid golden cupola of Montrose Academy, the neo-classical high school, to vary the monotony of the walk; but this place has long been a favorite vacation spot with city dwellers, especially families from Glasgow—and from much farther afield, you might imagine, when you hear American accents floating up from the doors of Montrose's little pubs. But these are servicemen from the U.S. Army Air Force's security base at Edzell, 15 miles up country. Dozens of local girls have married Americans, which has resulted in some comings and goings between the States and this unpretentious coastal community.

Montrose's fishing community, or what is left of it, inhabits Ferryden across the estuary, a double line of white-painted, low-built cottages. The serious maritime action takes place in Montrose harbor, which you approach by way of Baltic Street. The name hints at a far-flung trade of long ago, when Montrose's imports read like a bill of lading of argosies: flax from St. Petersburg, tar from Stockholm, tea and cloves from Antwerp and Amsterdam. Now she exports paper, barley and potatoes and does business with the oil rigs, 50 miles beyond the North Sea horizon.

Her most celebrated son, James Graham, Marquess of Montrose, was born in 1612 at Maryton on the south side of the Basin. He joined the Covenanters in 1638, fighting against his king, Charles I, in defense of Scottish Presbyterianism. Disillusioned with the Covenanters' bigotry, he then led a royalist army and virtually pacified Scotland for Charles I. But his victories came to nothing; in England the King was defeated and eventually executed at the hands of Cromwell's republicans.

After Charles II's restoration, the "Great Marquess" as he was called fought again for the Stuarts against the rebels. But private intrigues took precedence over national politics. Montrose fell into the clutches of a personal enemy, the Duke of Argyll, and in 1650 he went to the scaffold in Edinburgh: a military genius who believed in religious freedoms, but believed more strongly in loyalty to his king, however unworthy.

The Great Vale

At the North Esk bridge one and a half miles north of Montrose, the A92 swings into Grampian Region. However, our route turns inland on the A935 for Strathmore, the Great Vale of Angus, which runs southwest to Perth, 43 miles away. Near Brechin we join the main road to Aberdeen, the A94, a fast—perhaps too fast—road with some stretches of divided highway. Keep alert on it.

Brechin, now bypassed, is technically a city because it is an episcopal see. Its cathedral, founded about 1150, lies on the site of a 10th-century monastery. Of the monastery nothing survives and the cathedral's original structure is camouflaged by later "improvements." Adjoining it is the 87-foot round tower, tallest and most complete of the three in Scotland. (We have already mentioned Abernethy's; the third is on Egilshay island in Orkney.)

Pictish and Danish crosses and stones in the cathedral chancel proclaim Brechin's stormy ecclesiastical history, but on the whole it is a place of small industries and few buildings of note, a place the centuries have bypassed and left behind.

Forfar (A94), the county seat of Angus before regionalization, is a livelier town. It even has a culinary specialty: the Forfar bridie, a spiced minced-beef pasty. The town grew up round a castle of William the Lion (12th century), long demolished. At that period Forfar was an island in a swamp from which, now that it is drained, several Pictish stones have been recovered. Good examples are at Dunnichen off the A958 and Aberlemno on the B9134. Close to Dunnichen was Nechtans Mere (mere meaning lake) where the Picts gained a crushing victory over King Egfrith of Northumbria in 685. A tower-base and archway, dating from about 700 at Restenneth one mile east of Forfar on the B9113, are the oldest pieces of church masonry in Scotland.

Glamis

Continuing through Strathmore (A94), while the blue ridge of the roof of Angus falls away to the west, you enter the cattle-breeding country around Glamis. On those neat farms and well-kept policies, among the belts of trees and freshly-painted white five-barred gates the famous polled (hornless) Aberdeen-Angus bulls are bred. Stockbreeders come from all over the world to bid for them at the Perth livestock sales. The breed was originally developed, from the native small black Scottish cattle, by a local Angus farmer, Hugh Watson (b. 1789), who picked the best characteristics of the native stock and built up a championship herd. Even Queen Victoria and Prince Albert bought cattle from him. The breed was further strengthened by an Aberdeenshire family, hence its name Aberdeen-Angus.

Glamis (pronounced "Glahms") is a village green, a line of grace-and-favor cottages and the tall gates of Glamis Castle, the residence which, after Balmoral, most visitors to Scotland want to see. They have heard of its dark secret, its inaccessible chamber and the warning passed to Lord Strathmore's heir when he comes of age. A warning so dire that the heir never smiles again. From the look of the place, its gloomy turrets have heard the tale too; but your guide will smile and change the subject. The fact is that he knows no more about it than you do.

Glamis Castle connects Britain's royalty throught ten centuries, from Macbeth ("thane of Glamis") to the present Queen's sister, Princess Margaret, who was born there in 1930, the first royal princess born in Scotland for 300 years.

All this region conveys an agreeable impression of rural stability, simple lives and a disinclination to move with the times—a contrast with the humming traffic on the highways to Scotland's boomtown, Aberdeen. In the Glamis street called Kirkwynd, the Angus folk collection is kept, something out of the ordinary in folk museums. It portrays old country values, old notions of thrift and sobriety; not so different from the life around you in the calm little world of Strathmore.

Five miles northwest (A928) of Glamis is Kirriemuir, the weaving town which Sir J. M. Barrie immortalized as "Thrums." Peter Pan's creator was born and buried there. Seven miles south (A94) is Meigle, rich in Pictish stones. The museum is an old village school. Meigle is also the burial-place of a British Prime Minister (1905-08), Sir Henry Campbell-Bannerman.

Blairgowrie, 15 miles west of Meigle (A926) is the starting point for the wild ascent of Glenshee, the steep twisting section called the Devil's Elbow (no problem now, but a stern test on reliability trials in pioneer automobile days) and the lonely road past the ski slopes to Braemar (A92). It can be a busy road on winter weekends: Glenshee has the nearest natural winter-sports grounds to Edinburgh, Perth, Dundee and Aberdeen. Blairgowrie boasts a couple of good hotels and restaurants and excellent fishing in the contortions and cascades of the Ericht River above and below the town. If you have time to spare and the season is right you can get a holiday course in Pictish and Roman remains, and go blackberry, raspberry and strawberry picking in the lanes and market gardens.

Four miles south of Blairgowrie on the Perth road (A93), slow down to admire the remarkable beech hedge of Meikleour. It is 110 feet high and still growing, half a mile long and needing an army of gardeners to clip it every three years. It is said to have been planted in 1745, the year of Bonnie Prince Charlie. Continuing down the A93 you enter Perth near the old palace of Scone, one of the important house-and-garden sites of Tayside Region.

Glens of Angus

If possible, when you are in the northern parts of Strathmore, try to see at least one of the glens which penetrate the roof of Angus to the west. Long, silent and gently-winding, they were frequented until recently only by deer-stalkers and grouse-shooters. Now they are appreciated by touring motorists, but not in large numbers. One or two of the former shooting lodges—sizable little mansions, some of them—have become successful hotels.

Try Glen Esk, north from Brechin on an unclassified road; or Glen Clova (B955), Glen Prosen (unclassified) and Glen Isla ("Eye-la") on B951, all from Kirriemuir. After 12 miles or so they climb out of the Vale and approach the ridge of the high Grampians, growing rough and chilly. By the source of the Isla you may go (but only on foot) over the old robbers' road of the Monega Pass; at 3,300 feet, it is the highest right of way in the British Isles.

Dunkeld

The Great North Road (A9) leaves Perth by Atholl Street and the barracks of Perth's own regiment, the Black Watch, and after 14 miles comes to Birnam in the densely-wooded valley of the Tay. The Dunsinane ("Dun-synan") of Shakespeare's *Macbeth* is near Coupar Angus, 15 miles from here; a long march with a tree in your arms. But this riverside woodland, just opposite the larger town of Dunkeld, is the authentic Birnam Wood and on the Tay bank, behind the Waterbury Guest House, are two hoary trees, an oak and a sycamore, to prove it.

The main road bypasses Dunkeld. It crosses the turbulent Bran River west of the town and from the parking area at the roadside you may walk half a mile through larches and cedars (the first in Scotland, introduced by an arboricultural Duke of Atholl, affectionately known as Planter John, 200 years ago) to a small stone-built folly called The Hermitage. Tales of old-time travelers mention this place: it was a mandatory sight, a tiny summary of what Scotland had in store for them. Underneath the balcony the Bran foams and fusses among black rocks where you will often see fishermen precariously balanced, fighting the huge eels they have hooked while angling for salmon.

Spare half an hour, however, for Dunkeld, a charming town wedged among high hills. Its "little houses"—a row of 18th-century cottages along the cathedral approach—are one of the National Trust for Scotland's most successful renovations. In the ruined cathedral (12th–13th century), romantically situated in beautifully kept grounds on the river bank, lies Count Roehenstart of Bavaria, killed in a coach accident on Dunkeld bridge in 1854. He is described as the last descendant of Bonnie Prince Charlie.

A curious little museum in the square where the little houses begin is devoted to the history of the Scottish Horse, a yeomanry (rural volunteer) regiment raised by the Duke of Atholl's son. It started off on horses and ended up on bicycles.

Throughout the summer at the Loch o' the Lowes, one mile from Dunkeld on the A923, you may view ospreys and assorted waterfowl from a cleverly-constructed hide 200 yards from the carpark. This is one of two excellent public osprey-viewing sites in Scotland (the other is near Boat of Garten, Highland Region).

Pitlochry

Hotels and guest-houses in the main streets of little towns on Scotland's Great North Road no longer tremble to the midnight passing of fish trucks and oil tankers from the north: that highway, Edinburgh–Inverness–John o' Groats, which used to negotiate every insignificant village of the route, has, since 1976, been straightened out and carried clear of all bottlenecks.

It sweeps round Pitlochry, passing close to the Festival theatre, sometimes called the Theatre in the Hills, on a forest slope worthy of an Ibsen drama. Performances, which do not tax the intellect too heavily, take place most evenings in the summer.

Pitlochry's main street, a tartan bazaar in a graystone corridor, has become almost a pedestrians-only precinct. The small town is generally taken to be the midpoint of Scotland, though the geographical center is a few miles northwest, around Dalnacardoch. Pitlochry is equidistant from the three major winter-sports areas of Britain (about 40 miles from each): Glenshee, Aviemore and Glencoe.

Now the Highland fastnesses begin to crowd in. From here on, going north, you climb steadily. The town is well-built, with some comfortable stone villas of late-Victorian date. Among the many hotels which sprang up at that period is the inevitable Hydro, with a healing spring nearby. Forest paths to the deer-stalking country have now become nature trails. The salmon which used to make their way up the Tummel River into Loch Faskally above the town now go by way of a glass box, so you can see them.

Atholl

From Pitlochry to the northern boundary of Tayside Region lie hundreds of square miles of antediluvian forest and bare moorland. You are in Atholl country, the feudal domains of the Murrays of Atholl, offspring of royal Pictish lines and ancestors of the pre-Stuart monarchs. Medieval spellings have bequeathed a few inconsistencies. The Duke is "Atholl", but the whisky they distill at Pitlochry is "Athol." And the famous oatmeal-honey-and-whisky pudding, once the Hielandman's iron ration and now a delicacy of Taste of Scotland cookery, is "Athole" brose.

At Blair Atholl, seven miles north of Pitlochry, stands the clan seat, Blair Castle, in an estate of 300,000 acres. It is a building of suitable size and magnificence; and was the last British castle to be laid under siege (by its owner Lord George Murray when he returned from the Jacobite campaigns in 1746 and found strangers in possession). In and around Blair you may see something of the extravagant garb and stiff pageantry of an ancient body of troops: drums piled, pipes wailing, flags heaped and banners furled, possibly some antique piece of ordnance being touched off by the Master Gunner. These are the Atholl Highlanders, first formed under the "fire-and-sword" commissions which kings gave to self-governing lairds and now the last private army in the Queen's dominions. They pose no threat to the security of the state. They are recruited from among the

Duke's own friends and tenants. Retired generals and high court judges consider it an honor to serve as common soldiers. Their functions are to be His Grace's bodyguard, to wear fancy Highland costume and to preserve the old ceremonies.

It is another 15 miles to the watershed and the regional boundary (with Highland) at the Drumochter Pass. Here the winter snows linger late into the spring. A tough fence, built to protect the highway and the railroad from the weather, adds to the wildness of the scene. Those who regard Britain as over-populated might take a walk in these treeless wastes of Atholl. They may easily walk where no human foot has trodden before them.

Lochs Earn and Tay

We now return to Perth and complete our roundup of the Region with a few excursions into the western districts. First we go south towards Stirling on the A9, turning at Auchterarder to the A824 and A823. This now peaceful, bypassed village has a lot of antique shops. The reason is that Gleneagles hotel, with its clientele of well-heeled foreign visitors, is just up the road. This most prestigious caravanserai in the British Isles comprises 700 acres of parkland, 254 luxurious rooms, acres of gardens, a shopping complex, four 18-hole golf courses—and its own railroad station.

At Crieff, another clean, graystone, health-resort town on a hillside, we turn west (A85) to follow the River Earn to its loch, passing through Comrie, which is noted for slight earth tremors, being on an unstable plate of the Highland Line, and St. Fillan's. The healing saint Fillan had his cell here around the year 500 and his well, on the far side of the golf course, was at one period almost a Scottish Lourdes, to which invalids from all over the country were brought. The local archeological attraction is Dundurn, a hill close to the well. As a Pictish fort, Dundurn controlled the western approaches to the capital at Forteviot and the chronicles record a great battle there between Picts and Scots in 683.

Loch Earn, a typically long, thin loch embedded in steep hills, is becoming a notable water-sports venue. From here it is a short step to Killin (A827) where a rattling torrent bubbles over rapids in the main street. Then you coast the more elongated, more richly-wooded Loch Tay. Roads border each side of the loch for its whole 16 miles and then you are at Kenmore, which some have called Scotland's prettiest village. It is undoubtedly one of the most antiseptic; a tribute to the wealth and influence of the Marquess of Breadalbane who built it for the estate-workers at Taymouth Castle a half-mile away. The Breadalbanes (accent on the "al") were originally of the Campbell family, the Dukes of Argyll, the most rapacious landowners in Scotland and the most ruthless in holding their land down. "From the greed of the Campbells, good Lord deliver us" went the prayer of the inhabitants of the south-central Highlands. In 1842 the Marquess was still living in feudal splendor. He entertained young Queen Victoria at Taymouth that year with fireworks, gold plate and a procession of decorated barges on the loch.

An unclassified road out of Kenmore doubles back to the west and dives into the hills for a tranquil journey past Fortingall's yew tree of incalculable age and along Glen Lyon, on and on, a single track with occasional passing places, chopped and intersected by streams which race down from

3,000-foot heights. Glen Lyon, the longest accessible glen in Scotland, goes on for 27 miles until you come to a hydroelectric barrage. Here you retrace your route or attempt, at Bridge of Balgie, a high-level single-track road, not advised if the snow is lying, which goes past the Ben Lawers visitor center and drops to Loch Tay.

Six miles east of Kenmore on the A827 is Aberfeldy, yet another smart little town in an idyllic setting.

"Bless General Wade!"

The most-photographed feature of Aberfeldy is the Wade bridge over the River Tay, a neat pillared structure built in 1733 by General George Wade, and built to last.

Wade was the soldier whom the British Government commissioned to make roads and bridges through the Highland passes where no roads but the paths of cattle had existed before. "If you'd seen these roads before they were made / You would life up your hands and bless General Wade" says the couplet. While building his roads Wade lived at Weem, close to Aberfeldy, and after his death in 1748 he was buried in Westminster Abbey, London. His Scottish monument is the Wade Stone on a hillside near Dalnacardoch (A9).

The first map of the military roads of Scotland, published in 1755, computed their total length at 1,103 miles. Of the innumerable fine bridges that Wade built, Aberfeldy's is the most elaborate. Many others cross deep ravines, where you ought to stand in the torrent bed underneath to appreciate the magnitude of Wade's tasks. A few stand dilapidated at the roadside, having been rendered obsolete by the new lines of highway.

A Wade road will take you back from Aberfeldy to Dunkeld and Perth via Ballinluig, where a cottage claims the distinction of having provided breakfast for Bonnie Prince Charlie in 1746. That road follows the Tay all the way, but a more interesting route is the A826 to Amulree, joining the A822 to Crieff: two cattle passes, one bosomed in rich foliage and the other winding among stony hills. In the latter, the Sma' Glen, you can usually count on seeing a herd or two of genuine Highland bullocks; small, golden, shaggy, photogenic beasts and extremely docile despite their ferocious curving horns.

The Heart of Scotland

The old county of Perthshire, in the heart of Scotland, has sublime scenery on the old ways leading west to Rannoch Moor. For today's traveler there are a number of circular options, starting from the A9 near Killiecrankie, north of Pitlochry. The Pass of Killiecrankie was the scene of the first of the attempts by the supporters of the exiled King James VII—the Jacobites—to return him to the throne. Under their leader, Graham of Claverhouse ("Bonnie Dundee"), they defeated a superior army of King William, though Bonnie Dundee himself was killed and the revolt ultimately collapsed. The story is told in the National Trust for Scotland's Visitor Centre. This is also the starting point for easy walking in magnificent mature woodlands and impressive riverscapes. The Soldier's Leap, an 18 ft. jump across the River Garry, was successfully made by a Royalist soldier, to evade his Jacobite pursuers on the day of the Battle of Killiecrankie.

Killiecrankie is bypassed by the new A9 on a high deck. To find the Visitor Centre and the B8019 take the old road north of Pitlochry. The B8019 leads west to the Queen's View, with a sublime view of Loch Tummel and the western hills of Rannoch. There is a forest center nearby. The road continues west to join the B846 from Aberfeldy. The elegant cone of the mountain called Schiehallion ("Shee-halyon") is your landmark. It gradually drops behind as you make your way up Loch Rannoch by the B846, which beyond the loch's western end is a cul-de-sac, leading to the edge of Rannoch Moor. Rather surprisingly, you meet a railway here, the West Highland line to Fort William, which the late Victorian engineers took across the peaty wastelands by "floating" it on great rafts of turf and brushwood, which gradually consolidated to give safe passage.

If all this emptiness is a little intimidating, then return westwards by the south shore of Loch Rannoch, taking in the magnificent fragment of the ancient Caledonian pine forest, the Black Wood of Rannoch, an open woodland of great red-limbed Scots pines, with an exotic understory of juniper—so unlike the grim dark blocks of alien conifers preferred by modern forestry, all around. Crossbills, like exotic little brick-red parrots, are one of the wildlife specialties to look out for in this natural woodland. You might even see a capercaillie—a kind of dark, heavyweight, aggressive half-grouse, half-turkey!

PRACTICAL INFORMATION FOR TAYSIDE

HOW TO GET THERE. By train. Perth is a major rail center in Tayside with mainline trains from Edinburgh (1½ hours), Inverness (2¼ hours), Aberdeen (2 hours), Dundee (½ hour), and Kirkcaldy (1 hour). From London King's Cross the journey takes about 6½ hours; 7¾ from Euston.

There are several trains per day to Perth from Arbroath and Montrose on the east-coast line, and from Dunkeld, Pitlochry and Blair Atholl on the picturesque Highland line. The isolated station at Rannoch gives Tayside a toehold on the West Highland line, with access to Fort William and Mallaig in the north and the Clyde coast in the south.

By coach. Strathtay Scottish Omnibuses, Riggs Road (tel. 0738–26122), and Stagecoach, Walnut Grove, Kinfauns (tel. 0738–33481), both in Perth, run daily express coach services between Perth and London's Victoria, a 9-hour journey.

By air. There is an airfield for light private aircraft at Scone, and a small commercial airport at Dundee for Business Air flights from Aberdeen, Manchester and Esbjerg (Denmark). But for practical purposes the airports to and from Tayside are Edinburgh and Aberdeen.

HOTELS AND RESTAURANTS. The number of hotels, inns and guest-houses on Tayside's many country routes is ample proof of the Region's popularity as a touring area. Pitlochry alone—a mere village—has 30 hotels, more even than Perth! Dundee also has several good three- and four-star hotels.

Eating and drinking present no problems. Dundee, Perth, and the main routes all have restaurants and teahouses of a fairly stereotyped character, while country pubs offer bar lunches and snacks at reasonable prices.

Aberuthven (Just off A9, 10 miles southwest of Perth). **Restaurant.** *Smiddy Haugh* (I), tel. 076 46–2013. Low cost, superior value.

Alyth (A926). **Restaurant.** *Lands of Loyal* (M), tel. 0828–3151. Excellent light lunch, short dinner menu, above-average wines.

Auchterarder. *Gleneagles* (L), tel. 076 46–2231. 229 rooms with bath. One of the most famous hotels in the land, stands among endless golf courses and gardens, heated pool, tennis, squash, sauna, and excellent cuisine.

Auchterhouse (A927, midway between Dundee and Meigle). *Old Mansion House* (E), tel. 082 626–366. 6 rooms with bath. Small, luxury mansion with an expensive V.I.P. suite. Nice lawns and shrubbery. Tennis, squash courts, heated outdoor pool.

Blairgowrie (A923). *Altamount House* (E), tel. 0250–3512. 7 rooms with bath. Well-proportioned house secluded in large garden. Noted for imaginative cuisine.
Restaurant. *Blair* (I), High Street (tel. 0250–2287). Grills, salads, high teas, homebaked scones, filled potatoes. Also coffee bar.

Cleish (B9097). *Nivingston House* (E), tel. 057 75–216. 17 rooms with bath. Pretty country house with crow-stepped gables in 12 acres of gardens. Good-value bar meals but the set dinner is pricey. Rooms individually furnished and decorated.

Colliston (A993). *Lethan Grange* (E), tel. 0241–89373. 17 rooms with bath. Victorian country house hotel in 350-acre private estate. Own curling rink and golf course.

Crieff (A85). *Murraypark* (M), Connaught Terrace (tel. 0764–3731). 14 rooms, 13 with bath. High standard of comfort and service.
Restaurant. *Coffee Shop* (I), West High Street (tel. 0764–2308). Good wholesome fare including own doughnuts. Closes 5.30.

Dundee (A85). *Angus Thistle Hotel* (E), tel. 0382–26874. 60 rooms with bath. Modern, comfortable, and well-run. *Invercarse* (M), tel. 0382–69231. 39 rooms with bath. Excellent restaurant. In grounds overlooking the River Tay, fishing.
Restaurant. *Raffles* (I), Perth Road (tel. 0382–26344). Deservedly popular and worth the slight detour.

Dunkeld (A9). *Stakis Dunkeld House Hotel* (L), tel. 035 02–771. 100 rooms with bath. Former home of the Duke of Atholl. Solid-value restaurant. Attractive, riverside grounds. Leisure facilities. Fishing available.

Glenfarg (A90). *Bein Inn* (I), tel. 057 73–216. 14 rooms with bath. Historic tavern in wooded glen. Superior amenities at reasonable cost. Good restaurant.

Glenshee (A93). *Dalruzion* (I), tel. 025 082–222. 12 rooms, 5 with bath. Neat, clean, family hotel on main Braemar highway. Excellent value at modest rates. Free golf, fishing.

Kenmore (A827). *Kenmore* (E), tel. 088 73–205. 38 rooms, 35 with bath. Claims to be oldest Scottish inn. Standard country cuisine, superior wine cellar.

Restaurant. *Coshieville* (M), on B846 (tel. 088 73–319). Angus steaks, trout, bannocks, special ices, good wines.

Kinross (A9). *Green* (E), tel. 0577–63467. 44 rooms, 40 with bath. Venerable stage-coaching inn on Great North Road. Unostentatious excellence. Indoor curling, and swimming pool. Own golf course. Fishing on Loch Leven.

Restaurant. *Windlestrae* (M), tel. 0577–63217. Intimate Tudor-style, serves lobster, venison, Tay salmon, beef in Guinness.

Kirkmichael (A924). *The Log Cabin* (M), tel. 025 081–288. 13 rooms with bath. A ranch among the pines. Cordon bleu cooking makes it a popular stopover, halfway between Pitlochry and Blairgowrie.

Montrose (A92). *Park* (M), John Street (tel. 0674–73415). 59 rooms, 52 with bath.

Perth (A9). *Sunbank House* (I), 50 Dundee Road (tel. 0738–24882). 6 rooms, 4 with bath. Fine graystone mansion in best residential area near Branklyn Gardens. Views over River Tay. Unpretentious, solid comforts.

Restaurants. *Coach House* (E), North Port (tel. 0738–27950). Wall tables round spiral stair. Fresh ingredients, ever-changing menu. No background music. *Huntingtower* (M), Crieff Road (A85), tel. 0738–83771. Superior country restaurant in historic center close to city. *Timothy's* (I), 24 John Street (tel. 0738–26641). Cosmopolitan menu from Denmark to Delhi. Good reputation for snacks and light meals.

Pitlochry. *Hydro* (E), tel. 0796–2666. 64 rooms with bath. In own grounds above town; a bit old-fashioned. Tennis. *Green Park* (M), tel. 0796–3248. 37 rooms with bath. Overlooking Loch Faskally; a good touring base. *Birchwood* (M), East Moulin Road (tel. 0796–2477). 15 rooms with bath. Generally high standard and touches of refinement (fruit in bedrooms) at this pyramid-towered stone villa above town. Acres of gardens. Special terms for elderly.

St. Fillans (A85). **Restaurant.** *Four Seasons* (M), tel. 076 485–333. Fishy ingredients from loch and stream treated with flair. Bar snacks on panoramic terrace, midday and evening.

Scone (A94). *Murrayshall House* (E), tel. 0738–51171. 20 rooms with bath. Refurbished to impressive standards. Imaginative cuisine, local produce. Own golf, tennis, croquet. Three miles from Perth.

HOW TO GET ABOUT. By car. Main roads through Tayside are the A9 (Edinburgh–Perth–Inverness), A93 (Perth–Blairgowrie–Braemar),

A94 (Perth–Forfar–Aberdeen), A85 (Perth–Dundee) and A92 (Dundee–Aberdeen). The A93 is the quietest. The principal touring center, Perth, is 40 miles from Edinburgh, 115 from Inverness, and 81 from Aberdeen.

Minor roads throughout the Region are uniformly good. In the Angus glens and the western valleys toward Rannoch Moor it is possible to travel 20 miles without seeing a gas station; elsewhere the byways lead from village to village. Facilities for both people and automobiles are adequate.

Godfrey Davis Europcar have an office in Perth (tel. 0738–36888), in Dundee (tel. 0382–21281), and at Gleneagles Hotel (tel. 0738–31322). Budget Rent-a-Car are at Dundee (tel. 0382–644664). Ritchie's Self-Drive operate out of Arbroath (tel. 0241–72850), Brechin (tel. 0356–22343), and Montrose (telephone Brechin number).

By bus. There are bus services on all the major routes in Tayside, and mail or mini buses on most of the minor ones. Perth and Dundee are the principal centers for bus excursions.

TOURIST INFORMATION. If you enter Perth from the south by road, the Round House is one of the first buildings you see after crossing the South Inch. This is the Region's most impressive information center, serving Perth and district. You can "book-a-bed-ahead" and view audiovisual travelogues while you wait. Open Mon.–Fri. 9.30–7, Sat. 9.30–6, Sun. 12–6, Jun.–Sept.; normal office hours Oct.–May.

Other information centers are at Aberfeldy, Arbroath, Auchterarder, Blairgowrie, Brechin, Carnoustie, Crieff, Dundee, Dunkeld, Forfar, Kinross, Kirriemuir, Montrose and Pitlochry. They are also the accommodations bureaux for their districts and most of them will "book-a-bed-ahead." Opening hours are normally 10–6 daily except Sun. from Apr. to Sept.; shorter winter hours.

The Glenshee tourist office, Corsehill, Upper Allan Street, Blairgowrie (tel. 0250–5509), mainly for winter sports, handles only written and telephone inquiries.

FISHING. The Tay, its tributaries and their lochs provide rich salmon, brown and rainbow trout and sea-trout fishing. On certain Tay beats at Killin and Dunkeld you may fish for about £1.50 per day; permits available locally. Fishing on lochs Tay, Earn, Tummel and Faskally, with boatman or self-drive motor boat, may cost up to £20 per day; permits from lochside hotels.

If you like the look of a particular stream or loch, enquire at the nearest village post office, fishing-tackle shop or hotel. Among the hotels that offer excellent fishing to residents and nonresidents are Bridge of Cally, Blairgowrie; the Log Cabin, Kirkmichael; Fortingall, Fortingall; Ben Lawers, Aberfeldy; Kenmore, Kenmore; Dunkeld House, Dunkeld; Grandtully, Strathtay; and Ballathie House, near Meikleour. Permits for the Tay within Perth city boundaries are issued by the Director of Finance, 1 High Street, Perth, and for the Earn by Adam Boyd, Tackle Shop, 39 King Street, Crieff.

Crab boats at Arbroath will take you out for a day's sea-angling—cod, mackerel, haddock, flounder. There are good marks round the Bell Rock, 12 miles offshore. Sea fishing is available from central Dundee: tackle, bait and local wisdom from Gow's, 12 Union Street; and Shortcast, 8 Whitehall Crescent.

GOLF. There are about 50 golf courses in the Region; three good ones in Dundee and three more in Perth. Perth's King James VI club on Moncrieffe Island in the Tay (not really an island) has associations with that golfing monarch of 400 years ago. Carnoustie (A930), 11 miles east of Dundee, is Tayside's answer to St. Andrews, and you will pay around £6.50. for a round on the Medal (championship) course. The four 18-hole courses at Gleneagles are more costly: apply to Golf Secretary in advance (tel. 076 46–3543).

The superb and scenic small-town courses—Arbroath, Brechin, Forfar, Montrose, Aberfeldy, Comrie, Crieff, Dunkeld, Kenmore, Pitlochry and others—come much cheaper for the casual visitor. It is best to make arrangements beforehand if possible with the local secretary or professional.

HISTORIC HOUSES AND GARDENS. Blair Castle, Blair Atholl (A9). Great ducal château, dating from 1269. Jacobite relics. Open Easter–mid-Oct., weekdays 10–5, Sun. 2–5.

Castle Menzies, Weem (B846). Z-plan fortified seat of Menzies chiefs since 1500s. Open daily Apr.–Sept., weekdays 10.30–5, Sun. 2–5.

Glamis Castle, Glamis (A94). Much-visited 14th-century tower house with château-style additions. Old tapestries and needlework. Scene of Duncan's murder in *Macbeth.* Open May–Sept., daily except Sat., 1–5.

Hermitage, near Dunkeld. Gothick folly above cascade at end of 10-minute riverside walk. A favorite of old-time travelers. Always open. N.T.S.

Huntingtower (A85 near Perth). Gaunt 15th-century castellated house where Mary Queen of Scots spent her second honeymoon and her son James VI was seized in the Ruthven Raid. Open Apr.–Sept., weekdays 9.30–7, Sun. 2–7; Oct.–Mar., weekdays 9.30–4, Sun. 2–4.

Kinnaird Castle, Brechin (A94) (castle is 3 miles south on A933). 15th-century fortified house. Good paintings, furniture, domestic records. Open May–Sept. by arrangement (tel. 067 481–209).

Scone Palace, Scone (A93) (2 miles from Perth). Gothic house of early 19th century on ancient monastic structure. Large garden with Douglas fir raised from seed that David Douglas himself sent from U.S. in 1834. Moot hill where Celtic kings were crowned. Indoors, bed hangings embroidered by Mary Queen of Scots. Rare porcelains and ivories. Open mid-Apr.–mid-Oct., weekdays 9.30–5, Sun. 1.30–5; July–Aug., daily 10–5.

Private gardens open under Scotland's Gardens Scheme are **Bolfracks,** Aberfeldy (A827, 2 miles on Kenmore road), and **Cluny House,** also Aberfeldy (A827, 1 mile on Ballinluig road). Both open Apr.–Oct., daily 10–6.

Gardens that open occasionally in spring and summer include those at **Abercairny,** Crieff; **Airlie Castle,** Kirriemuir; **Ardvolich,** Lochearnhead; **Battleby,** Redgorton near Perth (headquarters of the Countryside Commission for Scotland); **Branklyn,** Perth (daily in summer, 9.30–sunset); **Cortachy Castle,** Kirriemuir; **Drumkilbo,** Meigle; **Drummond Castle,** Crieff (frequent high-season opening); and **Stobhall,** Guildtown, Perth. Consult Scottish or local press for opening details (normally weekends, once or twice a year). Beautiful, modern, subtropical rock gardens of Dundee University are newly opened on Riverside Drive (next door to Dundee airport). Open summer 10–4.30, winter 10–3.30.

MUSEUMS. Angus Folk Museum, Kirkwynd, Glamis (A94). The simple life of times gone by displayed in farmworkers' cottages. Open May–Sept., daily 12–5; June–Aug., daily 11.30–5.30. N.T.S.

Barrie's Birthplace, Brechin Road, Kirriemuir (A926). The humble cottage of Peter Pan's creator, with his homemade theater and costumes. Open May–Sept., weekdays 11–5.30, Sun. 2–5.30. N.T.S.

Black Watch Museum, Balhousie Castle, Perth (A9). Story of the Black Watch regiment from 1739 to present day. Open Easter–Sept., weekdays 10–4.30, Sun. 2–4.30; Oct.–Mar., weekdays only, 10–3.30.

Broughty Castle, Broughty Ferry, Dundee (A930). History and ecology of the Tay, whaling industry, old armor, in 15th-century castle. Open weekdays except Fri. 10–1 and 2–5.30, Sun. (May–Sept. only) 2–5.

Clan Museums. These include *Clan Menzies,* at Weem, Aberfeldy, and *Clan Donnachaidh,* at Bruar Falls, Blair Atholl.

Frigate "Unicorn," Victoria Dock, Dundee. Britain's oldest warship still afloat; served Royal Navy for 140 years. Shipboard life of Nelson's era. Open weekdays except Tues., 11–1 and 2–5, Sun. 2–5.

Glenesk Trust Museum, Tarfside, Glenesk (off A94). Old-time shepherd and farming life imaginatively reconstructed in a former shooting lodge, 10 miles into the hills beyond Edzell. Open June–Sept., daily 2–6.

Glenturret Distillery, Crieff (off A85). Claims, wrongly, to be Scotland's oldest. Free guided tours and tastings. Open Mar.–Oct., Mon.–Fri., 10–12 and 1.30–3.30.

"Little Houses," Dunkeld (A9). An important restoration of 20 picturesque cottages lining avenue between town center and cathedral. Several "lads o' pairts" born there, including a Canadian prime minister. National Trust shop and information center open Apr.–May and Sept.–Dec., weekdays 10–1 and 2–4.30; June–Aug., weekdays 10–6, Sun. 2–5. See also, at entrance square, **Scottish Horse Museum,** displaying history of a locally raised light cavalry regiment, 1901–1945. Open May–mid-Oct., weekdays 10–12 and 2–5, Sun. 2–5.

Meigle Museum, Meigle (A94). One of the best collections of Celtic sculptured stones in Europe. Open weekdays (contact caretaker in village).

Museum of Scottish Tartans, Comrie (A85). All you need to know about clans and their costumes. Open Apr.–Oct., weekdays 10–5, Sun. 2–5; Nov.–Mar., Mon.–Fri. 11–3, Sat. 10–1.

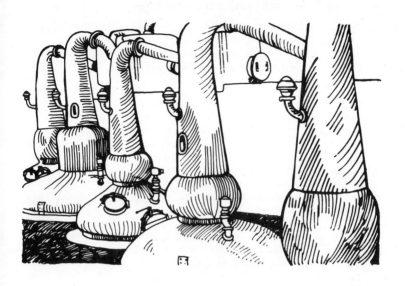

SCOTLAND'S GRANITE SHOULDER

Grampian

Scotland's most easterly Region has an east-facing seaboard of about 70 miles and a north-facing one of about 60. The east-facing coast is, particularly north of Aberdeen, gently sand-fringed, except where pink granites outcrop near Peterhead. The "grain" of the rocks—red sandstones, quartzite and other tough old heat-formed rocks—tilts to the north, however, forming spectacular cliffs and rocky bays in many places on the north-facing coast. There are also major fishing ports and several smaller old fishing communities. Grampian's coastline is one of the most beautiful and least spoilt of any in Scotland.

The Region is almost entirely north of the Highland Line, although much of it has Lowland characteristics. There are fertile river valleys, many square miles of agriculture and forestry, and, like the Lowland districts of Tayside, these areas are dotted with large farms and small hamlets and are the breeding-grounds of prize pedigree cattle, chiefly the Aberdeen Shorthorns.

But Grampian is not without Highland scenery. The region's name recalls the Grampians, the general name for the mountain massif of the central and eastern Highlands. The highest part of the Grampians, the Cairngorms, are a dissected plateau with several rounded summits over 4,000 ft.—only exceeded by Ben Nevis in Lochaber. The Cairnwell pass, south

231

of Braemar (A93), crosses into Tayside Region at 2,199 feet, the highest main road in Britain.

Grampian Region's A939 road, Cockbridge to Tomintoul, is often the first British road to be snowbound in winter and the last to be snow-free in spring.

By contrast, the Moray coastline on the northern shore, sheltered from the prevailing southwesterlies by the high Grampians, enjoys low rainfall and good sunshine records. The twin rivers Don and Dee flow out of granite uplands and make their way east to Aberdeen by scenic routes. Balmoral Castle, the Queen's summer residence, and Crathie church, which the royal family attends, stand beside the Deeside road; and Braemar, host village of the most renowned of Highland Gatherings, lies at the end of it. Not so many tourists know the country of the Don, or are aware of what they have missed. But, regarded purely as rivers, Scotland's most attractive pair are the Spey and the Findhorn, running north to the Moray coast.

The Dee and the Don are each 90 miles long—a good length for Scotland. Grampian is primarily a land of short rivers. They proceed in a series of linns—a topographical feature of the Region, a combination of deep pool, cascade and swirling channel. The atmosphere above these streams and the peat and melted snow which impregnate them are the secret of pure malt whisky production.

The chief city is Aberdeen which, if the recent rate of expansion is maintained, will in due course supersede Edinburgh as the second largest city in Scotland. Since 1969 Aberdeen has become Britain's metropolis of North Sea oil and natural gas, a base for offshore operations and oil-related construction industries and the pipeline terminus for the rich Forties field. Outside Aberdeen, no town of Grampian Region has more than about 18,000 people; though Peterhead, the next largest, is also riding the oil boom and steadily expanding.

Among the relics of primitive man are the Neolithic long cairns of Longmanhill (north coast, A98), Gourdon (near Inverbervie, A92) and Cults (near Aberdeen, A93). They date from around 3000 B.C. There are Bronze Age (1500 B.C.) stone circles at Old Keig (Alford, A944), Sunhoney (Echt, A974) and Tomnaverie (Tarland, A974). The hills above the Don have numerous Iron Age forts (A.D. 100-200) and the whole Region is strewn with Pictish stones of the period A.D. 600–1000, some of them intriguingly decorated. The best-known is the Maiden Stone at Chapel of Garioch, four miles north of Inverurie, off A96. The ruins of Deer Abbey (13th century) near Mintlaw on the A950 from Peterhead are close to the site of a vanished Celtic monastery where the precious *Book of Deer* (now in Cambridge University Library) was compiled and illuminated.

The Region is remarkable for the splendor of its many baronial castles. Among them you will see mottoes carved on stone shields and door-lintels which summarize a native philosophy of life. Inside the impressive Mitchell Tower, for example, in Aberdeen's Marischal College, is inscribed: "Thay haif said. Quhat say thay? Lat thame say." And above the staircase at Craigievar Castle: "Do not vaiken sleiping dogs."

The character of the people was formed by Grampian's geography: cut off by wild mountains on two sides and an inhospitable sea on the other two. Danes and Norsemen fought over it. Peterhead is only 300 miles from Stavanger in Norway. Grampian people have Scandinavian blood in their ancestry and they have tended historically to be slow, stolid, thrifty, industrious, self-sufficient and resentful of interference; paradoxically the least parochial people in Scotland.

Sir Walter Scott's *Old Mortality* and *The Legend of Montrose* are associated with this Region. The anarchic simplicity of the Mearns (the valley south of Stonehaven) is portrayed in Lewis Grassic Gibbon's trilogy *A Scots Quair.*

Stonehaven

The main A94, sweeping on its way to Aberdeen, bypasses the Mearns villages, and also Stonehaven, a clean, breezy little fishing town with some old-fashioned wynds and pends (passages) between main street and harbor. You see plenty of evidence of its popularity as a resort in its crowded caravan park and often-congested seafront swimming pool.

Stonehaven, like Montrose 23 miles south and Aberdeen 16 miles north, is built along a stretch of beach between two river mouths. The ruins of one of Scotland's biggest medieval castles are spread over a belligerent headland south of the town. Dunnottar Castle was the frontier post and toll-gate from which the Keith lords, hereditary Earls Marischal of Scotland, commanded the nation's eastern approaches. William Wallace captured it from the English in 1296, firing the interior and roasting alive the soldiers who had fled into the chapel for sanctuary. The armies of Balliol, Bruce, Montrose and Cromwell besieged it in their turn.

During the interregnum when Cromwell ruled in England, the Scottish regalia of crown, scepter and sword of state were deposited at Dunnottar for safe keeping. While under siege the defenders managed to smuggle out the regalia to the parish church of Kinneff (on the coast, six miles south), where they lay buried until the restoration of King Charles II. During the subsequent witch-hunt for the Covenanters the deepest dungeons of Dunnottar were a prison in which 167 men, women and children were starved and suffocated. They lie under the Covenanters' Stone in Dunnottar churchyard. This is where Sir Walter Scott first saw Old Mortality, the pious graybeard who went round Scotland tidying up the graves of the Covenant martyrs and who flits through the pages of Scott's novel of that name.

To reach Deeside, take the high-level Cairn o' Mount road (B974 Fettercairn–Banchory) for spectacular views across hill, forest and the Lowlands southwards. The Slug Road (A957) is a lower-level alternative. The Camp of Raedykes, a Roman station four miles along this road, interests archeologists. Some say that this must have been Mons Graupius where, in A.D. 84, the Romans under Agricola defeated the Picts. It is the Grampian massif's nearest approach to the sea, a fairly plausible site for the greatest battle in terms of numbers fought on British soil. What the Roman historian Tacitus called "Graupius", the Scottish historian Hector Boece misread as "Grampius"—thus the word "Grampian" came down to us.

Granite City

Major 20th-century novelist, Aberdeenshire-born Lewis Grassic Gibbon, called Aberdeen "the one haunting and exasperatingly lovable city in Scotland." Glaswegians of course say much the same sort of thing about *their* native town.

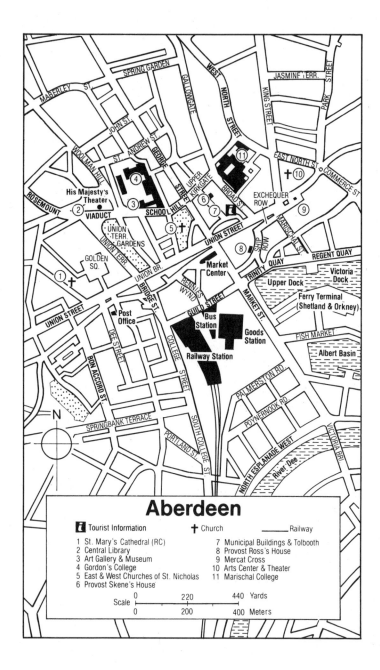

Aberdeen

i Tourist Information   **✝** Church   ———— Railway

1 St. Mary's Cathedral (RC)
2 Central Library
3 Art Gallery & Museum
4 Gordon's College
5 East & West Churches of St. Nicholas
6 Provost Skene's House

7 Municipal Buildings & Tolbooth
8 Provost Ross's House
9 Mercat Cross
10 Arts Center & Theater
11 Marischal College

Scale

| 0 | 220 | 440 | Yards |
| 0 | 200 | 400 | Meters |

In many respects Aberdeen is an archetypal British city and governments recognize this. When sociological experiments or nationwide surveys have to be carried out, Aberdeen is often the guinea-pig. Yet few British cities have undergone more violent changes in the past half-century and none have withstood the impact of change more successfully. Grim under low cloud or sparkling gray in the sunlight, Aberdeen still looks impregnable against the influx of the oilmen and their technology.

The gently undulating ground on which the city is built divides the estuaries of the Dee and the Don, two fine salmon rivers. (The city was called Aberdon long ago, and the citizens are still Aberdonians.)

She is the third city of Scotland, with cathedral and university (which is actually two universities combined) and clean, broad beaches on her doorstep. She is the Granite City, and has for centuries exported the durable, glittering stone of her suburban quarries which at the same time supply her own building needs. In the early 1970s she changed her personality from well-to-do over-grown market town to major oil capital, with her harbor area transformed into a front line base for North Sea exploration. Her role as a fishing port also continued, though somewhat eclipsed by her smaller neighbor Peterhead.

Most of central Aberdeen on either side of the mile-long straight thoroughfare called Union Street was built around 1800–1820: not as startling architecturally as Georgian Edinburgh, but handsome enough in its sparkling block granite. Union Street is carried downhill on low piers and where the main railroad goes under the viaduct there are flanking gardens like those of Edinburgh's Princes Street, but on a more modest scale. Note the solid range of buildings at the north end of the gardens. They comprise public library, church and theater: a landmark which Aberdonians know affectionately as "Education, Salvation and Damnation."

Perhaps the heart of the city today is the now-pedestrianized Castlegate, at the easternmost end of Union Street. Several features can be noted here, including the grand Salvation Army Citadel, its styling deliberately echoing Balmoral Castle. Close at hand is the impressive Mercat Cross (restored 1820), always the symbolic center of a Scottish medieval burgh. Note along its parapet, amongst its twelve panels, the portraits of the Stuart monarchs. Opposite is the handsome tower of the Town House or Tolbooth. It dates from the 17th century, with many later additions in silvery granite. Also in sight here is the handsome colonnaded facade of the Atheneum, built as a library, now mainly offices and eating places.

The old Shiprow, the main road into town in bygone days, goes off to the left. Here the house of Provost Ross, built in 1593, is worth looking at. The oldest house in Aberdeen is to your right, on the other side of Union Street, half-encircled by the city's administrative offices in St. Nicholas House. This is Provost Skene's house, built in about 1540. Both Ross and Skene were hardheaded Aberdonians who made their fortune in the import-export business, chiefly with the Baltic countries. The Government commander-in-chief, the Duke of Cumberland, stayed at Provost Skene's house in 1746 during his pursuit of the retreating Jacobite army.

Aberdeen's outstanding building in gleaming silver granite and in a flamboyant Gothic style, is Marischal (pronounced "Marshal") College, founded in 1593 as the city's second university. It was amalgamated with the first, King's College off King Street on the way to Bridge of Don (founded 1494), in 1826. Marischal College faces the north side of St.

Nicholas House on the site of an ancient monastery. When the new building was opened in 1906 it was the second largest granite hall in the world, the first being Spain's Escorial.

In Union Terrace Gardens you will find a number of statues, including monuments to William Wallace and Robert Burns (portrayed addressing the Daisy of his well-known poem). The Art Gallery on the other side of the railroad tracks contains sculptures by Epstein and Henry Moore and some good Impressionist and Post-impressionist paintings.

Aberdonians have a reputation for ultra-Scottish parsimony. They share it with citizens of several European cities and it usually stems from envy at their success in developing meager resources. Perhaps in Aberdeen they were once more thrifty than most and more inclined to drive hard bargains in commerce. They capitalized on the slur: the penny-pinching Aberdonian became an industry, and Aberdeen the fountainhead of jokes and comic postcards on the subject.

In truth Aberdeen is renowned for its generosity in entertaining delegations, visiting firemen and so forth and in contributing to worthy causes. She is not the tidy, sober city she used to be. Oil has sprayed her with something of a Klondike aroma and there is much movement of strangers at all hours of the day and night—though things have calmed down greatly since the heady days of the 1970s expansion. Prices of foodstuffs and services approach capital-city level, and if you come looking for accommodations in the tourist season you may be disappointed or have to pay extortionate prices, if you insist on a city-center hotel. On the whole, however, Aberdeen is the best-organized of the four large Scottish cities and her resilient citizens, like their tough stone, have stood up well to the socioeconomic earthquake of North Sea oil.

Scotland's Oil

As an energy source, oil is an infant barely 130 years old. We saw in the Central Region chapter how James "Paraffin" Young launched the world's first oil industry in Scotland after 1850. So rapidly did the demand increase with the invention of the automobile that by 1919 fuel economists were giving the industrial nations another 30 years before their oil ran out. Since then it has been discovered in previously undreamed-of quantities. The date of final exhaustion at current and projected rates of consumption keeps moving forward and now it stands somewhere in the second quarter of the 21st century.

North Sea oil was discovered in 1969 while engineers were prospecting for natural gas. Quantities have proved greater than forecast. Equally important, the oil is of very superior quality.

Scotland's oil lies in a straggling ribbon about 100 miles offshore, from a point southeast of Aberdeen to a point northeast of Shetland. There are about 70 exploration rigs continually working along this line and about 20 oil fields already in production.

The vision of a race of tartan sheikhs in Scotland has now evaporated somewhat, especially as the projected oil bonanza has not noticeably benefited the British taxpayer at large. But it has certainly benefited the economy in the east of Scotland and has created thousands of well-paid jobs.

Buchan

From Aberdeen you can coast the rugged northeast shoulder of Scotland on the A92 road to Fraserburgh and the A98 to the Moray Firth. This corner of Grampian Region is called Buchan. Though geographically north of the Highland line, Buchan is essentially a Lowland area, with historical and linguistic links with Scandinavia, in spite of its tourism authorities' willingness to participate in Scotland's tartan image. This cold and, in places, bleak shoulder of land spreads southwards in a great arc from Kinnaird Head, the turning point of the North Sea into the Moray Firth, gradually clothing its fields with increasing amounts of woodland as it nears the Grampian foothills.

Formerly it was rough moor and stony heathland, but the energy of generations of farmers, since the time of the 18th-century "agrarian revolution" have made it now a productive area for both cattle and wheat, and oats are still grown. The visitor traveling inland in this northeast corner is thus seeing a landscape of improvement: neat fields with dry-stone walls—"dry-stane dykes"—testifying to the back-breaking clearing, a few stands of shelter-belt timber, and gray-slated farmhouses tucked into the hummocky hills. The best starting point for discovering the story of this farming area is a visit to the North East Scotland Agricultural Heritage Centre in Aden Country Park, west of Peterhead.

Many of its inland communities also played their part in this landscape of improvement. They are "planned villages," such as New Pitsligo, Strichen or New Deer, set up by progressive landlords. The name New Leeds, for example, today an overlooked hamlet, testifies to the aspirations of its founder who tried to make it a textile center, using locally-grown flax. If the landscape shows the hand of man, then, by contrast, the coastline is a mainly untouched jewel. There are some spectacular chasms at places such as the Bullers o' Buchan (visited by Johnson and Boswell on their Highland journey) south of Peterhead, while Fraserburgh has one of the few British beaches to reach European Economic Community standards of cleanliness.

One beguiling feature of Buchan is its role as the heartland of the Scots language—not the Gaelic of the Highlands, but a northern form of "English" with a pedigree as respectable as southern or standard English, yet until recent times devalued by most Scots aspiring to ape southern speech. Generations of schoolmasters, and now the leveling influence of the mainly London-controlled media, have threatened it, but it survives, in all its charm and richness, in everyday life in Buchan, in farm, local shop or quayside.

The Rockbound Coast

Peterhead and Fraserburgh are sturdy little ports with a life of their own, most of it concentrated on fishing. Yet in this remote corner of Scotland a university was set up in 1595 (at Fraserburgh). With the two in Aberdeen, this short stretch of Grampian coast had for a few years more universities than in the whole of England and Wales, though not for long. Fraserburgh University's principal quarrelled with his patron, King James VI, and in 1605 the charter was withdrawn. Not to be outdone, Peterhead set itself up as a health resort on the strength of the curative properties of local springs. Around 1780 the town was doing good business with invalids from the south, but the vogue did not last.

As its name implies, Fraserburgh was the seat of the Fraser family. They changed its name from Faithlie. Kinnaird Castle, built in 1569 on Fraserburgh's promontory, proved too exposed for even the hardy Frasers. On top of it there still stands the first lighthouse built by the official Northern Lighthouses Trustees in 1787. Southeast of Fraserburgh (which, by the way, is usually known locally as "The Broch") is the internationally important wildfowl reserve of the Loch of Strathbeg. Also nearby are the villages of Cairnbulg and St. Combs, tucked gable-end against an open shore, whose menfolk have played an important part in the local fishery for generations. The villages here still hold curious events, Temperance Walks, accompanied by flute and drum bands, as part of their New Year traditions.

West from Fraserburgh, along the north-facing coastline there are other former fishing communities, though the boats' crews who have their homes there now usually work out of the main fishing ports of Peterhead, Fraserburgh or Macduff. The tiny village of Pennan gained temporary fame as part of the setting of the Burt Lancaster film *Local Hero,* while, west again, Gardenstown, always called "Gamrie", is noted for the variety of places of worship and strong faiths. (The fishing communities have often had bouts of fervent evangelical leanings, though the demands of running a hi-tech modern fishing vessel leave little time for religious sentiment.) The cliff scenery between Fraserburgh and Banff is among the finest on the British mainland.

The twin towns of Macduff and Banff face each other across the estuary of the River Deveron. Macduff was greatly expanded by the local landowner, the 2nd Earl of Fife, before the end of the 18th century. It has a modern harbor, and still builds vessels for the local fleet. Banff is an older foundation and, perhaps unexpectedly, has some fine Georgian architecture. In fact, the town has much character, as well as the Baroque splendor of nearby Duff House, built by William Adam for the Earl of Fife.

West of the town, the pattern of bright-painted, well-scrubbed coastal communities is continued by picturesque places such as Whitehills (still with its own fishing fleet) and Portsoy, with an atmospheric conservation area by its old harbor.

The Moray Riviera

The attractive little resort of Cullen shows a number of typical northeast features: firstly, the old seatown, clustered by the shore; secondly, the newer, planned town, laid out by the Earl of Seafield in the early 19th century; thirdly, the influence of local landowners. Between the two communities is a huge railway viaduct, pushed to the sea-edge as the Earl would not allow the tracks to cross his land. Beyond the town, the main way west, the A98 runs a little way inland through a prosperous well-clothed landscape of grainfields and woods, but there is the option of a series of coastal loops. These take in yet more well-established fishing villages— Portnockie, Findochty—positively Mediterranean in their color schemes, then more ribbons of sea-edge houses, glimpses of drying nets and jagged-edged rocks with a backdrop of faint blue hills northwards across the Moray Firth, all the way to the main port of Buckie.

Inland, back on the A98, Fochabers is yet another elegantly laid-out town (this time by the Dukes of Gordon). There is a variety of antique shops, and the local quality food factory, Baxters, welcomes visitors to its premises, while the local museum is an imaginative presentation of rural times past. You can walk the Speyside Way by the banks of the river and—timing it right—enjoy some sunshine. This is the "Moray Riviera," a harmless invention by the Victorian promoters of the hotel and golf courses of such resorts as Nairn (actually further west). Though the Gulf Stream does certainly warm the west coast, the main meteorological attractions in these parts are their fortunate position in the "rain-shadow" of the high Grampians. This protects the area from most of Scotland's prevailing moist southwesterlies.

Elgin

The ideal touring center for the district is Elgin, a cosy little market town which, by virtue of having a 13th-century cathedral, styles itself "city." The cathedral's interior was accidentally burned out in 1270 and deliberately fired in 1390. In 1506 the steeple fell down and 60 years later the Earl of Moray sold all the lead off the roof to clear a debt. The place now stands in fairly impressive but melancholy decay.

The ruins are associated with General Anderson (died 1824) who bequeathed his fortune to the town. His mother, left homeless and penniless at his birth, crept into a cell among the cathedral's wreckage. It is said that a stone basin in the vestry was Andrew Anderson's cradle. He enlisted in the East India Company's army as a drummer boy, made a great deal of money and retired at the top of his profession. The ornate Anderson Institute, a Corinthian building of 1831–32, established to give the young an education and make the old comfortable, stands opposite Panns Port, the cathedral's entrance gate.

South of Elgin on a roundabout route on the B9010 to Forres, is the hamlet of Dallas, prettily situated but otherwise quite insignificant. The Dallas which its emigrant families founded on the other side of the Atlantic was destined to be an entirely different sort of place. If you go to Dallas, Grampian Region, have a look at the parish cross in the kirkyard and then drive four miles north to Pluscarden Abbey, a foundation dating from 1230, and now undergoing substantial renovation by its community of Benedictine monks. It is open to visitors at all reasonable hours and its surroundings in the valley of the Lossie River, rich in both castles and distilleries, attract many visitors.

Elgin's north road (A941) brings you to the fishing harbor of Lossiemouth, lying on what its most famous son, Ramsay MacDonald, called "our Bay of Naples." MacDonald (1866–1937), first Socialist Prime Minister of Britain (1924 and 1929–31) was born in Gregory Place, Lossiemouth—a stone marks the cottage—and is buried in Spynie churchyard on the road to Elgin.

Lossiemouth had a naval air station during World War II, and this has since become an important Royal Air Force base. But the town and bay are also developing as a holiday resort. Five miles west, off the B9135, stands Gordonstoun, a 17th-century country house converted to a school in 1934 by the educationist Kurt Hahn. He attracted a royal pupil, Philip Mountbatten, later Duke of Edinburgh, and since then Prince Charles and his brothers have each received part of their education there.

The Whisky Trail

With enough sunshine to ripen local barley, pure water from the unpolluted Grampians and local peat for stoking the kilns, Speyside developed Scotland's largest concentration of whisky distilleries.

Millions of people the world over know Scotch whisky as a serious adjunct to gracious living. The word is a corruption of *uisgebeatha,* the Gael's "water of life." Tradition says that Scottish doctors practicing in London first popularized the drink outside the Highlands by recommending it as medicine: they all had shares in the whisky firms. Subsequently, for almost 200 years, while fashions in liquor have come and gone, whisky has maintained a steady and increasing popularity. Since 1960 it has been top of the world list for sales. The blending, bottling, transporting and selling keeps 20,000 Scots employed—rather more than does the fishing industry.

Yet the whisky most people drink is not, according to purists, the real stuff. Ordinary whisky is blended from a variety of grain spirits in relatively large-scale operations. The real stuff, the connoisseurs say, is the unblended or single malt whisky produced in a small distillery which, ideally, still uses peat in the malt drying process.

Memoirs of the Highland lairds nostalgically recall the "bothies" (mountain huts) of old with their well-built stone walls, watertight thatches and arrays of casks and tubs and iron pipes leading the cold spring water to the still-rooms. The permanence of the layout revealed that the one-man distillery stood in little danger of the law—maltster and excise officer were generally on the best of terms as the latter, appointed to some remote glen for life, soon learned discretion if he wanted to live peaceably with his neighbors.

The single malt distillery of today is a modest little building with pagoda-like chimneys. There are about 90 in Scotland, most of them scattered about the Grampian foothills, set on the banks of streams in the neighborhood of Elgin, Rothes, Keith, Dufftown, Tomintoul and Grantown-on-Spey. Their hygienic environment and sophisticated equipment are a world away from the "bothy" but the pale, sometimes colorless liquid which emerges is fundamentally the same as ever.

There are about 112 brands of malt whisky, but only some 20 are marketed commercially. They are usually matured for eight to 20 years and they cost about twice as much as blended Scotch. The best-known brands (Glenfiddich, Glen Grant, Glen Moray, Cardhu, Glenfarclas and a few more) originate within a few miles of each other but they differ as subtly as do the great wines produced in adjacent vineyards of Burgundy or Bordeaux. The most famous malt whisky is Glenlivet—"The Glenlivet," if it comes from Smith's distillery which, founded 1823, is the only one licensed so to describe the product, though several neighboring distilleries also take their water from the Livet stream. This river rises in the Ladder hills and crosses the B9008 road near Tomnavoulin en route for the Spey river. If you have time for only one distillery visit, make it The Glenlivet.

The tourist Whisky Trail starts at the Glenfiddich distillery in Dufftown and proceeds south to Tomintoul, then north to the Glenfarclas distillery, then to Knockando on the Spey for the Tamdhu distillery; north again past Craigellachie to Keith for the 18th-century Strathisla distillery and back south to Dufftown—an attractive run of 65 miles in green and hilly country, even if whisky does not interest you. The Trail is signposted and all the distilleries named have a traditional welcome for visitors. Many have visitor centers open at weekends as well as during working hours.

Among distilleries not on the trail but also open to visitors are Glendronach at Forgue (B9001 near Huntly); Glengarioch at Oldmeldrum (A947 from Aberdeen); Glen Grant at Rothes (A941 from Elgin); and The Glenlivet (B9008 from Dufftown). Opening hours are normally 10–4 on certain weekdays only, mid-April to mid-October.

The drive down Strathavon from Tomintoul (B9136) and along the Spey to its narrow estuary (A95, B9103) is of high scenic quality. The sights of the route are Ballindalloch Castle at Bridge of Avon, built in 1546 but enlarged many times; and the iron bridge which Telford, a 19th-century pioneer of civil engineering in Britain, constructed across the Spey under the Rock of Craigellachie in an exceptionally romantic setting. The main A941 road used to cross it, but now you have to make a short detour.

Romantic Castles

The Grampian summits are the backcloth of the malt whisky country, and on a day of rain and sleet it sometimes seems a long way round them to the hamlets of the upper Don and Dee, the nearest habitable valleys. On the Lecht road, Tomintoul to Cockbridge (A939), you may find snow as early as October and as late as April; you will probably see it on the hills as your road wriggles round their thrusting shoulders.

The Don valley is a soft, bright enclave which Scots love and strangers hardly know. The river is deep and swift and flows past farms and villages and great menacing fortresses like 13th-century Kildrummy (A97) and modern replicas like 19th-century Forbes (B992), where the road climbs out of a ravine called My Lord's Throat. Nearby is Alford ("*Aa*-furd") on the A944 where the "Great Marquess" Montrose fought a battle in 1645 for the lost cause of Charles I; and a little farther south Lumphanan (A980) with a peel tower and the wood where Macbeth suffered defeat and was killed in 1057 at the hands of Malcolm Canmore. There are a Macbeth Stone, a Macbeth Cairn and a Macbeth Arms hotel here—but nothing of Macbeth himself, despite what self-appointed guides may say. That man of blood, along with other Celtic kings of Scotland, was buried on the isle of Iona (Strathclyde).

Here we are in the midst of the land of fairytale castles. The most perfect of them, said to have been Walt Disney's model for the fairytale castles of his movies, is Craigievar, six miles south of Alford. It is one of those strange, pale-stone conglomerations of tall slender walls and turrets, winding stairs and crooked chambers that are the epitome of early 17th-century "Scottish baronial." They are found at their most graceful and esthetically satisfying in the valleys of Dee and Don. "Quite perfect, lightly poised on the ground . . . no infelicity of mass or exaggeration of detail . . . a serene assurance . . . a symphony in stone"—critics of various nations and centuries have enthused over Craigievar. Indoors the medieval and Renaissance elements are just as daring as the main fabric of the building. Until quite recently the castle was lived in by the Forbes-Sempill family. Older people can remember when rushes were freshly gathered in the meadows every morning and strewn on the floors. The place is now in the care of the National Trust for Scotland.

Scotland's Castle Trail

This part of Scotland has an extraordinary variety of castles. Some are in private ownership, tucked discreetly in thick woods and not always welcoming visitors. Much the best way of sampling the range is to follow *Scotland's Castle Trail,* a leaflet and map available from any of Gordon District's tourist information centers. The trail is clearly signposted.

Starting, for example, from the A920 west of Pitmedden—which has a unique formal garden in the care of the National Trust for Scotland— you can then circle to visit 15th-century Tolquhon ("Tu-*hoon*"—roughly), an Historic Scotland roofless ruin, then Castle Fraser, a magnificent 16th-century Z-plan structure. Craigievar, already mentioned, is a little west, then the mighty ruin of Kildrummy (HS), on the way to lonely Corgarff (NTS), a white fortified tower house in rolling dark moors. Northwards again, by way of contrast, Leith Hall (NTS) is a charming 17th-century mansion in peaceful grounds. Next signposted is Huntly Castle (HS), impressively ruined, which in turn leads on to Fyvie Castle, perhaps the most magnificent and certainly the most complex of this great treasury of castles. Finally, returning eastwards, Haddo House is an elegant and symmetrical 18th-century mansion.

Royal Deeside

We have left the Region's principal touring route until last. For the motorist—unhappily no longer for the rail traveler—the Deeside stretch divides into four: Aberdeen to Banchory (18 miles); Banchory to Ballater (25 miles); Ballater to Braemar (17 miles); and the minor road from Braemar to Linn of Dee, where the infant river comes bursting out of the Forest of Mar.

There are two Deeside roads and it makes sense to go up to Braemar on the A93 and return by the B976. The Dee glitters through a frame of pinewoods and birches, as the valley is richly clothed with woodland and lit with constantly changing colors.

Several beautiful houses cling to the lower banks. Note especially Drum Castle, a 13th-century hunting lodge with 17th-century additions (A93 near Peterculter); and Crathes, which has been in the hands of the same family, the Burnetts of Leys, since 1323 (A93 near Banchory).

All the valley towns are well-groomed and fresh-looking and the mica in their granite sparkles in the sun. They always look as though smartened up for a royal visit, as indeed they have often been in the past, for the Deeside roads have brought the crowned heads and potentates of Europe and farther afield to share a summer holiday with the reigning monarch at Balmoral. The Tsar and Tsarina of Russia once came this way and the cottages along Deeside were festooned in black and gold. In 1889 the Shah of Persia made a memorable visit to Queen Victoria and for him the color scheme was applegreen and pink. "What a beautiful climate," the Grand Vizier said enviously. "In our country it never rains like this."

Banchory is a modern village, though its golf course dates back to 1799 and the little monastery of St. Ternan stood in the 5th century where the churchyard is now. The Nature Conservancy Council studies the habits of grouse in a converted stables south of the river. The nearby Brig o' (Bridge of) Feuch is a local beauty spot, especially attractive in autumn, with rushing rocky waters and—sometimes—leaping salmon.

In former days, the life of the valley was bound up with its own little railway, but this has vanished without a thought given to its modern tourism potential. The line, closed in 1966, had many royal connections. Around Ballater station, the terminus where visitors for Balmoral disembarked and waited for their carriages to the castle, there survives some faded grandeur of the amenities provided for them.

Aboyne has a castle, some Bronze Age and Pictish remains, and there is also an annual Highland Gathering which usually takes place on the first Saturday in August. The highlight is the opening procession, traditionally led by the "Cock o' the North" (the head of the ducal family of Gordon) and his attendant chiefs. All the route between here and Ballater is dotted with handsome country houses and mock-baronial châteaux. When Queen Victoria acquired Balmoral, a number of self-made men with social and political ambitions thought it wise to stake a claim in the neighborhood.

On a plaque on Ballater's river bridge the disastrous history of several previous bridges is outlined. The Dee in spate is an awesome sight and there is said to be the masonry of a dozen castles as fine as Crathes or Craigievar rolling in its bed. Ballater is becoming devoted to tourism: every house a guest-house.

This is Royal Deeside. Ten miles on you pass Crathie church and know that you are almost at Balmoral. Crathie is the royal family's parish church and when they are holidaying at Balmoral crowds of 10,000 people have been known to line the road on which they walk to and from Sunday worship. Few locals join the crowds. One of Balmoral's great attractions for the monarch has always been the villagers' respect for royal privacy. In Queen Victoria's time there used to be an undignified scramble to go to church with Her Majesty; nowadays seats are reserved for parishioners.

Balmoral

Some credit Sir Walter Scott with having opened up Scotland for tourism through his poems and novels. Others say General Wade did it when he built the Highland roads. But it was probably Queen Victoria who gave tourism its real momentum when, in 1842, she first came to Scotland and when, in 1847—on doctor's orders: he thought the relatively dry climate of upper Deeside would suit her—she bought Balmoral.

At first sight she described it as "a pretty little castle in the old Scottish style." The pretty little castle was knocked down to make room for a much grander house in neo-baronial style. Year by year Victoria and her German husband Albert added to the estate, took over neighboring houses, secured the forest and moorland round about and developed the deerstalking and the grouse-shooting. Balmoral is now a large property: the grounds run for 12 miles along the Deeside road. Its privacy is protected by belts of pinewood and the only view of the castle from the A93 is a partial one, from a point near Inver, two miles west of the gates. But there is an excellent bird's-eye view of the castle in its wooded surroundings from an old military road, now the A939, which climbs out of Crathie, northbound for Cockbridge and the Don valley. This view embraces the summit of Lochnagar (3,786 feet) in whose "corries" (hollows) the snow lies late in the year; and, behind the castle, the Ballochbuie Forest, known as the "bonniest plaid in Scotland" from the alleged fact that its purchase price long ago was a length of tartan cloth.

As time went by the Queen and Prince Albert bought or leased for their relations and guests Birkhall House, Abergeldie Castle and Mar Lodge, all in the Braemar area. The royal connection brought prosperity to upper Deeside. It is now one of the most civilized districts of Scotland, in spite of the wildness of the scenery. In the early days, thanks to the Prince Consort's enthusiasm for the Highland tradition, a bad rash of tartanitis broke out. Stags' heads abounded, the bagpipes wailed incessantly and the garish Stuart tartan was used for every item of furnishing—carpets, curtains, chair-covers, wallpaper. This "Balmorality" was infectious and soon it was all the rage for the rich or aristocratic famous to play at mock-Highlanders on sporting estates all over Scotland. This is still prevalent even today on Deeside, where large acreages are bought by foreign millionaires for large sums.

From the brief glimpse the visitor is today allowed of Balmoral's interior, it is clear that royal taste today is more restrained. The Queen and other members of the royal family, however, follow their predecessors' routine in spending a holiday of about six weeks on Deeside, usually mid-August to the end of September; and these days the Queen often arrives as her great-great-grandmother did when she first came to Balmoral: by royal yacht to Aberdeen and then along the Deeside roads.

Springs of Dee

Nine miles west of Balmoral is Braemar, where the A93 takes a sharp turn south for the Devil's Elbow and Glenshee (Tayside Region). Here are the ruins of another royal seat, Kindrochit Castle, said to have been built by Malcolm Canmore in the 11th century.

The noisy torrent of the Clunie froths under an ancient bridge and Braemar village gets on with the business of accommodating its plentiful visitors and selling them souvenirs. Convalescing at The Cottage in Castleton Terrace in 1881, Robert Louis Stevenson wrote most of *Treasure Island*.

The Highland Gathering arena is half a mile west of the village. This biggest of clan events, always attended by a member of the royal family and sometimes by other, more exotic guests as well, takes place on a Saturday early in September. Though the Braemar Gathering is the main important event, there is also plenty in the way of short walking excursions available in the area.

A short drive west takes you to the end of the public road, which crosses the Linn of Dee and doubles back a little way. The Linn is a well-known beauty spot. Shaded by tall larches, the river foams through a narrow rocky neck, then spills into dark pools. Take your camera.

The straight journey from Aberdeen to Linn of Dee and back would be 130 miles but if you are going to explore Deeside thoroughly the by-roads would add a good deal of mileage to that.

PRACTICAL INFORMATION FOR GRAMPIAN

HOW TO GET THERE. By air. The airport for Grampian Region is Dyce, 7 miles north of Aberdeen. It has flights from Glasgow and Edinburgh (Air Ecosse, Air U.K., British Airways), Wick (British Airways), Orkney and Shetland (British Airways); also connections from London (Gatwick and Heathrow), Leeds/Bradford, East Midlands, Birmingham, Humberside, Manchester and Norwich, and from Amsterdam, Bergen, Stavanger and Copenhagen.

By train. There is a main railroad to Aberdeen from Stonehaven and the south via Dundee and Perth. The journey from London (King's Cross) by InterCity 125s takes only 7 hours. There are also motorail services from Euston carrying passengers and their vehicles. There is a service from Inverness to Aberdeen calling at Dyce, Inverurie, Insch, Huntly, Keith, Elgin and Forres. The journey takes about 2½ hours.

By bus. Stagecoach, Walnut Grove, Kinfauns, Perth (tel. 0738–33481), runs express coaches from and to Aberdeen/Stonehaven and London (Victoria Coach Station)/Birmingham (St. Chadsway). There are several direct bus services between Edinburgh/Glasgow and Aberdeen, journey time 3–3½ hours.

By boat. P. & O. Ferries, Jamieson's Quay, Aberdeen AB9 8DL (tel. 0224–589111) operate passenger and automobile shipping services to Lerwick in the Shetland Islands and Stromness in Orkney. Onward sailings from Shetland to the Faroe Islands, Iceland, Norway and Denmark, from May–Sept. Mini-cruises and excursions are also available from Aberdeen.

HOTELS AND RESTAURANTS. The Region has some splendid country hotels with log fires and rich furnishings, where you can be sure of eating well if you have time for a leisurely meal. Aberdeen restaurants have increased and improved to meet the demands of spendthrift oilmen. Elsewhere you will always get a pub lunch and a hotel high tea/dinner.

Aberdeen (A93). *Tree Tops* (L), Springfield Road (tel. 0224–313377). 90 rooms with bath. Has a glamorous restaurant called the *Garden Room.* *Caledonian Thistle* (M–E), Union Terrace (tel. 0224–640233). 79 rooms, 77 with bath. Old city-center hotel handsomely refurbished. *Royal* (M), Bath Street (tel. 0224–585152). 43 rooms with bath. Old-established, maintains standards without gimmicks. *Furain Guest House* (I), 92 North Deeside Road, Peterculter (tel. 0224–732189). 8 rooms, 4 with bath. Cheerful red granite house, family-run, on river 5 miles from city.

Restaurants. *Mr. G's* (E), Chapel Street (tel. 0224–642112); *Gerrard's* (E), Chapel Street (tel. 0224–639500), French cuisine; *Cooters* (M), North Deeside Road, Peterculter (tel. 0224–733289), welcoming, sensible layout, fresh food neatly presented, suburban location; *Yu* (M), 347 Union Street (tel. 0224–580318).

Pubs. For their central locations and bar meals on weekdays we recommend *Fiddlers,* 1 Portland Street; *Gabriel's,* 16 Dee Street; and the *Quarterdeck,* Blaikie's Quay.

Aboyne (A973). *Huntly Arms* (M), tel. 0339–2101. 36 rooms, 26 with bath. Impressive indoor and outdoor sporting amenities. Good food in generous measure.

Ballater (A93). *Tullich Lodge* (L), tel. 0338–55406. 10 rooms with bath. Late-Victorian atmosphere; great views; excellent restaurant. *Gairnshiel Lodge* (I), Glengairn (tel. 0338–55582). 14 rooms, 8 with bath. Delightful hunting lodge in quiet valley near Balmoral Castle. Guests are made cozy and kept well-fed on superior home produce.

Banff (A947). *County* (M), tel. 026 12–5353. 7 rooms, 6 with bath. Elegant small country house above bay, rooms furnished with taste and individuality.
Restaurant. *Fagins* (M), Whitehills, by Banff (tel. 026 17–321). Seafood a specialty, in unspoilt fishing village.

Braemar (A93). *Fife Arms* (M), tel. 033 83–644. 87 rooms, 40 with bath. Principal hotel of popular village. Don't expect peace and quiet in high season. *Schiehallion* (I), tel. 033 83–679. 11 rooms, 5 with bath. Tidy, friendly budget guest house.

Buckie (A98). **Restaurant.** *Old Monastery* (M), Drybridge (tel. 0563–32660). Excellent for fish. Atmospheric surroundings, wild coastal scenery.

Cruden Bay (A975). *Kilmarnock Arms* (I), Aulton Road (tel. 0779–812213). Good food and popular with golfers. Bram Stoker stayed here while writing *Dracula!*

Dyce (A947). *Skean-Dhu* (E), Farburn Terrace (tel. 0224–723101). 220 rooms with bath. The larger of two airport hotels.

Elgin (A96). *Eight Acres* (E), Sheriffmill (tel. 0343–3077). 57 rooms, 54 with bath. Admirably furnished with modern taste. *Mansion House* (M), The Haugh (tel. 0343–48811). 12 rooms with bath. Mock-baronial villa in riverside location a few minutes from town. Above average cuisine, dinners elaborately presented.

Ellon (A92). *Ladbroke Hotel* (E), tel. 0358–20666. 40 rooms with bath. Company consider this the brightest jewel in their upmarket motel chain.

Forres (A96). *Parkmount House* (I), St. Leonard's Road (tel. 0309–73312). 7 rooms, 2 with bath. Pleasant location between town center and golf course. Neat rooms. Sensible cuisine based on Scottish recipes. *Relais Routiers* recommended.

Glenlivet (B9008). *Blairfindy Lodge* (E), tel. 080 73–376. 12 rooms, 7 with bath. Shooting and fishing. Small rooms but first-class cuisine. *Minmore House* (M), tel. 080 73–378. 10 rooms with bath. Shooting, fishing and skiing available.

Huntly (A96). *Castle* (M), tel. 0466–2696. 24 rooms, 9 with bath. In own grounds, 1 mile from town center. Cuisine designed for strong, hungry people in a cold climate.

Insch (A979). *Station Hotel* (I), Commercial Road (tel. 0464–20604). 14 rooms, 11 with bath. Warm welcome and good "home cooking."

Macduff (A98). *Highland Haven* (I), Shore Street (tel. 0261–32408). 20 rooms with bath. Breezy location above picture-book harbor, but cozy inside. A new private hotel with Taste of Scotland cuisine and some ambitious leisure facilities, e.g., whirlpool spa and gymnasium. At present, remarkable value.

Oldmeldrum (A947). *Meldrum House* (M), tel. 065 12–2294. 11 rooms, 8 with bath. Best type of country-house hotel with much-praised cuisine, especially game pie and venison.

Peterhead (A952). *Waterside* (M), tel. 0779–71121. 110 rooms with bath. Big modern establishment with wide range of amenities and flexible meal service.

Pitcaple (A96, north of Inverurie). *Pittodrie House* (E), tel. 046 76–202. 14 rooms, 12 with bath. Secluded 15th-century tower. Spacious rooms with tapestries and antiques. Cordon bleu chef.

Rothes (A941). *Rothes Glen* (E), tel. 034 03–254. 19 rooms, 11 with bath. Fantasy creation of architect who built Balmoral. Patio, fountain, golf course, trout stream, Highland cattle. Cuisine almost matches expansive layout.

Tarland (A974). **Restaurant.** *Aberdeen Arms* (I), tel. 033 981–225. Above average for an area of undistinguished gastronomy. Worth trying for light lunch or evening (5–10 P.M.) meal.

Tomintoul (A939). **Restaurant.** *Glenmulliach* (I), Lecht Road (tel. 080 74–356). Home cooking. Lunch is good but tea and high tea with buttered scones and homemade shortbread are even better, and all at remarkably modest prices.

HOW TO GET ABOUT. By car. By road, Aberdeen is 120 miles from Edinburgh, 80 from Perth, and 105 from Inverness. Good centers for the coastal areas of the northeast are Fraserburgh, Macduff, Banff and Elgin; for the Grampian highlands, the Whisky and the Castle Countries, Keith, Huntly and Tomintoul; and for Deeside the small towns of Aboyne, Ballater and Braemar.

A dozen automobile hire firms operate from Aberdeen or Dyce (Aberdeen Airport) including Budget, Hertz, Avis, Godfrey Davis and Swan. You can also rent an automobile at Elgin (Budget Rent-a-Car, Macrae & Dick, Station Road, tel. 0343–45281), at Aberdeen (Mitchell Self-Drive, Chapel Street, tel. 0224–642642) and at Stonehaven (Mitchell's Garage, Barclay Street, tel. 0569–62077). Grampian roads, sometimes lonely and tortuous, are always in reasonable condition, but beware local farm-hands, inland, or fishermen, along the coast, driving at high speed on the otherwise quiet roads.

TOURIST INFORMATION. The Tourist Information Office for Aberdeen is at St. Nicholas House, Broad Street (tel. 0224–632727). It is open all year during normal working hours and until 8 P.M. in summer. An information kiosk on Aberdeen station, Guild Street, handles bed-booking June–Sept.

The Information Office at 17 High Street, Elgin, opens all year during normal working hours, and until 7 P.M. July–Aug.

Other local information offices are at Aboyne, Alford, Ballater, Banchory, Banff, Braemar, Buckie, Cullen, Dufftown, Ellon, Fochabers, Forres, Fraserburgh, Fyvie, Huntly, Inverurie, Keith, Peterhead, Stonehaven and Tomintoul. Normal hours 10–5, sometimes later in midsummer. All centers offer local accommodations and "book-a-bed-ahead" facilities.

Leaflets and booklets on the Grampian castles, malt whisky distilleries and other special features are available.

FISHING. The Region is rich in rivers and in burns and streams. The Spey, Dee, Don, Findhorn, Ythan and Deveron provide excellent sport for salmon and trout fishermen. At Bridge of Feugh (A943 near Banchory) you can see salmon leaping up slippery rocks. Prime beats tend to be privately owned or rather expensive, up to £20 per rod per day, but most large hotels along the river can arrange permits. Try Mar Lodge and Invercauld Arms, Braemar, Craigendarroch Hotel, Ballater and Banchory Lodge, Banchory, for the River Dee; Castle Hotel, Huntly, and County Hotel, Banff, for the Deveron; Grant Arms at Monymusk and Kildrummy Castle near Alford for the Don; and Craigellachie Hotel, Craigellachie, and Palace Hotel, Grantown-on-Spey, for the Spey. The Clerk of Fishings, Duke Street, Huntly, issues permits for stretches of the Deveron and Isla rivers. Fishing-tackle shops sell local permits elsewhere.

There is good sea-angling for cod, haddock, pollock and flatfish from rocks and harbor jetties at Lossiemouth, Buckie and Portsoy. Tackle, permits and information from The Angling Center, Moss Street, Elgin. You can fish from the long breakwaters of Peterhead and from boats at Fraserburgh and Stonehaven. Tackle, bait and list of local boatmen from sports shops or from the Information Caravan, The Square, Stonehaven.

The salmon/trout season runs February through September, with no Sunday fishing. Sea-angling is possible all year round, May to October being preferred. But among the old wrecks off Stonehaven there have been phenomenal catches of cod, 25–35 pounds in February and March.

GOLF. Grampian Region has 51 golf courses so you will never be far from one or perhaps two. They include numerous championship courses. All towns and many villages have their 18- or nine-hole municipal links. Among the notable private clubs are Royal Aberdeen and Deeside, Aberdeen; Duff House, Banff; and Royal Tarlair, Macduff. At municipal courses you will pay £1–£2 per round. The more prestigious clubs charge up to £10 a day and expect you to book by letter, or bring a letter of recommendation from a member.

HISTORIC HOUSES AND GARDENS. The medieval and Renaissance castles of Grampian Region are famous and a feature of the landscape everywhere. If you wish to explore them comprehensively, the leaflet *Scotland's Castle Trail,* available at information centers in the Region, is a useful guide. Many houses are also renowned for their gardens, and below we list some that are open under Scotland's Gardens Scheme.

Balmoral Castle, Ballater (9 miles west on A93). Exhibition in ballroom. Royal life of 19th century including Landseer paintings. Open May–July, weekdays only, 10–5.

Braemar Castle, Braemar (A93). Castellated mansion of 17th and 18th centuries. Among family treasures is 52-pound Cairngorm stone (semiprecious), the biggest ever found. Open May–Sept., daily 10–6.

Brodie Castle, Forres (3 miles west on A96). Ancestral home of ancient Brodie family. French furniture, plasterwork. Open Apr.–Oct., weekdays 11–6, Sun. 2–6; or by appointment.

Castle Fraser, Inverurie (8 miles south on B993). A great 17th-century tower house. Oak furniture and portraits. Open May–Sept., daily 2–6. N.T.S.

Craigievar Castle, Alford (7 miles south on A980). Outstanding 17th-century tower house with fine plasterwork and furnishings of three centuries. Open May–Sept., daily 2–6. Grounds open all year, 9.30–sunset. N.T.S.

Crathes Castle, Banchory (A93). A day's outing for the family. Eight gardens, ancient yews, nature trails, shops, restaurants. Most-visited of Grampian castles. Open Apr. and Oct., Sat. and Sun. 11–6; May–Sept., daily 11–6. N.T.S.

Fyvie Castle, Fyvie (A947 north of Old Meldrum). One of Aberdeenshire's most historic and civilized castles, newly opened to public. Rich Franco-Scottish architecture, fine parkland, walks, gardens, ornamental water. Open May–Sept., daily 11–6.

Huntly Castle, Huntly (A96). Evocative ruin with medieval heraldic embellishments. Stronghold of "Gay Gordons", despots of the north. Smashed down, rebuilt, burned, rebuilt 1450–1600. Open Apr.–Sept., weekdays 9.30–7, Sun. 2–7; Oct.–Mar., weekdays 9.30–4, Sun. 2–4.

Leith Hall, Huntly (at Kennethmont, 7 miles south on A97). Turreted house set around a quadrangle, dating partly from 1649. Relics and keepsakes, chiefly military, of Leith-Hay family. Open May–Sept., daily 2–6. N.T.S.

Gardens regularly open in the main season include **Innes House,** Fochabers (off A96), **Herb Garden,** Old Semeil (off A97), **Kildrummy Castle** (A97) and **Pitmedden** (B9000), the National Trust's great formal garden, with box hedges, bedding displays, as well as an agricultural museum and woodland walks. **Crathes Castle,** above, is also one of the area's outstanding gardens.

Among gardens open periodically under Scotland's Gardens Scheme are **Arbuthnott House,** Laurencekirk (A94); **Beechgrove,** Beechgrove Terrace, Aberdeen (B.B.C. Scotland's television garden); **Douneside,** Tarland (B9119); **Dunecht House,** Dunecht (10 miles west of Aberdeen on A944); **Gordon Castle,** Fochabers (A96); **Gordonstoun School,** Duffus (B9012); and **Tillypronie,** Tarland (A97). Details about opening days can be found in local newspapers and on posters in shop windows.

MUSEUMS. Adamston Agricultural Museum, Huntly (A96). Working farm with large collection of agricultural and domestic implements from the past, showing how the northeast was tamed. Open Wed., Sat., Sun. 9–7.

Aden Country Park (A950). Set in attractive parkland, restored farm building complex and vivid, high-quality display on northeast farming history. Park open all year. Heritage Centre May–Sept. 11–5. (Weekends Oct. and Apr.)

Gordon Highlanders' Regimental Museum, Viewfield Road, Aberdeen. History of Grampian's famous regiment from its formation in 1794. Open Wed. and Sun. 2–5.

Grampian Transport Museum, Alford (A944). Independent museum with major collection of vintage vehicles (over 100—claims to be largest in Scotland) in large exhibition hall. Nearby disused station has small rail museum, also narrow gauge train-rides to country park close by. Museum open daily Mar–Sept. 10.30–5.

Maritime Museum, Provost Ross's House, Shiprow, Aberdeen. History of fishing industry, shipbuilding, docks, gas and oil. A modern museum (1982) in an ancient setting. Open Mon.–Sat. 10–5.

Maritime Museum, Clunie Place, Buckie (A942). History of local fishing industry. Adjoins *Peter Anson Gallery,* where paintings and drawings by that well-known marine artist are displayed. Open Mon.–Fri. 10–8, Sat. 10–12.

GRANDEUR AND
TRANQUILITY

Highland and Islands

Broadly speaking, this Region includes all the landmass of Scotland north and west of the Grampian mountains as well as about 600 islands, most of which are gathered in four groups: the Inner Hebrides and Outer Hebrides to the west, the Orkney and Shetland isles to the north. Physically the Region occupies about one third of Scotland, but its population is small. Inverness, the "watchtower of the North," has 30,000 inhabitants, Thurso and Wick around 10,000. Dingwall, Kirkwall, Lerwick and Stornoway are hardly more than villages, but their situations as market centers and island capitals give them an importance out of proportion to their sizes.

With summer tourists these places more than double their populations. If you have not visited the "real" Highlands, you have not seen Scotland. In this Region is concentrated much of the romance of "Caledonia stern and wild," the glamor of the clans, the cattle, the red deer and the golden eagles, the Celtic mists and legends and a mixture of splendor and tranquility found hardly anywhere else in the world.

The best and easiest way to approach the Highlands is from the southeast. From coastal roads of Grampian, by Elgin and Forres; from Edinburgh, by the Great North Road through Perth and Pitlochry; from Glasgow or Stirling via Glencoe . . . some Highland roads follow the routes of now-vanished military roads built by the 18th-century Hanoverian government to move garrisons quickly in case of Jacobite rebellion. In those days the Highlands were more populated but the destruction of the clan system after the Battle of Culloden, and changing economic conditions (including the lowland Industrial Revolution) started waves of emigration, even before the brutal Highland clearances were carried out by new landlords seeking profits from sheep-rearing. The result is the empty glens you see today, which once had thriving populations. The way the exiles succeeded in new environments was as remarkable as the way they transmitted to their descendants a love of a homeland which had offered them only misery and betrayal.

Touristically, the great surprise is the changing scenery and the stunning effects of light and shade, cloud, sunshine and rainbows. In a couple of hours you may pass from heather, bracken and springy turf to granite rock and bog, to serrated peak and long sealoch, to the red Torridon sandstone of Wester Ross and ancient native pinewoods overlooking Loch Maree. Sea inlets are deep and fjord-like. The black shapes of the isles gather like basking whales on the skyline. Cliffs where quartzite gleams above crescents of hard sand lead round a northern shore which looks from the air as though it was trimmed by an axe. In the far north, Gaelic place names have mingled with a Norse heritage: Diabaig is "deop-vik" or deep bay and Cape Wrath on the northwest mainland tip has nothing to do with angry weather—the Norsemen named it "hvarf" or turning point. This Viking heritage prevails in dialect and historic sites in Orkney and Shetland.

In the northwest of the Region some people speak Gaelic, a language akin to Erse, Welsh and Manx. There are local disagreements about the correct vocabulary and pronunciation, but fine lyric poetry has been—and is still being—written in this "language of the heart." Love songs from the Hebridean crofts have their admirers in distant lands, not only among the 80,000 Gaelic speakers. Language societies campaign energetically and you may arrive in a Highland town where the annual *Mod* is being held—a competition for singers, pipers and bards, all in Gaelic.

Although the Region is rich in ancestral memories and folk tales, its art and architecture, with one or two exceptions, are negligible. The castles, mostly ruins now, were massive but not handsome. The outstanding ecclesiastical building is St. Magnus cathedral in Kirkwall, Orkney. In Glenelg and on Shetland there are a few Pictish brochs and ancient stone towers. Orkney and the island of Lewis have notable chambered tombs and standing stones. Coming to more modern times, the wanderings of Bonnie Prince Charlie through the western Highlands have added legendary and historical interest to many roads, houses and caves. And if you wish to track the Loch Ness monster, there are power-boats (cruisers) for hire. One company has even equipped a vessel with sonar.

Inverness

By way of Nairn, a clean, mild, upmarket vacation town, the A96 enters Inverness from the east. You can cross a modern road bridge (opened 1982) and proceed north without entering the town at all: this route takes you through the Black Isle, which is neither black nor an island, but an

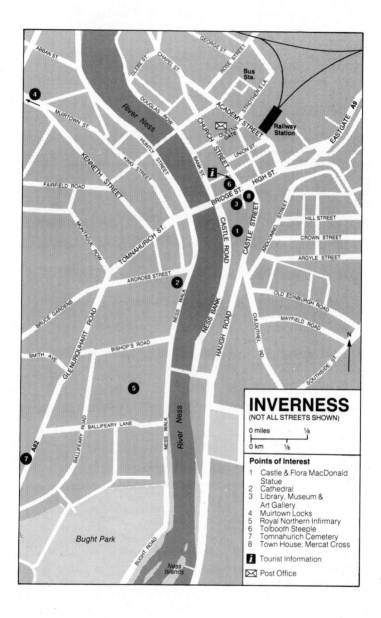

INVERNESS
(NOT ALL STREETS SHOWN)

0 miles ········ ⅛

0 km ········ ⅛

Points of Interest

1 Castle & Flora MacDonald
   Statue
2 Cathedral
3 Library, Museum &
   Art Gallery
4 Muirtown Locks
5 Royal Northern Infirmary
6 Tolbooth Steeple
7 Tomnahurich Cemetery
8 Town House; Mercat Cross

𝒊 Tourist Information

✉ Post Office

isthmus of peaceful farms and villages only gradually becoming known to visitors.

Inverness disappoints at first glance. It is an ordinary-looking place, though finely situated at the point where the River Ness and Caledonian Canal enter the narrows of the Inverness Firth; and its so-called castle, crowning a hill above the river bridges, is only a pseudo-Norman 19th-century edifice in red sandstone, housing local government offices. Incorporated in another office block is Queen Mary's House in Bridge Street, a lodging to which Mary Queen of Scots was reluctantly admitted for a few days in 1562.

But on a sunny day it is pleasant to wander round non-industrial Inverness, visiting old-established shops and admiring the paraphernalia of the clans, here displayed with an everyday air. Though the clan souvenirs recall the past, the fabric of Inverness is, in truth, short of very ancient buildings (though take a look at Abertarff House, among a few others). This came about simply because of its strategic Highland gateway position. The old town was frequently burned to the ground by marauding clansmen! Today Inverness is, instead, busy with traffic and has its share of modern "High Street" shops.

The cemetery here is also something of a tourist attraction. It spreads over the wooded slopes of Tomnahurich ("Hill of the Fairies") about a mile west of the town and overlooks a panorama of firth, river, canal and loch. It is not at all a melancholy spot and is well worth an evening stroll if you are staying in the town. At about the same distance from the town center, following the Ness upstream towards its loch, you come to the Ness Islands. They are neatly connected with each other by foot-bridges, and with either side of the river. Among them are bandstands and an open-air theater with regular programs of summer entertainment—nothing very sophisticated, but convincing demonstrations of the Highland capital's love and respect for the old piping and dancing traditions.

Thomas Telford

On the west bank of the river, a street named after Telford, early 19th-century pioneer of civil engineering in Britain, leads to the Muirtown locks on the Caledonian Canal. Thomas Telford wore himself out designing and constructing this 60-mile waterway through the Great Glen, from Inverness to Fort William. He started it in 1803 and died in 1834. He saw his great venture opened by 1822, though by the 1830s, in spite of growing traffic, certain works were already causing problems. Thereafter the story is one of renewals and repeated efforts to make the project viable.

Like the geological fault which formed the Great Glen, the Caledonian Canal runs in a fairly straight line, passing through the narrow lochs of Ness, Oich and Lochy and splitting Scotland into two portions. There are 29 locks to cope with variations in the water levels, and at the southern end, just above Fort William, a chain of eight locks (which Telford christened Neptune's Staircase) carries the Canal down to Loch Linnhe and the sea. The trip was therefore never a fast one; but for the shipping between east and west coasts it was an alternative to the dangerous passage round Scotland's northern shores, where the tides of the Pentland Firth run at 13 miles an hour.

The trouble was that in the 40-odd years between conception and completion ship sizes increased enormously; and steam replaced sail. Though the canal played an important role in moving mines in World War I, its economic role remained uncertain for decades afterwards. Today, still used by fishing vessels and some commercial traffic, its main role is as a tourism asset.

The Great Glen

Loch and Canal excursions are available in summer from Inverness and Fort William. An excellent highway (A82) goes through the Glen, offering better views and a much faster trip. You hit the Loch Ness shore five miles from Inverness and in another ten you are at the Drumnadrochit inlet, the site, at the Drumnadrochit Motor Inn, of the "official" Loch Ness monster exhibition.

Still hugging the shores of the loch, a further 13 miles brings you to Invermoriston where you can take the A887 and A87 into Glen Moriston, past the Five Sisters of Kintail (five peaks in a row) and along the banks of Loch Duich and Loch Alsh; a route which brings you to the ferry for Skye at Kyle of Lochalsh. This road is another "road to the isles"—perhaps the most scenic of all—and along it, near Dornie, you pass that sturdy little castle on the islet, with a causeway to the mainland, which features on the covers of so much tourist literature and in advertisements for Scottish products worldwide. It is called Eilean Donan. Empty and neglected for years, it is now a private house again. Bonnie Prince Charlie was never there, but the castle did have the distinction of being bombarded by frigates of the Royal Navy during an abortive Spanish-Jacobite landing in 1719. This curious incident did actually involve action on shore. A group of Spaniards made their way up Glen Shiel but were scattered and routed by superior Hanoverian mortar fire. The incident is recalled in the place name Coirein na Spainteach, "The Spaniards' Corrie." Much of Glen Shiel, including the Five Sisters of Kintail, is in the care of the National Trust for Scotland and offers superb high-level walking for the capable.

We have come some way from the Great Glen, so now we shall return to Invermoriston and continue down the A82 to the foot of Loch Ness: its volume greater than any other freshwater loch in Scotland ($24\frac{1}{2}$ miles long and 750 feet deep in places), it is one of the loveliest too, with a width never greater than one and a half miles.

Fort Augustus is a popular stopping-off place at the southern end of the loch. It was one of the forts built to accommodate the troops that pacified the Highlands after the first Jacobite rebellion of 1715. Much later (1876) it acquired a Benedictine monastery, which was built on the site of the original fort.

Here the Caledonian Canal and the A82 cut across a neck of valley, traverse the small Loch Oich where the Great Glen Water Park has been established, and run by Loch Lochy and Inverlochy to Fort William, a seaport 60 miles from the sea. The deep inlet, Loch Linnhe, is characteristic of the Region. Inland lochs have lengths disproportionate to their widths, but the sea-lochs seem to go on for ever. You may find the Corran Ferry, south of Fort William, helpful in shortening your journey times to Ardgour, if car touring.

Fort William nestles on an elbow of lochs. It is a great tourist nexus in the season although it has only one real street. Ben Nevis, highest mountain in the British Isles (4,406 feet) looks over the town and if you do not want to make the climb (a surprisingly straightforward one) you should at least drive five miles up Glen Nevis (unclassified road) for a glimpse of the wild district of Lochaber. South of Fort William, the A82 turns at Ballachulish bridge for Glencoe and Strathclyde, while the A828 continues along the sea-loch shores, tortuous but smothered in flowers in spring, towards Oban and the hills of Lorne (Strathclyde).

The Great Glen roads and their offshoots are heavily-trafficked in summer and susceptible to flooding and landslips during torrential rains. For many visitors this Inverness–Fort William route is the baseline for explorations of Scotland's northwestern Highlands and islands.

Glen of Weeping

South of Fort William the A82 crosses a modern bridge over the narrows of a loch at Ballachulish. (To go round the head of the loch would add 25 miles to your journey.) Here the main roads divide, the A828 going round the coast to Oban and the A82 climbing on the Rannoch Moor by way of Glencoe and heading for Loch Lomond and Glasgow.

There is always a chill in Glencoe (Glen of Weeping) even on the hottest day. The pass is hemmed in with 3,000-foot rocks and over the top, where the Kingshouse Inn (long ago the only tavern for miles around, therefore visited by every notable traveler) stands on an old disused road, the formidable rock bastion of Buchaille Etive Mor, the "Great Shepherd of Etive," frowns down from 3,345 feet.

Glencoe is the best-known of Highland passes as a result of the massacre of 1692. It involved fewer than 100 deaths, but has been remembered where many much larger and equally brutal clan massacres are forgotten. MacIain, local chief of the MacDonalds, was late in taking an oath of loyalty, required of Jacobite-sympathizing clans. Subsequently, Campbell militia (i.e. government troops) were billetted with the clan. They were hospitably received for some days before falling upon the MacDonalds with fire and sword—in accordance with secret government orders to destroy the clan to teach others a lesson. It is remembered today because it broke a Highland code of trust. A Highlander's home was open to all, even bitter enemies, should they require food and shelter.

The National Trust for Scotland now has care of 14,000 acres of high mountain in Glencoe and neighboring Dalness. There is a NTS shop and visitor center at Clachaig on the old road halfway up the glen (open daily in summer 9–6.30 and in spring and autumn 10–5.30). Though magnificent, the walking terrain is suitable only for the careful and well-equipped.

Culloden

At the other end of the Great Glen, on the shores of the Moray Firth, the pages of history flutter with other dark deeds of assassination and massacre. Cawdor Castle (B9090), where Shakespeare placed the murder in *Macbeth,* is a well-organized house and park open to the public. You can eat in the castle restaurant or share a picnic with an amiable herd of Highland cattle; roam the gardens which hang above the River Nairn; and examine the domestic life of the laird from stable and kitchen to drawing-room and bedchamber. There are other fine castellated mansions in this district—Kilravock, pronounced "Killrawk," is a gem and at Darnaway you can glimpse the workings of a Scottish estate at its farm visitor center. There are nature trails and woodland walks, as well as high-season castle tours.

Culloden Moor is five miles east of Inverness. This wide-open, breezy moorland, with views across the Moray Firth to the north, is the place of the last battle fought on British soil, between exhausted Jacobites and the well-drilled British Army (which included a number of Scottish regiments). The story is movingly told in the National Trust for Scotland's audio-visual presentation. The NTS have also restored the battle site, even re-routing a minor road that formerly ran through it. It is certainly an atmospheric, somber place, curiously at odds with jingling cash registers and chattering coach parties.

Through January and February 1746 Bonnie Prince Charlie's Jacobite army continued its retreat from England, sporadically harried by the Duke of Cumberland's troops and steadily losing numbers as disenchanted Highlanders deserted and made for home. The Prince's idea was to recruit and re-form in the Highlands, to appeal to the French for reinforcements and launch another campaign. But first there had to be a confrontation with his pursuers, and it came in April on Culloden Moor.

When battle commenced the Jacobite command was gloomy, but the Prince was briefly his old optimistic self and full of dash. The skills and the numbers (9,000 against 5,000) were all on his opponents' side. It was over in 40 minutes. On the Moor lay 1,000 Jacobites, dead and dying, and the rest were scattered into hiding. Bundled away to safety the Prince stood dazed. "He neither spoke nor enquired after the absent."

The Prince in the Heather

General "Butcher" Cumberland, commanding the government forces at Culloden, earned his nickname for the atrocities committed after Culloden on guilty and innocent alike in the Highland area—often described as the most shameful chapter in the history of the British Army. The rebel Prince, meanwhile, escaped from the battlefield and was to endure an extraordinary Scottish journey. He found his way to Fort Augustus (A82), then to Loch Arkaig (off B8005), then to Arisaig (A830) where he escaped to the isles of Harris and South Uist. There he met Flora MacDonald, the young lady who took him, disguised as her maid, "over the sea to Skye" and back to the mainland.

The local lairds, Jacobites to a man, then cooperated in moving the Prince around the wastes of the central Highlands, first to Loch Affric (off A831) and to Loch Arkaig for a second visit (there was supposed to be a treasure-chest of louis d'or, French gold coins, waiting for him, but it still remains hidden in the hills!) and at last to Loch nan Uamh on the Arisaig road (A830), close to the spot where he had landed 15 months earlier, to re-embark for France. "Never was there dawn so brilliant, never sunset so clouded," it was said of the Young Pretender's life. A biographer summed up his tragedy as: "In Rome a Protestant, in Britain a Papist"—in other words, fated always to be in the wrong place at the wrong time.

Despite a dragging sordid end which overshadowed The Adventure, the Prince remains a Scottish hero. He suits the pedestal on which song writers and sentimental novelists have placed him. His Scottish exploits were the stuff that myths are made of. *Will ye no' come back again . . . Speed, bonnie boat . . . Charlie is my darling . . .* the tunes and lyrics of Lady Nairne, jaunty or mournful, composed long after the events, are as good an epitaph as any adventurer could wish for.

Memories of the Prince cluster thickly on our West Highland routes, especially the 39 miles of the A830 from Fort William to Arisaig and Mallaig. The Fort William museum has a room dedicated to him; relics are shown at Culloden House (off B9006); Glenfinnan (A830) has the great monument to the clans who joined him there (a column aptly described by Queen Victoria as "rather ugly . . . like a sort of lighthouse surrounded by a wall"); seven beech trees at Kinlochmoidart (B850) commemorate the seven men of Moidart who befriended him; and there are numerous caves on coastline and loch shore which now bear his name.

Flora MacDonald has a statue in front of Inverness Castle; a memorial cairn at Milton, her birthplace on South Uist; and her last home and grave at Flodigarry and Kilmuir respectively (A855) near the northern tip of the island of Skye.

The Highest Restaurant in Britain

The Great North Road (A9) and railroad come in from Tayside Region at the summit of the Drumochter pass. From that watershed they descend with the infant Spey in a valley which broadens quickly and acquires a green and golden fleece of pinewood and birch. We are as far from the sea as we can be in Scotland, yet there are tangs of ozone and the clean look of a maritime vacationland about us. Newtonmore and Kingussie depend almost wholly on tourism; on city people who want to unwind in the silence of the hills, to do a little fishing and play a little golf. From Newtonmore in the 1950s some riders set out to cross the mountains to Braemar; and the new activity called pony-trekking was born.

Kincraig (still A9) has the Highland Wildlife Park, open daily mid-March to October; and Carrbridge the ambitious Landmark Visitor Centre, a sculpture park, tree walks, nature trails, entertainments and a multivision theater with travelogues and narratives of Highland history.

Hereabouts you skirt the Cairngorm winter-sports complex, the biggest in Scotland. Access is from Aviemore (A9) and Coylumbridge or from Grantown-on-Spey and Nethybridge on two branches of the B970 road. A bus service links Aviemore with Coire Cas ("Corry Cass") at 2,000 feet, where there are parking lots, cafes and restaurants, two chairlifts and seven ski-tows. The principal chair-lift rises to 3,600 feet, only 500 feet from the summit of Cairngorm. At the halfway station there is a self-service restaurant. At the top stands the Ptarmigan restaurant, the highest in Britain, with a panorama of Strathspey and the blue hills beyond Inverness.

The Aviemore Centre has numerous modern hotels where lively evening entertainment is offered; ceilidhs (song-and-dance parties) and country dancing the specialties. There is a big ballroom, a theater, a cinema, a curling rink and facilities for children: the sort of things you will not see again in many miles of Highland travels—though many visitors may be thankful about that and consider the hi-tech developments a gross intrusion. However, Strathspey, now anglicized as Spey Valley, is big enough to absorb not only skiers, but vacationers old and young, all year round.

North of Inverness

In former times, beyond Inverness, the northbound motorist had little choice but to trace laboriously round the outlines of the great firths of Beauly, Cromarty and Dornoch. However, the A9 has been greatly improved in recent years. Inverness is bypassed by a fast road over the Kessock Bridge, then across the Black Isle to another bridge, over the Cromarty Firth. The Dornoch Firth bridge is also being built. Some of the improvements were to help the area share in North Sea oil prosperity. But this district, known as Easter Ross, should not be hurried through. If possible, go a little out of your way to see Cromarty (A832), once an important port on the narrows of its firth, now a sleepy period-piece; Fortrose and Rosemarkie (A832), also on the Black Isle, with their relics of 15th-century cathedral and 7th-century monastery, their Pictish stones and Fairy Glen and Eathie Burn, the stream in whose banks locally-born Hugh Miller "dug his reputation" as a renowned geologist; Contin church and Rogie falls near Dingwall; the lighthouse and ruined castle at Portmahomack (B9165); the spa town of Strathpeffer (A834), its railroad station now a craft center, locked in hills, dreaming almost undisturbed dreams of a fashionable 19th-century clientele; and Dornoch (B9167), population only 750 but cathedral city, county capital, golf mecca since 1619 and baronial stronghold.

North of Dornoch, near Golspie, the A9 passes through the woods of Dunrobin Castle ("o" as in "robe"), an ancient seat elaborated by its 19th-century lord, the Duke of Sutherland, into a flamboyant white-turreted enormity. Another transformation is pending: into a leisure complex. A 19th-century Duke loved railroads so much that he actually had built part of what is today's north line—including his own private station—when the original undertaking ran out of funds. The line goes by the coast as far as Helmsdale, then takes a wide sweep across the heathery hinterland of Caithness, a detour which removes it from the view of the Langwell grouse moors and deer forests. Langwell was the stamping-ground of the Duke of Portland, who detested trains.

A branch road from the A9 accompanies that railroad, riding high over bare moorland to Kildonan (A897), where prospectors used to pan for gold, to a lonely hotel at Forsinard, and then to Melvich at the foot of Strath Halladale on the north coast of Sutherland. Staying with the A9, you run along a coast where cliffs are steep and harbors few. The best views are to be had from the Ord of Caithness, where you cross a 750-foot bluff within a mile of the sea before dipping perilously to the mouth of a glen at Berriedale. In the glen is Langwell House, a palace by ordinary standards, a mere hunting lodge for the ducal Portlands.

Caithness

Dunbeath is another lost village, huddled in an angle of the cliffs where a torrent races down and with a castle ruin on the cliff edge. The castle was a fortress of the Sinclairs who controlled this country. The simpler life, everyday work and play of long ago, is displayed at the Laidhey Croft, a museum a few yards along the A9 from the village.

The largest of these little coastal refuges is Lybster, a center for archeological exploration. Within a few minutes of the village you may see the Camster cairns, dating from about 1000 B.C., the Standing Stones of Achavanich, the Hill o' Many Stanes and other relics of early Pictish and Norse occupation.

Wick, 121 miles from Inverness, lies on the coast athwart the Wick River. In the heyday of the Scottish herring it was a prominent port and it is still something of a metropolis for white fish and a market center for Caithness farmers.

Thurso, northernmost town on Britain's mainland, dates from Viking times. Its harbor too was once prosperous. From it was shipped the blue-gray Caithness stone which paved the streets and courtyards of many European towns. Like Wick, the place is developing as a modest family resort, its principal attractions the awesome cliff scenery and spacious firm sands. Considering the latitude (equivalent to that of Juneau, Alaska), the climate on this northern shore can be astonishingly mild. The port of Thurso, called Scrabster, is a terminal for Orkney.

Roads leading north from Wick and Thurso converge at John o'Groats, the Land's End of Scotland, though not precisely the most northerly point. The approach is shabby and dull. It is sad to see Caithness, not the most picturesque of Scottish counties at the best of times, petering out in a rash of shacks, small-holdings and caravan parks. But the beach and breakwater are usually remote from this unsightliness, while the cliff paths towards Duncansby Head on one side and Dunnet Head on the other offer dramatic seascapes. And at low tide you may find the lucky "groatie buckie," a type of cowrie shell found only here.

Summer boat-trips are offered from John o' Groats to Orkney through the swirling Pentland Firth. The tomb of Jan de Groot, the Dutch settler who gave the place its name, is in Canisbay church, two miles west. Six miles from John o' Groats stands the Castle of Mey near a desolate foreshore. It is the property of the Queen Mother, to which she briefly retired after the death of her husband King George VI in 1952, and which she has since transformed. A dangerous reef in the Pentland Firth, called the Merry Men of Mey, throws up spectacular fountains of spray in stormy weather.

Ten miles west of Thurso, at Dounreay ("Doonray"), you can stop for a conducted tour of one of Britain's earliest fast breeder nuclear reactors.

Sutherland

Norse marauders gave the district its name: "Southland." But along with Caithness it forms the northern limits of Britain's mainland and it has the most savage and majestic of Scotland's sea-cliffs, cascades, caves and capes. From John o' Groats via Thurso, the A836 to Tongue and the A838 to Durness link the hamlets of the coastal strip.

Caithness and Sutherland are sparsely-populated and neglected-looking regions. Fishermen, mountaineers and walkers have long visited them and the hotels and self-catering cottages are designed to meet their needs.

Sutherland's coastal backcloth is the mountain ranges of Reay Forest and Assynt, studded with glassy lochs and split with foaming torrents.

Ben Loyal, south of Tongue, is called the "Queen of Scottish Mountains" for its grandeur rather than its height (2,504 feet). As you travel west, the peaks of Ben Hope (3,040 feet) and Foinaven (2,980 feet) are disclosed. At Durness, the A838 turns south for Laxford Bridge. To reach Cape Wrath itself, you must take a passenger-only ferry across the narrow Kyle of Durness, than go by minibus to the remote tip.

From Laxford Bridge the A894, over the graceful Kylesku Bridge, runs southwards into some of Scotland's grandest hill scenery. From the ancient lochan-dappled, ice-scoured rock platforms rise strangely terraced hills, such as Quinag and Suilven, with a grandeur which is slightly intimidating; in this region of lonely road-junctions, it can be almost a relief to find busy little villages such as Lochinver, tucked on the serrated sea-edge.

"I would not exchange these lochs and isles with their passionate tides and skies loaded with mists for all the archipelagos of the eastern seas," wrote Jules Verne after his northwestern pilgrimage—sentiments echoed by some famous diarists who followed him. Splendor and tranquility, an ever-changing sky, a kaleidoscope of brilliant colors revolving on the hills . . . there is something indefinable, too, which makes this district memorable for the visitor. Magical and eerie are words frequently used. Sunset over Badcall Bay (near Scourie, A894) has been known to inspire feelings too deep for words or tears in some fairly hard-bitten tourists. Now they know why a Highlander's nostalgia in exile lasts him all his life.

An occasional turning from the A9 on the east coast between Bonar Bridge and Wick takes the motorist across Sutherland to these western sea-lochs by way of mountain passes and serpentine lochs. Close to Bonar Bridge at Carbisdale Castle (a modern building on the site of the last battle fought by the "Great Marquess" Montrose, 1650), the A837 crosses Scotland from east to west, passing through the wilderness of Assynt on its way to Lochinver. A branch of this road (A835) heads south for Ullapool on Loch Broom. Above the forest east of Inchnadamph the peak of Ben More Assynt (3,273 feet) is prominent; and the grim ruin of Ardvreck Castle sticks up from Loch Assynt as you descend towards the sea at Lochinver.

Another coast-to-coast highway, single-track for many miles, is the A838 from Bonar Bridge to Loch Laxford via Lairg. Study your route map closely. For all the sense of remoteness of these far communities, note that the roads radiating northwest from Inverness will return you to the east in a surprisingly short time. Ullapool and Inverness, by the fast A832/A835, are only an hour or so apart.

Lairg, which also has a fine cascade, the Falls of Shin, famous for its leaping salmon, is a grand junction of roads to far west and far north and is correctly called the gateway to Sutherland. From here the rough and hilly A836 and B873 make straight for the north coast at Tongue and Bettyhill respectively.

Wester Ross

South of Sutherland and Caithness, the old county of Ross, formerly inhabited by the descendants of Celtic earls of that name, spreads across the full width of Scotland. Around the Cromarty and Dornoch firths on the A9 we traversed East Ross. The deeply-indented shores and multitudinous islets of the other side of Scotland, 80 miles away, are known as Wester Ross. The land is still rough and desolate and scenic, but the villages are more numerous than in the far north.

Ullapool was custom-built as a herring station in the 1780s. Then the herring vanished and for a time Ullapool was a ghost village. But its well-built stone cottages attracted inhabitants and now it deals in mackerel and seafood—and tourists.

The Inverpolly area, in that part of Wester Ross north of Ullapool, specializes in weird mountain shapes such as Stac Polly. The main road from the north (A837/A835) is fast and *not* single-track from Lochinver, with worthwhile single-track coastal options giving breathtakingly wild views. There is plenty of easy walking but the higher summits, such as the An Teallach ridge above Little Loch Broom and Slioch (3,217 feet) above Loch Maree, are best left to mountaineers.

South of Ullapool, only side-roads are now entirely single-track. Though the Atlantic southwesterlies beat on the coastline, there is very little frost thanks to the Gulf Stream. This has encouraged spectacular displays at the famous "cool temperate" gardens of Poolewe, often described as tropical—hereabouts a relative term!

Beyond Loch Maree, much-praised scenically, you find one of the real gems of Wester Ross—Torridon. The road becomes single track through a glen with sublime mountainscapes: red sandstone cliffs and scars, topped with shattered quartzite. The west end of the glen is a National Nature Reserve; the east end is cared for by the National Trust for Scotland. South again, you can reach the tiny village of Applecross by a coastal road from Shieldaig, then climb out by the spectacular hairpins of the Bealach na Ba, "The Pass of the Cattle."

Prehistoric cairns and "wheelhouses" break the curve of hills in several places. The most remarkable antiquity in the northwest, however, is Dun Dornadilla, which is a broch. (These are mysterious Pictish stone towers, built, it is speculated, as protection against sea raiders.) You will find it by a narrow road below Ben Hope, south of Loch Hope, between Durness and Tongue.

Continuing south through Wester Ross, beyond Lochcarron—quite a center for these unpopulated parts—touring around will reveal Plockton, with its unexpected palm trees, and, elsewhere, sublime views to the blue hills of Skye.

Isle of Skye

Coming south down the west coast of Scotland you reach the first of the ferry ports to Skye at Kyle of Lochalsh, terminus of the A87 from Invermoriston in the Great Glen. On the five-minute boat trip to Kyleakin ("Ky-lakkin") your eye is caught by Moil Castle, a gap-toothed ruin. The owner was a Danish noblewoman of the Middle Ages called Saucy Mary, who stretched a chain to the mainland and demanded a toll from passing ships.

Skye is the largest of the Inner Hebrides group, 50 miles from tip to tip; celebrated for its Coolins, or Cuillins, a range of jagged black mountains which kill one or two rock-climbers every year. Roads are good. Castles, hotels and topographical features are soaked in the mystique of Bonnie Prince Charlie and Flora MacDonald but the person who did most to popularize the island by visiting it 30 years later and praising its landscapes and seascapes and natives' hospitality was Dr. Johnson. You may assimilate the violent history of the clans at the 800-year-old Dunvegan Castle (A850), ancestral seat of the MacLeods; at Duntulm (off A855), the ruin of a 15th-century citadel of the MacDonalds, Lords of the Isles; and at mock-Tudor Armadale Castle (A851) with its flower-beds and guided walks through a fertile strip of shoreline called the Garden of Skye.

You can make the crossing to Skye by the very frequent Kyle-Kyleakin ferry, but there are also ferries from Glenelg to Kylerhea (summer only) and from Mallaig to Armadale in the south of the island.

The Cocktail Islands

South of Skye, across the Coolin Sound, lie the isles of Rhum, Eigg, Muck and Canna, a constellation known as the Small Isles. (The first three are sometimes facetiously called the Cocktail Islands.) Public access has long been restricted in the interests of conservation but nowadays Rhum attracts 4,000 visitors annually, some of whom stay a night or two at the ostentatious Kinloch Castle, which is part hotel, part hostel and part craft center. The wild life of Rhum includes goats, red deer and shaggy ponies. Most of the isles are bare and rocky but low-lying Canna, now in the care of the National Trust for Scotland, has a farm, a bird sanctuary and a few Stone Age and Celtic remains. Canna House contains a library of traditional Gaelic songbooks and other literature. The National Trust for Scotland hopes one day to provide limited accommodations for ornithologists and folklorists.

Eigg is remarkable for its oddly-shaped sgurr (rock pinnacle) which rises to 1,289 feet. A 16th-century massacre by the MacLeods of Skye, who trapped and suffocated 395 of their hereditary foes the MacDonalds in a cave on Eigg, is described in Scott's long narrative poem *The Lord of the Isles*.

Visiting the Small Isles presents problems. It is best to adapt yourself to the schedules of mainland trains and inter-island mail-boats. You might, for example, leave Glasgow at 6 A.M., step aboard the Mallaig mail-boat at 11, having traveled the beautiful West Highland railroad; and spend the rest of the day island-hopping, calling at Skye and all the Small Isles and returning to the mainland about 7 P.M. There are also summer ferries and cruising from Arisaig. A small amount of high-quality accommodation is available on Eigg and Muck. Careful timetable planning is needed!

Mallaig, like Ullapool, is an important fishing harbor in a magnificent setting. Here you return to Bonnie Prince Charlie country. The A830 to Fort William passes, south of Arisaig, the cave where the Prince lived while awaiting the French ship sent to bring him off; and a tablet at the roadside in Borrodale, near the head of Loch nan Uamh ("Bay of Caves") marks the spot where he stepped on board and said farewell to Scotland. Halfway to Fort William you pass the Glenfinnan monument and Highland Gathering arena. In that bowl of the hills, where the view opens on Glen Shiel's misty length, the young Prince raised the standard of revolt in August 1745.

The lands to the south, the peninsulas of Moidart, Sunart, Morven and Ardnamurchan, are empty West Highland sheep-cropped landscapes of birch and crag. Prince Charles Edward Stuart wandered here, and today's visitor can also wander in a great loop, with superb views of the Small Isles from the sound of Arisaig, then across to Loch Moidart, where Castle Tioram sits broken on a brackeny islet. Further on, Acharacle straggles along the marshy end of thin Loch Shiel. Salen gives the choice of the Ardnamurchan excursion—worth it for the cliffs and lighthouse, but the road is narrow, blinded in places by birchwoods and rhododendron thickets. Return east by Strontian, at the foot of a populated glen in which lie old lead mines, where the mineral strontium was discovered, hence the name.

Outer Hebrides

The oldest inhabitants call them the Long Island, this splintered line of many islands from the pugnacious Butt of Lewis in the north to the 600-foot Barra Head on Berneray in the south, whose lighthouse has the greatest arc of visibility in the world. They stretch about 130 miles from end to end, and lie about 50 miles from the Scottish mainland.

These are the Outer Hebrides. Lewis, the most northerly island, is the largest and also has the only town, Stornoway, on a big land-locked harbor. A few miles west (B8012) are the neolithic Standing Stones of Callanish—a central cairn surrounded by 13 monoliths and others which may have formed concentric circles dotted about—and the shapely broch of Carloway. These legacies of the aboriginal islanders are rated second only to Stonehenge in British antiquities.

Harris, which has the highest mountain in the islands (Clisham, 2,600 feet), was the home of the world-famous Harris tweed. A few weavers still practice their ancient craft, weaving and spinning by hand and coloring the material with natural dyes, but Harris tweed as an industry is now centered in Stornoway on Lewis, where mill shops have been established for individual sightseers and buyers.

From Leverburgh on Harris (a name which recalls the philanthropist Lord Leverhulme; his attempts to drag the islanders into the 19th century met with little success) a ferry-boat crosses to Newton in North Uist. From there you may travel through Benbecula and South Uist without stopping, thanks to connecting causeways.

North Uist is rich in monoliths and chambered cairns and other reminders of a prehistoric past. The temple of the Trinity (13th century) at Carinish, close to the southern causeway, is worth a visit.

Benbecula ("Mount of the Fords") is less bare and neglected-looking than the islands to the north; and in South Uist in summer there are wild gardens with riots of Alpine and rock plants. Ruined forts and chapels abound (this was a refuge of the old Catholic faith) and at Eochdar you will find the Black House museum, which gives a picture of Hebridean life as it was up to the 20th century. "Black" houses are cottages of undressed boulders, sometimes built half underground, sheeted down against the Atlantic gales with a dense straw thatch. The biggest religious monument in the isles, some say the biggest ever sculpted in Britain, stands on the Hill of Miracles at Rueval. It is the statue of Our Lady of the Isles and it was done by Hew Lorimer in 1957. South Uist's famous daughter, Flora MacDonald, was born at Milton; her cottage still stands. (All these hamlets are on or near the A865.)

Eriskay, known abroad for the haunting *Eriskay Love Lilt,* and its group of islets almost block the six-mile strait between South Uist and Barra.

Barra, an isle you can walk across in an hour, has formidable peaks, some sandy beaches and one huge old castle, the largest ancient monument in the western isles. This is Kishmul or Kismuil, on an islet in Castlebay, the principal harbor of Barra. The 45th MacNeil of Barra, its feudal laird, restored it earlier this century and local boats take visitors out to it on Saturday afternoons in summer. Barra is a friendly, flowery little island. Its airport is a stretch of sand, washed twice daily by the tide.

Within living memory it was hard to find a place to stay in the Outer Hebrides outside Stornoway. Now the hotels, guest-houses and self-catering developments proliferate and some natives complain that second-home buyers, many from England, are destroying a way of life. Communications by sea and air are excellent and you will have no difficulty with accommodations.

Orkney

The northern archipelagos, two groups totaling 200 islands of which about 40 are inhabited, are linked historically with Scandinavia. "Shetland for scenery, Orkney for antiquities," the saying goes—and both for bird-watchers. The islands teem with sea-birds of many kinds, including migratory swarms of rare Arctic waterfowl.

Cartographical convenience usually dictates that Orkney and Shetland are tucked away in the corners of maps (as they are on ours), often on reduced scale. When you tour them you appreciate the spread of latitude that they cover: no hope of doing them justice in a couple of hours, or even in a couple of days.

Orkney's isles are mostly smooth and round-topped, enclosing bays and straits called flows. The off-lying stack rocks have land-based counterparts in important Stone Age and Old Norse monuments: Skara Brae, a 5,000-year-old complex of cottages; Maeshowe, of similar age, the finest chambered tomb in western Europe; the Ring of Brogar, 36 standing stones in a broken circle which once contained 60 of them . . . all these sites are close to, or on, the shallow loch of Stenness on Orkney mainland (A965 from Kirkwall). Local information leaflets will help you locate these antiquities and many more.

At Kirkwall harbor the lobster boats, coastal steamers and inter-island ferryboats come and go. Behind the waterfront the flagged streets and passageways resemble those of some prosperous little town of the Zuider Zee. The principal building, St. Magnus cathedral, is of modest and rather militant appearance, built in pink sandstone on foundations laid by the Norse Earl Rognvald in 1137. The St. Magnus Festival (arts, music, drama) takes place annually in June and its activities are centered on Kirkwall and the island's other "town," Stromness (A965), also on Orkney's mainland.

More recent history has left its mark. The twin Martello towers guarding Longhope, isle of Hoy (B9047) were built to stave off a possible French landing in the Napoleonic wars of two centuries ago. The Churchill Barriers across the eastern exits from Scapa Flow make it possible to drive 22 miles from Kirkwall across three islands. They are reminders of a nasty moment for the British Fleet in October 1939, when a German submarine braved ripping tides and hidden rocks to penetrate the great naval anchorage and sink a battleship.

Shetland

Here the Norse heritage lives on as nowhere else, exploding in celebration in Lerwick on the last Tuesday in January at the winter fire festival of Up-Helly-Aa. But Lerwick is a cosmopolitan port all the year round. Flags of all nations fly at the mastheads of the fishing boats which come in to land their catches: Russian, Polish, Spanish, French, German. And if you travel Shetland's mainland as far as Sullom Voe ("voe" means inlet) on the A970 from Lerwick you will hear the accents of Texas and California at the great North Sea oil terminal.

Small ferries, taking automobiles, provide daily connections between Shetland's mainland, on which most inhabitants live, and some of the other 16 islands, of which Yell (80 square miles) is the largest, and served by a frequent roll-on-roll-off service. The nearer inhabited isles of Burra, Trondra and Muckle Roe are linked to the mainland of Shetland with bridges.

Stone towers or brochs keep watch from many headlands. That of Mousa, off the A970, 12 miles south of Lerwick, stands 43 feet high and you can climb the stairway in its walls. The most impressive archeological site is Jarlshof, close to Sumburgh airport in the extreme south: a village sunk to its roofs in the earth, formerly inhabited by Bronze Age, Iron Age and Viking settlers.

The diminutive Shetland ponies are by no means extinct; but are kept more as pets in the south of England than as working animals on Shetland crofts.

Fair Isle

Every year a handful of tourists visit the Fair Isle, midway between Orkney and Shetland; attracted perhaps by its reputation for the patterned knitwear which is still produced by a few of its 75 inhabitants, chiefly for mail-order customers. The distinctive patterns and the sheep with their exceptionally soft, shaded wool are not exclusive to the Fair Isle: Shetland does business in this kind of thing too. But Fair Isle patterns do retain a distinguishing mark—odd symbols of which the row of crosses and circles locally known as Oxo is most common.

If you want to visit Fair Isle, then Loganair fly from Tingwall airport (near Shetland's main town, Lerwick); or the island boat will take you there (small charge) from Sumburgh, a 24-mile trip. Accommodations are available at the Fair Isle Bird Observatory Lodge.

The Life Style

Those who work in the Highlands and islands are fully occupied wresting a living from barren land and inhospitable seas. Fishing is still vital to the economy of larger villages; and many girls, once unemployable, now find jobs in fish processing factories. Others work seasonally at hotels and guest-houses, which have multiplied rapidly.

Well-paid jobs, an influx of workers from far away and some disturbance in life-style and environment were brought in with the development of the major oil and gas terminals at Sullom Voe in Shetland and Flotta in Orkney and the oil-platform construction yard at Kishorn near Loch-carron (B857). Forestry is a growth industry too: you will notice as you travel the western Highlands how many neglected hill-slopes are being planted with Sitka spruce, Scots pine and Douglas fir.

Crofting, farming on a family scale, was once considered the solution to the problems of rural communities. It is nowadays practised only on a part-time basis. Very few Highlanders or islanders make a living from the land; but enough is produced to while vegetables are delivered daily from a neighborhood plot.Unemployment is higher than the national average. Drink is a problem. Old Roman Catholic traditions persist but life is influenced much more by the stern fundamentalism of the "Wee Frees"—the Free Kirk of Scotland which, among other restrictions, ensures that shops are shut on Sundays, that no frivolous activities take place on that day, that few ferries operate and that other transport services are cut to a minimum. The native Highlander and islander regards other Scots as foreigners, no better than the English or the Americans; but he is friendly and courteous as a rule. Scotland's Tourist Community Award (sponsored by the Scottish Tourist Board) for the warmest welcome went to the small Orkney islands of Shapinsay in 1986 and Eday in 1987.

PRACTICAL INFORMATION FOR
HIGHLAND AND ISLANDS

HOW TO GET THERE. By air. The Region has mainland airports at Inverness and Wick and island airports on Lewis, Benbecula, Barra, Orkney and Shetland, with inter-connecting services and links with the south. London–Inverness takes 75 minutes. Local aircraft serve most inhabited isles. One airstrip is washed twice daily by the tide!

By train. Inverness is the region's railhead, with overnight sleeper services from London Euston. Daytime departures are from King's Cross. From here lines serve the far north (Thurso/Wick) and the Kyle of Lochalsh in the west via the spectacular Kyle Line. Also lines lead south to Glasgow/Edinburgh and Aberdeen. Speeds on the remote lines are slow, trains few—even fewer on Sundays—but the scenery can be superb.

Mallaig, Fort William and Oban are served by the West Highland Line, beginning at Glasgow Queen Street. The overnight sleeper from London Euston to Fort William means the visitor leaves London at night and sees Rannoch Moor by morning.

By boat. P & O Ferries, Jamieson's Quay, Aberdeen AB9 8DL (tel. 0224–589111) operate daily car-ferry services to Shetland. Reservations tel. 0224-572615 (for Shetland), tel. 0856-850655 (for Orkney). Also summer ferries between Orkney and Shetland. Caledonian MacBrayne, Ferry Terminal, Gourock PA13 1QP (tel. 0475-33755) connect Oban with South Uist and Barra, and Mallaig with Skye. From Skye they run ferries to North Uist and Lewis, and they also run out to Lewis from Ullapool.

HOTELS AND RESTAURANTS. One of the regions where you can rent a self-catering cottage (contact local information center for details).

Most large country hotels have restaurants with international cuisine. Game, fish, seafood and venison are often presented in interesting forms. Much of the Region comprises countryside that has never known supermarkets, delicatessens or wine bars.

Achiltibuie (off A835). *Summer Isles* (M), tel. 085 482–282. 12 rooms, 10 with bath. Remote but nicely furnished. Subtle cooking from exclusively homegrown produce. Set menu.

Ardgay (A9). *Croit Mairi* (I), tel. 086 32–504. 6 rooms. Modern house on Dornoch Firth.

Arisaig (A830). *Arisaig Hotel* (M), tel. 068 75–210. 13 rooms with bath. Old Jacobite inn enthusiastically renovated. Warm praise from food experts.

Aultnamain (A836, on Struie Hill). **Restaurant.** *Aultnamain Inn* (M), tel. 086 282–238.

Aviemore. *Coylumbridge* (L), on A951, tel. 0479–810661. 175 rooms with bath. Tennis; close to Loch Morlich for yachting and skiing on slopes above. French and English food. *Post House* (E), tel. 0479–810771. 103 rooms with bath. In Sports Center, lively and modern with high-quality bedrooms; sauna. *Badenoch* (M), tel. 0479–810261. 81 rooms, 60 with bath. Modern; in the Sports Center. *High Range* (M), tel. 0479–810636. 8 rooms with bath. Central building with surrounding chalets, on outskirts of town, extensive mountain views, set in lovely wood.
Restaurants. *Old Bridge* (M), Dalfaber Road (tel. 0479–811137). English-style pub with pub grub. *Winking Owl* (M), Grampian Road (tel. 0479–810646). Popular licensed restaurant, also bar meals.

Cromarty (A832). **Restaurant.** *Le Chardon* (M), Church Street (tel. 038 17–471). Amazingly rich and exotic *table d'hôte;* vegetarians catered for.

Gairloch (A832). *The Old Inn* (M), tel. 0445–2006. 7 rooms with bath. Cheerful oasis in wilderness of the west.

Halkirk (B874). *Ulbster Arms* (M), tel. 084 783–206. 31 rooms, 22 with bath. Modernized Victorian house on Thurso River. Sat. spot for Caithness youth.

Inverness (A9). *Kingsmills* (L), Culcabock Road (tel. 0463–237166). 54 rooms with bath. Country-house elegance in pleasant gardens. Squash courts. *Ballifeary House* (M), Ballifeary Road (tel. 0463–235572). 9 rooms, 8 with bath. Victorian villa, nice situation, professionally run. *Kerrisdale* (I), Muirfield Road (tel. 0463–235489). 3 rooms. Spacious 19th-century house where favored few receive full attention.

Kincraig (A9). *Invereshie House* (M), tel. 054 04–332. 9 rooms with bath. Historic house incorporates restaurant with above average cuisine. Game and shellfish presented with flair.

Lewis, Isle of. *Caberfeidh* (E), Stornoway (tel. 0851–2604). 40 rooms, with bath. The most expensive hotel in Outer Hebrides.

Lochinver (A837). *Hillcrest Guest House* (I), tel. 057 14–391. 3 rooms. Friendly, willing service; home cooking.

Lybster (A9). **Restaurant.** *Portland Arms* (M), tel. 059 32–208. Nourishing country and marine diet.

Nairn (A96). *Golf View* (E), tel. 0667–52301. 55 rooms with bath. Famous seaside and sporting hotel, spacious location. Imaginative Highland cuisine. *Windsor* (I), Albert Street (tel. 0667–53108). 60 rooms, 54 with bath. Privately owned, near sandy beach. Gourmet evenings (seafood) and live entertainment.
Restaurant. *Tastebud* (I), Harbour Street (tel. 0667–52743). Keeps one of the more authentic Taste of Scotland tables.

North Uist, Isle of. *Langass Lodge* (M), tel. 087 64–285. 5 rooms. Seascapes, nature reserve, fishing. Good shellfish menu.

Onich (A82, south of Fort William). *Onich* (M), tel. 085 53–214. 27 rooms with bath. Family-run hotel on shore of Loch Linnhe; games room, putting green, fishing, boat trips. Venue for local dances and ceilidhs (Gaelic songs and stories).

Orkney, Mainland of. *Ayre* (M), Ayre Road, Kirkwall (tel. 0856–2197). 32 rooms, 10 with bath. View over bay. Not all rooms equipped to modern standards, but atmosphere is pleasant and food above average. *Royal* (M), Victoria Street, Kirkwall (tel. 0856–3477). 33 rooms, 17 with bath. Clean and neat. Good solid fare, but some finesse about it too.
Restaurants. *Foveran* (I), Kirkwall (tel. 0856–2389). Noted for hot squid and giant crab claws. British Tourist Authority commendation. *Woodwick* (I), Evie (tel. 085 675–221). Fine situation 12 miles from Kirkwall. Favored by discerning visitors to the islands.

Rosemarkie (A832). *Marine* (M), tel. 0381–20253. 52 rooms, 23 with bath. Golfing and family hotel. Terraced lawns, fine sailing and bathing.

Shetland, North Mainland of. *Shetland* (M), Holmsgarth Road, Lerwick (tel. 0595–5515). 64 rooms with bath. Enterprising modern establishment keen to impress. Good large bedrooms, undistinguished food. Offers travel-inclusive vacations by sea from Aberdeen.

Skye, Isle of. *Skeabost House* (E), near Portree (tel. 047 032–202). 27 rooms, 18 with bath. Dignified building in fine surroundings. Island cuisine, good seafood. Full range of amenities including golf. Closed Oct.–Apr. *Rosedale* (M), Portree (tel. 0478–2531). 22 rooms with bath. *Harlosh* (I), Dunvegan (tel. 047 022–367). 8 rooms, 2 with bath. At lochside. The usual shellfish, nice and fresh, and first-class haggis. *Coolin Hills* (M), Portree (tel. 0478–2003). 26 rooms with bath/shower. Good cooking, superb loch and mountain views, and quiet situation.

Restaurant. *Glenview Inn,* Culnacnoc (tel. 047 062–248). Intimate, with above average cuisine. Booking essential. Accommodation available.

Torlundy (A82, north of Fort William). *Inverlochy Castle* (L), tel. 0397–2177. 13 rooms with bath. Regal welcome in a Highland castle where Queen Victoria once slept. Gastronomic cuisine.

HOW TO GET ABOUT. By car. Vehicles towing caravans can be a nuisance on some Highland roads in summer, but in general motoring in this Region is a pleasure and principal routes are well-built and maintained. Inverness, Dingwall and Lairg are good centers from which to launch your assault on the wilds of Wester Ross and Sutherland. Mainland ferry ports include Mallaig and Kyle of Lochalsh, for Skye, and Ullapool, for Lewis and Harris.

Please remember you are traveling in a region where the local inhabitant's daily routine takes precedence over the tourist's desires. This certainly applies to driving techniques on single-track roads. Never hold up a following vehicle. It might be the local doctor on his or her way to an emergency. Use passing places sensibly—and do not park in them.

Cars can be rented, with or without driver, in Inverness, Dingwall, Fort William and elsewhere. Call *Hi-Line* for details (see Tourist Information below).

By boat. P & O Ferries, Jamieson's Quay, Aberdeen AB9 8DL (tel. 0224–589111) operate daily car-ferries between Aberdeen and Lerwick (Shetland); and between Scrabster (Caithness) and Stromness (Orkney). Caledonian MacBrayne, Ferry Terminal, Gourock PA13 1QP (tel. 0475–33755) offer five services a week from Mallaig to the Small Isles; six days a week from Mallaig to Armadale (Skye); a shuttle service on weekdays (reduced service Sundays) from Kyle of Lochalsh to Kyleakin (Skye); six days a week from Sconser (Skye) to Raasay; six days a week from Oban (Strathclyde) to Barra and South Uist; daily from Uig (Skye) to North Uist and Harris; and six days a week from Ullapool to Stornoway; with appropriate return services. Caledonian MacBrayne also offer summer mini-cruises among the islands, with or without your own automobile.

Contact Caley Cruisers (tel. 0463–236328) or Jacobite Cruises (tel. 0463–233999), both Inverness, for power-boat rental or excursions on Loch Ness.

By train. The islands have no railroads. The Region's mainland has three: the main line from Perth to Wick and Thurso, with intermediate stations at 22 places, including Inverness and Dingwall; the Kyle route, Inverness to Kyle of Lochalsh, with many stops at wayside halts; and the line from Fort William to Mallaig (considered the most spectacular train ride in Britain), a continuation of the dramatic West Highland route from Glasgow to Fort William.

By bus. Highland Scottish Omnibuses, Seafield Road, Inverness (tel. 0463–233371) provide daily services to Ullapool, Gairloch, Aultbea and Kyle of Lochalsh and, in summer, they run many excursions and tours from Inverness, Dingwall and Fort William.

By air. British Airways fly between main airports and Orkney, Shetland and the Outer Hebrides. Between individual islands there are numerous light aircraft connections.

TOURIST INFORMATION. In some parts of the Outer Hebrides, notably Lewis and Harris, Sunday is a day of rest and "recharging of batteries"—an institution which reflects the islanders' own sense of values. Year-round information centers are at Aviemore, Inverness and Wick, opening weekdays, usually 9–8 in summer and 9–6 in winter; as are Dornoch, Fort William, Gairloch, Grantown-on-Spey, Kirkwall (Orkney), Lerwick (Shetland), North Kessock, Portree (Skye) and Stornoway (Lewis).

There are also some 30 part-time information centers scattered among villages and small resorts of the Highland and Islands Region. These centers open seasonally, normally 10–6 from May to Sept.; a few are closed on Sundays. Hotel bookings and all kinds of information, however, are handled by *Hi-Line,* Dingwall, Ross-shire IV15 9SL. Write or telephone 0349-63434, daily up to 8 P.M., including weekends in summer. The free booklet *Highlands and Islands Holiday Ideas,* from Hi-Line or any information center, contains details of many hotels, guest houses and cottages.

FISHING. Splendid game fishing is to be had on freshwater lochs and streams all over the Region. In Shetland alone there are 200 lochs. Sea trout are found in the bays and sounds of the islands and congregate round the outfalls of the rivers. Almost every Highland and Island hotel offers its guests fishing from a neighboring river bank or from a boat. Casual visitors pay around £3 a day. American Express, 115 Hope Street, Glasgow G2 6LX (tel. 041–221 4366) organize inclusive trout-fishing vacations in Orkney (May–Sept.) with flights from principal English and Scottish airports.

There is scarcely any coarse fishing. Sea-angling (skate, whiting, mackerel, cod and other varieties) is popular in the islands and at the mainland resorts of Thurso, Dunnet, Brora, Dornoch, Fortrose and Nairn. Record catches of heavy skate are regularly reported from Shetland.

The Hydro-Electric Board's fish-lift at Torrachilty Dam near Marybank, A832 from Beauly, is open to the public.

GOLF. In many areas there is hardly enough level ground for a green, but most east-coast towns and villages have at least one golf course apiece. There is one in Shetland, three in Orkney, two in the Outer Hebrides and one on Skye. The best golf course in the Region, over 360 years old, is Royal Dornoch (B9167, off A9). It offers full catering facilities, a practice area and a light-aircraft strip adjoining the course. Book a round in advance at about £5. Rather less expensive and exclusive are the fine courses at Nairn (A96), Fort William (A82) and Fortrose and Rosemarkie (A832). Speyside, south of Inverness, is good golfing country and at Newtonmore and Kingussie you will pay about £4 per day.

HISTORIC HOUSES AND GARDENS. Setting aside the rambling fortresses of a few clan chiefs, the Highland and Islands Region is noted more for desolate ruins than civilized castles and country houses. The following attract many visitors:

Bualadhubh, Eochar, South Uist (off A865). Traditional "black" house appropriately furnished. Open May–Sept., weekdays 10–5.

Cawdor Castle, Nairn (5 miles south on B9090). Handsomely-kept castle and park of 14th–17th centuries. "Upstairs Downstairs" insight into a building that is still very much a home. Open May–Sept., daily 10–5.30.

Dunrobin Castle, Golspie (A9). Parts date from 14th century, but most is flamboyant 19th century. Rich furnishings. Estate exhibits include steam fire engine and hunting trophies. Open mid-June–mid-Sept., weekdays 10.30–5.30, Sun. 2–5.30. Last entry 5 P.M.

Dunvegan Castle, Isle of Skye (west coast, on A863). Impressive medieval pile stained with blood and alive with the stormy history of the MacLeod clan. Relics include Fairy Flag and Rory O'Mor's Horn. Open May–Sept., weekdays only, 10.30–5; Apr. and Oct., weekdays only, 2–5.

Fort George, Ardesier, Inverness (off A96). Not a stately home but an 18th-century garrison headquarters with interesting exhibits of Seaforth, Cameron, and Queen's Own Highlanders regiments, from 1778 to present day. Open Apr.–Sept., weekdays 9.30–7, Sun. 2–7; Oct.–Mar., weekdays 9.30–4, Sun. 2–4.

Cawdor and Dunvegan have beautiful formal gardens but the horticultural paradise of the Region is **Inverewe,** near Poolewe on the northwest coast (A832). A variety of temperate species are set in a magnificent landscape. It is open daily throughout the year, 9.30–sunset. Visitor Centre opens Apr., Sept.–Oct., weekdays 10–5, Sun. 12–5; May–Aug., weekdays 10–6.30, Sun. 12–6.30. Restaurant. An N.T.S. property.

Among gardens regularly open to the public between May and Sept. are **Ardtornish,** Lochaline (off A884); **Duirinish Lodge,** Kyle of Lochalsh (off A87); and **Kyle House,** Kyleakin, Skye (A850). Gardens occasionally open—see local press and posters for details—are the **Castle of Mey,** the Queen Mother's Caithness retreat 7 miles west of John o' Groats (off A836); **Dundonnell** on Little Loch Broom (A832); **Langwell,** Berriedale (A9).

MUSEUMS. Many isolated community centers have displays of children's work illustrating the old life in their districts. Geological material is collected in town museums, sometimes with costumes and memorabilia of local events. The following short list includes some museums of special character:

Clan Museums. These can be found at Kintail on the A87 (Clan MacLennan); at Newtonmore on the A9 (MacPherson); and at Armadale, Skye, on the A851 (Donald).

Culloden Visitor Centre, Culloden Moor, Inverness (A9). (Actually 6 miles from Inverness on B6009.) Jacobite rebellion, Gaelic history, battle of 1746. Open June–mid-Sept., daily 9–7.30; Apr.–May and mid-Sept.–Oct., daily 9.30–5.30. Battlefield always visitable.

Deer Museum, Torridon (A896, west of Kinlochewe). Old travelers said this remote district of west Highlands "exhibited more wild beauty than any other part of Scotland" and Torridon is also geologically renowned. National Trust for Scotland's visitor center presents audio-visual travelogs, mostly about the red deer, wild cats, and golden eagles. Open June–Sept., weekdays 10–6, Sun. 2–6.

Glencoe and Dalness Visitor Centre, Clachaig (off A82 near foot of pass of Glencoe). Historical displays, walks, shop, picnic area in somber "Glen of Weeping." Open Apr.–May and Sept.–Oct., daily 10–5.30; June–Aug., daily 9.30–6.30.

Glenfinnan Visitor Centre, Glenfinnan (A830). In an appropriate setting, the word-and-picture story of Bonnie Prince Charlie's ill-fated campaign of 1745–46. Open Apr.–Oct., daily 10–5.30; July and Aug. 9.30–6.30.

Heritage Centre, Bank Row, Wick (A9). Life of old port displayed in a cluster of restored cottages. Open June–Sept., Tues–Sat., 10–12.30 and 2–5, Sun. 2–5.

Heritage Museum, Auchtercairn, Gairloch (A832). History and folklore of western seaboard. Furnished croft house. Winner of Scottish Museum of the Year award in 1980. Good licensed restaurant. Open Apr.–Sept., Mon.–Sat. 10–5.

Highland Folk Museum, Duke Street, Kingussie (A9). Senior Scottish folk museum, established 1934. Open-air exhibits include "black" house, mill, and turf-built kailyard. Open Apr.–Oct., weekdays 10–6, Sun. 2–6; Nov.–Mar., weekdays only, 10–3.

Hugh Miller's Cottage, Church Street, Cromarty (A832). Birthplace and fossil collection of famed writer and geologist (1802–56). Open May–Sept., weekdays 10–12 and 1–5; also Sun. 2–5, June–Aug. N.T.S.

Landmark Centre, Carrbridge (A9). Multivision theater portraying Highland history. Craft exhibitions, bookshop, sculpture park. Open June–Sept., daily 9.30–9.30, Oct.–May, 9.30–5.

Loch Ness Centre, Drumnadrochit (A82). The official Monster ("World's Greatest Mystery") museum. Unashamedly a tourist trap. Open June–Sept. daily 9–9.30; other timings vary, check in advance (tel. 045 62–573).

Pier Art Centre, Stromness, Orkney (A965). Modern paintings, sculpture in two 18th-century buildings. Ben Nicolson, Barbara Hepworth. Children's workroom. Open Tues.–Fri. 10.30–12.30, Sun. 1.30–5, Mon. 2–5.

Shetland Museum, Lower Hillhead, Lerwick, Shetland (A970). Agriculture, fishing, marine biology. Spanish armada relics. Open Mon., Wed., Fri., 10–1, 2.30–5 and 6–8; Tues. 10–1 and 2.30–5; and Thurs. 10–1.

Strathspey Railway, The Station, Boat of Garten (A95). Locomotives, rolling stock, railroad history in the north. Steam trains operate between Boat of Garten and Aviemore, an 8-mile trip. Open Easter–mid-May, Sun. 12–5; mid-May–mid-Oct., weekends 12–5; also Mon.–Thurs in July and Aug. 12–5.

Stromness Museum, Alfred Street, Stromness, Orkney (A965). Stereotyped natural history collection enlivened with relics of Orkney's international links—whaling, Hudson's Bay Company, Royal Navy at Scapa Flow, scuttling of German High Seas Fleet. Open daily except Thurs. P.M., 11–12.30 and 1.30–5.

Tankerness House, Kirkwall, Orkney (A964). Scene from island life in far-off times, displayed in 16th-century merchant laird's residence. Open Mon.–Sat. 10.30–1, 2–5; May–Sept. also Sun. 2–5.

West Highland Museum, High Street, Fort William (A82). Relics of Lochaber history, old clan maps, wanderings of Bonnie Prince Charlie. Open weekdays Jun. and Sept., 9.30–5.30; July and Aug. 9.30–9; Oct.–May 10–1 and 2–5.

Index

(The letter H indicates Hotels and other kinds of accommodations.)

(The letter R indicates Restaurants.)

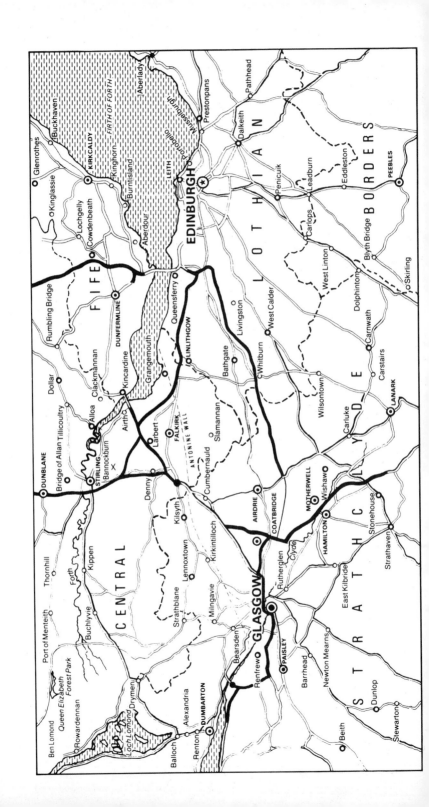

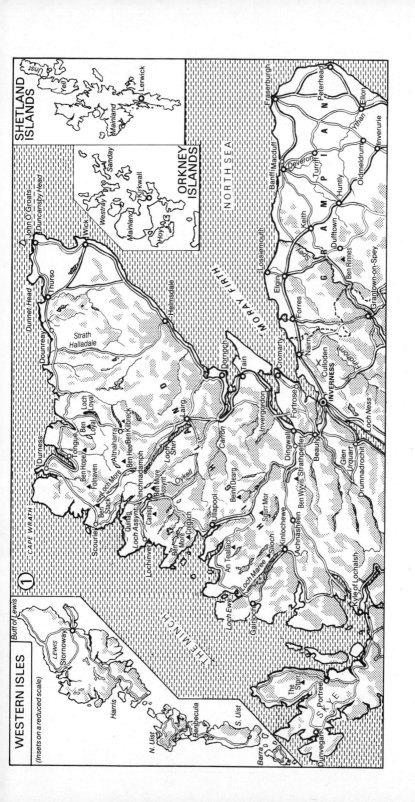

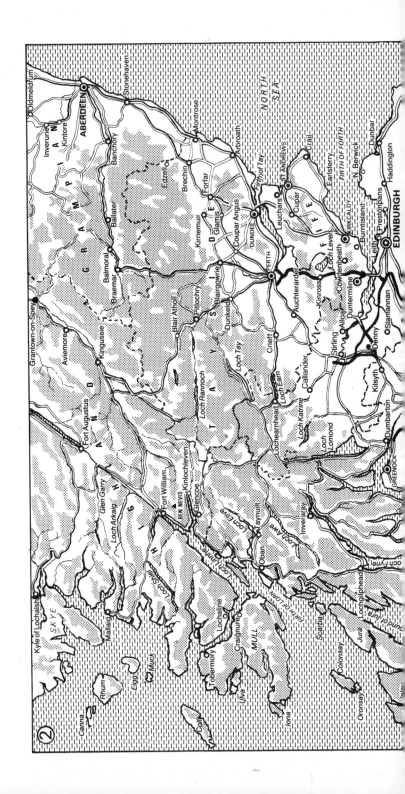

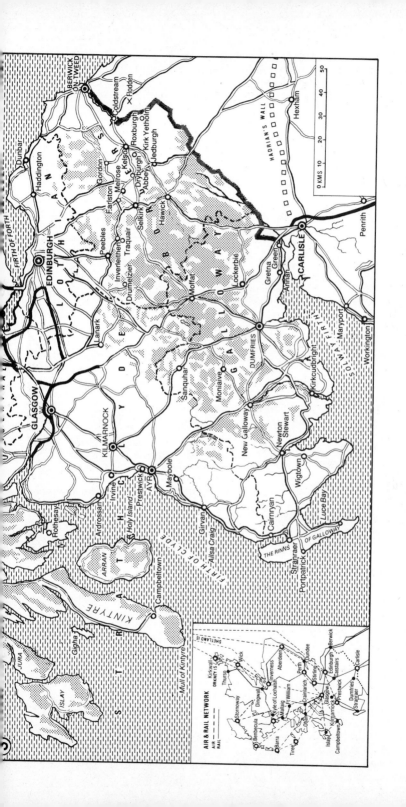

Fodor's Travel Guides

U.S. Guides

Alaska
Arizona
Atlantic City & the
  New Jersey Shore
Boston
California
Cape Cod
Carolinas & the
  Georgia Coast
The Chesapeake Region
Chicago
Colorado
Dallas & Fort
  Worth

Disney World & the
  Orlando Area
Florida
Hawaii
Houston &
  Galveston
Las Vegas
Los Angeles, Orange
  County, Palm Springs
Maui
Miami, Fort Lauderdale,
  Palm Beach
Michigan, Wisconsin,
  Minnesota

New England
New Mexico
New Orleans
New Orleans (Pocket
  Guide)
New York City
New York City (Pocket
  Guide)
New York State
Pacific North Coast
Philadelphia
The Rockies
San Diego
San Francisco

San Francisco (Pocket
  Guide)
The South
Texas
USA
Virgin Islands
Virginia
Waikiki
Washington, DC
Williamsburg

Foreign Guides

Acapulco
Amsterdam
Australia, New Zealand,
  The South Pacific
Austria
Bahamas
Bahamas (Pocket
  Guide)
Baja & the Pacific
  Coast Resorts
Barbados
Belgium & Luxembourg
Bermuda
Brazil
Britain (Great Travel
  Values)
Budget Europe
Canada
Canada (Great Travel
  Values)
Canada's Atlantic
  Provinces
Cancún, Cozumel,
  Mérida, the
  Yucatán
Caribbean

Caribbean (Great
  Travel Values)
Central America
China
China's Great Cities
Eastern Europe
Egypt
Europe
Europe's Great Cities
Florence & Venice
France
France (Great Travel
  Values)
Germany
Germany (Great Travel
  Values)
Great Britain
Greece
The Himalayan
  Countries
Holland
Hong Kong
Hungary
India, including Nepal
Ireland
Israel

Italy
Italy (Great Travel
  Values)
Jamaica
Japan
Japan (Great Travel
  Values)
Jordan & the Holy Land
Kenya, Tanzania,
  the Seychelles
Korea
Lisbon
Loire Valley
London
London (Great Travel
  Values)
London (Pocket Guide)
Madrid & Barcelona
Mexico
Mexico City
Montreal &
  Quebec City
Munich
New Zealand
North Africa
Paris

Paris (Pocket Guide)
Portugal
Rio de Janeiro
The Riviera (Fun on)
Rome
Saint Martin &
  Sint Maarten
Scandinavia
Scandinavian Cities
Scotland
Singapore
South America
South Pacific
Southeast Asia
Soviet Union
Spain
Spain (Great Travel
  Values)
Sweden
Switzerland
Sydney
Tokyo
Toronto
Turkey
Vienna
Yugoslavia

Special-Interest Guides

Bed & Breakfast
  Guide: North America
Health & Fitness
  Vacations

Royalty Watching
Selected Hotels of
  Europe

Selected Resorts
  and Hotels of the U.S.
Shopping in Europe

Skiing in North
  America
Sunday in New York